Dostoevsky's Political Thought

Dostoevsky's Political Thought

Edited by Richard Avramenko
and Lee Trepanier

LEXINGTON BOOKS
Lanham • Boulder • New York • Toronto • Plymouth, UK

Published by Lexington Books
A wholly owned subsidiary of The Rowman & Littlefield Publishing Group, Inc.
4501 Forbes Boulevard, Suite 200, Lanham, Maryland 20706
www.rowman.com

10 Thornbury Road, Plymouth PL6 7PP, United Kingdom

Copyright © 2013 by Lexington Books

All rights reserved. No part of this book may be reproduced in any form or by any electronic or mechanical means, including information storage and retrieval systems, without written permission from the publisher, except by a reviewer who may quote passages in a review.

British Library Cataloguing in Publication Information Available

Library of Congress Cataloging-in-Publication Data
Dostoevsky's political thought / edited by Richard Avramenko and Lee Trepanier.
p. cm.
Includes bibliographical references.
ISBN 978-0-7391-7376-3 (cloth : alkaline paper) — ISBN 978-0-7391-7377-0 (ebook)
Dostoyevsky, Fyodor, 1821–1881—Political and social views. 2. Dostoyevsky, Fyodor, 1821–1881—Philosophy. 3. Dostoyevsky, Fyodor, 1821–1881—Criticism and interpretation. 4. Politics in literature. I. Avramenko, Richard, editor of compilation. II. Trepanier, Lee, 1972– editor of compilation.
PG3328.Z7P629 2013
891.73'3—dc23
2013006981

∞™ The paper used in this publication meets the minimum requirements of American National Standard for Information Sciences Permanence of Paper for Printed Library Materials, ANSI/NISO Z39.48-1992.

Printed in the United States of America

Contents

Introduction   1
    Lee Trepanier

I: Dostoevsky's Political Theology

1. Dostoevsky's Discovery of the Christian Foundation of Politics   9
    David Walsh

2. The Politics and Experience of Active Love in *The Brothers Karamazov*   31
    Lee Trepanier

3. This Star Will Shine Forth from the East: Dostoevsky and the Politics of Humility   51
    John P. Moran

4. Dostoevsky's Heroines: Or, on the Compassion of the Russian Woman   73
    Richard Avramenko and Jingcai Ying

II: Dostoevsky's Political Thought

5. Philosophical Anthropology and Dostoevsky's "Legend of the Grand Inquisitor"   93
    Ellis Sandoz

6. Ugliness, Emptiness, and Boredom: Dostoevsky on the Secular Humanist Social Religion   115
    Ethan Alexander-Davey

7. Between Compassion and Misanthropy: On Moral Reasoning in Fyodor Dostoevsky's *Crime and Punishment*   141
    Khalil M. Habib

8. Freedom from Freedom: On the Metaphysics of Liberty in Dostoevsky's *Crime and Punishment*   159
    Richard Avramenko

III: Dostoevsky and the Modern Hermeneutic

9. Speaking on the Lower Frequencies: *Notes from Underground* in Ralph Ellison's America   181
    Steven D. Ealy

10 The End of the Ancient World: Dostoevsky's Confidence
  Game 201
  Ron Srigley

11 How Bodies Read and Write: Dostoevsky's *Demons* and
  Coetzee's *Master of Petersburg* 223
  Michael S. Kochin

Bibliography 237
Index 247
About the Contributors 253

Introduction

Lee Trepanier

Recognized as one of the world's great novelists and philosophical thinkers, Fyodor Mikhailovich Dostoevsky continues to influence us today. As we navigate ourselves in a world filled with religious visionaries, cynical revolutionaries, and political ideologues, we often refer back to Dostoevsky to make sense of the melodrama and the grotesque of our own times. His portrayals and analyses of the moral and spiritual dilemmas still haunt us today because they penetrate to the deepest concerns of the human condition regarding the nature of God, freedom, and human identity. Although we live in a different cultural and political context than Dostoevsky's nineteenth-century Russia, we still return to his writings for lessons of what it means to be human in the most fundamental sense. It is his answers—and lack of answers—that prompt us to come back to his thought for further reflection and mediation.

Dostoevsky's influence on literature and literary scholarship persists in the likes of J. M. Coetzee, Malcolm V. Jones, and Gary Saul Morson, and has led to theatrical and opera productions, art exhibitions, and cinema based on both his works and life.[1] For the fields of psychology, philosophy, and theology, Dostoevsky remains a source of inspiration for movements such as psychoanalysis, existentialism, and dialectical theology; and in terms of politics, Dostoevsky has been seen as one of the prophets of twentieth-century totalitarianism and twentieth-first century religious fundamentalism.[2] In short, there is very little of contemporary thought and culture that has escaped the influence and imagination of this nineteenth-century epileptic, gambling-addicted Russian writer.[3]

Recent theoretical approaches to Dostoevsky's works have focused on religious interpretations, usually adopting a Bakhtinian perspective, which looks at biblical and liturgical sources and Orthodox Christian motifs.[4] Complementing this new scholarship, this volume seeks to understand Dostoevsky as a political thinker in terms of his theology, philosophy, and relevance for contemporary culture. Despite the abiding interest in his works, Dostoevsky has not been comprehensively analyzed as a political thinker per se. This absence in the literature on Dostoevsky is puzzling, given his influence in theology, philosophy, aesthetics, literature, and other disciplines. We hope this volume both remedies this deficiency and directs future conversation on Dostoevsky in a different and equally productive direction in the future.

Having stated our purpose, we do not think this volume is exhaustive on the subject of Dostoevsky as a political thinker. By gathering a diverse group of political theorists and philosophers into a focused conversation concerning Dostoevsky's political thought, we hope this volume prompts the reader into reflecting upon broader questions about freedom, love, evil, suffering, and God. With each contributor engaging in a careful exegesis of Dostoevsky's works and combining it with fundamental questions of political philosophy and politics, the volume will not only shed new insight about Dostoevsky's writings to the readers but prompt them to return to Dostoevsky's works themselves in order to deepen their understanding of him. Like other scholarship on Dostoevsky, this one ultimately does not attempt to outshine the author but merely stand in his shadow.

The first section of the volume concentrates on Dostoevsky's political theology: the metaphysical or religious foundation of his thought and its relationship to political philosophy and politics. David Walsh starts this analysis in his chapter, "Dostoevsky's Discovery of the Christian Foundation of Politics," where he presents Dostoevsky's Christian philosophy of existence as dramatically portrayed throughout his fictional works. The various characters in Dostoevsky's world undergo the most ancient law of the cosmos of gaining wisdom through suffering: the revelation that a transcendent order of existence ultimately governs all humans whether they will it or not. For Dostoevsky, this revelation came through Christ and therefore Christ was the only possible response to the spiritual crisis of modern civilization. According to Walsh, Dostoevsky ultimately believed that the necessity of a Christ-like love was the only principle that could spiritually renew and genuinely revolutionize civilization.

Lee Trepanier explores the nature and dynamics of this principle of love in his chapter, "The Politics and Experience of Active Love in *The Brothers Karamazov*." Challenging contemporary interpretative uses of Bakhtin's concept of polyphony, Trepanier contends that the unity in the novel is rooted in Zosima's teachings of active love and responsibility for all. The understandings of these teachings are not only the interpretive keys to understanding the novel as a whole but also provide a compelling defense of Christianity against the alternative vision of Ivan and his tale of the Grand Inquisitor.

In chapter 3, "This Star Will Shine Forth from the East: Dostoevsky and the Politics of Humility," John P. Moran explores another aspect of Dostoevsky's political theology: Christian humility as an antidote to the humiliation from which characters in *The Brothers Karamazov* suffer as Russia herself. The humiliation of Dmitri, Ivan, and Smerdyakov—and their respective responses of romanticism, rationalism, and nihilism—is contrasted with Alyosha's humility as a monk. Moran concludes how these understanding of humility can be transposed from individual existence to the nation itself as a possible path that Russia could have taken.

The last chapter of this section, "Dostoevsky's Heroines: Or, on the Compassion of the Russian Woman," looks at Dostoevsky's heroines, particularly those in *The Devils*, as the embodiment of Dostoevsky's idea of compassionate love. Whereas the men in Dostoevsky's Russia have departed from the feminine principle, thereby losing their moral compass and continuously overstepping all moral boundaries, Russian women have preserved the life-affirming and organic values of Russian folk beliefs and Christian faith. The women in Dostoevsky's works—Marya Lebyadkina, Darya Shatova, Sofya Ulitina—all illustrate the value of suffering and compassion which only can lead Russia on a path towards spiritual renewal.

The second section of the volume focuses on Dostoevsky's political philosophy. Whereas the contributors in the first section primarily examine the nature of Dostoevsky's sources of religious and spiritual renewal for both individuals and nations, the authors in this section explore the political and philosophical consequences for individuals and people when those sources of love, compassion, and humility are ignored or rejected. The pathologies that plague modern civilization—materialism, boredom, utilitarianism—are examined by our contributors as Dostoevsky diagnosed them during his own time and how they remain relevant for us today.

In "Philosophical Anthropology and Dostoevsky's 'Legend of the Grand Inquisitor,'" Ellis Sandoz adopts a Platonic perspective to analyze Dostoevsky's philosophical anthropology on the problem of good and evil and its relationship to ethics and political philosophy. In the "Legend of the Grand Inquisitor," we discover a philosophical anthropology of atheistic humanism that leads to rebellion, negation, and ultimately to political tyranny. Sandoz concludes with how one should interpret this tale in contrast to commentators who have drawn diametrically opposed conclusions from it.

Whereas Sandoz's analysis of Dostoevsky's prophecy of totalitarianism was relevant for the Cold War era, Ethan Alexander-Davey brings Dostoevsky's political thought into the post–Cold War period when democratic elites attempt to implement their programs of transforming humanity into a world of cosmopolitan liberalism and global capitalism. Dostoevsky himself was confronted with a similar choice between liberalism and socialism and sought a third way in a Russian conservatism that exposes the materialistic and individualistic philosophical anthropologies of both ideologies. In "Ugliness, Emptiness and Boredom: Dostoevsky on the Secular Humanist Social Religion," Alexander-Davey examines Dostoevsky's public writings, such as *Diary of a Writer* and *Winter Notes on Summer Impressions*, to illustrate the commonalities that liberal and socialist ideologues share and how these characteristics still inform contemporary ideologies of our own day.

In his chapter, "Between Compassion and Misanthropy: On Moral Reasoning in Fyodor Dostoevsky's *Crime and Punishment*," Khalil M. Habib reveals how this materialistic and individualistic philosophical anthropology is dramatically and psychologically portrayed by Dostoevsky in the character Raskolnikov. In the belief of his own superiority, Raskolnikov justifies his "small crime" on the philosophical grounds of utilitarianism. But in spite of his most strenuous efforts, Raskolnikov is unable to suppress his innate moral sentiments that are in direct conflict with his abstract thinking and inner spiritual isolation. It is only when he accepts Sonia's redemptive love does Raskolnikov appreciate and understand the limits of human agency and the ethical need for conscience and a belief in God.

The importance, definition, and use of freedom are further analyzed by Richard Avramenko in his chapter, "Freedom from Freedom: On the Metaphysics of Liberty in Dostoevsky's *Crime and Punishment*." Dostoevsky foresaw the problems that "approximate freedom," which is about power, would pose for the West. By contrast, "proximate freedom," which is about love, is a possible path for spiritual salvation for both individuals and nations. Avramenko shows how these types of freedom are dramatically contrasted with each other in various characters in *Crime and Punishment* as well as comparing Dostoevsky's own life with Raskolnikov's to show how political solutions sought only in approximate freedom will fail.

The final section of the volume is entitled, "Dostoevsky and the Modern Hermeneutic," where our three contributors reveal how Dostoevsky enriches not only our understanding of contemporary literature but literature that wrestles with political problems unique to different countries, whether in the United States, France, or South Africa. Here we see not only the enduring importance of Dostoevsky's political philosophy but also its universality in its ability to speak with other authors who are attempting to understand their own moral, social, and political questions in their countries. Dostoevsky's political philosophy consequently continues to provide us a source to evaluate and re-evaluate our own moral and political traditions from which we can glean greater insight.

In "Speaking on the Lower Frequencies: *Notes from Underground* in Ralph Ellison's America," Steve Ealy compares the dehumanizing effects of scientism and racism on Dostoevsky's Underground Man and Ellison's Invisible Man. This comparison teaches not only the peculiar problems that each political regime possesses but also explores the role that liberty plays as a potential remedy to these problems. Although both Dostoevsky and Ellison have different conceptions of freedom, they both share a vision of the importance of embracing one's cultural heritage and maintaining a healthy relationship to one's historical roots, both of which liberty asks and demands.

In "The End of the Ancient World: Dostoevsky's Confidence Game," Ron Srigley engages Camus's interpretation of Dostoevsky's *The Brothers Karamazov* and contends that Dostoevsky's novel is a type of confidence game similar to Herman Melville's *The Confidence Man*. Both works present a type of "game" that is amenable to the totalizing impulses of the Christian tradition. For Srigley, instead of representing nihilism, Ivan's difficult and honest questions concerning the Christian tradition opens the possibility of reflecting upon God and morality without the mediating influence of any tradition. Although Dostoevsky himself is closed to this prospect, he at least points to its possibility in his portrayal of the Grand Inquisitor.

The final chapter considers the ethics of reading and writing by asking what moral obligations, if any, does a writer have towards his characters and the real-world suffering that he or she represents in art. In "How Bodies Read and Write: Dostoevsky's *Demons* and Coetzee's *Master of Petersburg*," Michael Kochin explores these and other questions concerning the nature of community and the ethics of writers communicating certain experiences to readers. For instance, how can and should demonism—the possessed Stavrogin who withdraws from himself, society, and God—be represented and portrayed to readers without corrupting them? Does Coetzee's Dostoevsky believe that fictional portrayals are more real than reality itself? And is writing itself conducive to the alleviation of suffering imagined or merely affords readers a spectacle from a safe aesthetic distance? Kochin shows how both Dostoevsky and Coetzee wrestle with these questions and formulates an artistic response that attempts to answer and satisfy these various ethical concerns.

Again, this volume is not intended to be exhaustive on the topic of Dostoevsky's political philosophy but merely an introduction to it and to hopefully nudge its scholarship in a different direction. We believe that political philosophy can contribute to the broader conversation about Dostoevsky and generate insights that are also relevant to the fields of theology, philosophy, history, literature, and aesthetics. Thus our hope is not only to bring Dostoevsky into the mainstream of our discipline but also afford a unique and illuminating perspective that can form useful connections with other fields on the same subject.

We would like to close with acknowledgements of those who made this project possible. First, we would like to thank Justin Race, Alissa Parra, and their predecessors at Lexington Books for their understanding and support of this project. We also would like to recognize Dr. Donald Bachand for his university support on this volume. Finally, we would like to express our love, compassion, and humility—values that Dostoevsky calls for within us—for our family and friends. Specifically, MiJung and Sara for their patience and suffering while we labored on this project. This volume is dedicated to you.

NOTES

1. For an excellent summary of Dostoevsky's influence on contemporary culture, refer to Sarah Young and Lesley Milne, eds. *Dostoevsky on the Threshold of Other Worlds: Essays in Honor of Malcolm V. Jones* (Ilkeston, Derbyshire: Bramcote Press, 2006). See also Alexander Burry, *Multi-Mediated Dostoevsky: Transposing Novels Into Opera, Film, and Drama* (Evanston: Northwestern University Press, 2011).

2. For example, refer to William J. Leatherbarrow, ed. *The Cambridge Companion to Dostoevskii* (Cambridge: Cambridge University Press, 2002), Louis Breger, *Dostoevsky: The Author as Psychoanalyst* (New York: New York University Press, 1990), Walter Kaufmann, ed. *Existentialism from Dostoevsky to Sarte* (Cleveland, OH: Meridian Books, 1968), P. H. Brazier, *Barth and Dostoevsky: A Study of the Influence of the Russian Writer Fyodor Mikhailovich Dostoevsky on the Development of the Swiss Theologian* (Eugene, OR: Wipf & Stock Publishers, 2008), George Grant, Ian Angus, Ron Dart, and Randy Peg Peters, eds. *Theology, Philosophy, and Politics* (Toronto: University of Toronto Press, 2009), Ellis Sandoz, *Political Apocalypse: A Study of Dostoevsky's Grand Inquisitor* (Wilmington, DE: ISI Books, 2000), John P. Moran, *The Solution of the Fist: Dostoevsky and the Roots of Modern Terrorism* (Lanham, MD: Lexington Books, 2009).

3. For more about Dostoevsky's life, refer to Joseph Frank's five-volume biography: Joseph Frank, *Dostoevsky: The Seeds of Revolt, 1821–1849* (Princeton: Princeton University Press, 1976), Joseph Frank, *Dostoevsky: The Stir of Liberation, 1860–1865* (Princeton: Princeton University Press, 1986), Joseph Frank, *Dostoevsky: The Years of Ordeal, 1850–1859* (Princeton: Princeton University Press, 1990), Joseph Frank, *Dostoevsky: The Miraculous Years, 1865–1871* (Princeton: Princeton University Press, 1995), Joseph Frank, *Dostoevsky: The Mantle of the Prophet, 1871–1881* (Princeton: Princeton University Press, 2002).

4. For the influence of Bakhtin on interpreting Dostoevsky, refer to Mikhail Bakhtin, *Problems of Dostoevsky's Poetics* (Minneapolis: University of Minnesota Press, 1984), Gary Saul Morson, *The Boundaries of Genre: Dostoevsky's Diary of a Writer and the Traditions of Literary Utopia* (Evanston: Northwestern University Press, 1988), Malcolm V. Jones, *Dostoevsky After Bakhtin: Readings in Dostoevsky's Fantastic Realism* (Cambridge: Cambridge University Press, 2005). For recent interpretations of Dostoevsky as a religious thinker, refer to George Pattison and Diane Oenning Thompson, eds. *Dostoevsky and the Christian Tradition* (Cambridge: Cambridge University Press, 2001), Steven Cassedy, *Dostoevsky's Religion* (Stanford: Stanford University Press, 2005), Malcolm V. Jones, *Dostoevsky and the Dynamics of Religious Experience* (London: Anthem Press, 2005), Rowan Williams, *Dostoevsky: Language, Faith, and Fiction (Making of the Christian Imagination)* (Waco: Baylor University Press, 2008), William Peter van den Bercken, *Christian Fiction and Religious Realism in the Novels of Dostoevsky* (London: Anthem Press, 2011).

I

Dostoevsky's Political Theology

ONE

Dostoevsky's Discovery of the Christian Foundation of Politics

David Walsh

The neglect of Fyodor Dostoevsky as a political theorist can be explained in part by his choice of imaginative literature rather than discursive argument as his primary mode of communication.[1] Add to this the impression so readily accepted by many of his readers that the novelist remained an inconclusive searcher to the end of his life, and there seems to be little incentive for students of political thought to explore further. But by far the greatest obstacle to the acknowledgement of his achievement is the radically unfamiliar character of his theory of politics. In an age of unquestioned acceptance of autonomous secular reason as the starting point for all discussion of man, society and history, Dostoevsky had the audacity to reject the reigning assumption out of hand. In its place he maintained that the point of departure for any study of human nature must be Christ, for no personal or political order can be sustained unless it is rooted in a universal, self-sacrificing love. He insisted that the moral regeneration of society could never be achieved without a rediscovery of the transcendent spiritual order from which all reality is ultimately derived. As a consequence, he elaborated the essential elements of a Christian philosophy of politics, and did it outside the context of any confessional apologetics. Therein lies the challenge of his work for contemporary political theory.

Dostoevsky's political vision is the exemplary modern statement of the necessity for Christianity as the foundation of politics, and it is so precisely because Dostoevsky's open exploration of reality followed the logic of experience rather than specific dogmatic preconceptions. It was his own confrontation with the chaos of the modern world that convinced him of the truth of Christ as both the source and criterion of order in human existence. The arguments were not resolved intellectually but were painfully worked out in the harsh reality of life. "My hosanna has passed through a great furnace of doubts."[2] Beginning as a utopian socialist, he had embraced atheistic communism and was on his way to becoming a Nechayev-like terrorist when he was arrested, imprisoned and eventually encountered the reality of human nature and the redemptive image of Christ still living within the Russian people.[3] His searching plumbed the depths of modern nihilism at least as profoundly as Nietzsche, but where Nietzsche sought to overcome it through the resources of his own will, Dostoevsky discovered the infinite love of God as the grace that saves man from the abyss.[4] Their analyses are parallel so far as the critique of the modern ideological movement goes; each regards the schemes of the world-immanent salvation as only thinly veiled disguises for the imposition of universal slavery. But in place of Nietzsche's determined acceptance of the will to power as the means of preserving human freedom, Dostoevsky insisted on mutual forgiveness as the way to fully respect the uniqueness and freedom of every individual. The answer to the lust for power is not its expansion, but the self-sacrificing love of Christ that dissolves the *superbia vitae* at its root. Deeper than the level of argument is the witness of living truth that Dostoevsky discovered during his imprisonment, where he met the ordinary Russian people and found that

> a heart-knowledge of Christ, a true conception of Him, does fully exist. It is being passed from generation to generation, and it has merged with the heart of the Russian people. Perhaps, Christ is the only love of the Russian people, and they love His image in their own way, to the limit of sufferance.[5]

The communication of this insight as the only means of restoring the human image (*obrazil*) in man became the central preoccupation of Dostoevsky's work (DW 183). He accepted from the start an ineluctable condition that the constitutive spiritual truth of man's existence could not be conveyed directly. It could only be communicated through an evocative reactualization of the movements of the soul by which its order is apprehended; there is no meaning of life that can be possessed apart from the concrete participation in its truth. Even the distorting ideas of modern liberalism and socialism, Dostoevsky realized, cannot be refuted by logic for they do not arise strictly from reason. They can only be answered "by faith, by the deduction of the necessity of faith in the immortality of man's soul; by the inference of the conviction that this faith is the only source of 'living life,'" which, once "you have beheld it you know that it is the Truth and that there can be no other" (DW 678), must be portrayed within the struggle to achieve it and never simply dispensed as the end result of a process. Such was the problem of Dostoevsky's art. It was not that the author could not make up his mind as to how his characters should develop, but that he intended to introduce us to the inner existential conflict in which the decision of life and death was being made. Dostoevsky's genius is in depicting the moment of wholly free choice where the fate of a personality is about to be determined. This is why the outcome remains uncertain for so long and why the author's own position cannot intrude while he heightens the dramatic tension of the moment.[6] Indeed it is in the tendency for the writer himself to disappear, allowing his own views to be "pinned to the wall," that "the whole trick" of Dostoevsky's art consists.[7]

The truth of a Christian philosophy of existence is shown rather than described or professed in his work. It speaks directly to the fundamental need of the modern world for a regeneration of the spirit, to find again the power of transcendent love that can lead us away from destruction and toward life. For Dostoevsky presupposes nothing. He takes men as they are and leads them through the desolation of revolt, self-assertiveness and pride to recognize that reality of an order of beauty, forgiveness and love that is true because it is the ultimate order of the universe. The characters of his "novel-tragedies" undergo the most ancient law of the cosmos: wisdom through suffering. They bring to light the consequences of their respective responses to the human condition and thereby reveal the transcendent order of existence that ultimately governs all men whether they will it or not. Ideas are tested within the concreteness of "living life." The truth or falsity of existence is apprehended directly, as individual moral dramas disclose their meaning as part of the larger struggle between good and evil within society and reality as a whole. In this way Dostoevsky succeeded in demonstrating the existential truth of Christianity and in making it the foundation for modern political philosophy. His secret, as we will attempt to show, was in penetrating the spiritual crisis of our civilization to the point where the revelation of Christ was the only possible response. We will follow first his analysis of human nature as it is revealed by the paradigm of Christ, and then his application of this insight into the problems of social and political order in history. The necessity for a Christ-like love in individual existence is the principle that alone can supply, in Dostoevsky's view, what is missing in the modern revolutionary movement.

I.

In Dostoevsky's novels there are very few passages that provide lyrical descriptions of the beauty of nature. His tales are almost exclusively focused on the inner struggle within the souls of his characters, and accounts of the physical surroundings are strictly subordinated to the action of this human drama. The theme that absorbed his interest from the very start was man in his tragic duality, the innermost center of the person where the forces of good and evil are engaged in a mysterious battle leading either to death or life. Dostoevsky recognized his vocation when he was only eighteen. In a letter to his brother, Dostoevsky wrote with newfound confidence that he wants to "study the meaning of man and of life."[8] This preoccupation with human nature was what made Dostoevsky into a consummate psychologist of the human soul, deftly exposing its minute twists and turns and the hidden recesses unsuspected even by the individual himself. Yet he was always more than a psychologist and rejected that label because he never regarded psychological analysis as an end in itself. It was only the means of probing the spiritual forces that reach into man and struggle for resolution in the *anima animi* of human freedom. The study of man, if it is a fully open exploration, must unfold into a study of the order of reality with its transcendent foundation. Through his anthropological inquiry Dostoevsky became a metaphysician in the classical sense.[9]

It is the essence of man's nature that he cannot be bound by any finite categories. His nature is not something fixed and given, but an openness or mystery in which the form it is to take is not predetermined. The outcome is decided by the choice of directional pull to which man responds—the immortalizing height or the moralizing depth—to use the language of the classic philosophers to whom Dostoevsky is so close. He places in the mouth of Dmitri Karamazov, the man who represents the regenerative force of the earth, his description of this tensional or between status of human existence.

> I can't endure the thought that a man of lofty mind and heart begins with the ideal of the Madonna and ends with the ideal of Sodom. What's still more awful is that a man with the ideal of Sodom in his soul does not renounce the ideal of the Madonna, and his heart may be on fire with that ideal, genuinely on fire, just as in the days of youth and innocence. Yes, man is broad, too broad, indeed. I'd have him narrower.[10]

But it is the fate of humankind not to be allowed to rest within those narrower limits, for each is called to play his or her part in that drama of free response where the contest between good and evil in existence is decided. The fall and redemption of individual man becomes transparent in the social process and the cosmic whole in which it finds its place. "God and the devil are fighting there," concludes Dmitri Karamazov, "and the battlefield is the heart of man" (BK 127).

This inexorable tension of existence Dostoevsky elaborated in terms of the tragic duality of human nature. He considered his artistic device of the double to be one of his most original contributions to the exploration of these problems. Throughout Dostoevsky's writings we find a constant concern with the bifurcation of human consciousness, which is capable of such utter self-renunciation that it can virtually lose itself in love of another, or of such utter self-absorption that it can only be satisfied by attaining total tyrannical control over another. The unending struggle between these different selves was what Dostoevsky referred to as "my usual substance." Indeed it absorbed his attention to the point of becoming the principal structural device for the organization of his great novels. "The hero's personality," Mochulsky explains, "appears as the axis of the composition."[11] This is particularly clear in *The Possessed* where the principle of centralization has reached its limit, for everything revolves around the enigmatic figure of Stavrogin. As Dostoevsky observes, "the Prince is everything."[12] The other characters retain their own independent centers of consciousness, but are held together within the most comprehensive drama of the hero's self-revelation and his fate. All of the action is centered on the enigma of the personality resolving itself in the moment of critical free decision.

It is at that point that freedom itself is discovered to be the problem. Nothing predetermines the choices a man will make, and even the principle by which they will be decided must be discovered within the process. Dostoevsky's characters are like many of the participants within the Platonic dialogues, souls who are confronted with the fundamental choice of a pattern of life with its fate and are desperately in search of that guiding knowledge by which the decision can be made rightly. Superfluous discussion and casual exchanges are brushed aside in order to concentrate on the heart of the matter: testing the ideas by which men live in order to discover their truth and falsity. Ivan Karamazov describes the situation exactly when he asks what brothers who have not met before and will not meet again talk about in these exchanges in the tavern.

> Of the eternal questions, of the existence of God and of immortality. And those who do not believe in God talk of socialism and anarchism, of the transformation of all humanity on a new pattern, so that it all comes to the same, they're the same questions turned inside out. (BK 275)

Dostoevsky's heroes are individuals who by and large have not finally answered these questions. Their fate has not yet been determined. In the interim of struggle and indecision they explore the moral alternative that beckon them, thereby unfolding the experiential logic of responding to the pull of one or the other direction.

At one extreme stands the possibility of the closed self. This is the "underground man," most elaborately developed in *Notes from the Underground*, but a fundamental type in all the later novels because Dostoevsky regarded this as the characteristic individual of the modern world. It is the type of all who are cut off from the world of common humanity, all who are detached from their own language, their own soil, their own people, their own history. They are the Russian intelligentsia and nobility of the nineteenth century who had nothing of value to do in their own society and looked slavishly to European liberalism to define their meaning and purpose. Within the kind of "haphazard household" they set up when everything that could give their lives significance had fallen away, they—and especially their afflicted children—were ultimately thrown back on the resources of the self to create a world in which to live. Now the ideal became self-sufficiency and independence. The highest good was to insulate oneself from the outside world so as to experience one's own limitless freedom. They sought, in a word, the sense of superiority to all.[13] European liberalism with its deism, its faith in reason and science, its trust in the natural goodness of human nature, and its boundless confidence in the ability of progress to bring about the perfection of man and society, had been the starting point. The self-defensive cynicism of the underground man was its inevitable consequence, once the brittleness of such rational expectations stood revealed in the confrontation with reality.

Yet the search for refuge within one's shell was not the final stage in this psychological progression. The collapse of rational humanism could just as easily develop into the demonically self-assertive force of the strong personality. This type, which Dostoevsky encountered in prison, began to appear in his stories after that time.[14] Like the underground man, the titanic personality is also in revolt against the confinement of the human spirit within rational limits—a cage remains a cage even if it is a crystal palace—but the thirst for freedom within such individuals can only be assuaged by reducing all others to the status of the ant-hill. Dostoevsky's favorite image for this temptation is the spider awaiting its victim. It is a possibility that is never so close as when it is stirred by love of the dependency of another on oneself. The hollowness of liberal humanitarianism is seen to be motivated at its most fundamental level by the will to power.

This is the dynamic that was explored in the first of Dostoevsky's great novel-tragedies, *Crime and Punishment*. Raskolnikov begins as a utilitarian dreamer, contemplating the murder of the old pawnbroker as a means of benefiting others, but proceeds to assert his own absolute prerogative as a Napoleonic individual beyond good and evil. After that, it is only a question of whether he will have the strength of will to demonstrate the claim, whether he will be able to remain superior to the vicissitudes and appeals offered to him by life. This logic of experience unfolds inexorably from humanitarianism to murder. For Raskolnikov has already committed the crime in his heart when he allows himself to fantasize freely about it. He had separated himself from the bonds of mutual obligation that form a community of human beings, with the result that there was no longer anything to restrain him from carrying out his benevolent impulse through murder. Once he had stepped outside of the recognition of the transcendent worth of each individual, nothing stood in the way of a descent into the destructive abyss of nihilism. Without the acknowledgement of every person as an absolute end in himself or herself, no other value is worth having. The existence of individuals whose importance extends beyond life itself is the *sine qua non* for obtaining all other benefits. Any other love of mankind that, for example, sees us all eventually "reduced to zero," is only too easily transformed into hatred for men. "I assert," Dostoevsky concluded, "that love of mankind is unthinkable, unintelligible and altogether impossible without the accompanying faith in the immortality of man's soul" (DW 540).[15]

The impression of having reached a hitherto unknown freedom by discarding this ultimate spiritual order and becoming a law unto oneself is sheer illusion. Dostoevsky's analysis of the empty freedom of the closed self heightens the classical understanding of the tyrant as the least powerful individual in the state. He meticulously explores the emerging realization of futility within the strong individual's self-consciousness. Stavrogin's confession is in part motivated by his awareness of the abyss he is approaching:

> It wasn't simply that I had lost the feeling of good and evil, but that I felt there was no such thing as good and evil (I like that); that it was all a convention; that I could be free of convention; but that if I ever attained that freedom, I'd be lost. (P 426)

Yet even in this admission of his sins Bishop Tikhon discerned the same spirit of unrepentant spiritual pride at work, only now more subtly and more dangerously. He appealed to Stavrogin to overcome his longing for martyrdom, for conflict, for a testing of his strength against the world. "You'll conquer your pride and put your demon to flight. You'll end up the winner and gain your freedom" (P 441). The demon of self-will, however, proved too strong for the "Russian Hamlet"; as Tikhon had warned, he plunged further into crime with no other purpose than to sense his own limitless strength. For the man who has finally closed himself off from the common spiritual truth of humanity there remains only one tormenting question, "What was I to apply my strength to?" Its absolute unanswerability eventually could only be expressed by the hero's suicide.[16]

Ivan Karamazov is a personality subject to the same temptations. He too had set himself up as a superior to the universal moral order that has its source in God. In his case Dostoevsky explored the component of revolt within the nihilistic assertion that "everything is lawful," for it is in the name of innocent suffering humanity that Ivan rejects the God whose injustice has been the cause of all this misery. Indeed there is probably no more profound expression in all modern literature of the revolt of man against God than the famous passage in which Ivan throws down the gauntlet of his "even if."

> I don't want harmony. From love for humanity I don't want it. I would rather be left with the unavenged suffering. I would rather be left with my unavenged suffering and unsatisfied indignation, *even if I were wrong*. (BK 291, emphasis in original)

He cannot accept such an unjust God, and by calling Him to account before his own "pitiful, earthly, Euclidean understanding," Ivan proclaims his own greater ability to realize justice on earth. The starting point is his impassioned declamation, "I must have justice, or I will destroy myself" (BK 259), but the conclusion exposes its true origins in his willingness to destroy everyone else as well. Justice, when it assumes the task of a comprehensive reordering of reality, can no longer function as the principle of order within human existence. Particular actions come to be viewed, not as they are in themselves, but in relation to the one absolute goal of universal justice, its attainment, as it recedes more and more into the future, provides the rationalization for the multiplication of injustice and rapacity in the present. Missing is the recognition that no future state of justice can be realized by shortchanging justice in the present, that without the subordination to transcendent justice here and now we abandon all criteria to define our goal of justice in the future. From the tortured logic of his rebellion against God, Ivan became chiefly responsible for instigating the murder of his father. The contradiction is exemplified most clearly in his own account of the Grand Inquisitor who claims to love humans with a love exceeding Christ's, yet contemptuously tramples on their dignity as free spiritual beings in the name of providing for their happiness. He pictures men as not better than beasts who "crawl to us and lick our feet and spatter them with tears of blood," eventually coming to "lay their freedom at our feet, and say to us, 'Make us your slaves, but feed us'" (BK 300).[17]

What saves Ivan from this extreme is the "frantic and perhaps unseemly thirst for life" that is the elemental force of the Karamazovs. Like all of Dostoevsky's heroes who are saved (e.g., Raskolnikov in *Crime and Punishment*, Versilov in *The Adolescent*), he loves life more than the meaning of it. His head may reject the injustice of God's creation, but his heart is still capable of being moved by "the sticky little leaves as they open in spring" (BK 273). This is why he is torn between belief and disbelief, suffering from an "aching heart," as the Elder Zosima diagnoses, unable to either accept or reject his own arguments against immortality and God. Unlike the actual murderer, the illegitimate son Smerdyakov, Ivan cannot fully accept that "everything is lawful." His love of "living life" pulls him back from the precipice as he is revolted by the demonic self-closure of Smerdyakov and finally overcomes his last double, the "paltry, trivial devil" who echoes back to him all his own ideas about the new god-man of the future. Ivan again becomes capable of acknowledging his connection with other men and of shouldering the common obligations that arise from it. He feels sympathy for the peasant he had knocked down and returns to help him, and he finally confesses before the court his guilt in inciting Smerdyakov to murder their father. In the struggle of his "aching heart," Ivan had chosen life rather than death, once his proud self-determination had been dissolved by the truth of God entering his soul.[18]

Ivan Karamazov had discovered the "law of the planet": wisdom through suffering. The scriptural passage that dominates this novel is John 12:24: Except a grain of wheat fall into the ground and die, it abideth alone: but if it die it bringeth forth much fruit. It forms not only the motto but the refrain to which each of the characters returns in recognizing the way to order in existence. Life cannot be obtained as a gift or without cost, rather man is required to accept the cross of self-renunciation to the point of death if the freedom of true love is to be reached within his soul. Only then does the mysterious oneness of reality become transparent. We realize that we are all responsible for all, that the unseen bonds between us call us to forgive one another for everything and to ask one another forgiveness for everything, that we already possess paradise within if only we will open our eyes to see it. In other words, the regeneration through suffering that Dostoevsky underwent in his own life became the pivot around which the struggle of his characters unfolded. Each discovers in his own way that life can only be attained through death. On the day after his first wife's death the author wrote in his notebook:

> Masha is lying on the table. Will I see Masha again? To love a person as one's own self, as Christ commanded is impossible. On earth the law of personality binds us; the *I* stands in the way. . . . Christ was able, but Christ was eternal, from all ages the ideal toward which man strives and according to the law of nature must strive. After Christ's appearance, it became clear that the highest development of personality must attain to that point where man annihilates his own "I," surrenders it completely to all and everyone without division or reserve. . . . And this is the greatest happiness. . . . This is Christ's paradise.[19]

Of all Dostoevsky's heroes, only Prince Myshkin (*The Idiot*) is not subject to this law of the cosmos, and this is because he is not fully incarnated in existence. He is the static image of the "beautiful individual." He exists as a glimpse of paradise but is incapable of showing us the way to it, and his love is eventually proved ineffectual in the contest with evil in existence.

"On earth," Dostoevsky explained, "there is only one positively beautiful person—Christ."[20] He is the still point around whom Dostoevsky's art is constructed. The answer to the revolt of man who sets himself up in judgment over creation is the God who takes on himself the burden of suffering and evil in existence. The answer to the man who kills God in order to save mankind is the God who allows himself to be sacrificed for the redemption of all men. The answer to the man-god is the God-man.

This is the meaning of the confrontation that takes place in the famous "Legend of the Grand Inquisitor," where the representative of imperial humanitarianism stands in judgment before the fullness of incarnate divine Love. No amount of explanation and rationalization can conceal the evil that lies at the heart of the Inquisitor's scheme for universal salvation through the destruction of man's humanity. The suffering, unspeaking Christ is the presence that powerfully dominates the encounter precisely because of the intensity of response he evokes in the other. His loving silence testifies more profoundly than words to the truth of God's redemptive forgiveness that can overcome the evil perpetrated by man's freedom. It reveals the transcendent love of Christ that alone calls man to the true inner freedom of God. So effective is the depiction that it has, not without justification, been considered an appropriate addition to the Christian cannon.

> Never before in all world literature has Christianity been advanced with such striking force as the religion of spiritual freedom. The Christ of Dostoevsky is not only the Savior and Redeemer, but also the Sole Emancipator of man.[21]

It has rightly become the *locus classicus* for an understanding of the political necessity of Christianity in the modern world, for it provides an iconographic image of the unconditioned divine love that is the ultimate foundation of human freedom.

From the example of Christ, Dostoevsky received the principle of universal forgiveness that is the radiant center of order in human existence. His insistence that we are responsible for all and must forgive and be forgiven would be unthinkable without the reality of Christ in whom the perfect forgiveness and reconciliation of all men has already taken place. At the heart of Dostoevsky's thought is the conviction that there can be no love of man that does not finally lead us to Christ as the one truly adequate source. The unconditioned divine acceptance of each individual in his or her unique strengths and failings is the truth of Christ beyond which there can be no other, as Dostoevsky declared in his most famous confession to N. D. Fonvizana, the woman who had given him the copy of the gospels that had been his only reading in prison.

> I will tell you regarding myself that I am a child of the age, a child of nonbelief and doubt up till now and even (I know it) until my coffin closes. What terrible torments has this thirst to believe cost me and does still cost me, becoming the stronger in my soul, the more there is in me of contrary reasoning. And yet sometimes God sends me moments in which I am utterly at peace; in those moments I love and find that I am loved by others and in such moments I have constructed for myself a symbol of faith in which everything is clear and holy for me. The symbol is very simple; here it is: to believe that there is nothing more beautiful, profounder, more sympathetic, more reasonable, and

more courageous and more perfect than Christ and not only that there is nothing, but I tell myself with jealous love that never could be there. Moreover, if someone were to prove to me that Christ is outside the truth, then I would prefer to remain with Christ than with the truth.[22]

Those of Dostoevsky's heroes who have not entirely closed themselves off to the truth of living life all eventually make the same connection, that the love of man is ultimately the presence of Christ among them. Even Versilov, the spokesman for an autonomous morality and the new golden age of brotherhood to arise from it, acknowledged that he "mostly ended with Heine's vision of 'Christ on the Baltic Sea.' I realized I couldn't manage without Him altogether and so, in the end, He appears in the midst of the abandoned men" (A 473).[23]

At the other end of the human continuum from the underground man with his titanic striving is the beautiful soul who has been formed by the truth of Christ. Dostoevsky became more successful at depicting such individuals as his work progressed, though they remain more the center of illumination in the novels than the center of the action. The Elder Zosima, for example, is juxtaposed with the Grand Inquisitor and was intended as an immediate response to the Inquisitor's arguments.[24] Of course it is here more important than ever to remember that the "whole novel" serves as Dostoevsky's own response to these issues, and that the discourse of Book VI is the speech of the Elder and not the author. Zosima is the voice of the traditional monastic leaders of Russian piety with all their "infinite, naïve hopes for the future of Russia," which did not necessarily coincide with Dostoevsky's own more somber assessment of history.[25] It is for this reason that he was concerned that the "answer" might not be enough.

> For this 6th book, *The Russian Monk* . . . was intended as an answer to this whole negative side. And therefore I also tremble for it in this sense—will it be a *sufficient* answer? The more so that this answer now is not direct, not point by point to the theses that were expressed earlier (in the G. *Inquisitor* and before), but is only implied. Here something is presented directly opposed to the world-outlook expressed above, but again it is present point by point, but, so to speak, in an artistic picture. This is what disturbs me, that is, will I be understood and will I attain even a particle of my aim?[26]

The uncertainty, moreover, is justified inasmuch as Dostoevsky's intention was to remain faithful to the tensions within reality itself: there is a truth of Ivan's revolt against innocent suffering and to the Inquisitor's complaint that men are incapable of shouldering the burden of freedom. Most strikingly, the Elder Zosima adds nothing further by the way of argument or information to change their position. The presentation has to be oblique, a juxtaposition rather than a confrontation, because the opposing sides live within different worlds. What is required is not a mere listening to the words of the Elder but a real hearing of them, in which event the reality to which they refer can penetrate our hearts and the world of Christ's love can overcome the world of man's revolt.

Only then can we recognize Zosima's tale as a revelation of the way to paradise on earth and beyond it, in contrast to the hell on earth that is promised by the words of the Inquisitor. His proclamation is that paradise is already present within us and is only waiting to burst forth as soon as we are willing to admit that "each of us has sinned against all men, and I more than any" (BK 344). If we are to perceive the divine mystery in all things, we must be prepared to abandon our pride in asking one another for forgiveness and in forgiving one another in turn. "There is only one means of salvation," he replies to Ivan's rebellion:

> Take yourself and make yourself responsible for all men's sins, that is the truth, you know, friends, for as soon as you sincerely make yourself responsible for everything and for all men, you will see at once that it is really so, and that you are to blame for every one and for all things. But throwing your own indolence and impotence on others you will end by sharing the pride of Satan and murmuring against God. (BK 384)

The love that loves a man even in his sin discloses the reality that endures, in light of which even the evil in man's existence fades into insignificance. We attain to that mystic sense of the unity between our transient world and its eternal foundation, which is the source of Zosima's ecstatic worship of the whole creation. Reality formed such a continuous vision that he could call on the birds for forgiveness, insisting that "all is like an ocean, all is flowing and bending; a touch in one place sets up movement at the other end of the earth" (BK 383ff). This is why he exhorted Alyosha to "water the earth with the tears of our joy and love these tears" as the way of opening his soul toward the same visionary truth. For it was only when Alyosha had undergone the same experience, when "something firm and unshakeable as the vault of heaven had entered his soul," that he recognized "the threads from all those innumerable worlds of God" by which all that grows lives and is alive (BK 436).

The struggle within the soul of man reveals the struggle within the soul of society. Dostoevsky understood Plato's anthropological principle that the polis is man written in large letters, that the substance of society is psyche, and that the exploration of social-political reality, if it is to be critical, must penetrate to the different human types that dominate the public realm. This is what he sought to do by means of his analysis of the underground-titanic man and paradigmatic Christ-like individual, whose opposition had come to define the social and historical setting. It enabled him to explore the same underlying tension on this comprehensive level: to understand that the dream of liberal humanitarianism would become a nightmare if it were not firmly anchored in the spirit of Christian self-sacrifice. Through novels and other writings, Dostoevsky focused his inquiry on those whom this civilizational crisis was most compelling and whose response would most crucially determine the outcome. This is the new urban class of petty officials, disaffected intellectuals and former gentry whose overriding characteristic is that they now exist beyond the support of restraint of most traditional Russian institutions. In them have been concentrated all the consequences of "the two-century-long detachment [of the Russian upper classes] from the soil and from work of every kind" (DW 545).[27] Tolstoy and others who write about the true Russian aristocracy were confined, in Dostoevsky's view, to the creation of historical novels, since the world they described had not become "an insignificant and segregated little corner of Russian life." By contrast, if one were concerned with the other more numerous corners of national life one must feel compelled "to elucidate even a fraction of this chaos, even without the hope of finding the guiding thread." Dostoevsky saw himself as definitely transcending the historical "land-owner literature" of his contemporaries by resolutely fixing his attention on the disorder of the society that surrounded him, in the hope of eventually finding therein "the laws of both his decomposition and the new construction" (DW 592).[28]

The new class of rootless wanderers that replaced the previously dominant landowning class had their origins in the segregation of the nobility and intelligentsia from the Russian people. A process that began with the Europeanizing reforms of Peter the Great culminated in the liberation of the serfs, as the severing of the final link with the life of the people. Even the Russian language was abandoned in favor of French and the cultural heritage of the West in general. The disconnected gentry looked disdainfully on the rudeness of the Russian peasant with his superstitious attachment to Orthodoxy and his tendency toward reckless excess. As a modern intelligentsia their mission was to rescue the people from their ignorance, by introducing the light of universal liberal reason everywhere they went. The hollowness of this humanitarian project became all too apparent in its consequences, as Dostoevsky relentlessly exposed the impotence of a merely human love that flourishes in the abstract but finds in practice "that man is physically unable to love his neighbor" (A 214).[29] Not that the ideal of a universal love of mankind is false, but that it can never be realized without the true inner transformation in the image of Christ. In turning their backs on the people, the liberal dreamers had, Dostoevsky was convinced, turned away from the one enduring source of this truth.

The sectarian viewpoint fundamentally characterized the outlook of the Russian educated class of the nineteenth century. They defined themselves by means of segregations. The sense of possessing a superior wisdom in science, material progress and autonomous morality was so pervasive that they felt at last as if they had escaped the human condition. It began to seem as if the road to spiritual growth could be bypassed, if only men were willing to follow the promptings of enlightened self-interest. No more would the attainment of inner maturity involve the painful renunciation of self; the golden age of reason had made realization of the free personality available to everyone for the asking. But the real nature of this liberal enlightenment did not escape Dostoevsky: contempt for human freedom. In refusing to pay the price of dying to oneself—the only way to true self-realization—they reveal the low esteem in which they hold man's most previous possession. Everything that is of value in man arises out of the inviolability of his free response. By making man the creature of his social circumstances and his material interests, which have only to be changed in order to change his character, modern socialists have deprived man of responsibility for his actions and, as a consequence, of his dignity as a man. Dostoevsky was a close student of the new reformed courts and repeatedly opposed the inhumaneness of their "humane" acquittals of criminals on account of their social environment (DW 13).

The microcosm of this spiritual crisis is the Russian family. Dostoevsky was fascinated by the disintegration of the family—the appearance of "casual households" and "accidental families"—as both reflecting and promoting the larger collapse of the Russian civilizational ethos. Fathers who saw themselves called to a universal liberal mission felt free to neglect the concrete responsibilities to their children (Versilov, Stepan Verkhovensky), and were eventually followed by others for whom the itch to debauch was rationalization enough to neglect their familial duties (Fyodor Karamazov). Without paternal authority and love the sons grew up in the private world of their own resentment and rebellion. Some gave themselves over to revolutionary activity believing that the destruction of the present is the way to future regeneration (Stepan Verkhovensky, Ivan Karamazov in part); others abandoned themselves to the underground world of their own dreams of superiority to all that is (Arkady Dolgoruky, Ivan Karamazov in part); and others simply threw themselves into the reckless, passionate life of their fathers (Dmitri Karamazov). Those who could be saved were frequently saved by encountering the living soul of life within their mothers or within the other women, whose enduring suffering of everything in patience had made them transparent with the mystery of life through death in all creation (Arkady's mother, Sonya Marmeladov, Maria Lebyatkin). Dostoevsky's painstaking exploration of these relationships reveals the extent to which the fate of the nation is being decided within the struggles of the Russian family.

No more than the family can the nation survive without the love of fathers for their children (DW 776ff.). True brotherhood exists only where love has called forth the free response of love, in creating the bond of mutual obligation on which alone the social-political union can be based. The Western substitution of reason, science and self-interest cannot provide an enduring foundation; its results were graphically evident to Dostoevsky in the spiritual and political decay of modern Europe. He formulated it as an empirical rule that

> if nations fail to live by superior disinterested ideas, by the lofty aims of serving mankind, and merely serve their own "interests," they must unfailingly perish, grow benumbed, wear themselves out, die. (DW 901)

For the moral idea comes first. It provides the nation with its *raison d'etre*, and with its disappearance the survival of the nation ceases to serve a purpose.[30] Saving one's skin at the cost of what makes life worth living is, neither for individuals nor for states, a course that achieves either virtue or safety. In opposition to the fashion of *realpolitik,* Dostoevsky insisted, while recognizing the necessity for a balance of power, that "the policy of honor and disinterestedness is not only the supreme but, perhaps, the most advantageous policy for a great nation, exactly because it is great" (DW 381). These and similar reflections emerged within the context of the debate about Russian self-sacrifice in aiding their fellow Slavs of Eastern Europe against the Turks, but they form part of Dostoevsky's larger concern with the restoration of order in the modern world. The ideal end of such a renovated political philosophy Dostoevsky envisioned as "individual self-betterment" through moral growth (DW 1000).

It is because they have lost sight of this truth that Russian fathers fail to take responsibility for raising their children in the light of responsibility itself. Their failure is a reflection of the pervasive abdication by the intelligentsia of any responsibility for preserving the moral foundations of society. In order to bring about the general improvement of social life, all that is needed is progress in the material conditions of existence and the removal of all institutional restraints on autonomy. The real character of this idealism is to be recognized, not only in the suggestion that man does live by bread alone and can be controlled by it, but much more significantly in the train of disorder that is invariably let loose in society. Dostoevsky understood the political dynamics of the modern revolutionary process, and indicated them most clearly in his tale of the Grand Inquisitor. Utopian dreamers represent only the first stage of the revolution; they are capable of destroying the old, but when the expected transformation of human nature does not occur, they are left in helpless chaos. The process is finally concluded only when a strong personality comes on the scene. Such a one is the old Inquisitor who recognizes that men are "vile and weak" and that, having failed to build the Tower of Babel, they now seek him out after a thousand years of agony.

> They will find us and cry to us, "Feed us, for those who promised us fire from heaven haven't given it!" And then we will finish building their tower, for he finishes the building who feeds them. (BK 300)

The attempt to produce good behavior through manipulation is now completed by the ruler who understands that men will only become brothers through the utter destruction of their human freedom.[31] He is successful because he is uninhibited by any respect for the inner person. He embodies the "everything is lawful," for the secret of the Inquisitor is, as Alyosha guesses, that he no longer believes in God and therefore can no longer believe in man.

But his tragedy is that he once did believe in God. "I too prized the freedom with which Thou hast blessed men, and I too was striving to stand among Thy elect. . . . [before] I turned back and joined the ranks of those *who have corrected Thy work*" (BK 308). Mixed with the pride of the man who thinks he can do better than God is the true divine ideal of making all men brothers. The problem arises from the mistaken conviction that brotherhood can be achieved by eradicating man's untrustworthy freedom, not from the ideal itself, to which Dostoevsky remained loyal all his life. Indeed it could be said that he remained from first to last a "Christian socialist." What changed completely was his conception of how a Christian socialism was to be realized. From an advocacy of change in the institutional structure of society as paramount, he came to insist on the primacy of an inner spiritual regeneration of the person as the principle and goal. In place of a change through revolution, he sought a transformation through conversion. The heroes who are closest to Dostoevsky's own Christian socialism of the 1840s and who, as a consequence, do not develop into the demonic extremes of "unrestricted despotism," are frequently the ones who recover and restore the ideal of brotherhood to its true Christian foundation. Stepan Verkhovensky, father of the fanatical revolutionary, recognizes the nihilistic abyss of socialism and proclaims that "the final word in this business must be general forgiveness"; it is the only way for Russia to be freed of the devils that possess her (P 504, 671). Without this underlying change of heart, no genuine political order is possible.

The temptation, however, to yield to the illusory efficacy of power is so universal that Dostoevsky found in it the basis for his philosophy of history. He considered the devil's three temptations to Christ in the wilderness to have been extraordinary in the extent to which they predicted the whole future history of mankind. "The statement of these three temptations was itself the miracle" (BK 299). In them was revealed the great heresy in the history of Christianity which Dostoevsky identified as the central idea of the Catholic Church: "Christianity cannot survive on earth without the earthly power of the Pope" (DW 225).[32] It implied the acceptance of the devil's suggestion that man is only material and capable of living by bread alone, that men are unsuited to the spiritual achievement of faith and must be given tangible proof, and that political power must be obtained first even at the price of man's humanity. This was the great turning point at which Orthodoxy had broken away from Western Christianity, which followed its own logical unfolding into the modern world. Dostoevsky regarded socialism as merely an extension of the Catholic principle that had now largely dispensed with the religious component, while Protestantism was no more than the recurrent ineffectual protests against this principle in the name of individualism (DW 563ff).

This is the setting from which Orthodox Russia derives its world-historic mission. As the preserver of the true Christian faith, it is the indispensible vehicle for the political and spiritual salvation of mankind. In contrast to the West where the Church was absorbed into the state, in the East "the state was conquered and destroyed by the sword of Mohammed, and there remained only Christ detached from the state." The conflict that had originated with the confrontation between Christianity and the Roman Empire, when "the man-god encountered the God-man, Apollo of Belvedere encountered Christ," has now reached its culmination in the opposition between European socialism and Russian Orthodoxy (DW 1005). It is the apocalyptic character of this conflict that impressed Dostoevsky, the sense of living at a decisive turning point that, while "by no means solving *all* human destinies, brings with it the beginning of the end of the whole former history of European mankind" (DW 565). He had contemplated the abyss of European nihilism and recognized it as the death of a civilization. The only non-nihilistic alternative was a restoration of the inner spirit of Christian love that he found preserved nowhere else but within Orthodoxy. In framing the problem thus, Dostoevsky was careful to avoid chiliastic or millenarian excesses, for it was precisely against the reduction of man to a historical future that he was reacting. And while much has been made of his messianism and his occasional militarism (that Russia must take Constantinople as part of its pan-Slavic mission), it must always be remembered that the primary means to be employed is the power of suffering love, the power of Christ.

Even the avowedly Russocentric nature of the vision does not invalidate its content, since it arises from Dostoevsky's own experience with the Russian people as the means for his personal reception of the grace of salvation. It was because of them, he explains in the *Diary*, that "I again received into my soul Christ Who had been revealed to me in my parents home and Whom I was about to lose when on my part, I transformed myself into a 'European liberal'" (DW 984). In this experience he came to recognize the political importance of the Russian peasants as the one segment of society in which the spiritual reality of man, the core of Orthodoxy, has been preserved without dilution. They may be ignorant or unlearned, they may be deceived or weak-willed, they may be debauched or even cruel, but they never attempt to conceal the moral truth of human existence. Most importantly, for Dostoevsky, people never will accept their sins for truth (DW 985). Before the witness of the simple peasant all argument is superfluous; the testimony of living life itself is all the proof we need that the knowledge of good and evil is innate and not acquired. Everyone, Dostoevsky asserted, is able to understand "Thou shalt love thy neighbor as thyself." "Essentially this knowledge comprises man's whole *law* and so it was enunciated to us by Christ" (DW 790). The peasants are the ones who truly know the meaning of Orthodoxy, because their school has been the centuries of suffering which they have endured in their history and continue to remain with Christ—"the Counselor Whom they embraced forever in their soul, and Who, as a reward for this, has saved their soul from despair" (DW 983). They carry the image of Christ within them because their sufferings have been united with the redemptive sacrifice of Christ.

It is this capacity to die to themselves that gives the Russian people their universal mission. They have become capable of transcending their own specific interests and culture to serve as the medium of universal spiritual truth to mankind. Dostoevsky repeatedly calls attention to the facility with which Russians have adopted the language, manners and civilization of the European nations, as a preparation for their role as carriers of the universal ideal. At the same time, he emphasized, they find within themselves the spiritual truth of existence—their unity with the suffering of Christ—which has made the words "peasantry" (*Krestianstvo*) and "Christianity" (*Christianstvo*) virtually synonymous (DW 452). The special character of the Russians is that they find their identity in the love of two motherlands, Russia and Europe; the service of the universal and the tendency toward cosmopolitanism are the impulses that have united Russians of every social stratum (DW 342, 581). It is on this basis that Dostoevsky made his famous appeal, in the Pushkin Speech, for a reconciliation between the Westernizing liberals and the conservative Slavophiles. Their unification is made possible by the identity of their goals: the Westerners have submerged their Russianness in order to pursue the idea of universal human progress, the Slavophiles have discovered that the Russian is defined by his devotion to the one spiritual truth in all men. Everything hinges on the recognition that the service of all men consists precisely in the service of each individual man in the unique, irreplaceable freedom of his or her person. To be a genuine Russian means in his view

> to show the solution of European anguish in our all-humanitarian and all-unifying Russian soul, to embrace in it with brotherly love all our brethren, and finally, perhaps, to utter the ultimate word of great universal harmony, of the brotherly accord of all nations abiding by the law of Christ's gospel. (DW 980)

Yet there was nothing inevitable about this vision of a new golden age that Dostoevsky carried within, because it is almost entirely based on a love that calls forth and depends on a free response. This is why the qualification "perhaps" is always present. It was above all a truth he apprehended within his own experience and found embodied in all that is best within the Russian people. He powerfully evoked the example of Pushkin who was the first to recognize the people's truth as the answer to the modern search for true humanizing progress. Pushkin prefigured the Russian destiny of "universality acquired not by the sword but by the force of brotherhood," and thereby pointed the way toward the building of a new world "through the universal communion in the name of Christ." Dostoevsky referred to this as "our Russian socialism," or "the establishment of an oecumenical Church on earth in so far as the earth is capable of embracing it" (DW 979, 1029). Its foundation is the recognition that "individual self-betterment" is the beginning and the end of all political organization, that the regeneration of the inner person is more important than institutional reform and that the suffering appeal of individual example is the way toward it. His faith in the transformation of the modern revolutionary spirit into the Christian personal *metanoia* was illustrated by the French writer, George Sand, whom he much admired. His reflections at her death brought him back to his own beginnings.

> ... George Sand, I repeat, was perhaps, without knowing it herself, one of the staunchest confessors of Christ. She based her socialism, her convictions, her hopes and her ideals upon the moral feeling of man, upon the spiritual thirst of mankind and its longing for perfection and purity, and not upon "ant-necessity." All her life she believed absolutely in human personality (to the point of its immortality), elevating and broadening this concept in each one of her works; and thereby she concurred in thought and feeling with one of the basic ideas of Christianity, i.e., the recognition of human personality and its freedom (consequently, also of its responsibility). (DW 349)

Dostoevsky could range back and forth over the history of his own convictions without encountering a contradiction because he was dealing first and foremost with an openness to reality, rather than with any dogmatic propositions of assent. Whether one begins as a socialist or a Christian is less significant than how one responds to the truth disclosed by the directional pull of experience. A belief in autonomous morality can unfold into an insistence on the absolute independence of man's private conscience from any higher reality, and may be so proposed in the name of human freedom; but the inexorable result will be the radical separation from any enduring criterion of truth. The nihilism of "everything is lawful" sets at nought the value of human freedom itself. A more open unfolding of the moral intuitions of the heart would reveal the law of reality that binds all things because it has its source in God. Man cannot set himself in judgment over all things without thereby destroying the very principle of justice in whose name he has revolted; he can live rightly only by fulfilling his own concrete obligations within the mysterious process of the whole. In this way he comes to penetrate the essential meaning of existence as the divine plan of redemption. He begins to discover the One in whom the victory of good over evil has been completed, and to see in Christ the one in whom the true freedom of man attains its highest recognition. It is Dostoevsky's achievement as a political philosopher to have articulated this dynamic of "living life" and to have recovered, as a result, the vision of Christianity as the core—previously lacking—which alone could provide the only true inspiration of the modern revolutionary movement.

NOTES

Originally published as David Walsh, "Dostoevsky's Discovery of the Christian Foundation of Politics," *Religion and Literature* 19 (1987). Reprinted with permission with slight modifications.

1. Notable exceptions are the studies of Ellis Sandoz, "Philosophical Dimensions of Dostoevsky's Politics," *Journal of Politics* 40 (1978), Jean Drouilly, *La Pensée Politique et Religieuse de F. M. Dostoevsky* (Paris: Libraire des Cinq Continentes, 1971), and Jack F. Matlock, "Literature and Politics: The Impact of Fyodor Dostoevsky," *The Political Science Reviewer* 9 (1979).

2. Konstantin Mochulsky, *Dostoevsky: His Life and Work* (Princeton: Princeton University Press, 1967), 650.

3. For his revolutionary years see Joseph Frank, *Dostoevsky: The Seeds of Revolt, 1821–1849* (Princeton: Princeton University Press, 1976), Chs. 17–19. On the prison experience and his conversion see Joseph Frank, *Dostoevsky: The Years of Ordeal, 1850–1859* (Princeton: Princeton University Press, 1990), Chs. 1–11. And on the period of his release, Joseph Frank, *Dostoevsky: The Stir of Liberation, 1860–1865* (Princeton: Princeton University Press, 1986). Dostoevsky's own account of the prison years is available in Fyodor Dostoevsky, *The House of the Dead* (New York: Dutton, 1962).

4. See Hendri de Lubac, *The Drama of Athiest Humanism* (New York: New American Library, 1963), 167–87 for an excellent discussion of the comparison with Nietzsche.

5. Fyodor Dostoevsky, *The Diary of a Writer* (Santa Barbara: Peregrine Smith, 1979). This "Diary" which consists of Dostoevsky's reflections published monthly (with interruptions) between 1873 and 1881, is an indispensable source for his mature understanding of politics, philosophy, literature and religion. Hereafter cited in-text as DW.

6. Mikhail Bakhtin, *Problems of Dostoevsky's Poetics* (Minneapolis: University of Minnesota Press, 1984), 20 explains Dostoevsky's technique of polyphonic novel as "the principle of seeing and understanding the world and its formulation from the viewpoint of a given idea only for the characters, not for the author himself, not for Dostoevsky" (20). "It is not a world of objects, illuminated and ordered by his monological thinking, that unrolls before Dostoevsky, but a world of mutually illuminating consciousness. . . . He searches among them for the highest, most authoritative orientation, and he thinks of it not as his own true thought, but as another person and his world. The image of the ideal man or the image of Christ represents for him the solution of ideological quests. This image or this highest of voices must crown the world of voices" (90). See also Robert Louis Jackson, *The Art of Dostoevsky* (Princeton: Princeton University Press, 1981).

7. Dostoevsky provides an appreciative recognition of the use of the same technique by Herzen in Dostoevsky, *The Diary of a Writer*, 5.

8. Mochulsky, *Dostoevsky: His Life and Work*, 17.

9. See Vyaacheslav Ivanov, *Freedom and the Tragic Life* (New York: Noonday, 1952), George Panichas, *The Burden of Vision: Dostoevsky's Spiritual Art* (Grand Rapids: Eerd-

mans, 1977), and A. Boyce Gibson, *The Religion of Dostoevsky* (Philadelphia: Westminster, 1973).

10. Fyodor Dostoevsky, *The Brothers Karamazov* (New York: Modern Library, 1950), 127. Hereafter cited as BK.

11. Mochulsky, *Dostoevsky: His Life and Work*, 17.

12. Fyodor Dostoyevsky, *The Possessed* (New York: New American Library, 1962), 434. Hereafter cited as P.

13. Arkady Dolgoruky, the young narrator of *The Adolescent*, explains his ideal of becoming a Rothschild: "I don't really need money, or rather it's not money that I'm after, nor power for that matter. What I'm after is something that can be acquired through power and only through power: that is self-sufficiency and a calm awareness of my strength. And this is the most complete definition of the freedom that the world is striving for! Freedom! I have finally written down the great word" (Fyodor Dostoevsky, *The Adolescent* (New York: Norton, 1971), 87). Hereafter cited as A.

14. The reader first encounters them in Dostoevsky, *The House of the Dead*.

15. Lebedev in *The Idiot* tries to identify the "whole trend" of the modern world and finds its essence not in the new technology of railroads and large-scale industrialization, but in the false humanitarianism at its core: "But a friend of humanity with shaky moral principles is a devourer of humanity, not to speak of his vanity; for if you wound the vanity of one of these innumerable friends of humanity he's ready to set fire to the four corners of the earth to satisfy a petty revenge, like all of us would, and, to speak fairly, like I would, the vilest of all" (Fyodor Dostoevsky, *The Idiot* (New York: New American Library, 1969), 396).

16. The character and fate of Svidrigailov in Fyodor Dostoevsky, *Crime and Punishment* (New York: Dutton, 1961) follows a similar course.

17. Shigalov, the ideological planner of the revolutionary cadre in *The Possessed*, expressed it thus: "I have become entangled in my own data and my conclusions directly contradict my original premises. I started out with the idea of unrestricted freedom and I have arrived at unrestricted despotism. I must add, however, that any solution of the social problem other than mine is impossible" (P 300).

18. See Alyosha's reflections on Ivan in *The Brothers Karamazov*, 796.

19. Mochulsky, *Dostoevsky: His Life and Work*, 261.

20. Mochulsky, *Dostoevsky: His Life and Work*, 345.

21. Mochulsky, *Dostoevsky: His Life and Work*, 622. See also Ellis Sandoz, *Political Apocalypse: A Study of Dostoevsky's Grand Inquisitor* (Baton Rouge: Louisiana State University Press, 1971), 218 and *passim*. For a more ambivalent assessment see Vasily Rozanov, *Dostoevsky and the Legend of the Grand Inquisitor* (Ithaca: Cornell University Press, 1972).

22. Mochulsky, *Dostoevsky: His Life and Work*, 152.

23. The Elder Zosima in *The Brothers Karamazov* expresses it thus: "On earth, indeed, we are as it were astray, and if it were not for the precious image of Christ before us, we should be undone and altogether lost, as was the human race before the flood" (384).

24. See also Makar Dolgoruky, the pilgrim in *The Adolescent*, and Bishop Tikhon in *The Possessed* for other examples of this type.

25. Mochulsky, *Dostoevsky: His Life and Work*, 589.

26. Mochulsky, *Dostoevsky: His Life and Work*, 590.

27. Cf. James H. Billington, *The Icon and the Axe: An Interpretive History of Russian Culture* (New York: Vintage, 1966), esp. Chs. IV and V.

28. *The Adolescent* was originally entitled "Disorder" and was intended to portray the obsolescence of "landowner literature" as Dostoevsky referred to it. See the *Adolescent*, 564–66 and Mochulsky, *Dostoevsky: His Life and Work*, 497ff.

29. Ivan in *The Brothers Karamazov* similarly exclaims: "I could never understand how one could love one's neighbours. It's just one's neighbours, to my mind, that one can't love, though one might love those at a distance" (281).

30. *Diary of a Writer*, 1000ff.

31. See *Diary of a Writer*, 620 on the proletarian intention of compelling the bourgeoisie to become a "brother," the principle of *fraternité ou la mort*.

32. See also *The Idiot*, 560ff. Dostoevsky's anti-Catholicism is almost as notorious as his anti-Semitism and therefore just as much in need of explanation. The most important aspect to emphasize is that his opposition arises in each case from a hatred of the principle that he saw represented by Catholicism or Judaism, the subordination of faith to power or the unbridled pursuit of wealth. He always retained the awareness that specific individuals may not fall under the abstract classification of the group, that their hearts are still capable of being guided by the light of inner moral truth. Moreover, he explicitly defended himself against the charge of anti-Semitism and called for brotherhood between Jews and Christians which, as Joseph Frank remarks, "is not the same as calling for a pogrom" ("Introduction" to *Diary of a Writer*, xxiii).

TWO

The Politics and Experience of Active Love in *The Brothers Karamazov*

Lee Trepanier

INTRODUCTION

Early reception of *The Brothers Karamazov* ranged from praise to condemnation, with most of the criticism and debate focused on Book V's *The Tale of the Grand Inquisitor*. Both liberal atheists and conservative believers upbraided Dostoevsky for his alleged identification with the Inquisitor's position against God, while a minority of critics, such as Vladimir Soloviev, applauded Dostoevsky's exploration and defense of Christianity.[1] In the West interest in *The Brothers* also focused on *The Tale*, with commentary ranging from Dostoevsky's literary techniques to his theories of psychology, philosophy, and theology.[2] Perhaps the most influential of these criticisms both in Russia and the West was M. M. Bakhtin's *Problems of Dostoevsky's Creative Works* that was published in 1929 and later reissued and expanded in 1963 as *Problems of Dostoevsky's Poetics*.[3] Crucial to Bakhtin's criticism was his concept of polyphonism as the interpretative key to understanding Dostoevsky's works. According to Bakhtin, there exist multiple points of view as represented by the characters in Dostoevsky's novels, with no one view or position privileged over another: each character possessed a fully valid voice that was either consciously or subconsciously engaged in a dialogue with other characters. Although the author abstained from his authoritative voice in the work, Dostoevsky's novels nonetheless had a unifying structure in them; or what Bakhtin referred to as a "unity in diversity": there was an underlying harmony in Dostoevsky's works in spite of their polyphonic nature.[4]

Unfortunately, this suggestion has been ignored by most commentators on *The Brothers*; and instead of looking for such a "unity in diversity," critics have focused on the polyphonic aspect of Bakhtin's theory to interpret *The Brothers*. On the one hand, the critics agree that *The Tale* is the crux to understanding *The Brothers*; but, on the other hand, they disagree on the significance of *The Tale* and how it is related to the rest of the book. Some identify Dostoevsky's position with Christ; others equate his position with the Inquisitor's; and most, by employing Bakhtin's polyphonic theory, select one or two characters in the novel for their own philosophical speculation.[5] By adopting Bakhtin's polyphonic theory, these critics can claim that the author's beliefs are irrelevant to the interpretation of the novel, because the characters all possess equally valid positions. Within this interpretative context, the critic can adopt a postmodern stance in dismissing the author's viewpoint and construct any significance to the novel that he wishes.

But not all critics have subscribed to Bakhtin's polyphonic theory: another group, usually post-revolutionary émigrés and post-Soviet writers, have focused on the religious themes in Dostoevsky's works.[6] These critics start from the opposite assumption of the Bakhtin camp: the author's views are relevant to the interpretation of the novel. In spite of occasionally lapsing into a too reverential attitude towards Dostoevsky, these critics acknowledge the attractive power of Book V but contend it is Book VI where Dostoevsky's own philosophical and theological positions are presented. The chief spokespersons for Christianity, Alyosha and Zosima, refute Ivan and the Grand Inquisitor not by logic and reason but rather by indirection and example.

My own interpretation of *The Brothers* concurs with these critics and builds upon their analyses with a focus on the experiential nature of active love and its role in forging a community of responsibility and memory modeled after the ideals of Christianity. The episodes that best exemplify how active love accomplishes these tasks are found in Zosima's memoirs, Alyosha's encounter with Grushenka, and the portrayal of the children in the novel. These episodes represent the "unity in diversity" that Bakhtin had claimed in his study of Dostoevsky's works. In a sense, I try to reclaim Bakhtin from those who have misused his theoretical concept of polyphony for their own philosophical agenda in the interpretation of the novel: underneath the valid and opposing viewpoints is a unity rooted in Zosima's teachings of active love and responsibility for all. Thus, contrary to the claim that *The Brothers* is a polyphonic novel, where the author's own views are irrelevant to its interpretation, and the claim that Dostoevsky was unable to furnish an adequate defense of Christianity, I contend that the often neglected doctrines of active love and the responsibility for all are the interpretive keys to the novel — Bakhtin's "unity in diversity" — thereby providing a compelling alternative vision to Ivan's and the Grand Inquisitor's.

THE CHALLENGE OF THE GRAND INQUISITOR

The Tale of the Grand Inquisitor begins as a dialogue between the two brothers, Ivan and Alyosha, where the former acknowledges his incapacity to experience Christian love for one's fellow neighbors. "I could never understand," Ivan says, "how one could love one's neighbors . . . though one might love them at a distance."[7] Ivan can only see the possibility of Christian love as a Kantian categorical imperative: something required or imposed upon by duty. The cruelties of humans, especially on innocent and helpless children, had led Ivan to conclude that humans are nothing more than monsters of destruction. Adopting a rationality of cause-and-effect, "Euclidean reason," Ivan finds the suffering of the innocent intellectually incomprehensible and emotionally unendurable, for "The innocent must not suffer for another's sins, and especially such innocent [children]!" (14:215). He rejects the idea of a higher and universal harmony, such as a Christian Paradise where all is forgiven and reconciled: "I don't want harmony. From love of humanity, I don't want it. I would rather be left with unavenged suffering . . . *even if I were wrong*" (14:223). The depth of Ivan's rejection is so great that he declares, "And so I hasten to give back my admission ticket, and if I am an honest man I must give it back as soon as possible. . . . It's not God that I don't accept, Alyosha, only I most respectfully return Him my ticket" (14:223).[8]

This sense of outrage against God is dramatically portrayed in Ivan's unfinished poem, *The Tale of the Grand Inquisitor*. In *The Tale* Christ returns to Seville during the darkest days of the Inquisition, where "everyone recognized Him . . . He moves silently in the people's midst with a gentle smile of infinite compassion. The sun of love burns in His heart. Light, Enlightenment, and Power shine from His eyes, and their radiance, shed on the people, stirs their heart with responsive love" (14:226). While Christ performs His miracles, prompted by the "responsive love" between Him and the people, the Grand Inquisitor, "an old man, almost ninety, tall and erect with a withered face and sunken eyes," orders the arrest of Christ and throws Him into prison where the two confront each other face-to-face. While Christ remains silent, the Grand Inquisitor asks why Christ had returned "with empty hands, with some promise of freedom," when He could have accepted the first temptation in the desert of turning stones into bread. If He had done so, "mankind will run after Thee like a flock, grateful and obedient"; instead, Christ refused because it would deprive "man of freedom . . . thinking, what is freedom worth if obedience is brought with bread?" (14:230). Christ's refusal therefore is a refusal to command human conscience—a refusal that is reinforced by Christ's rejection of the second and third temptations: proof of His own divinity and acceptance of temporal power to enforce His faith on earth.

By refusing to "take possession of man's freedom," the Inquisitor charges Christ, "You have increased man's freedom and burdened his spiritual kingdom with suffering forever. . . . In place of the rigid ancient law, man now must with a free heart decide for himself what is good and what is evil, having only Your image before him as a guide" (14:232). But because humans are "weak, vicious, worthless, and rebellious," incapable of acting out of the self-sacrifice that Christ had demanded, His message will fail. In its place the Grand Inquisitor has taken upon himself the burden of freedom to provide meaning to humans under the guise of Christ's name: "We corrected Your work and [instead of freedom of conscience] have founded it upon miracle, mystery, and authority" (14:234). Initially humans will attempt to discover the meaning of existence for themselves—whether in science, reason, or waiting for the return of Christ—but eventually they will grow weary and look upon the Inquisitor to provide them a universal happiness: "we shall persuade them that they will become free only when they renounce their freedom to us and submit to us," and humankind will be reduced to the level of children, with every detail of their lives under the Inquisitor's control. "Peacefully they will die, peacefully they will expire in Your name, but beyond the grave they will find nothing but death," for immortality does not exist (14:235-236).

Although the Grand Inquisitor's secret is that he works for the Devil and not for Christ—"We are not with You but with *him*—that is our mystery"—he is not an atheist who has joined the forces of Enlightenment and reason (14:234). For Ivan, the Grand Inquisitor is a tragic figure who genuinely suffers, because he "has wasted his whole life in the desert and yet could not shake off his incurable love for humanity"; and this suffering only increases because he "leads men consciously to death and destruction and yet deceive them all the way . . . in the name of Him in whose ideal the old man had so fervently believed all his life long" (14:237–239). Perhaps recognizing his suffering, Christ responses to the Inquisitor's monologue with a kiss on the lips, prompting the Inquisitor to shudder and open the cell door for Christ. "Go," he commands Him, "and come no more—come not at all, never, never." After Christ has left, "'the kiss glows' in his heart, but the old man sticks to his idea" (14:240).

By itself, *The Tale* provides a compelling argument against Christianity; but in the context of the entire novel, it is one of a series of lacerations (*nadryv*) that various characters exhibit, which only active love can heal. Throughout *The Brothers*, particularly in the characters Dmitry and Feodor, the reader is reminded of the "Karamazov baseness"—the earthly drive for sensuality—to which Ivan himself admits of possessing. "It is a feature of the Karamazovs, it's true that the thirst for life regardless of everything, you have it no doubt too, but why is it base?" (14:209). This baseness can be channeled into an indulgence of gross sensuality, as demonstrated by Feodor's and Dmitry's exploits, but it also can be transformed into a life-sustaining force, as Ivan acknowledges:

[E]ven if I didn't believe in life, if I lost faith in the order of things, were convinced in fact that everything is disorderly, damnable, and perhaps devil-ridden chaos, if I were struck by every horror of man's disillusionment—still I would want to live, and having once tasted of the cup, I would not turn away from it until I have drained it. . . . I have a longing for life, and I go on living in spite of logic (14:209).

The attempt to rise above this "Karamazov baseness" is usually to deny one's material, sensual nature, resulting in a fragmentation or laceration of oneself. The assumption of higher motives for one's actions—honor, nobility, love—at the expense of our material nature is to both objectify ourselves and others that in turn create a condition of incoherence and self-fragmentation. An example of this is Katrina's alleged love and devotion to Dmitry. Disgraced earlier by Dmitry, Katrina's profession of love is really a form of vengeance or baseness, although she refuses to admit it and causes harm both to herself and others exposed to her.

Ivan also engages in a type of laceration with his Euclidean compassion and concern for humankind—a "laceration of falsity," as Alyosha suspects (14:215–216). Ivan's claim of love and compassion for humankind disguises his "Karamazov baseness"—his love of nature's "sticky little leaves as they open in spring"—and has transformed itself into a life-sustaining force that compels him to search for a meaning of existence. Of course, Ivan's intellect and logic had led him to conclude that life is meaningless, with his declaration of committing suicide when he turns thirty, because he is torn between his reason and "baseness." This conflict causes Ivan's laceration of falsity with his claims of love and compassion for humankind instead of acknowledging his own base need for companionship and love—something which the author implicitly suggested in the beginning of Book V when he pointed out that Ivan has no friends. Ivan's rebellion therefore is nothing more than a laceration of himself in the denial of his need of companionship and love—a theme that surfaces throughout the novel in such characters like Grushenka, Alyosha, and Kolya.

Given this understanding of Ivan's laceration, *The Tale* is not a conflict between faith and reason, Christianity and Enlightenment, or Christ and the Anti-Christ; rather it is a dramatic account of Christianity in its lacerated form.[9] The Grand Inquisitor's project is a fusion of both strands of Western Christianity: the Catholic provision of happiness to all people with a Protestant elect shouldering the burden of freedom. Ivan sees the choices that Christianity can offer as either the Catholic realization of happiness in a totalitarian state or the Protestant responsibility of individual freedom that eventually collapses into a Hobbesian state of war of all against all. The only possible solution to this problem is the Grand Inquisitor's project of claiming Christian love but ruling as a totalitarian state. Thus, the conflict between the universal happiness of Roman Catholicism and the individual freedom of Protestantism ultimately become reconciled in the Grand Inquisitor's solution.

But Ivan's presentation of Christianity is de-contextualized from the Christian community: individual freedom does not occur in a vacuum but within a community that cultivates and supports people to make the right choices from their consciences. Furthermore, Ivan's presentation of Christianity is incomplete, with Orthodox Christianity absent except for Christ's (and Alyosha's) kiss, representing the mystical and experiential nature of Christianity. By presenting a de-contextualized Christianity, Ivan is able to offer to the reader a false dichotomy of two lacerated versions of Christianity; but, it will be in Book VI, with its examination of Orthodox Christianity, that will re-contextualize the aspirations of Christianity in its unlacerated form and provide a response to *The Tale*. Dostoevsky himself wrote about this account of Christianity in its Catholic, Protestant, and Orthodox forms:

> On one side, at the edge of Europe, there is the Catholic idea—condemned and waiting in great torment and perplexity: Is it to be or not to be? Is it still to live or has its end come? . . . In that sense, for instance, France over the ages has seemed to be the most complete incarnation of the Catholic idea. . . . This France, who developed from the ideas of 1789 her own particular French socialism—i.e., the pacification and organization of human society without Christ and outside of Christ . . . is and continues to be in the highest degree a Catholic nation wholly and entirely, completely contaminated by the spirit and the letter of Catholicism. . . . For French socialism is nothing other than the compulsory union of humanity, an idea that derived from ancient Rome and that was subsequently preserved completely in Catholicism. . . . On the other side rises up old Protestantism. . . . This is the German. . . . Through his entire history he dreamed only of and longed only for his unification so he could proclaim his own proud idea. . . . And meanwhile, in the East, the third world idea—the Slavic idea, a new idea that is coming into being—has truly caught ablaze and has begun to cast a light that has never before been seen; it is, perhaps, the third future possibility for settling the destinies of Europe and of humanity (25:6–9).

From his entries in *Diary of a Writer*, personal correspondences, and private writings, we know that Dostoevsky believed that Orthodox Christianity was the remedy and answer to an Enlightened Europe and Western Christendom. Contrary to Bakhtin's followers, Dostoevsky did not envision *The Brothers* as a polyphonic piece without a unifying structure or had subconsciously sided with the Grand Inquisitor, although he acknowledged his anxiety if he were to fail in his vindication of Orthodox Christianity.[10] As he wrote, "As an answer to all this *negative side*, I am offering this sixth book, 'A Russian Monk.' . . . And I tremble for it in this sense: will it be a *sufficient* answer? All the more so because *the answer here is not a direct one, it is not a point-by-point response to any previously expressed positions* (in the Grand Inquisitor or earlier) but only an oblique response . . . so to speak, in an *artistic pictures*" (IV: 209).

THE RESPONSE OF THE RUSSIAN MONK

For Zosima, the modern predicament for humankind is radical individualism where people are isolated and alienated from one another. This isolation, alienation, and radical individualism are a product of laceration, where humans reject God and therefore deny their proper place in the world, with their pride and egoism dictating their "Karamazov baseness" toward continual sensual and material pleasure. The cure for this modern condition is *kenosis*: the negation of selfhood where we feel a responsibility for everyone and everything, thereby prompting us to engage in active love to improve our individual and communal condition. These two doctrines—responsibility for all and active love—are presented in Book VI, *The Russian Monk*, as an indirect refutation against *The Tale*. The actual content of the Book is the Elder Zosima's memoirs and sermons, with the former divided into three narratives: 1) the death of Zosima's older brother, Markel; 2) the early life of Zosima whose abuse of a servant leads him to change his life; and 3) Zosima's encounter with a mysterious stranger who, after conversations with Zosima, declares his guilt as a murder.

In the first narrative, Markel is portrayed as an atheist freethinker, but upon succumbing to a terminal illness, "a marvelous change passed over him, his spirit was transformed" (14:261). By accepting his own death, Markel was awaken to the value of life to the point of desiring to trade places with his servants and begging for forgiveness from nature because he "did not notice the beauty and glory" of it (14:263). Markel's experience of the value and beauty of life is similar to Ivan's love of life, even if it is against "logic," and what Zosima passes down to Alyosha. The rest of this narrative recounts Zosima's reading of the Book of Job as "a mystery—that the passing earthly scene and the eternal verity are brought together in it" for "it's the great mystery of human life that old grief gradually passes into tender joy"; and urges priests to spread the Gospel among the people rather than performing their assigned clerical duties (14:265).

The second narrative describes Zosima's vicious, debased behavior after military cadet school in St. Petersburg (14:268). He forms an attachment with a respectable young lady but delays marriage for two months in order to continue his debaucheries. When he returns, Zosima discovers she is already married to someone else and that she had been engaged to this suitor while Zosima was courting her. Furious, Zosima challenges the husband to a duel and strikes his orderly, Afanasy; but, on the morning of the duel, he regrets his challenge, with the beauty of nature filling him with shame—the lesson of Markel has reawaken in Zosima's soul—and leads him to ask for forgiveness from Afanasy (14:270). At the duel Zosima allows the husband the first shot, which misses, and refuses to fire in return, asking for forgiveness for his insult. Zosima's refusal to return fire causes a scandal in his regiment and he resigns his commission, announcing that he will enter the monastery.

The final narrative is about the visits of a respected, philanthropic family man to the young officer Zosima, who now has earned a reputation for following his own conscience rather than the expectations of society. The mysterious visitor is interested in what had motivated Zosima to follow his own conscience, because he has "a secret motive of my own, which I may perhaps explain to you later on" (14:274). His secret is that, when he was young, he had murdered a girl who had refused his suit and managed to escape prosecution. The visitor had hoped that his philanthropic activities and later his marriage and family would erase the memory of his crime, but he has become more haunted by it. He agrees with Zosima's assertion that "all men are responsible to all for all, apart from our sins . . . the Kingdom of Heaven will be for them not a dream but a reality"; but wonders whether such a condition is possible, given the nature of modern society, where everyone is isolated and alienated from one another (14:275). Zosima replies that it is possible but it is a long spiritual and psychological process: "Until you have become really, in actual fact, a brother to everyone, brotherhood will not come to pass. No sort of scientific teaching, no kind of common interest, will ever teach us to share property and privileges with equal consideration for all" (14:275). The visitor eventually accepts Zosima's advice and makes a public declaration of his crime, even furnishing evidence to support it. Nobody believes this exemplary citizen, and instead of prosecuting him they have him declared insane, where he ultimately is taken ill and dies.

Zosima concludes with a sermon about two ways of life: the material world with its pursuit of pleasure and desire, and the ecclesiastical world with its obedience, fasting, and prayer. The fundamental difference between these two worlds is their conception of freedom: freedom in the material world is the unbridled pursuit of one's desires; freedom in the ecclesiastical world is to restrain and control these desires. To counteract this material understanding of freedom, Zosima urges Orthodox monks to spread the Gospel and to save the Russian people from the ailments of modernity. They should strive to emulate Christian ideals, in particular they should continue to pray and practice active love, for it is necessary "to love a man even in his sin, for that is the semblance of the Divine love and is the highest love on earth . . . [and] all of God's creation, the whole and every grain of sand in it. Love every leaf, every ray of God's light, love the animals, love the plants, love everything" (14:288–289). Children are especially singled out by Zosima for love, "for they are sinless like the angels, they live to soften and purify our hearts and as it were to guide us."

Zosima's exhortations reside on the mystery, beauty, and value of all life, and Christ was sent down to remind humans of God's love for all of life: "God took seeds from different worlds and sowed them on the earth, and His garden grew and everything came up that could come up, but what grows lives and is alive only through the feeling of its contact with other mysterious worlds. Once contact is lost, then you will be indifferent to life and even grow to hate it" (14:290–291). This need for human contact can be fulfilled by active love, as Zosima speculates on the creation of humanity: "Once, only once, there was given him a moment on his coming to earth, the power of saying: 'I am and I love. . . . Once, only once, there was given him a moment of active *living* love, and for that earthly life was given him" (14:292). Active love therefore is part of human nature which individuals should embrace and practice in order to counteract the rationalism, secularism, and materialist understanding of freedom in the modern world.

Dostoevsky dramatically portrays how active love, and its accompanying doctrine, the responsibility for all, actually work in Book VI, where Markel teaches his younger brother to love and value life, a lesson that in turn Zosima passes down to Alyosha. The transmission of active love is not doctrinal in the sense of memorizing a set of teachings or logical procedures; rather, it is experiential in nature that passes mysteriously from one person to another. As Zosima had told Madame Khokhlakova, such subjects like the immortality of the soul cannot be proved, but "one can be convinced by the experience of active love" (14:52).[11] Of course, appeals to the experiential nature of active love automatically will be rejected by those who rely upon reason; but it may be the only possible avenue available for Dostoevsky given the limitations of language. At best, language can only point to or indicate human experience; it cannot fully capture it and transmit it like a data set to another person—a view that Dostoevsky himself held about the inherent inability of language to reveal the deepest truths of human existence (29:2).[12]

By appealing to experience, Zosima's doctrine of active love reintegrates isolated individuals back into a community where the aspirations of Christianity become re-contextualized. Whereas Ivan had presented Christianity as either happiness for all or individual freedom, Zosima furnishes an account of Christianity that emphasizes both happiness and individual freedom within a community. Within the context of a community, the aspirations of Christianity are possible: people possess freedom to make choices for their individual and for the community's happiness. This condition only is possible with Zosima's understanding of freedom: not the pursuit of pleasure but the restraint on human desires for the individual and communal good. Ivan's understanding of freedom is ultimately self-defeating: the pleasure principle leads to conflict among individuals over limited resources, resulting in the Inquisitor's totalitarian state as the only viable political solution.[13] By contrast, Zosima's definition of freedom provides an escape from the cycle of satisfaction and emptiness that accompanies those who follow the pleasure principle: genuine happiness is the acceptance of life, including all its pain and suffering, for "It's a great mystery of human life that old grief passes gradually into quiet tender joy" (14:265).

Although Zosima's acceptance of the mystery of existence may strike some as hopelessly naïve, it is epistemologically consistent with the Christian account of human nature. The possession of reason is a great advantage for humans to navigate themselves in the world, but it cannot stand outside of the realm of reality, since humans are bounded spatially and temporally. The tragedy of Ivan is that he wishes to transform Euclidean reason from a finite viewpoint to a vantage point outside of space and time—an impossible feat. In fact, the attempt to make reason survey all of reality—and therefore transform it according to the person's will—is reflective of the individual who is isolated from his community. Thus, the presentation of a de-contextualized Christianity reflects Ivan's own experience in the novel, as a young, intellectually gifted man with no friends—no community—to which he can reach out for mutual support. But when someone exists within a community, with all their demands, obligations, and requests, the person is aware of the limited cognition of his own situation and therefore is more receptive to the mystery of reality.

Finally, Zosima's rebuttal of Ivan's position is not only epistemological but social and political with his doctrine of responsibility for all, where "the moment you make yourself responsible in all sincerely for everyone in all sincerely for everyone and everything, you will see at once that it really is so and that you are, in fact, responsible for everyone and everything" (14:291). The experiential sense of interconnectedness with others propels us to not only accept that we are complicit in the suffering that exists in the world but that we are obligated to improve things through active love. Zosima's continual emphasis on active love suggests that acceptance of the mystery of existence does not equate into social and political passivity; rather, it implies the opposite. When people engage in active love, they will experientially expose others to Zosima's vision of epistemological humility, self-constrained freedom, and a socially bound community where the ideals of Christianity become contextualized and consequently can become possible.

THE EXPERIENCE OF ACTIVE LOVE

Dostoevsky continued his indirect response to *The Tale* in the dramatic actions of the character Alyosha and his engagement with the children.

Earlier, Alyosha had urged Ivan to love life "regardless of logic as you say, it must be regardless of logic, and it's only then one can understand the meaning of it" (14:209–210). The model for discovering the meaning of life is Christ, who has forgiven "everything, all *and for all*, because He gave His innocent blood for all and everything. You have forgotten Him, and on Him is built the edifice, and it is to Him they cry aloud, 'Thou art just, O Lord, for Thy ways are revealed!'" (14:223–224). Because Christ has sacrificed himself for all of humanity, everyone becomes indebted to Him and thereby are responsible to everyone else and to everything. The foundation for the regime is not based on the innocent blood of the victim, as Ivan had proposed; rather, the regime is rooted in the self-sacrifice of Christ that allows humans to accept the happiness and suffering of everyone in the Christian community. The doctrine of the responsibility for all is prompted by the action of active love—which is why Zosima instructs Alyosha to leave the monastery in order to marry Liza Khokhlakova and to prevent parricide in his family. Alyosha obeys and departs from the monastery but only possesses a lacerated understanding of Zosima's teaching: a doctrinal and dogmatic knowledge instead of an experiential and mystical one.

Alyosha tries to follow the Christian ideals of sacrifice, responsibility, and love by preventing Dmitry from killing their father in Book III and later, imitating Christ in *The Tale*, he kisses Ivan when they leave in Book V; however, the experiential nature of Zosima's teachings do not attach themselves onto Alyosha's soul until he practices active love with Grushenka in Book VI. Depressed over the death and disgrace over Father Zosima's death—people expected the body to remain odorless because Zosima was such a holy man, and when the body began to stink, people saw it as a sign of God's disapproval—Alyosha asked why had God disgraced "the holiest of holy men ... as though involuntarily submitting to the blind, dumb, pitiless laws of nature" (14:306). Like Ivan, Alyosha looked for a higher justice that would reconcile the laws of nature with the goodness of God. When this higher justice failed to appear, Alyosha became distraught to the extent that he allowed the career seminarian Rakitin to arrange a visit to Grushenka, who wishes to seduce him.

The ease which Alyosha loses his faith in the Christian ideals of sacrifice, responsibility, and love can be attributed to the fact that "all the love that lay concealed in his pure young heart for 'everyone and everything' had, for the past year, been concentrated—and perhaps wrongly so—primarily on his beloved elder, now dead" (14:306). This is Alyosha's own laceration: although Alyosha recognizes the teaching of the responsibility for all, he lacks the experiential understanding of this truth due to his youth and his misattribution of the doctrine to Zosima. This misattribution is not surprising, given the nature of the institution of the Elders, where novices who have voluntarily submitted themselves to an elder commit their will entirely to his guidance in "the hope of self-conquest, of self-mastery" (14:28). Alyosha submitted himself to Zosima in this way and misinterpreted the latter's teaching to Zosima instead of to everyone and everything. When Alyosha had accepted the devil's second temptation of miracles, he became disillusioned with Zosima and his teaching, correcting Rakitin that "I am not rebelling against my God; I simply 'don't accept his world'" (14:308).

But when Alyosha arrives at Grushenka's home, the planned seduction goes awry after she hears of Zosima's death and reacts with genuine sorrow. Alyosha in turn is moved—"and a light seemed to dawn in his face"—by Grushenka's pity, telling Rakitin that "I've found a true sister, I have found a treasure—a loving heart. She had pity on me just now . . . I'm talking about you, Grushenka. You've just restored my soul" (14:318). This prompts Grushenka to express remorse over her intention to seduce Alyosha, as she had done with his father and brother, Dmitry, and how this experience has transformed her life, triggering her childhood memory of a folktale she heard from a peasant she still employs. The tale is about a wicked old woman who was in the fiery lake of Hell. Her guardian angel wondered what good deed she had done in order to tell God, and he remembered that she had once given an onion to a beggar. God replied to "take that onion and hold it out to her in the lake, let her catch hold of it and pull it, and if you can pull her out of the lake, let her come to Paradise, but if the onion breaks, then the woman must stay where she is" (14:319). The angel lowers the onion to pull her up, but when the other sinners cling to her as she rises, she began kicking them, crying out, "It's me who's being pulled out and not you." At that moment, the onion broke, with the woman falling back into the lake and the angel departing.

This "onion" tale is not only a condemnation of self-centered egoism and radical individualism but a correction to *The Tale*. Both egoism and individualism precludes a sense of community, thereby making it impossible to be responsible for anyone besides oneself. In the context of self-centered interest, people are seen as competitors over limited resources instead of participants in a common enterprise, and stability only can be restored through a totalitarian regime. The wicked old woman's willingness to remain in Hell with her comrades rather than allow a few of them to join her in Paradise is the more accurate portrayal of the Grand Inquisitor's regime than an elect who sacrificed himself for the many. The purported nobleness and sacrifice of the Grand Inquisitor is exposed by the wicked old woman's self-centered egoism: it is acceptable if she were to enter Paradise because of her one act of charity, but it is not acceptable for others, who have done nothing of the sort, to enter Paradise with her, because it violates the cause-and-effect of Euclidean reason. By contrast, in taking responsibility for everyone and everything, the cause-and-effect of Euclidean reason becomes inconsequential for someone like Zosima, who accepts the mystery of existence with the belief that eternal life, as assigned by God, will be the true, higher justice.

This vision of a higher justice is experienced by Alyosha when he returns to the cell where Father Paissy holds vigil besides Zosima's corpse. Alyosha begins to pray with "a sweetness in his heart . . . and joy, joy was glowing in his mind and in his heart" (14:325). This sweetness and joy in his heart is the experiential understanding of the responsibility for all as prompted by his encounter of active love with Grushenka. It becomes further cemented with his dream of the wedding feast in the "Cana of Galilee," where Christ performs his first miracle by transforming water into wine. Alyosha sees Zosima in the dream who explains his presence by saying, "I gave an onion to a beggar. And many here have given only an onion each—only one little onion . . ." (14:325–327). Zosima urges Alyosha to continue his work and look at Christ who is a guest at the wedding feast. "He is terrible in His greatness, awful in His sublimity, but infinitely merciful"; He "had made Himself like unto us from love and rejoices with us." Alyosha awakens with "tears of rapture" in his soul and walks out into the night where he experiences religious awe:

> The silence of the earth seemed to merge into the silence of the heavens, the mystery of the earth came in contact with the mystery of the stars. . . . Alyosha stood, gazed, and suddenly he threw himself down upon the earth. He could not have explained to himself why he longed so irresistibly to kiss it, to kiss it all, but he kissed it weeping, sobbing and drenching it with his tears, and vowed frenziedly to love it, to love it forever and ever. . . . It was as though the threads from all those innumerable worlds of God met all at once in his soul, and it was trembling all over "as it came in contact with other worlds." He wanted to forgive everyone and for everything, and to beg forgiveness—not for himself, but for all men, for all and for everything (14:328).

When Alyosha rose from the earth, he was "a weak youth" but now "a resolute fighter for the rest of his life," and he never forgot that moment in his life: "'Someone visited my soul at that hour!' he used to say afterwards with firm faith in his words . . ."

Dostoevsky's ambiguous and vague description of Alyosha's experience is perfectly suitable, since, as stated previously, language is unable to convey experience with complete accuracy from one human being to another.[14] This is why Dostoevsky must respond to *The Tale* indirectly, because the response rests on an experiential foundation that to which at best can be pointed or indicated. A set of syllogism to prove something like the responsibility for all would not convince the reader that *The Tale* was the inferior argument because such a presentation at the outset epistemologically favors reason over experience. The adoption of a dramatic interplay between characters is a better strategy by showing how characters experience for themselves the doctrine of responsibility of all through active love. From Alyosha's encounter with Grushenka, the reader sees that Christ's demand upon humans is not impossible, as the

Inquisitor had claimed: both Alyosha and Grushenka reveal the depth of unselfish love and how it restores lacerated people. Christ's demands of humans are shown to be perfectly just; and, as the "Cana of Galilee" illustrates, He inspires his followers to give their own "little opinion" to their fellow humans. This vision prompts Alyosha to embrace the earth and the stars, for his "Karamazov baseness" has been transformed, and he has healed himself. By accepting both the material and spiritual aspect of his nature, Alyosha is able to restore his fragmented self, as initiated by the sinner Grushenka's pity for him, and he can go forth to heal other lacerated people in the community.

THE POLITICS OF LOVE AND MEMORY

Alyosha's attempt to heal lacerated people is dramatically portrayed throughout the novel, but it is probably best illustrated in his engagement with the children who represent the new generation in Russia with Alyosha eventually becoming their spiritual guide. Of particular importance is the relationship between Alyosha and Kolya, who is intellectually advanced and the future leader of the group of boys. Kolya is resistant to emotional displays and "read some things unsuitable for his age" from his father's library (14:463). He reveals his precociousness to Alyosha by telling him that "God is only a hypothesis" and that "it's possible for one who doesn't believe in God to love mankind"; and he repeats what Rakitin, who has become a rival to Alyosha in the education of the boys, has taught him: "I am not opposed to Christ. . . . He was the most humane person, and if He were alive today, He would be found in the ranks of the revolutionaries, and would perhaps play a conspicuous part" (14:499–500).

Given these views, albeit second-handed, Kolya has engaged in a series of escapades that exhibited his intellectual ability and emotional control: lying between railroad tracks while a train passes over him, persuading the slow and stupid to destroy other people's property, and refusing to visit his ailing friend, Ilyusha. Although the other boys have visited Ilyusha and have searched for his dog, Zhuchka, to relieve Ilyusha's guilt for putting a pin into a piece of bread for dogs to eat, Kolya has refused to visit because he wishes to demonstrate his independence from Alyosha's influence and that he himself has found Zhuchka, teaching the dog to do tricks and wanting to complete its training. Kolya is not evil but rather immature, as to be expected from children, for if he "had known what a disastrous and fatal effect" of hiding Zhuchka from Ilyusha "might have on the sick child's health, nothing would have induced him to play such a trick on him" (14:491). In fact, when Kolya finally visits his dying comrade, "his voice failed him . . . his face suddenly twitched and the corners of his mouth quivered" (14:488). His composure of emotional restraint and rationalism gives ways to feelings of empathy and compassion.

Kolya's laceration is similar to Ivan's, except that his views are acquired rather than self-created and that he is still young enough to change, which eventually happens to him under Alyosha's influence. Alyosha's growing influence over Kolya is representative of the work that Zosima commanded Alyosha to do in the world outside the monastery, as Kolya learns from Alyosha that his pride has misguided him in the treatment of Ilyusha. He first listens to Kolya's second-hand opinions about God, socialism, and other revolutionary ideologies, responding "quietly, gently, and quite naturally, as though he were talking to someone of his own age, or even older" (14:500). The need of children to be taken seriously by adults is a powerful one that can propel intellectually gifted children like Kolya into revolutionary ideologies when their ideas are dogmatically dismissed from their religious elders. A better strategy is to engage with children as their equals in the hope that they will expose their insecurities. Kolya does exactly this, confessing that "I am profoundly unhappy, I sometimes fancy all sorts of things, that everyone is laughing at me, the whole world, and that I feel ready to overturn the whole order of things" (14:503). He admits that it was his vanity and pride that precluded him from visiting Ilyusha, to which Alyosha asks him to overcome his faults and fear of failures by visiting his friend. The scene concludes with Kolya, Ilyusha, and the captain embracing one another as a community united by suffering, pathos, and the Christian hope of eternity.

The funeral of Ilyusha is the final scene in the novel, with the family distraught over their little boy's death. When the group of boys pass the stones under which Ilyusha had wished to be buried, Alyosha calls the boys together and asks them to make a pact to never forget Ilyusha or one another, cherishing the memory of Ilyusha and "how good it was once here when we were all together united by a good and kind feeling" (15:195). Alyosha then proclaims that "there is nothing higher and stronger and more wholesome and good for life in the future than some good memory, especially memory of childhood and home." The boys promise to remember and shout out, "Karamazov, we love you," to which Alyosha adds, "And may the dear boy's memory live eternally!" The reference to eternity prompts Kolya to inquire whether that bodily resurrection is true and whether they "shall live and see each other again, all, Ilyushechka too?" Alyosha replies in the affirmative that it shall be so, and "hand in hand" they all go to the funeral dinner to eat pancakes, for "it's a very old custom."

The death of Ilyusha is remembered as a community of friendship based on the Christian hope of the bodily resurrection instead of the tragic death of an innocent child—another indirect response to *The Tale*. This transformation of memory connects the new community of believers and cements their bonds of friendship.[15] The slow conversion of Kolya from his atheist socialism to his tepid acceptance of Christianity was the result of Alyosha's active love, revealing how active love can experientially transform lacerated individuals into a community of friendship, hope, and memory. This experience has been demonstrated dramatically from Markel to Zosima to Alyosha to Kolya and, finally, to the reader himself. Again, this appeal is indirect because of the inherent limitations within language, but Dostoevsky more than meets the challenge of the Inquisitor. Dostoevsky can lead the reader to the experience of active love in illustrating how it operates, although ultimately it is up to the reader to see whether such an experience exists within him.

CONCLUSION

Dostoevsky's indirect appeal to the reader is best demonstrated when one discovers that the arguments of both the Inquisitor and Zosima in Books V and VI are structurally and logically identical, as Cassedy demonstrates.[16] For example, the argument of the Inquisitor is as follows: justice does not exist in the world because it is not perceptible to our senses, with the proof being that events fail to correspond to our conception of God's justice. The assumption to the Inquisitor's position is that reality does not exist outside of our senses (or either God is fundamentally unjust or not omnipotent), which leads us to the conclusion that justice does not exist either in this world of the next. When we examine Zosima's argument in Book VI, we see the structure and logic of the argument are the same as the Inquisitor's: justice exists in the world but it is imperceptible to us, with the proof being that, even if events do not correspond to our conception of God's justice, we accept this condition because God is not accessible to our senses. The assumption is a reality that does exist outside the realm of our senses (and that God is just and omnipotent), which leads us to conclude that justice exists in both this world and the next. The only way the reader can decide between these two positions is based on his own subjective belief in God: on the one hand, if he lacks a belief in God, then he will agree with the Inquisitor; on the other hand, if he believes in a God, then he will accept Zosima's teachings. Since the arguments are structurally and logically identical, reason cannot decide which argument is superior. Dostoevsky can only resort to indirection and example to persuade the reader to accept Zosima's teaching over the Inquisitor's.

Whereas the Inquisitor offers miracle, mystery, and authority irrespective of the divinity of Jesus, Zosima offers all three rooted in the experience of divinity as emphasized in Orthodox Christianity and prompted by active love. Zosima's miracle is illustrated in Alyosha's vision of the wedding feast in the "Cana of Galilee"; the mystery is the acceptance of responsibility of suffering in our lives, since we are all responsible for each other in a community of believers; and authority is the voluntary binding of people together in active love and the transformed memory with Christ as their model. Dostoevsky's dramatic portrayal of Alyosha and his engagements with Grushenka and the children demonstrate how Zosima's miracle, mystery, and authority can be realized in a social and political community. By accepting our "Karamazov baseness" as well as the spiritual model that Christ offers, Dostoevsky suggests that a coherent self can emerge and assist in the healing of lacerated individuals who have been cut off and isolated from themselves, others, and divinity. This vision of a Christian and his Orthodox community therefore is the underlying harmony—the "unity in diversity"—that Bakhtin seemed to suggest in his criticism.

The Brothers therefore is not a polyphonic novel in the sense that there is no one view or position privileged over another; rather, the "unity in diversity" that Bakhtin had proclaimed can be located in the teachings of Zosima. Furthermore, such a position of polyphony—all diversity and no unity—is clearly repudiated by Dostoevsky's own personal and public writings. Although Ivan and his Inquisitor may appear to some to be more attractive than Alyosha or Zosima, it may be a reflection of the reader's own personal experiences rather than requiring Dostoevsky to furnish a direct refutation to *The Tale*. Dostoevsky imparted to us a vision of a Christian community based on love, memory, and responsibility that requires the reader to make the necessary connections in the novel, thereby forcing him to reflect upon his own experiences and compare them with the characters in the novel. By challenging us to respond to the Inquisitor's challenge with the material given in the novel, Dostoevsky is asking whether the capacity for active love exists within ourselves and whether, like Alyosha, we have the courage to practice it in our own communities.

NOTES

Originally published as Lee Trepanier, "The Politics and Experience of Active Love in *The Brothers Karamazov*," *The Political Science Reviewer* 38 (Fall 2009). Reprinted with permission.

1. For more about Russian reaction to *The Brothers*, refer to Marina Kostalevsky, *Dostoevsky and Soloviev: The Art of Integral Vision* (New Haven: Yale University Press, 1997); George Pattinson and Diane Thompson, *Dostoyevsky and the Christian Tradition* (Cambridge: Cambridge University Press, 2001).

2. For more about Western reception to *The Brothers*, refer to Rene Wellek, ed. *Dostoevsky: A Collection of Critical Essays* (Whitefish, MT: Literary Licensing, LLC, 2011); Malcolm Jones, *Dostoevsky after Bakhtin: Reading in Dostoevsky Fantastic Realism* (Cambridge: Cambridge University Press, 1990); Steven Cassedy, *Dostoevsky's Religion* (Stanford: Stanford University Press, 2005).

3. Michael Holquist, ed. *The Dialogic Imagination* (Austin: University of Texas, 1981); Mikhail Bakhtin, ed. *Problems of Dostoevsky's Poetics* (Minneapolis: University of Minneapolis Press, 1984).

4. Bakhtin himself never elaborated about this unity which was probably due to the restrictions on writing about religious and philosophical subjects in the Soviet Union.

5. For the influence on Bakhtin on Dostoevsky studies, refer to Malcom Jones, "Dostoevskii and Religion" in *The Cambridge Companion to Dostoevskii*, ed. W. J. Leatherbarrow (Cambridge: Cambridge University Press, 2002). A sample of different and conflicting interpretations of *The Tale* are found in Edward Wasiolek, *Dostoevsky: The Major Fiction* (Cambridge: Harvard University Press, 1964); Roger L. Cox, *Between Earth and Heaven: Shakespeare, Dostoevksy and the Meaning of Christian Tragedy* (New York: Holt, Rinehart, and Winston, 1969); Stewart R. Sutherland, *Atheism and the Rejection of God: Contemporary Philosophy and* The Brothers Karamazov (Oxford: Basil Blackwell, 1977); Robert Belknap, *The Genesis of* The Brothers Karamazov: *The Aesthetics, Ideology, and Psychology of Text-Making* (Evanston, IL: Northwestern University Press, 1990); Liza Knapp, *The Annihilation of Inertia: Dostoevsky and Metaphysics* (Evanston: Northwestern University Press, 1996); Bruce K. Ward, "Dostoevsky and the Hermeneutics of Suspicion," *Literature and Theology* 11 (1997), 270–83; Ellis Sandoz, *Political Apocalypse: A Study of Dostoevsky's Grand Inquisitor* (Wilmington, DE: ISI Books, 2000); Susan Leigh Anderson, *On Dostoevsky* (Boston: Wadsworth, 2001); Diane Oenning Thompson, "Dostoevskii and Science" in *The Cambridge Companion to Dostoevskii*, ed. W. J. Leatherbarrow (Cambridge: Cambridge University Press, 2002), 191–211; James P. Scanlan, "Dostoevsky's Arguments for Immortality," *Russian Review* 59 (2000), 1–20; Harriet Murav, "From Skandalon to Scandal: Ivan's Rebellion Reconsidered," *Slavic Review* 63 (2004), 756–770; and Cassedy, *Dostoevsky's Religion*.

6. Pattinson and Thompson, *Dostoyevsky and the Christian Tradition*, 6–11; Jones, "Dostoevskii and Religion" and Joseph Frank, *Dostoevsky: The Mantle of the Prophet, 1871–1881* (Princeton: Princeton University Press, 2002).

7. Translations are my own from G. M. Fridlender, ed. *Polnoe Sobranie Sochinenii* (Leningrad: n.p. 1972–1990). Subsequent citations will be volume and page number.

8. Ivan's "returning God's ticket" is a rejection of God's world instead of God Himself. As Dostoevsky wrote to K. P. Pobedonostev on May 19, 1879, "Our socialists today are not concerned with scientific and philosophic arguments against the existence of God (as were the whole last century and the first half of this century); these have been given up. Rather, they are interested in denying as strongly as possible the creation of God, his world, and his meaning. Only in these questions does contemporary civilization find meaning" (4:55–57).

9. Dostoevsky was familiar with the works of both Roman Catholicism and Protestantism as well as Enlightenment accounts of Christianity. Victor Terras, *A Karamazov Companion: Commentary on the Genesis, Language, and Style of Dostoevsky's Novel* (Madison: University of Wisconsin Press, 1981), 21.

10. Dostoevsky expressed this sentiment in separate letters to his editor, N. A. Liubimov, on May 10, 1879, and to K. P. Pobedonostev on August 24, 1879 (30:1, 63–65, 120–121).

11. For more about the debates on Dostoevsky's views on the immortality of the soul, refer to Scanlan, "Dostoevsky's Arguments for Immortality."

12. Refer to Dostoevsky's letter of July 16, 1876 (29:2).

13. Dostoevsky believed that the only viable political solution from a condition of competition over limited resources was a totalitarian state. The possibility of liberalism as a political solution was ridiculed by Dostoevsky in his portrayal of such characters like Miusov. Interestingly, Dostoevsky failed to consider the free market solution as a mechanism to manage social and economic conflict—in fact, he never considered economic solutions in both his personal and public works.

14. Jones makes a similar point, "This emphasis on the silence of heaven has been associated by some with the apophantic strain in Orthodox theology, according to

which the essence of God is unknowable and a sense of the presence of God is to be attained only through spiritual tranquility and inner silence, for which all mental images are obstacles. At all events it harmonises with Dostoevskii's view that human language is incompetent to express the deepest truths" (Jones, "Dostoevskii and Religion," 170–171).

15. For more about the role of memory in the novel, refer to Diane Thompson, The Brothers Karamazov *and the Poetics of Memory* (Cambridge: Cambridge University Press, 1991).

16. Cassedy, *Dostoevsky's Religion*, 101.

THREE

This Star Will Shine Forth from the East

Dostoevsky and the Politics of Humility

John P. Moran

As Isaiah Berlin once noted, Fyodor Dostoevsky is perhaps the most "centripetal" of all Russian writers.[1] This is to say that all of his thoughts and inquiries ultimately gravitated toward addressing one central question: can human society exist without God? Famously, Dostoevsky was pessimistic about this. However, instead of relying upon theological or rational justifications for the role of religion in public life, he based his pessimistic analysis of godlessness on the effects of such a condition upon the individual psyche.[2] His message is clear: the human psyche is, by nature, not fit to exist without God, and any attempt to do so results in self-destruction.

It is perhaps for this reason that *The Brothers Karamazov*, his latest and arguably greatest work, is generally not viewed as a political work. Exceptional in this regard are those who have focused specifically upon the novel's most famous chapter entitled "The Grand Inquisitor."[3] In this chapter, we take a different approach by arguing that other sections of this novel contribute to the understanding of Dostoevsky's final and most complete statement on the appropriate role of Christianity within the Russian state. Such an approach begins with a speech given near the end of *The Brothers Karamazov* where Dostoevsky has the chief prosecutor refer to the Karamazov family as being similar to Nikolai Gogol's reckless troika. He states, ". . . in this [Karamazov] family portrait it is as if one can gain a glimpse of certain fundamental features of today's educated society—not all the features, but a snapshot, and in miniature..."(15:125).[4]

How is the Karamazov family like a miniature snapshot of Russia? How is it like a reckless troika? As the name of this characteristically Russian vehicle implies, a troika is propelled forward by three horses.[5] Similarly, the Karamazov family consists of three legitimate brothers, each of whom represents visions of a fundamental feature of nineteenth-century Russian educated society: the romantic vision, the rational vision, and the Christian vision. While the romantic (Dmitri) and rational (Ivan) visions are quite different for Dostoevsky, they ultimately result in a common end—the simultaneous destruction of themselves and of Russia (as represented by Fyodor/Fatherland). To state it differently, the murder contemplated by Dmitri and Ivan, and accomplished by Smerdyakov, is not merely *patricide*, but *patriacide*.

What is overlooked by many readers is the problematic nature of the third horse—the Christian vision. It is assumed by most that Dostoevsky looked to this third horse as Russia's salvation. This is only partially true. In point of fact, Dostoevsky divides Christianity into two camps. In the first, we find the "institutional" church as so famously depicted in "The Grand Inquisitor." This is the camp that relies on "miracle, mystery, and authority" to exercise worldly power and to provide for human happiness. Importantly, "The Grand Inquisitor" is not merely an anti-Western or anti–Roman Catholic screed. Dostoevsky also, albeit in a somewhat veiled manner, criticizes the Russian "institutional" church. This is found in his depictions of Zosima's fellow monks, most of whom seem equally wedded to the power of ecclesiastical authority (Paisiy) or miracle and mystery (Ferapont).

These individuals are clearly contrasted with those in Christianity's second camp—the most reclusive element within the Christian church—the monastic hermits. Importantly, the key trait distinguishing these monastic hermits from their fellow Christians is their embrace of the virtue of *humility*. This is the case within both Eastern and Western Christianity. In Western Christianity, the rule that governs both monks and hermits, the Rule of St. Benedict, outlines a twelve-step ladder of humility, which provides, "... the heart of Benedict's presentation of the way to God."[6] Once the monk or hermit arrives at the top of this ladder of humility, he achieves "that perfect love of God which casts out fear."[7] In other words, humility allows a hermetic monk to achieve the ultimate Christian goal of attaining a soul that loves perfectly and is in union with God.

The mainstream Russian Orthodox hermitic approach does not differ from this. Nil Sorsky, a fifteenth-century founding figure of the Russian *staretz* movement writes, "Let us in every way conduct our life in humility. And this is the beginning of it: to hold oneself beneath all others, to reckon oneself the most sinful and worthless of all men, and, as being beyond nature, the filthiest of all creations, and worse than the demons, as one violated and defeated by them."[8] Dostoevsky seems to agree on the importance of humility, but he emphasizes a more worldly, or political, outcome of its exercise. This is seen when he has Zosima use the following words, "When you ask yourself in times in which you are faced with certain thoughts, particularly at the sight of human sin, 'Should I use force or loving humility?,' you should always state, 'I will decide upon loving humility.' If you commit yourself to this position forever you shall be able to subdue the entire world. A loving humility is a frightening power, it is the most powerful power, nothing else like it exists" (14:289).

This somewhat non-monastic or non-hermetic goal to what is commonly seen as a monastic virtue is unconventional. Indeed, Zosima himself admits to the startling aspect of this approach when he declares, "And how astonished men would be if I were to say that from these meek monks, who yearn for solitary prayer, the salvation of the Russian land will perhaps come" (14:284). It is thus that Dostoevsky not only provides a critique of the three horses of the Russian ideological troika, but also his own vision for the role of religion in Russia. As will be seen below, Dostoevsky uses the characters of *The Brothers Karamazov* to illustrate or to personify the social dynamics at play in nineteenth-century Russia. Dmitri, who personifies romanticism, embraces at least a form of love, but he rejects the route of humility to get there. His loving sentiments are worldly, proud, and self-interested. He, and the Russia that embraces his vision, end badly. Ivan, who personifies rationalism, rejects the existence of love in the first place. Much as Dmitri, his story ends badly. The institutional Christian Church, as illustrated in both "The Grand Inquisitor" as well as the characters of Paisiy and Ferapont, also illustrate a form of love that is proud and worldly. Taken in this light, Dostoevsky's political message is clear: a politics of humility is required for Russia's salvation. A paradoxical "monk in the world" will be necessary. This, of course, is the role of the novel's hero, Alyosha Karamazov.

FYODOR KARAMAZOV: HUMILIATED RUSSIA

The first question Dostoevsky must answer for any thoughtful reader is: Why humility? Is this a solution that is particularly important for Russia? Why? One of the first things we learn about Fyodor Karamazov is that he is a uniquely "national" character (14:7).[9] He is a "father" (*otets*) not just in the biological sense; he is a "father" in the sense that he represents the root or origin of the Russian people. Ultimately, this is the sense of *otets* that provides the root word for "fatherland" (*otechestvo*).[10] Fyodor's three legitimate sons arrive in the order that the three visions of nineteenth-century Russia's future appear. Just as romanticism appeared in Russia first in the 1820's, so the first son—Dmitri—is also a romantic. He is of the generation of Pushkin, the poet with whom he is frequently mentioned. The next son, Ivan, represents the generation of the 1840's. He is a "Westerner," politically liberal and/or socialistic and secular in orientation. The third son, Alyosha, represents not so much a different generation of thinkers but rather the conservative, Christian reaction to the Westerners.[11] Smerdyakov, the last son, represents the generation of the nihilists and terrorist revolutionaries, born in the 1860's and active in the 1880's. Although Dostoevsky was never able to personally witness the end of this movement, he regarded Smerdyakov as the logical conclusion to the thought processes of the "Westerners."

At the same time, Dostoevsky describes Fyodor as a buffoon (*shut*), a role he plays for psychological reasons. Although he claims to do it because he wants to make himself "agreeable" (14:39), his behavior is primarily motivated by insecurity and shame. This becomes clear at the very beginning of the book when Zosima says to Fyodor, "Above all else, do not be so ashamed of yourself, for it is precisely this that causes everything else" (14:40). In other words, as a result of the shame he feels, he lashes out at others to counter-shame them. Indeed, at the moment he is about to play the buffoon, Fyodor thinks to himself, "Well, now there's no rehabilitating myself. So let's shame them for all I am worth. I'll not feel shame at what they think—that's all" (14:80).

What causes Fyodor to feel this shame originally? Fyodor himself gives us the critical clue when he states, "I'm taking revenge for my youth, for all my humiliation" (14:83). For Dostoevsky, this is pivotal primarily because children are so vulnerable psychologically.[12] Indeed, the hearts of children are particularly defenseless with regard to the treatment they receive from their parents. There is little that can be more humiliating or shameful to a child than to be neglected by his or her parents. Neglect is perceived by the child as the withholding of love. Such a condition is, of course, intolerable to a child. They logically conclude that if their own parents do not love them, it is unlikely that anyone else will. They ultimately become fixed in their conviction that they are unlovable.[13]

It follows that Dostoevsky is implying that the spirit of Russia's early period is one of humiliation (or lovelessness). Part of this, no doubt, is due to Russia's youthful humiliation—the Mongol yoke. As Orlando Figes has written, "It is hard to overstress the sense of national shame which the 'Mongol yoke' evokes in the Russians. Unless one counts Hungary, Kievan Rus' was the only major European power to be overtaken by the Asiatic hordes."[14] This humiliation from Russia's past is compounded by a collective spirit of inferiority widely felt by Russians during the nineteenth century toward Europe. Once again, Orlando Figes quotes the great nineteenth-century Russian intellectual, Alexander Herzen, with the following illustrative quotation: "Our attitude to Europe and the Europeans . . . is still that of provincials towards the dweller in a capital: we are servile and apologetic, take every difference for a defect, blush for our peculiarities and try to hide them."[15] Figes accurately points out that this put Russians in a highly precarious emotional position. After all, Russia's ". . . rejection by the West could equally engender feelings of resentment and superiority to it."[16] This paradoxical combination of resentment and superiority is clearly represented in the character of Fyodor Karamazov. Of course, the ramification of this is the neglect of his children. The next generation of Russians is thus reared in their own pot of humiliation.

DMITRI KARAMAZOV: THE ROMANTIC

Perhaps the most important utterance in the novel with regard to Dmitri Karamazov occurs when he yells at his father (and others in the room), "Why is such a man alive? . . . Tell me, can he be allowed to go on dishonoring the earth?" (14:69).[17] On the one hand, through this sentence, the reader is immediately made aware of the rage that Dmitri feels toward his father. This is obvious. However, the message becomes far more sublime when we keep in mind that Dmitri personifies romanticism and its political manifestation: nationalism.

Let us begin with the first question: what is at the root of Dmitri's rage toward his father? The first is obvious: they are competing for the same woman. On a psychological level, we may also consider the irony that the man who withheld love from him as a child is now attempting to keep him from experiencing love with another. Both of these facts are obvious. However, in them we do not find the whole story. The question must arise: why Grushenka? In many ways, Grushenka is a female version of Fyodor. She is vulgar, crass, and seems resentful about how others treat her, both past and present. Dmitri subconsciously sees this. In seeking her love, Dmitri is attempting to compensate for the fact that his own father neglected and abandoned him. By attaining her love, he is, in essence, capturing his father's love as well—a primal form of love he should have received as a child. In doing so, he is proving that he is "lovable." This explains, in part at least, Dmitri's desperate need to be loved by Grushenka.

His desperation is clear when he states, "When [her] lover comes, I'll go into the next room. I'll clean her friends' dirty galoshes, light their samovar, run their errands" (14:110). When Dmitri learns that Grushenka's first love (a Polish gentleman) had returned to town and taken her away, he responds by stating, "She's now with him. . . . Now I shall see what she looks like with him . . . [and then] I will disappear" (14:370). At that moment he felt an even greater arousal of his love for her and declares that he will efface himself to her.

The only man Dmitri objects to as her lover is his own father. Psychologically, this is perfectly understandable. It is not that he objects to Grushenka desiring his father, but the opposite. In seeking out and seducing Grushenka, Fyodor is, in Dmitri's mind, seeking out and seducing himself. In other words, he is loving himself. In Dmitri's mind, this self-absorbed love is what led to his childhood neglect to begin with. This strikes at the core of his deep psychological need for love—and he subconsciously knows this.

This psychological narrative is combined with Dmitri's "romantic" spirit. Indeed, the youthful Dmitri fits the Russian romantic mold insofar as he lived a wild, extravagant life in the Caucasus as a young officer. While there he fought a duel, was broken to the ranks, and earned promotion again. Of course, he became involved with a young, beautiful woman. Similarly, and somewhat humorously, Dostoevsky has Dmitri share Pushkin's notorious obsession with women's feet (14:109).[18] Dostoevsky clearly paints Dmitri in the image of a romantic, and in doing so illustrates the psyche, or perhaps the psychopathology, of a romantic. Indeed, Dmitri is the personification of the romantic spirit itself.

ROMANTICISM AS MOVEMENT

Although Romanticism is notoriously difficult to define—or even characterize—there is a consensus that it finds its roots in eighteenth-century Germany. As Isaiah Berlin so accurately summed up, "What people [romantics] admired was wholeheartedness, sincerity, purity of soul, the ability and readiness to dedicate yourself to your ideal, no matter what it was."[19] It is a movement most often contrasted with rationalism. A romantic does not justify what he does through reason, he simply does it based upon pure emotion. Passionate emotional engagement is the fundamental virtue of this movement. As Berlin continues, "You would have found that common sense, moderation, was very far from their [a romantic's] thoughts."[20]

With Dmitri's courtship of Grushenka, Dostoevsky conveys the spirit of romanticism, but in a negative light. His mental transformation of Grushenka, from whore to Goddess, is not only ridiculous, but dangerous. Indeed, his unruly passions ultimately result in devastating human tragedy in other parts of the novel. Perhaps the best illustration of this is when Dmitri's uncontrollable rage compels him to senselessly attack Captain Snegiryov in the presence of the Captain's son, Ilyusha. The trauma experienced by the son as a result of this humiliating attack is so severe that it significantly contributes to his death. Even more indicative of Dostoevsky's indictment of romanticism lies in the patricide that is at the center of the novel's plot.

As mentioned above, Dostoevsky hints that Dmitri's patricidal psyche is born of parental neglect. Therefore, if Dmitri is meant to represent the spirit of romanticism, this implies that the spirit of this movement must be driven by both a hatred of its host country as well as a certain self-hatred. This is somewhat ironic, as romanticism is commonly seen as the antecedent movement to nationalism. Indeed, nationalism is the political manifestation of romanticism. It is commonly assumed that nationalism is a political doctrine that insists ethnic boundaries not cut across political boundaries.[21] Nationalists make this demand under the assumption that every nation has the right to self-determination. National identity functions as the primary determinate of justice and defines the good. It is also assumed, on a deeper level, that the spirit of nationalism is animated by a love of one's own people. In keeping with Dmitri's romantic psyche, he is a Russian nationalist. Toward the end of the novel he makes an enormously illustrative statement in which he states, "I hate America, damn it. Even though Grushenka will be with me. . . . And how will I put up with the crowded hordes out there, though they may be better than I, everyone of them. I really hate America already! And though they may be wonderful with machines, every one of them, damn them, they are not my people, not of my soul. I love Russia, Alyosha, I love the Russian God, though I am a villain" (15:186).

This statement must be understood within the context of Dmitri's hatred for his father. To hate his father while loving Russia he must ignore the reality that his father *typifies* Russia, that he is the "national" type. In other words, to love Russia he must ignore reality. Not coincidentally, this is an oft-noted tendency of the nationalist as well. As E. J. Hobsbawm once wrote, "Nationalism requires too much belief in what is patently not so."[22] Yet another scholar of nationalism, Benedict Anderson writes, "In an anthropological spirit, then, I propose the following definition of the nation: it is an imagined political community—and imagined as both inherently limited and sovereign."[23] This then begs the question: why must an individual go so far out of his way to imagine this false political community? Through Dmitri, Dostoevsky illustrates that a nationalist's love is motivated by a psychological need to be loved by an individual who is desperately in need of love. On a personal level, Dmitri's psychological need to be loved by Grushenka is a compensatory attempt to be loved by his father.

For Dostoevsky, Dmitri's flaw is his demand to be loved. The logic used by Dostoevsky (through Zosima) is somewhat counter-intuitive. Humility provides the path to the "perfect love" that heals the soul of the humiliated from the trauma of past humiliation. The humiliated must practice humility to master the exercise of a love of which they themselves were deprived. Once achieved, they escape the ravages of shame and humiliation. This two-fold paradox flies in the face of natural intuition—that the humiliated should be shown respect by *others* and the unloved should be loved by *others*. Thus, the first step in soothing the loveless humiliation of the Karamazov family (and by implication Russia itself) is the practice of humility.

Dmitri's need to love and be loved by Russia—and thus exhibit Russian nationalism—is also a compensatory love. Thus, when Dmitri states that he hates America, he is readily admitting that he sees that country as superior and resents his underappreciated status as a Russian.[24] His love for his country is not a real love, but a reaction to a feeling of being unappreciated and unloved. In the end, Dostoevsky's depiction of the romantic and nationalistic movement through the character of Dmitri is ingenious in that he cuts to the psychological core of the movement and finds an unexpected spirit (of humiliation and self-hatred). Simultaneously, he illustrates that the movement is, paradoxically, bent on destroying the very object of its purported love—through *patricide* nationalists are committing *patriacide*.

Interestingly, and in spite of every intention, it is not Dmitri who ends up killing his father. Dostoevsky purposefully keeps the individual representing nationalism from killing Russia. While he certainly regards nationalism as a sickness, both for the individual and for the Russian nation, Dostoevsky swims against the current. Rather than the collective psychopathology of romanticism as the greatest threat to Russia's salvation, he looks to Ivan and the rationalist approach as being far more culpable and dangerous.

THE RIDDLE OF IVAN KARAMAZOV'S RATIONALISM

Ivan Karamazov is arguably the most misunderstood character in this novel because of the commonly held belief that he represents pure rationalism. It is more accurate to approach this character as does Alyosha near the beginning of the novel when he states, "I love you, Ivan. Brother Dmitri says of you: Ivan is a tomb! I say of you, Ivan is a riddle" (14:209). We can surmise that Dmitri regards Ivan as a "tomb" because, as a rationalist, he has renounced love. Alyosha, however, hits closer to the mark, for he clearly sees the riddle of Ivan: on the one hand, he renounces love, but on the other he cannot control his human impulse to love. Much like Bazarov in Turgenev's *Fathers and Sons*, Ivan is a nihilist who believes in neither God nor morality.[25] He is an empiricist. He explains to Alyosha, "I have a Euclidian, earthly mind and so therefore I can not solve problems that are not of this world. And I advise you never to think about it either, my friend Alyosha, especially about God, whether He exists or not. All such questions are utterly inappropriate for a mind created with an idea of only three dimensions" (14:214). The riddle, of course, is that Ivan's mind perforce does drift to another dimension.

This is precisely why Dostoevsky has Ivan write a scholarly article discussing the proper role of ecclesiastical courts in society. Here he makes the argument that "every earthly State should be, in the end, completely turned over to the Church and should become nothing else but a Church, rejecting every purpose incongruous with the aims of the Church" (14:58). Because this was an unusual argument for a rationalist to make, readers are often unsure what to make of it. Members of the "Church faction" regarded Ivan as their ally in the battle with the atheists, while the atheists thought that the article was nothing more than "an impudent farce and mockery" (14:16).

Bakhtin may have had a point when he wrote that "everything in his [Dostoevsky's] world lives on the very border of its opposite."[26] At least this is the case with both Dmitri and Ivan, whose natures are so conflicted that they seem doomed to self-destruction. While Dmitri's conflict centers upon the *nature* of love, Ivan's conflict hinges upon the *existence* of love. Indeed, the otherwise unlikable divinity student, Rakitin, correctly guesses that Ivan had written the aforementioned ecclesiastical courts article as a way to gain the respect (and ostensibly the love) of Katerina (Dmitri's fiancé!). This is the riddle of Ivan's rationalism. Throughout the novel, he is perpetually stuck in a conundrum. In one of his most famous statements, he declares, "I want to travel from here to Europe, Alyosha. And yet I know that I am only going to a graveyard, but it is a most precious graveyard.... I know I shall fall on the ground and kiss those stones and weep over them even though I'm convinced in my heart that it has long been nothing but a graveyard" (14:210). By stating that Europe is a graveyard, Ivan elaborates a grand theme of nineteenth-century Russian literature—Western Europe has lost its soul. This loss of soul results in the catastrophic condition of lovelessness. In other words, Ivan knows that by embracing utilitarianism and empiricism he embraces a "dead" set of European ideals, a spiritually empty set of principles.

Even though he is aware that his rationalist approach is a graveyard, Ivan does his best to maintain his rationalist façade. In yet another of his famous pronouncements, he declares, "One can love one's neighbors in the abstract, or even at a distance, but at close quarters it's almost impossible" (14:216). At the same time, he is aware that he can not maintain this position in the long run and explains to his brother that "when I approach the age of thirty and I want to 'dash the cup to the ground,' wherever you may be I'll come to have one more talk with you, even if I have to come from America" (14:240). It is his conflicted soul that is driving him to "dash the cup to the ground." On the one hand he is a man of reason. On the other, he experiences emotional states more akin to that of Dmitri: For example, he declares, "Though I may not believe in a universal order of things, yet those sticky little leaves as they open in spring are dear to me. The deep blue sky is dear to me" (14:210). Perhaps even more inexplicable are "his ardent and insane passion for Katerina

Ivanovna" (15:48) and his almost pathological desire for his own father's murder (15:66). None of these intensely felt emotions are the hallmark of a strictly rational creature.

The fact that Ivan is tormented in his rationalism—that his rationalism is but a riddle—is seen most clearly by Zosima. Just after he hears Ivan's theory about the ecclesiastical courts, he says to Ivan, "in your despair, even you divert yourself with magazine articles and discussions in society though even you don't believe your dialectics—and with an aching heart you mock at them inwardly" (14:65). Ivan, rather than even attempting to deny this, rises from his chair, receives his blessing, and kisses his hand.[27] Of course, most of the novel devoted to Ivan focuses on his attempts to resolve this doubt. Toward the end of the novel, he comes close to resolving this doubt in his interviews with Smerdyakov. It is only at this point that he realizes that the ultimate end result of his rationalism is nihilism. He is appalled by this. This turning point is symbolized by his return to the place where, on his way to interview Smerdyakov, he had knocked unconscious a drunken peasant and had left him lying in the snow (which certainly would have resulted in his death). He retrieves the man and offers sufficient aid for his recovery.

The experience of helping the drunken peasant made him "feel" good. It is as if at this point he sees more clearly precisely what Zosima saw and thus resolves to change his ways. However, by not acting immediately upon the most pressing issue of his life—facing the issues associated with his father's murder—he postpones his salvation. By waiting until the following day to report to the police Smerdyakov's guilt as well as his own (perceived) complicity, he dooms himself to insanity. He spends that evening tormented by the devil, unable to completely let go of his rationalism and embrace charitable love. Ultimately, Ivan attempts to admit to the murder of his father in an effort to expiate his feelings of guilt over his secret desires to see this murder happen. Of course, he also feels complicit because he taught Smerdyakov that "all things are permitted" (15:67). In the end, he is driven to insanity; for Dostoevsky, the incompatibility of being a rationalist and being truly human is simply too profound.

THE CONFLICTED SPIRIT OF RATIONALISM

Through Ivan, Dostoevsky portrays both the spirit of the rationalist society as well as its fate. In short, rationalist societies are profoundly conflicted societies that will ultimately destroy themselves. The process by which this occurs on the social level is most clearly illustrated in the most famous chapter of *The Brothers Karamazov*—"The Grand Inquisitor." To state it differently, Ivan's internal moral and intellectual dynamics are played out on a social level in this chapter.

The first point to be made here is the fact that Ivan calls the story of "The Grand Inquisitor" a "poem." A poem, of course, is distinct from prose insofar as it expresses feelings and emotions. One would not expect to find in a young man committed to rational thought such emotional sentiments. Even more ironic is that the poem illustrates the perfect rationalist conundrum in which he finds himself: one pitting love against rationalism. At first glance, the story of "The Grand Inquisitor" seems to be a critique of the Catholic Church.[28] Indeed, the story takes place in Catholic Spain during the Church's darkest hour: the inquisition. This, however, is not the main point. The main point of this *poem* is to illustrate the feelings within Ivan and his inner turmoil. The poem itself tells of Christ's return to sixteenth-century Seville, in inquisitorial Spain, and is recognized as such. Predictably the town's people are drawn to him. They felt, "The Sun of Love which burned in his heart" (14:227). The Archbishop of Seville eventually approaches Christ and confronts him with the paradoxical words, "Why, have you come to hinder us? . . . tomorrow I shall condemn you and burn you at the stake as the most evil of heretics" (14:228). He then denounces the freedom Christ gave to mankind fifteen hundred years ago, and resents that Christ gave man the freedom that makes him unhappy. He resolves to "correct" Christ's work and to take this freedom away. In the place of this freedom, he offers to man true happiness: "miracle, mystery, and authority" (14:232).

From a political point of view, this "poem" creates a problem. If the earthly goal of a leader is to make man happy, he *should* take away this freedom. As D. H. Lawrence has famously argued, "The recognition of the weakness of man has been a common trait in all great, wise rulers of people."[29] Lawrence concludes that Christianity is impossible because it makes "demands greater than the nature of man can bear."[30] A great political system recognizes this and relieves man of this freedom.[31] For Dostoevsky, this is perhaps the most seductive argument in support of socialism. At its core, socialism promises a society that allows for the blossoming of human happiness. Once the material conditions of man's existence are corrected through the elimination of private property, man can be expected to attain his highest state of happiness. This end goal must be contrasted with the end goal of Christianity, which is the realization and expression of God's love. This end goal is not only fundamentally different, but it involves an internal conversion rather than an external political or material configuration.[32] The key problem here is that the Inquisitor approaches Christ's freedom from a political perspective. Indeed, Christ no doubt disappointed some in his day by not being a political actor—a liberator from Roman political oppression. Christ's message, however, was one of spiritual rather than political salvation. His was a freedom from the internal or spiritual oppression. It is not a political freedom from external constraints.

The goal of the Christian is inner salvation through God's love. Thus, when Christ states that "the Truth will set you free" (John 8:31), he is, in essence, saying that God's love will set you free. Anything opposed to God's love—namely, sin—keeps mankind from experiencing true freedom. In Christ's words, "Everyone who sins is a slave to sin" (John 8:34). To state it differently, sin enslaves and imprisons mankind. Thus, when the Inquisitor states that mankind has rejected God's freedom, he is basically stating his observation that man persistently slips into sin in pursuit of his own immanent happiness. This precludes his true freedom—and, ironically, his happiness. Rather than espousing a path to true freedom so consistently rejected by mankind (which requires the hard work of internal conversion), the Inquisitor offers a sort of "short-cut" to happiness— miracle, mystery, and authority. Again, these provide an external focus, rather than an internal conversion. Ironically, the Inquisitor does none of this out of malice. Indeed, he claims to be doing this out of a genuine concern for human happiness. He truly believes in the rightness of his actions. He recognizes that what he is doing is a "lie," but selflessly bears the burden of this for the happiness of mankind.

Famously, the poem ends with an unexpected twist. At the end of his long-winded justification of his rationalist approach, the Inquisitor stops, expecting a response. Christ says nothing, but approaches the old man in silence and softly kisses him (14:239). The Inquisitor shudders and declares, "Leave, and do not return. . . . Never return at all, never, never!" (14:239) Ivan concludes the poem with the words, "The kiss glows in his heart, but the old man holds to his earlier idea" (14:239). He recognizes the conundrum of Christ's love, but, like Ivan, rejects it. Alyosha, of course, immediately understands that this poem depicts the conflicted state of Ivan's soul and indicates this with his first response to it. He responds sadly, "And you with him, you too?" (14:239). Indeed, Ivan is very much stuck in a spiritual conundrum. On the one hand, it sounds ludicrous for a Christian leader to "correct" Christ, yet on the other, it is difficult to deny the merit of the Inquisitor's argument (mankind is burdened with his moral freedom: it makes him unhappy).

The Grand Inquisitor legend thus illustrates Ivan's moral quandary. Can man live happily without love? If so, the Inquisitor is correct. Man is in his happiest state deprived of his freedom, living by mystery, miracle, and authority. If, however, man cannot live happily without love, the Inquisitor's argument falls apart. For Dostoevsky, this is the *fundamental* problem with any *political* system predicated on the promise of immanent happiness. Although Ivan is conflicted about this conundrum, he clearly is the intellectual source for the moral justification used by Smerdyakov to kill their father. Dostoevsky is, ultimately, arguing that rationalism applied to the political realm results in patri(a)cide. In other words, the more significant threat to Russia comes from this conflicted rationalist quarter rather than romanticism/nationalism. This is precisely why Dostoevsky has Fyodor anticipate this when he asks, "What does Ivan say? Alyosha my dear, my only son, I'm afraid of Ivan. I'm more afraid of Ivan than of the other one. You're the only one I'm not afraid of" (14:130).

SMERDYAKOV: THE NIHILIST AGENT OF RATIONALISM

Toward the end of the novel, Smerdyakov accuses Ivan of patricide with the following words, "You killed him. You are the real killer! I was only your stooge, your faithful servant Licharda, and it was following your words I did it" (15:59).[33] Ivan eventually acquiesces to this accusation. How are we to understand this? Why did Dostoevsky not have Ivan kill his father rather than Smerdyakov?

The main literary purpose of Smerdyakov-as-a-murderer is to further emphasize the effect of profound humiliation. In point of fact, it would be difficult to create a character more humiliated than Smerdyakov. His mother was, in Dostoevsky's words, "an idiot girl, who wandered about the streets and was known to the whole town by the nickname of Stinking Lizaveta (Lizaveta Smerdyastchaya)" (14:89). Fyodor raped her on a bet. Fyodor found it "amusing" that the people in the town began to use the patronymic "Fyodorovich" with Smerdyakov, but he denied paternity. He ended up, however, assigning a thoroughly humiliating nickname for him—Smerdyakov ("The Stinker")—ostensibly in honor of his raped mother.

Smerdyakov's humiliation does not stop there. Gregory, who had taken it upon himself to raise the child, also demeaned him regularly. At one point Gregory yells at him, "You are not a human being. You emerged from the mildew in the bathhouse. That's what you are" (14:114). He then observes that the child grew up with "no sense of gratitude," and that "he [Smerdyakov] doesn't care for you or me, the monster" (14:114). It makes some sense that this degree of humiliation would result in certain unique behavioral characteristics. While Smerdyakov displays little interest in cultivating friends or romantic relationships, he does attempt to salvage some measure of dignity with regard to his physical appearance. He also displays, in his early childhood, the classic trait of many modern serial killers insofar as he "liked to hang cats and bury them with great ceremony. He used to dress up in a sheet as though it were a vestment, and sing and wave some object over the dead cat as though it were a censer" (14:114). Smerdyakov is, in essence, Dostoevsky's illustration of what can happen in the most extreme cases of humiliation and shame. He does not simply suffer from a damaged self-image—he is psychologically and spiritually destroyed. This condition ultimately results in a rage so intense that he would rather die than to continue living with this humiliation. As Smerdyakov puts it, "I would have welcomed their killing me before I was born so that I might not have come into the world at all" (14:204–205).

As evidence of his "self-death" and the "numb" sensation that accompanies such a supremely humiliated and unloved state, after murdering his own father, Smerdyakov displays no remorse.[34] His psychological motivation for killing his father is clear: he murdered the man primarily responsible for his humiliation. Because Ivan had provided for him a justification for it, he had no moral or ethical brake on committing this crime. He commits suicide not to escape justice (there is no incriminating evidence) but to avoid the further humiliation of a courtroom trial. For him, suicide is not even a dramatic event; it is nothing more than a merciful release from a numb and burdensome life.

Another reason Dostoevsky has Smerdyakov commit the murder rather than Ivan revolves around the chronology of Russian history. For Dostoevsky, the liberal "Westerners" of the 1840's set the stage for the violent revolutionaries of the next generation. Indeed, this is the theme of his book *The Possessed* (written just before *The Brothers Karamazov*). In a letter that Dostoevsky sent to the future Tsar, Alexander III, he explains his chronological thinking with regard to the origins of Russia's nihilistic terrorists:

> It's almost a historical study, in which I've sought to account for the possibility of such monstrous phenomena as the Nechaev movement occurring in our strange society . . . Our Belinskys and Granovskys would never have believed it if they'd been told they were the direct spiritual fathers of the Nechaev band. And it's this kinship of ideas and their transmission from fathers to sons that I've tried to show in my work.[35]

The idea that the importation of even seemingly innocuous Western rational secular ideas was somehow damaging to Russia was, of course, not unique to Dostoevsky (both Turgenev and Tolstoy agreed with this). He differed primarily in what he thought would be the end result of the West's Godless ideas. In *The Brothers Karamazov*, he brought together all of the political musings stretching from *Notes from the Underground* to *The Possessed* about the dangers of a Godless society—such Godlessness could only result in patri(a)cide through nihilistic violence.

ALYOSHA KARAMAZOV: A MONK IN THE WORLD

Alyosha Karamazov is clearly the hero of this novel, and as such he is very different than his brothers. Why is Alyosha so different? If shame and humiliation are the key elements leading to self-loathing and violence, why is Alyosha not as hateful as the other brothers? Dostoevsky clearly wants to point to Alyosha's Christian faith and loving humility that saves him from his brothers' fates. He first hints at this when describing his early childhood. His mother, Sophia (*reason*), was Fyodor's second wife and the mother of both Ivan and Alyosha. In spite of her name, she appears to have lost her reason (*teryala rassudok*) and sought religion between the time she gave birth to Ivan (in the first year of her marriage to Fyodor) and to Alyosha (in the fourth year) (14:13). Her conversion stemmed from the abuse and humiliation at the hands of Fyodor. It was thus that the rationalist first child was not exposed to Christianity, but the second one was. Indeed, the most cherished memory Alyosha retains of his mother was of her kneeling before an icon in the corner of a room praying to the Mother of God, "in hysterics, sobbing with cries and moans" (14:18).

Key, however, is not that Alyosha is merely a Christian as a result of his mother's conversion, but that he is a monastic novice under the spiritual guidance of a *staretz*. In placing himself under the guidance of a *staretz*, he chose the most humble of an already humble "career" choice. He sought neither fame nor glory; he sought a life of solitude, prayer, and obscurity. His life was to be geared toward the worship and contemplation of God and of God's love. Humiliation—the feeling of lovelessness by others—is impossible for someone who has no expectations of receiving worldly love in the first place. It is, of course, Zosima that provides the source for Alyosha's psychological health.

At the very beginning of the novel, Zosima immediately understands the problem that festers at the root of the Karamazov family—humiliation. He makes this clear when he tells Fyodor, "Do not trouble yourself. Make yourself quite at home. And, above all, do not be so ashamed of yourself, for it is from this that all the other things come" (14:40). This statement is followed by one of the most powerful symbolic actions of the novel when Zosima, "distinctly and deliberately bowed down at Dmitri Fyodorovich's feet till his forehead touched the floor" (14:69). This is followed by the words, "Forgive me! Forgive me, all of you!" (14:69). This dramatic display of loving humility is intended by Zosima to be illustrative of the key to addressing the problem of humiliation within the Karamazov family. It is here that we find the source of Alyosha's immunity to the humiliation experienced by his brothers. As a humble novice, Alyosha feels none of the psychological disturbances experienced by Dmitri and Ivan. He was just as neglected as they were, but as a humble novice he shows no sign of disappointment over his childhood neglect. In essence, Alyosha's humility shields him from the humiliation of not being loved by his father.

This humility not only protects Alyosha from an intolerable past but provides a potent *psychological power* that can transform even the most despicable of characters in the novel. To state it differently, he is not just experiencing a "conversion of soul" through his practice of "loving humility," he is able to transform the people around him—even the two most hideous characters of the novel: Fyodor and Grushenka. For example, within two weeks of his return home, Fyodor "took to embracing him [Alyosha] and kissing him terribly often, with drunken tears, with sentimentality. It was evident that he felt a real and deep affection for him, such as he had never been capable of feeling for anyone before" (14:18–19). Fyodor concludes, "I feel that you're the only creature in the world who has not condemned me" (14:24). Grushenka echoes a similar sort of transformation when she declares to Alyosha, "I believed that, nasty as I am, someone would really love me, but not only in a shameful manner" (14:323).

This very worldly power of loving humility cannot be underestimated for Dostoevsky. Indeed, Alyosha's functions as an intermediary between the hermetic world and the outside world. It is up to him to fulfill the seemingly impossible task of applying the hermetic ideals of loving humility to the world. This is precisely why Zosima tells Alyosha that "this is not the place for you in the future . . . you should get married, too" (14:71). Later in the novel, he explains that he will live as a "monk in the world" (14:259). Within three days of Zosima's death Alyosha does precisely this. Alyosha is, in essence, the antidote to the conditions that allow for patri(a)cide. By bringing loving humility into the world, a healthy, Russian alternative to romanticism and rationalism become available to a world otherwise pervaded with Karamazov-like humiliation.

A STAR RISES IN THE EAST: POLITICAL CHRISTIANITY?

In this light, it is difficult to imagine that the Christianity of Alyosha and Zosima could really be considered as the third leg of this reckless Russian troika. After all, both Dmitri and Ivan are not only self-destructive but harm most of those around them. Even worse, they contemplate and contribute to *patricide* and *patriacide*. Alyosha and Zosima do none of these things—they actually attempt to stop them. For Dostoevsky, however, Alyosha and Zosima do not represent the complete Christian vision as seen in nineteenth-century Europe. For him, Christianity—or at least a prominent part of it—still represents the third horse of this reckless troika. To see this, we must distinguish between the two visions of Christianity found in the novel. On the one hand, we see a Christianity based on "loving humility." This is Zosima's hermetic, and humble, Christianity. This is to be contrasted with the Christianity of the Inquisitor, which is based on "miracle, mystery, and authority." The crucial difference between these two approaches is in their conceptions of humility. While the Inquisitor's motivation may well be his "love" for the people (as he claims), by stating that he is "correcting" Christ's work by taking away man's freedom, he is displacing God himself. In becoming God, he is violating the principle of *humility* to the extreme. His actions may be grounded in love, but they are not grounded in loving *humility*. They are grounded in "miracle, mystery, and authority." Moreover, "The Grand Inquisitor" is not merely a critique of the Roman Catholic Church—a Church to which he was famously opposed. In point of fact, Dostoevsky is primarily opposed to any Christian Church that attempts to exercise the type of Inquisitorial authority we see in this chapter. To illustrate this, Dostoevsky provides a Russia-based analogy in chapters 3 through 5 of Book I with the narrative dealing with Ivan Karamazov's ideas about the appropriate role of the ecclesiastical courts within the Russian state.

What is most striking about this discussion is the enthusiasm with which the monastery's monks embrace the idea of political reform that would enhance the role of the Church in the state. This argument is neatly summed up in the words of Father Paisiy, who declares, "It is not that the Church is transformed into the State, understand this! That is Rome and its dream. That is the third temptation of the devil. It is the opposite: the State is to be transformed into the Church, will ascend and become the Church over the whole world. This is the complete opposite of Ultramontanism and Rome, and your interpretation. It is *the* great worldly destiny ordained for the Orthodox Church. This star will arise in the east!" (14:62). For Paisiy, this transformation will begin with the abolition of civil courts.

Paisiy's assertion, of course, is in reaction to Ivan's article, where he claims that "if there were only the ecclesiastical courts, the Church would not sentence a criminal to prison or to death. Crime and the way of viewing it should inevitably change, of course, little by little, not suddenly, not now, but fairly soon" (14:58–59). The point is that for Dostoevsky, even within a Russian Orthodox Monastery, one finds the dangerous temptation of authority. Zosima recognizes this. In principle, Zosima agrees with Father Paisiy's notion that the state should become the Church, but he disagrees with the notion that political reform should make this happen; it should only happen when society itself is ready for it. He argues, "The Christian society is currently not yet ready and is only resting on seven righteous men, but as they are never lacking, it will continue unshaken in expectation of its complete transformation from a society almost pagan in character into a single universal and all-powerful Church. So be it, so be it!" (14:61).[36] In other words, the Church must transform society in order to create a Kingdom of God on Earth, but not through a forceful state. It must happen through the conversion of the heart of each individual within society, not through the exercise of "the third temptation of Christ." In other words, it is not through authority that the lost sheep will be gathered, but through loving humility.

Through the character of Father Ferapont, Dostoevsky also warns of the first and second temptations of Christ—that of miracle and mystery. The first point to be made here is obvious—Father Ferapont is a Russian Orthodox hermit. Significantly, he is not a *staretz* (he is actually opposed to this institution). Nonetheless, he has, in theory at least, left the world to seek salvation in poverty, silence, solitude, obscurity, and obedience to God's will. The temptations to which Ferapont surrenders appear to be the first two temptations of Christ—miracle and mystery. As an ascetic mystic, he has committed himself to silence. However, when he does speak, he speaks of demons and exorcisms. In a characteristic passage he states:

> I'm telling you—I see, I see through them. As I was coming out from the Superior's, I looked—there was one, behind the door, hiding from me—and a full-grown one, a yard and a half or more high, with a thick, long, brown tail, and the tip of his tail was in the crack of the door and I, not being an idiot, instantly slammed the door and pinched his tail. He squealed and began to struggle and I made the sign of the cross over him three times. He dropped dead, like a squashed spider. He must be rotten and smelly, but they don't see or smell anything. I haven't gone there in a year. I reveal it to you as you are a stranger (14:153–154).

In this crazed passage, we can discern an element of insanity within Father Ferapont. It is here that we find a sobering parallel with the message of the Inquisitor. Ferapont is not Inquisitorial with regard to the principle of authority, however, he does embrace the powers of miracle and mystery. Through these powers he is able to attract an astonishing number of followers—both inside and outside the monastery. *All of this in spite of the fact that he is clearly insane.* For Dostoevsky, the seductive power of "miracle, mystery, and authority" is almost irresistible—even to monks in a monastery who have at least formally committed themselves to lives of poverty, silence, solitude, and obscurity.

THE POLITICS OF HUMILITY

For Dostoevsky, individuals must embrace "loving humility" to escape and recover from humiliation. Humiliated Russia must take the same route. Because they are grand political movements that reject loving humility, neither nationalism (with its roots in romanticism) nor socialism (with its roots in rationalism) can address the problem of national humiliation. Even worse, because of their inner contradictions, these movements represent grave threats to the Russian fatherland. In *The Brothers Karamazov*, Dostoevsky aims to show, through the Karamazov family members, how they ultimately result in *patricide* and *patriacide*.

Surprising to many, even Christianity can be ineffective at addressing the problem of national humiliation. Inquisitorial-style Christianity, be it in Spain or a Russian Orthodox monastery, lacks the key element for addressing humiliation—humility. Indeed, for Dostoevsky, Russia's political salvation can *only* be addressed through the practice of national humility. As Zosima depicts, it will come from the meekest and mildest—

the *startsy* of Russia. It will also come from another humble section of the Russian people—the Russian peasants. Indeed, Russians must trust in the Christian and peasant spirit of the people. As Zosima states, "The salvation of Russia comes from the common people. . . . An unbelieving reformer will never do anything in Russia. . . . Take care of the people and guard their hearts. Quietly educate them. This is your monastic duty, for the common people are Chosen People of God" (14:285). In addition, "when the time comes they will show it to the wavering truths of the world. That is a great thought. This star will shine forth from the East" (14:284). Importantly, all of this must be accomplished in a spirit of humility, for "Russia is great in her humility" (14:286).

A great deal is at stake here, and not just the salvation of Russia. Europe itself has an interest in all of this. This is where we must return to the symbol of Gogol's reckless troika, used by Dmitri's prosecutor toward the end of the novel. The prosecutor argues,

> Our deadly troika is speeding headlong and, possibly, to destruction. And for quite some time throughout the whole of Russia, hands have been extended and have appealed to stop this furious, shameless sprint. And if yet other nations step aside from this sprint at breakneck speed, than maybe, it is not at all from respect of it, as the poet [Gogol] had wanted, but from horror. Take note of this! From horror, or maybe from disgust. And it is good that they step aside, but perhaps they will be led to position themselves as a solid wall in front of this rushing phantom and they themselves will stop this crazed sprint of our licentiousness for the sake of their own safety, enlightenment and civilization. We have already heard alarmed voices from Europe" (15:150).

Clearly, for Dostoevsky, this troika, representing nineteenth-century Russia's three philosophical visions (romanticism, rationalism, and Christianity), is galloping out of control and will lead not just to Russia's destruction, but to that of Europe as well. The irony, of course, is that these three visions arrived in Russia from Europe itself.

In essence, Dostoevsky's solution is therefore not a political solution, but an anti-political solution. For this reason, the use of individual, novelistic characters provides an ideal stage upon which to suggest this. In using the psychological dynamics of Dmitri, Ivan, and Alyosha as microcosms of romanticism, rationalism, and Christianity, Dostoevsky ingeniously provides illustrations of the spirits of these movements, their origins, their inner tensions, and their fates (as movements). The humiliation of these characters, as well as that of Russia, can only be dealt with by the humble. The psychological illustration of this process on the individual level is compelling. The application of it to the social level seems equally as compelling.

NOTES

An earlier form of this chapter, "This Star Will Shine Forth from the East: Dostoevsky and the Politics of Humility," was delivered at the Annual Meeting of the American Political Science Association, Seattle, Washington, 2011.

1. Isaiah Berlin, *The Hedgehog and the Fox: An Essay on Tolstoy's View of History* (London: George Weidenfeld & Nicolson Limited, 1988), 4.

2. Indeed, it is generally accepted that Dostoevsky's true genius lies primarily within the realm of psychology. In fact, Sigmund Freud once said that everything he had discovered in the first seventy years of his life had already been found in the works of Fyodor Dostoevsky (attributed to Edward Wasiolek in Richard Pope and Judy Turner, "Toward Understanding Stavrogin" *Slavic Review* 49 (Winter 1990), 543–553. Yet another notable thinker made a similar observation: Friedrich Nietzsche wrote that "Dostoevsky was the only psychologist from whom I had anything to learn" (Friedrich Nietzsche, *Twilight of the Idols; and The Anti-Christ* (Baltimore: Penguin Books, 1968), #45).

3. See Ellis Sandoz, *Political Apocalypse: A Study of Dostoevsky's Grand Inquisitor* (Baton Rouge: Louisiana State University Press, 1971); Jack F. Matlock, "Literature and Politics: The Impact of Fyodor Dostoevsky," *The Political Science Reviewer* 9 (1979), 36–90; Joseph Alulis, "Dostoevsky and the Metaphysical Foundation of the Liberal Regime: 'Legend of the Grand Inquisitor,'" *Perspectives on Political Science* 38 (2009), 206–216; Lee Trepanier, "The Politics and Experience of Active Love in *The Brothers Karamazov*," *The Political Science Reviewer* 38 (Fall 2009), 197–205; David Walsh, "Dostoevsky's Discovery of the Christian Foundation of Politics," *Religion and Literature* 19 (1987), 49–72.

4. F. M. Dostoevsky, *Polnoe Sobranie Sochineii i Pisem* (Leningrad: Nauka, 1972–1990). All parenthetical references within this chapter are by volume and page number to this Academy edition. I am responsible for translations. Several translated quotes within this chapter can also be found in: John P. Moran, *The Solution of the Fist: Dostoevsky and the Roots of Modern Terrorism* (Lanham, MD: Lexington Books, 2009b) and John P. Moran, "The Roots of Terrorist Motivation: Shame, Rage and Violence in *The Brothers Karamazov*," *Perspectives on Political Science* 38 (2009a), 187–196.

5. I would like to thank William L. Taylor for pointing this out.

6. Michael Casey, *A Guide to Living in the Truth: St. Benedict's Teaching on Humility* (Liguori, MO: Liguori/Triumph Publications, 2001), 4.

7. Saint Benedict, *The Rule of St. Benedict in English* (Collegeville, MN: The Liturgical Press, 1982), 32.

8. Nils Sorsky, *The Authentic Writings* (Kalamazoo: Cistercian Publications, 2008), 185.

9. Of course, the name Karamazov seems to imply a certain "dark stain." *Kara* meaning black, and *maz'* meaning ointment or oil. But the fact that a distinctly Turkic rather than a Russian root was used is perhaps to indicate a certain non-European element to a nation that is in many other ways European.

10. Famously, the alternative word in Russian for this concept, usually translated as "motherland" ("rodina") does not find its root in the word for "mother" but rather in the word for "birth" or "origin" ("rod").

11. It makes some sense that Dostoevsky would have these two characters be of the same generation. Dostoevsky himself shifted from the "Westerner" to the "Christian" positions within his own lifetime. The story of how this occurred is wonderfully covered in Joseph Frank, *Dostoevsky: The Years of Ordeal, 1850–1859* (Princeton: Princeton University Press, 1990).

12. Indeed, Dostoevsky has Zosima address this specifically later in the novel (14:289–290). For more, see Laurie Langbauer, "Ethics and Theory: Suffering Children in Dickens, Dostoevsky, and Le Guin," *English Literary History* 75 (2008); Joseph R. Yacoub, "Children in Dostoevsky: The Case of *The Idiot* and *The Brothers Karamazov*" in

Proceedings of the 2004–2005 Midwest Philosophy of Education Society, ed. Jason Helfer (Bloomington, IN: AuthorHouse, 2007).

13. James Gilligan, "Shame, Guilt, and Violence," *Social Research: An International Quarterly* 70 (2003), 1153.

14. Orlando Figes, *Natasha's Dance: A Cultural History of Russia* (New York: Picador, 2002), 366.

15. Figes, *Natasha's Dance*, 66.

16. Figes, *Natasha's Dance*, 66.

17. Dostoevsky felt that this exclamation was so important that he named the entire chapter "Why Is Such a Man Alive?"

18. To ensure that the reader understands the Pushkin reference here, Dostoevsky had already put the following words in the mouth of Rakitin, "Pushkin, the poet of women's feet, sung of their feet in his verse. . . ." (p. 86). For more see Helena Goscilo, "Feet Puskin Scanned, or Seeming Idee Fixe as Implied Aesthetic Credo," *The Slavic and East European Journal* 32 (Winter 1988), 562–573.

19. Isaiah Berlin, *The Roots of Romanticism* (Princeton: Princeton University Press, 1999), 9.

20. Berlin, *The Roots of Romanticism*, 9.

21. Ernest Gellner, *Nations and Nationalism* (Ithaca: Cornell University Press, 1993), 1.

22. E. J. Hobsbawm, *Nations and Nationalism Since 1780: Program, Myth, Reality* (Cambridge: Cambridge University Press, 1995), 12.

23. Benedict Anderson, *Imagined Communities: Reflections on the Origin and Spread of Nationalism* (New York: Verso, 1991), 5–6.

24. It is commonplace to suggest that nationalism flourishes in areas where a particular national identity is most threatened by a dominant nation or by a neighboring country (Ireland and Poland are two classic examples).

25. Ivan Turgenev, *Fathers and Sons* (New York: Bantam Books, 1981).

26. Mikhail Bakhtin, *Problems of Dostoevsky's Poetics* (Minneapolis: University of Minnesota Press, 1984), 176.

27. Even Rakitin notices his doubt by stating: "His soul is stormy; his mind is in a prison. Within him, his thought is great and unresolved" (14:76).

28. Dostoevsky was notably anti-Catholic. His main objection to Catholicism, as voiced by two of his most sympathetic characters, Myshkin in *The Idiot* and Alyosha in *The Brothers Karamazov*, revolves around his concern about conflating temporal and spiritual power. See Joseph Frank, *Dostoevsky: The Miraculous Years, 1865–1871* (Princeton: Princeton University Press, 1995), 335.

29. D. H. Lawrence, "Preface to Dostoevsky's 'The Grand Inquisitor'" in *Dostoevksy: A Collection of Critical Essays*, ed. Rene Welleck (Englewood Cliffs, NJ: Prentice-Hall, 1962), 93.

30. Lawrence, "Preface to Dostoevsky's 'The Grand Inquisitor,'" 91.

31. Based upon this logic, Lawrence concludes that Lenin was ". . . surely a pure soul . . ." (Lawrence, "Preface to Dostoevsky's 'The Grand Inquisitor,'" 94).

32. Perhaps the best statement on this is made by Carl Linden when he writes, "Marx . . . is not aware of a need to rectify the inner regime of his own being, but only of the regime of the outer city. The fruits of the works of Marx and his Leninist following prove them to be not the savior of the modern city of man, but rather its angry and tyrannous despots" (Carl A. Linden, *The Soviet Party-State: The Politics of Ideocratic Despotism* (New York: Praeger, 1983), 28).

33. The Notes in the David McDuff translation explain that *Licharda* is a Russian version of the name Richard. Here it refers to the servant of King Guidon in Bova Korolevich (Prince Bova), a chivalric legend originally translated from medieval French (Fyodor Dostoevsky, *The Brothers Karamazov: A Novel in Four Parts* (London: Penguin Classic, 2003), 1001).

34. Gilligan, "Shame, Guilt, and Violence," 1149–1181.

35. As cited in Michael R. Katz, "Introduction" in *Devils* (Oxford: Oxford University Press, 1992), ix. Also quoted in Moran, *The Solution of the Fist: Dostoevsky and the Roots of Modern Terrorism*, 13.

36. This reference to "seven righteous men" refers to the seven general councils that defined the Orthodox Church's teaching about the fundamental doctrines of the Christian faith. For an excellent background on these councils see Timothy Ware, *The Orthodox Church* (New York: Penguin, 1997), 18–42.

FOUR

Dostoevsky's Heroines

Or, on the Compassion of the Russian Woman

Richard Avramenko and Jingcai Ying

INTRODUCTION

Readers of Dostoevsky's political novels recognize well that he is engaged in pitched battle against the West for the spiritual direction of Russia and his Russian brethren. He regards Russia as the last bastion of hope in the fight against secularism, materialism, rationalism, and individualism. That Russia is moving in the direction of the West is nothing less than a "political apocalypse," as Ellis Sandoz puts it.[1] The bulwark against this Western invasion is, of course, Russian Orthodoxy, which is manned by a uniquely appropriate warrior, the Russian Soul.[2] Representatives of this type tend to be holy men, like Fathers Zosima and Paissy (*Brothers Karamazov*), Bishop Tikhon (*The Possessed*), Myshkin (*The Idiot*), and Dolgoruky (*The Adolescent*). In their battles against the West, these holy men are armed with what Dostoevsky regards as the chief weapon against the West: Christian love. This Christian love, however, is distinct for Dostoevsky because it is rooted in a shared history of suffering, and this suffering allows for his holy men to manifest their love as compassion. As Dostoevsky puts it, "If you love, you will belong to God. . . . With love all things may be redeemed, all things may be rescued."[3] Like Christ, the Russians have suffered, and from their suffering the rest of the world will be saved.[4]

The holy men in Dostoevsky's novels, however, are not the only characters whose compassionate love is exemplary. Overlooked almost universally by political theorists are Dostoevsky's women. Sonya's love for Raskolnikov in *Crime and Punishment* and Darya's love for Stavrogin in *The Possessed* is quintessentially self-sacrificial love. Its essence is compassion, i.e., the willingness to share others' suffering.[5] Sonya shares Raskolnikov's suffering from his guilt. Darya takes upon herself Stavrogin's suffering from his nihilism. Male characters, of course, follow this pattern, but it is only with the more "feminine" characters that we witness a self-sacrificial individual relinquishing his own happiness to help a particular, non-abstract sinner find salvation: Myshkin's love for Nastasya in *The Idiot*, and Alyosha's love for his brothers in *The Brothers Karamazov* are prime examples. Prince Myshkin shares Nastasya's suffering from debauchery and Totsky's mistreatment of her. Alyosha suffers his brothers' debauchery and godlessness. In all four examples, this compassionate love is either exemplified by women, or by males who are quite outside the hyper-masculinity of the typical male character.

The following sheds light on the feminine character of compassionate love in Dostoevsky's work. In doing so, we will foreground some feminine characters that are rarely noticed. But rather than a broad survey of the feminine characters in Dostoevsky's work, we will focus on the heroines in *The Possessed*—it is in this novel, after all, that we find the most self-assertive, violent men. To illustrate the feminine character of compassionate love, we will first attempt to explain why women are important in Dostoevsky's vision of Russian salvation and then expound the meaning of compassion that paves the way to salvation. We will then focus on three heroines in *The Possessed* (i.e., Marya Lebyadkina, Darya Shatova and Sofya Ulitina) and analyze them in light of our theoretical framework. From this analysis, we will argue that the compassion of Russian women is Dostoevsky's most poignant example of Russian love. The three heroines we will look at all manifest Sonya's beseeching to Raskolnikov: "We are going to suffer together, we will bear the cross together!"[6]

DOSTOEVSKY'S WOMEN

Few political theorists have made much of love in Dostoevsky's work. Perhaps the best account of the theme comes from Lee Trepanier, who points to Father Zosima's idea of "active love" as the basis of Russian Orthodoxy—or at least Dostoevsky's gloss on Russian Orthodoxy. As Trepanier puts it, active love is exemplified by "Zosima's vision of epistemological humility, self-constrained freedom, and a socially-bound community where the ideals of Christianity become contextualized and consequently can become possible."[7] Missing from Trepanier's account, however, is the central point of this paper: that the kind of love of which Zosima speaks is made active most effectively through Dostoevsky's heroines. Other scholars, of course, recognize the role love plays in Dostoevsky's work. Nathan Rosen, for example, recognizes that for Dostoevsky love is "a movement toward the preservation or creation of a moral order" that reveals the good in heroes and saves them from chaos and nihilism.[8] Richard Chapple recognizes that what is unique about this active love is that it embraces "the concrete individual rather than the abstract masses."[9] Neither of them, however, connects love to the compassion of Dostoevsky's heroines.[10]

In fact, even fewer readers of Dostoevsky connect compassionate love to Dostoevsky's heroines, especially the heroines in *The Possessed*. Katherine Briggs, for example, in her monograph on the women in Dostoevsky's novels, completely ignores the heroines in *The Possessed*.[11] Those who do look at the women tend to pick and choose the heroines to discuss rather than recognizing the centrality of the feminine to Dostoevsky's politics. Linda Ivanits, for example, praises Marya Lebyadkina's spirituality as a Russian peasant, proclaiming her the only "positive heroine" in *The Possessed*.[12] Nina P. Straus, in her analysis of Nikolai Stavrogin's mistresses, argues that they all seek independence of their lover's sado-masochistic masculinity and counterbalance it with their feminine strength.[13] Elsewhere, Straus does associate Dostoevsky's view of maternity with "the idea of the feminine components of faith, with earth and Russia as a mother, and with Jesus as the mother's son incorporating traits of suffering, self-sacrifice, and compassionate love associated with maternity" but seems to overlook the most important examples of this pattern.[14]

Nevertheless, it is in the Russian woman—especially the Russian peasant woman—that Dostoevsky sees the hope for the salvation of Russia and her ill sons. As a Russian slavophile and Christian, he wants to defend both the Russian folk-belief in Mother Earth and the Orthodox faith in a more general sense. For him, the Russian peasant woman possesses both, which makes her the ideal healer for the Russian man's Western disease. As Nicolai Berdyaev puts it, the Westernized Russian man "has departed from the feminine principle" and "renounced his mother-earth. . . ."[15] He has lost his moral compass, continuously overstepping all moral boundaries (e.g., Raskolnikov in *Crime and Punishment*) and lusts for every sensual pleasure (e.g., Stavrogin in *The Possessed*). In the face of the Russian man's degeneration, the Russian woman preserves the "life-affirming and altruistic values" inherited from Mother Earth, the sacred soil that remains the regenerative source for all Russians.[16] Dostoevsky is not merely hoping for such a heritage in the Russian woman, he actually finds it in her: "In the Russian woman resides our only great hope, one of the pledges of our revival. The regeneration of the Russian woman during the last twenty years has proved unmistakable."[17] The heroines in Dostoevsky's novels embody this "great hope" and exemplify the Russian woman's striving to reunite the degenerated Russian man with Mother Earth. Therefore, it is not surprising that nearly all the heroines in Dostoevsky's work are peasants because the Russian peasants have always been closest to the soil. In fact, Dostoevsky is so hopeful of the peasant's spiritual health that in *Crime and Punishment* he even lets Sonya, a peasant, give Raskolnikov the cypress-wood cross, a symbol of the Russian peasantry, to ensure the murderer's salvation and reconciliation with the Russian soil.[18] To Dostoevsky, the Russian peasant woman might be the only way back to Mother Earth for the fallen Russian men.

Of course, Dostoevsky's heroines are more than daughters of Mother Earth—they are also the followers of Christ from whom the Russian man will regain his faith in God. The Russian peasant woman's messianic identity is revealed in the words of Stepan Verkhovensky, a failed scholar in *The Possessed*. Representing the Russian idealists of the 1840s, Stepan admires the European civilization but lacks aims and resolution in his opinions and sentiments to save Russia.[19] Yet, from him, a Russian man who loves anything but Russia, we learn the messianic mission Dostoevsky places upon the Russian peasant woman:

> "Oh, blessed is he to whom God always sends a woman and . . . I fancy, indeed, that I am in a sort of ecstasy."[20]

> He simply bowed down at her feet and kissed the hem of her dress. . . .
> "My savior," he cried, clasping his hands reverently before her (*P* 612).

Through this Westernized liberal who comes back to Russia and Russian Orthodoxy on his deathbed, Dostoevsky highlights the Russian woman's unique mission on the earth—to heal the Russian man who has withered spiritually from his genuflection before the altar of Western rationalism and materialism. In seeking the salvation of Russia in Western ideas, the Russian men have turned their backs on the Russian God, losing their way to salvation and bringing their nation suffering and chaos. The way back is through the Russian peasant woman. Prostrating himself before a peasant woman, Stepan turns to the Russian God for salvation and realizes that there is nothing but death in the West—a truth later confirmed by Stavrogin's suicide. Kneeling before a Russian peasant woman, Stepan understands that the meaning of being a Russian lies in Mother Earth and God. To be sure, depicting the peasant woman as representative of both Mother Earth and Christianity, Dostoevsky suggests a rather heretical Christian belief of which the Othrodox Church would have disapproved. This is a point to which we will return in our analysis of Marya Lebyadkina. For now, it suffices to reiterate that the Russian woman, as the apostle of Mother Earth and Christ, is the key to the salvation of Russia and her wayward sons.

DOSTOEVSKY'S WOMEN'S COMPASSION

In all the heroines Dostoevsky depicts, compassion is the common characteristic. For the novelist, only those women who love *compassionately* possess the regenerative capacity. Here compassion retains its etymological sense: *compatior*, to suffer with one, the impulse that compels Dostoevsky's heroines to share the Russian men's suffering. As the willingness to share suffering, compassion justifies suffering in love, paves the way to salvation, cleanses egoism in love, and remains as the spirit of the Russian community. First of all, compassionate love means the acceptance and sharing of suffering. In *Crime and Punishment*, for example, Sonya's compassion for Raskolnikov first manifests in her willingness to partake in his suffering by accompanying him to Siberia. Sonya's commitment to Raskolnikov exemplifies the sort of Russian love Dostoevsky envisions, a love that entails little happiness but much suffering. As Berdyaev puts it:

> The common bond between two human beings, the love-cult of woman, is a beautiful flower sprung from European Christian culture, and Russia had no age of chivalry with its garden of *trouvère*. This spiritual lack gives a flavour of affliction and pain, of melancholy and often of distortion, to all Russian manifestations of love. There has been no real romanticizing of love in Russia, for Romanticism is a purely Western phenomenon.[21]

Instead of romantic tales with happily-ever-after endings, Dostoevsky sees suffering in love. For him, love is never merely a companion from whom endless joy and reassurance will flow. Rather, Russian love is bound up with pain. When "suffering is [the Russian] life," no love can escape into a Romantic utopia.[22] Therefore, Russian love is not the joy individuals experience in each other. It is realized only when people suffer with each other, when they are compassionate for each other. Its immensity is the intensity of suffering. In *Crime and Punishment*, love is realized only when Sonya assures Raskolnikov that they will "bear the cross together," suffer with each other. In short, to realize love is to share suffering—that is, to have compassion.

For Dostoevsky, the meaningfulness of compassion and its necessity are never doubted because shared suffering is the Russian way to salvation. In Father Zosima's words, Dostoevsky reveals to us that the attainment of compassionate love is faith in God:

> Try to love your fellow human beings actively and untiringly. In the degree to which you succeed in that, you will also be convinced of God's existence, and of your soul's immortality. And if you attain complete self-renunciation in your love for your fellow creatures, then you will unfailingly come to believe, and no form of doubt will ever be able to visit your soul. That has been tested, that is precisely true.[23]

"To love your fellow human beings" is to suffer with them. As Ellis Sandoz asserts, only through suffering can a Russian find God and Russian love and therefore transcend "the common bond between two human beings" because it allows the person to enter the relationship with God.[24] Raskolnikov receives from Sonya not only the warmth of companionship but also God's grace in her compassionate love. After failing to become a superman without God, he understands that a man "left to his own resources . . . can do nothing."[25] With shared suffering, Sonya shows Raskolnikov, who once admired Napoleon for his individualistic heroism, that a Russian man will find no salvation in the Western cult of individualism; he can only be saved by divine grace while rooting himself in Mother Earth/the Russian God. Following this truth, Raskolnikov lays himself down in the soil and confesses his sins at the crossroad. Sonya realizes her compassionate love for Raskolnikov as the murderer admits his sin and begins his return to God, to Russia, and to salvation.

However, Raskolnikov's salvation does not come without sacrifice; it is achieved at the cost of Sonya's self-renunciation. As with Father Zosima in *The Brothers Karamazov*, Dostoevsky reminds us that salvation (i.e., the realization of compassionate love) requires self-renunciation. As such, compassionate love stands in contrast with self-assertive love that only empties personality. Zosima recognizes this well and declares that this self-assertive love does nothing to heal the sickness of the soul:

> Fanciful love thirsts for a quick deed, swiftly accomplished, and that everyone should gaze upon it. In such cases the point really is reached where people are even willing to give their lives just as long as the whole thing does not last an eternity but is swiftly achieved, as on the stage, and as long as everyone is watching and praising. Active love, on the other hand, involves work and self-mastery, and for some it may even become a whole science.[26]

Fanciful love only gratifies the ego. An individual besotted with fanciful love accepts suffering not because he selflessly shares others' suffering, but because he desires the praise brought by his own suffering. As such, fanciful love is nothing more than self-love, *amor sui*. Its realization is essentially the assertion of egoism, which reduces personality to "the abyss of its own nothingness."[27]

It is into this abyss that Raskolnikov had fallen. To realize his dream of Napoleonic heroism, he kills two innocent women. He is only rescued from this abyss by Sonya's compassionate love, a love founded on self-renunciation as opposed to the assertion of the ego. A truly compassionate individual must break from the desire to gratify his or her ego and reconstruct his or her personality by partaking in others' suffering. As Father Zosima tells us, self-renunciation does not diminish personality but paves the way to God. Therefore, faith, fortified in shared suffering, guarantees the fullness of Sonya's personality. In turn, Sonya's personality embodies the idea of compassion. To Dostoevsky, ideas without embodiment are as imaginary as the tales of Western romantic love. Sonya actualizes compassion as much as compassion fulfills her personality. To be sure, a truly compassionate individual never takes pleasure in suffering because he understands that pain is incompatible with gratification. Nor does he seek suffering as an ascetic, for the point of compassion is never suffering itself. The essence of compassion lies in togetherness ("com"), not suffering ("passion")—or, in the Russian, the "so" of "*sostradanie*."

In the form of its shared suffering and fulfilled personality, compassion is the culmination of the Russian spirit of community. Although the preceding analysis focuses on suffering, it is a mistake to think that Dostoevsky values suffering intrinsically; to him, it is only a means to personality, to God, and to the Russian community. More important than suffering ("*patior*") is togetherness ("*com-*") in compassion. Togetherness is the basis of the Russian community, a community Berdyaev describes as "the unity of love and freedom which has no external guarantees whatever."[28] Compassion is the fundamental stratum of this community because, as an idea distinct from mere suffering, its emphasis lies in sharing more than suffering.

Sonya is a heroine because she does more than accept suffering—she not only suffers for her family but, more importantly, suffers with Raskolnikov. In Sonya, suffering is no longer personal but interpersonal and communal. Because the choice to suffer with others can be imposed by no external authority but only by an inner urge to bear others' suffering, compassionate love retains freedom. Shared suffering, hence, becomes a spiritual bond uniting all individuals who freely submit to the community without losing their personality. Out of their free will, individuals who suffer with each other constitute the base of this organic Russian community. This free community needs no "external guarantees" because God sanctions its spiritual bond with freedom. We know from Father Zosima that compassion connects man to God: "In the degree to which you succeed in that [i.e., loving others compassionately], you will also be convinced of God's existence, and of your soul's immortality."[29] Because self-assertion leads to empty personality and obstructs the way to salvation, faith and salvation only exist in the Russian community, a community of compassion. It is precisely in this kind of love, as exemplified by a heroine, that Dostoevsky sees "the inner mystery binding all beings to each other as fellow creatures in a common world." Love as compassion is "the corporate experience of love."[30]

In *The Possessed*, Dostoevsky offers three sterling examples of this "corporate experience of love" in three separate heroines: Marya Lebyadkina, Darya Shatova, and Sofya Ulitina. Each of these women naturally sacrifices herself for the sake of another suffering person. Each of them is, in a sense, a nurse to the soul of suffering Russia. The success of their spiritual ministrations depends, of course, both on how far advanced the disease and the nature of the disease itself. Their success, in other words, reveals Dostoevsky's thoughts on which disease poses the most danger for the Russian Soul. We shall begin this diagnosis and analysis with Marya Lebyadkin.

MARYA LEBYADKINA: A HOLY FOOL FOR MOTHER EARTH

Being a holy fool, Marya Lebyadkina seems odd among the heroines in *The Possessed*. Different from Darya Shatova and Sofya Ulitina, Marya does not necessarily suffer with others, but her own suffering is exemplary. Crippled and feebleminded, she lives with an abusive, alcoholic brother and is tricked into marrying Stavrogin, who marries her in defiance of conventions. She may indeed be the most miserable woman in the story. Yet, as a holy fool, she causes no discomfort or repugnance on the part of others. To the Russian peasants, a holy fool's infirmity lends itself to a "higher sensibility" that allows the Holy Spirit to manifest in them: "Severe asceticism, feigned madness, and at times feigned immorality were the outstanding characteristics of this type of spirituality."[31] In other words, Marya's feeblemindedness is a veil covering her inner spirituality. From this woman who suffers excruciatingly, we will hear the most spiritual passage Dostoevsky writes in *The Possessed*, a spiritual insight that equates the Mother of God to Mother Earth.

Marya exhibits her spiritual insightfulness during Shatov's visit to her apartment. After combing Shatov's hair, Marya speaks of his boredom: "You may be a very sensible man but you're *bored*. It's strange for me to look at all of you. I don't understand how it is people are *bored*. Sadness is not *boredom*. I'm happy" (*P* 131, translation modified). People like Shatov are bored because they accept neither God nor suffering. Their boredom is the kind of atheism springing from the difficulty reconciling "belief in God and divine providence with the existence of evil and unjust suffering."[32] Marya, however, is not bored because she believes in God. The world's suffering and her own miseries may render her melancholic but never bored. She endures evil and sin cheerfully because faith strengthens her with hope.

Marya's cheerfulness stems not only from the orthodoxy of her Christian faith but also from her peasant belief in Mother Earth. Recalling her conversation with a lay sister, Marya reveals her conviction that the Mother of God is Mother Earth, in whom lies the joy of life:

> "What is the mother of God?" "What do you think?" "The great mother," I answer, "the hope of the human race." "Yes," she answered, "the mother of God is the great mother—the damp earth, and therein lies great joy for men. And every earthly woe and every earthly tear is a joy for us; and when you water the earth with your tears a foot deep, you

will rejoice at everything at once, and your sorrow will be no more, such is the prophecy." That word sank into my hearts at the time. Since then when I bow down to the ground at my prayers, I've taken to kissing the earth. I kiss it and weep. And let me tell you . . . there's no harm in those tears; and even if one has no grief, one's tears flow from joy. The tears flow of themselves, that's the truth (*P* 132–133).

Marya blends Mother Earth and the Mother of God into a personal incarnation that is neither true to the folk religion nor approved by the Orthodox Church. In Linda Ivantis's words, "This outright equation of the earth and Mary exhibits shadings of a heretical cult."[33] This heretical cult, according to Joanna Hubbs, is a fourteenth-century dissenting sect called *Strigol'niki*, from which the confession to earth originated.[34] However, their ritual of confession did not warrant forgiveness; Mother Earth still condemned murderers and "those damned by their parents" eternally.

The merciful image of Mother Earth is Dostoevsky's view of the folk religion, which is bound with his Christian faith, and more specifically, with the Virgin Mary. Although not identified with Mother Earth, the Mother of God has long been solicited as "a merciful protector, an intercessor for men before the heavenly justice."[35] Mary, to Dostoevsky, supplies the unconditional mercy Mother Earth lacks, whereas Mother Earth provides a national faith. This heretical integration points to Dostoevsky's slavophile/Russophile sentiments in his Christian faith, echoing his diatribe against Western Catholicism in the *Idiot*. Therefore, the women who will save Russia can never be Westernized, like Nastasya Filippovna in the *Idiot*. Russia's saviors can only be Russians in touch with both Mother Earth and the Mother of God. Indeed, it is the integration of both beliefs that sets Marya aside from other Westernized female characters in Dostoevsky's work. As we will see in what follows, the Russian women who share Marya's peasant background and her faith are the best candidates for saving Russia's sons.

It is by the connection of God and Mother Earth that Marya's peasant Christian faith stores the strength of life amid suffering. As aforementioned, Marya may be the most miserable character in the novel, yet she is also the most cheerful one. The reason for this juxtaposition is her faith in Mother Earth and God. To the Russian peasants, Mother Earth herself is the source of every life, from which every life will also return.[36] Therefore, to confess to Mother Earth is to seek life, to shed tears on Mother Earth is to water life, and to worship Mother Earth is to consecrate life. No sorrow can drown this joy flowing out of such a life-affirming faith, as Christ preaches to his disciples in the Gospel of John (John 16:20–24). Marya's joy for life is later substantiated by Shatov's excitement for the birth-giving of his wife, another Marya: "Shatov spoke in an incoherent, stupefied and ecstatic way. Something seemed to be tottering in his head and welling up from his soul apart from his own will" (*P* 556). To embrace Mother Earth is to relish the creation of life, an event of "a great joy."

Like the pain of labor preceding the joy of new life, suffering always overshadows the joy of life. Marya's joy does not come from the abundance of a happy life but from the miseries of her painful life—joy alone is not enough to support life. From this perspective, to be spiritually alive, one must suffer, as Christ did. In Marya, we see both the culmination of suffering and faith, which, to Dostoevsky, is the birthright of the Russian people:

> I believe that the main and most fundamental spiritual quest of the Russian people is their craving for suffering—perpetual and unquenchable suffering—everywhere and in everything . . . Even in happiness there is in the Russian people an element of suffering; otherwise, felicity to them is incomplete. . . . [T]hey do know Christ, [. . .] the heart-knowledge of Christ, a true conception of Him, does fully exist . . . it has merged with the heart of the people.[37]

More than the endurance of physical pain, suffering is the ground of life, "the most fundamental spiritual quest." As such, suffering is "everywhere and in everything." All human experiences, including happiness, must rest upon suffering, or they will be meaningless. Why? Because only the acceptance of suffering leads to true faith. The Russian conception of Christ is a God who suffers with human beings. To reject suffering is to reject God and the ground of all human life. Christ can only be understood in suffering, as Marya exemplifies, and, therefore, to follow Him is to suffer. This is the spiritual journey on which all Russians must embark. Through Marya, who is already on this journey, Dostoevsky shows us that cheerfulness, the affirmative attitude towards existence, comes not from the absence of suffering but from the acceptance of suffering with faith in God. As Stefan Zweig puts it, the basis of existence for Dostoevsky is "I suffer, therefore I exist."[38] The vicissitudes of Marya's life best exemplify Zweig's formulation. Suffering imbues her entire existence and fortifies her faith in God.

DARYA SHATOVA: THE "FAILED" NURSE

In our analysis of Marya Lebyadkina's suffering, we conclude that to retain faith means to accept suffering, which, to Dostoevsky, is the ground of existence. However, it would be misleading to assert that suffering only belongs to the poor, oppressed Russian peasants like Marya. To Dostoevsky, suffering is the ground of existence precisely because of its universality. It is imperative for human beings to seek, gain, and reinforce faith in suffering. This search for suffering is not masochistic but compassionate. It stems not from the thirst for distorted pleasure but from the communal spirit of shared suffering. In Darya Shatova, we see such a spirit. Unlike Marya, Darya is not disabled, destitute, or oppressed. She is adopted by Varvara Stavrogina and raised in an aristocratic, wealthy household. However, similar to Marya, Darya is also a peasant woman of faith. In her love for Stavrogin, we see nothing but compassion, her will to share Stavrogin's suffering. In their conversations, it is clear that she fights Stavrogin's nihilism while holding deep concern for him. Although Darya is unsuccessful in helping Stavrogin regain his faith, her failure does not betray a limit to the saving capacity of compassion. As the epigraph of the novel suggests, Stavrogin might well be the possessed pig that ought to die off the Russian soil.

To understand Darya's compassion for Stavrogin, we must first understand Stavrogin himself, the anti-hero who suffers from his nihilism and alienation from Russia. In his letter calling for Darya's company, Stavrogin reveals the rotten state of his soul:

> As always I blame no one. I tried the depths of debauchery and wasted my strength over it; but I don't like vice and didn't really want it. . . .
>
> Dear friend! Great and tender heart which I divined! Perhaps you dream of giving me so much love and lavishing on me so much that is beautiful from your beautiful soul that you hope to set up some aim for me at last by it? No, it's better for you to be more cautious, my love will be as petty as I am myself and you will be unhappy. Your brother told me that the man who loses connection with his country loses his gods, that is, all his aims. One may argue about everything endlessly, but from me nothing has come but negation, with no greatness of soul, no force. Even negation has not come from me. Everything has always been petty and spiritless (*P* 635).

In this confession, Dostoevsky depicts the inner character of "a complete nihilist" who "has no horizon orienting him to earth or the heavens."[39] Without any sense of an objective standard, he finds everything "trivial and stale" and, therefore, becomes bored of everything. His boredom results not from his contempt for traditional values but from his self-will. Throughout his life, nothing but his selfhood matters to Stavrogin. He is an "individual" through and through. He indulges in debauchery, which, in Berdyaev's words, is "love and affirmation of self, conducing to the ruin of self" and "the most frozen isolation to which a man can condemn himself, a decline to a sentient nothingness."[40] In the end, he finds that self-will and debauchery only isolate him, deprive him of purpose, and eventually reduce him to pettiness. He can negate nothing because he has no belief to negate, i.e., the ground for all negations. Even his dislike of debauchery is not a negation of sensual pleasure but only a disbelief in sensual pleasure, which stems from his hollow self. As Stavrogin quotes Shatov's words, he knows that the cause for his perdition is his separation, his disconnection, from Russia. Yet, Stavrogin still misquotes Shatov because Shatov's original word is God, not gods. Stavrogin's nihilism has depleted his spirit to the extent that he can no longer tell the difference between Christianity and paganism. After all, to a complete nihilist, differences in faith provoke nothing but indifference. David Walsh is indeed right to conclude that "atheists' freedom is also self-closed and empty."[41] Moreover, Stavrogin's nihilism precludes him from any chance of participating in the organic and life-spirit emanating from the soil of Russia herself. As he puts it, "I have no ties in Russia—everything is as alien to me there as everywhere" (P 634). He is alienated from Russia because he has neither faith nor compassion, the two essential characteristics of the Russian Soul. From the start of the novel, Stavrogin loves only himself. His life is purposeless because he has no faith in Russia and is unable to suffer with others, the very purpose of a Russian's life. He is dead to the suffering of others, just as he is dead to himself.

Knowing well that Stavrogin's soul is empty, Darya is still determined to take some of his suffering on herself. At their first meeting at Stavrogin's house, Darya reveals her intention to be Stavrogin's companion. However, Stavrogin, full of self-will, cannot comprehend her compassion. Without understanding Darya, he mocks her determination, comparing her to "pious old women who frequent funerals and find one corpse more attractive than another" (P 273). Stavrogin's necrophilic joke worries Darya because the joke is self-referential. If Darya were the old lady, then Stavrogin would be the corpse that interests her. In truth, the joke does allude to his spiritual death—his disconnection from God, Russia and the Russian people—and foreshadows his suicide. Stavrogin's reference to death makes Darya concerned with his general well-being: "'Are you very ill?' she asked sympathetically, looking at him in a peculiar way. 'Good heavens! And this man wants to do without me!'" (P 273). Darya is afraid that without her, Stavrogin could not even physically survive in this world, let alone regain his spiritual health. Her desire to share his suffering is uncanny. She wants to save him through compassion.

Darya is determined to accompany and save Stavrogin even after enduring his mockery. She recognizes his dead soul, but is nevertheless shocked when she learns that he has accepted Fedya's offer to murder Marya Lebyadkina and her brother. She fears that Stavrogin has been implicated in a potential murder: "Surely you must see that you're being caught in their nets on every side!" (P 273). The net here likely refers to a spider's web. As Briggs observes, Dostoevsky often presents in his novels the spider "as a spiteful, evil insect which lurks in dark corners to prey on others . . . a metaphor for the dark and unadmitted feeling which lies within the human psyche."[42] Here the spiders are Fedya who kills for money and Stavrogin who consents to Fedya's assassination contract. Both of them prey on Marya Lebyadkina. For Darya, Stavrogin's spider-like action is a clear sign of possession: "God save you from your demon, and . . . call me, call me quickly!" (P 274). Stavrogin's demon is his nihilism, his inability to love.[43] Still, Darya displays genuine concern for his well-being and offers to share in his suffering. Her willingness to suffer with others and Stavrogin's inability to love forms a stark contrast between a compassionate heroine and a rapist.[44]

Dedicating herself to saving a westernized Russian man, Darya fits Dostoevsky's profile of the female savior for Russia. She is a godly peasant woman who represents the healing power of Mother Earth and the Christian salvation. As a compassionate heroine, she is at least as admirable as Sonya. Although Stavrogin repeatedly rejects her companionship and mocks her love, she is steadfast in her willingness to renounce her own happiness and become his spiritual nurse. Even after reading his letter, in which he reveals his disrespect for her sacrifice and the gloomy future of accompanying him, Darya still chooses to go to his side and bury her life with him. By doing so, Darya follows Father Zosima's principle of active love to the letter. In her, we see the same Russian spirit we have seen in Sonya—that is, the communal spirit that compels individuals to alleviate the suffering of others through self-sacrifice. Darya's compassion, like Sonya's, is also an act of free will. Thus, her altruistic personality can stand as an exemplar of Christian freedom, as opposed to Stavrogin's atheistic freedom that centers on self-will and ends in self-destruction.

SOFYA ULITINA: THE "SUCCESSFUL" NURSE

Sofya Ulitina is a minor character in the novel, and only appears near the end. However, she might well be one of the most telling characters. To begin, she shares many characteristics with Darya. Both of them are godly peasants who, out of compassion, try to save westernized Russian men (i.e., Stavrogin and Stepan) with Christian faith. Darya wants to be a nurse at a convent and sell bibles while Sofya used to be a nurse and is now selling Gospels. What distinguishes Sofya from Darya is Sofya's marital status. She is a widow whose late husband fought Europeans in the Crimean War—which is of especial interest in this context because France was a major belligerent against Russia in the Crimea, and Stepan, the man she sacrifices herself for, speaks French like a Parisian. In any case, following her husband's anti-European legacy, Sofya appears in the novel to be the healer for the spiritual disease Stepan contracts from Europe, and especially from the French. Although she is only a minor character in the novel, she embodies the hope Dostoevsky places upon the Russian women. Without Sofya, Stepan would be doomed to die alone on his search for Russia. It is Sofya, the common Russian peasant woman, who makes possible the only salvation scene in the novel. Simply put, no Sofya, no salvation.

Before encountering Sofya, Stepan has already experienced the sort of hospitality and care for others that is *de rigeur* with the Russian peasants. After being offered a free ride by a peasant woman, Stepan is stunned and thinks to himself: "'How wonderful it is,' he thought to himself, 'that I've been walking so long beside that cow and it never entered my head to ask them for a lift. This 'real life' has something very original about it'" (*P* 597). For a man immersed in Western culture where individualism, materialism, and self-interest trump community, it is indeed hard for him to imagine being offered a free ride from a strange Russian peasant. As Stepan later confesses to Sofya, in French no less, that he has never seen them close up (*P* 605). Therefore, it is only natural that he cannot understand "this real life." This "something" Stepan will later understand with the help of Sofya is compassionate love, the Russian community spirit, the Russian Soul.

Deeply moved by the peasants' hospitality, Stepan perceives the dignity of a Russian peasant woman in Sofya. When he sees Sofya, he murmurs: "There's something noble and independent about her, and at the same time—gentle. *Le comme il faut tout pur*, but rather in a different style" (*P* 603). Sofya is "noble" because she harbors a noble faith, a faith rooted in both Mother Earth and Christianity. She is "independent" because she lives on her own. Spiritually, she is also a self-standing believer without external guarantee, just like the Russian community itself. Sofya is "gentle" because, like the peasant woman who offers Stepan a free ride, she is raised in a community of hospitality. As such, she is a lady "in a different sense," different from those westernized Russian ladies who concern themselves with nothing but debauchery (e.g., Nastasya in *The Idiot*). Later, Stepan recognizes that Sofya (and the peasant woman who gave him a ride) are the real Russian people, the people who know compassion in their heart (*P* 605). Therefore, it is safe to assert that the dignity Stepan perceives in Sofya is the radiance of the Russian spirit. Stepan, whose compassion is awakened by Sofya's dignity, returns to the real people when he offers to take Sofya to Spasov, the village for which she desperately wants to leave. In contrast with Stavrogin who repeatedly rejects Darya's compassion and the Russian spirit, Stepan hears the call of compassion and embarks on his journey to salvation with Sofya his nurse.

Dignified and compassionate, Sofya becomes not only Stepan's travel companion but his nurse. Like Darya who is worried about Stavrogin's possession, Sofya is anxious about Stepan's well-being when she hears his dreaming of "a gaping jaw full of teeth" (*P* 607). However, the demon in Stepan does not drive Sofya away. To share and alleviate Stepan's suffering, she stays. At first, she resists his request for her overnight company, fearing for her reputation. Eventually, she remains with him to nurse him because, despite the risk to her reputation, she understands that he is suffering, really suffering (*P* 609). Sofya stays up all night caring for Stepan, running in and out of the room. Even though her frequent movement provokes other residents to abuse her, we hear not a single complaint from Sofya. On the contrary, she even decides to stay with him when he is too ill to board the steamer departing for Spasov. To ease his suffering, she foregoes the opportunity to start a new life. Later, she fully commits to Stepan when he begs her not to leave him alone. What motivates her to make such a commitment is compassion in its most unadulterated form. Out of compassion, Sofya is constitutionally incapable of abandoning a physically and spiritually ill man and thus remains to nurse Stepan and share his suffering.

Sofya's compassionate care of Stepan rekindles his Russian faith. He shares this revelation with Varvara Stavrogina: "I've learnt to know real life in Russia . . . *et je precherai l'Evangile*" (P 617). Stepan finally realizes the bond Dostoevsky is suggesting between Russians and Christianity. Deciding to preach the Gospel, Stepan has taken the first and most crucial turn back to the Russian spirit and his own salvation. As death closes in, Stepan, inspired by Sofya's compassionate care, enunciates his insights of the Russian spirit in his profession of faith:

> My immortality is necessary if only because God will not be guilty of injustice and extinguish altogether the flame of love for Him once kindled in my heart. And what is more precious than love? Love is higher than existence, love is the crown of existence; and how is it possible that existence should not be under its dominance? If I have once loved Him and rejoiced in my love, is it possible that He should extinguish me and my joy and bring me to nothingness again? If there is a God, then I am immortal. *Voilà ma profession de foi* (P 623).

Stepan's profession of faith echoes Father Zosima's interpretation of love and God. For both of them, love leads to faith in God and God, in return, guarantees the meaningfulness of love. Love is compassion, the willingness to suffer with others, and being means only the earthly existence full of suffering. Compassion is higher than earthly existence because it transcends the world through sharing. Out of shared suffering, the genuine Russian community is created and the Russian path to God is paved.[45] By sharing others' suffering and self-sacrificing, individuals can forge a communal bond that leads to salvation. Thus, suffering ceases to be meaningless pain and turns into the basis of a historical, corporeal community. If a Russian, like Stavrogin, loses himself to the loveless rationalism of the West, then only passionate self-love informs his existence—which is empty and destructive. For Dostoevsky, Russian love can only be compassion, not passion. This is what Stepan learns from Sofya and what cures him from the spiritual ailments of the West.

CONCLUSION

For Dostoevsky, the way to salvation is by dwelling in the nexus of suffering and compassion. It is on this same canvass of compassion that salvation for Russia herself will be drawn. That is, in the reciprocity of suffering and compassion, Dostoevsky sees hope for Russia's future. By sharing one another's suffering—through renunciation of the self—the great schisms in Russian society can be healed. Through the abandonment of individual well-being and the love of other sufferers, none will be ostracized from this community that places forgiveness over judgment, unity over individuality, and godly hope over atheist progressivism. In *The Possessed*, like much of the rest of Dostoevsky novels, Russian women are the last line of defense in the battle against secularism, materialism, rationalism, and individualism. Marya Lebyadkina, the peasant woman who endures the most miserable of miseries, joyfully proclaims the godly hope in Mother Earth, the Russian embodiment of the Mother of God. In Marya's words, Dostoevsky suggests to us that the basis of human existence is never happiness. Even spiritually, man is unhappy, for suffering is the foundation of human life. Only in suffering can man find God and the meaning of life. However, such discovery is not the attainment of salvation. To be saved, man must either love or be loved. That is, man must share others' suffering or share his suffering with others. Stavrogin is destined for self-destruction because he rejects Darya's love, her compassion for him. Stepan, in contrast, is saved because he accepts, even begs for, Sofya's compassionate care. Marya, Darya, and Sofya, three peasant women, are the agents of compassion whose activities in the novel manifest nothing but the Russian spirit (i.e., compassion for all mankind). Their heroism is indeed Dostoevsky's formula of salvation—that is, the way to God is through the feminine—through the compassion best exemplified by the Russian peasant women.

NOTES

1. Ellis Sandoz, *Political Apocalypse: A Study of Dostoevsky's Grand Inquisitor* (Baton Rouge: Louisiana State University Press, 1971).
2. For a brilliant analysis of this, see Nikolas Berdyaev, *The Russian Idea* (London: Geoffrey Bles & The Centenary Press, 1947) and Nikolai Berdyaev, *Dostoevsky* (New York: Meridian Books, 1957).
3. Fyodor Dostoyevsky, *The Brothers Karamazov: A Novel in Four Parts and an Epilogue* (London: Penguin, 2003), 72.
4. For more on Dostoevsky's messianic vision of Russia, see his *Pushkin Speech*, in Fyodor Dostoevsky, *The Dream of a Queer Fellow and the Pushkin Speech* (New York: Barnes and Noble, 1961), 57–58.
5. The Russian word for compassion, *sostrandanie*, is etymologically parallel to the Latin, "suffering with." The root, incidentally, also lies at the heart of Father Zosima's name.

6. Fyodor Dostoyevsky, *Crime and Punishment* (Oxford: Oxford University Press, 2008), 405.
7. Lee Trepanier, "The Politics and Experience of Active Love in *The Brothers Karamazov*," *The Political Science Reviewer* 38 (Fall 2009). Reprinted as chapter 2 in this volume.
8. Nathan Rosen, "Chaos and Dostoyevsky's Women," *The Kenyon Review* 20 (1958).
9. Richard L. Chapple, "A Catalogue of Suffering in the Works of Dostoevsky: His Christian Foundation," *The South Central Bulletin* 43 (1983).
10. Frank Friedeberg Seeley, "Dostoyevsky's Women," *The Slavonic and East European Review* 39 (1961). More explicit than Rosen and Chapple, Seeley offers a tripartite definition of love that includes humility, the perception of the soul, and compassion. Without ranking these three components of love, Seeley fails to emphasize the saving and communal powers of compassionate love. Thomas A. Idinopulos, on the other hand, highlights the communal element in love by suggesting that for Dostoevsky "love . . . consists of compassion, fellow suffering—a love which does not forsake but rather which forgives the sinner, accepts tragedy as well as joy in life, a love which perceives and celebrates the inner mystery binding all beings to each other as fellow creatures in a common world" (Thomas A. Idinopulos, "The Mystery of Suffering in the Art of Dostoevsky, Camus, Wiesel, and Grünewald," *Journal of the American Academy of Religion* 43 (1975)).
11. Katherine Jane Briggs, *How Dostoevsky Portrays Women in His Novels: A Feminist Analysis* (Lewiston, NY: Edwin Mellen Press, 2009).
12. Linda J. Ivanits, "Dostoevskij's Mar'ja Lebjadkina," *The Slavic and East European Journal* 22 (1978).
13. Nina Pelikan Straus, "Every Woman Loves a Nihilist: Stavrogin and Women in Dostoevsky's *The Possessed*," *NOVEL: A Forum on Fiction* 27 (1994b).
14. Nina Pelikan Straus, *Dostoevsky and the Woman Question: Rereadings at the End of a Century* (New York: St. Martin's Press, 1994a), 84. Straus, for example, has little to say about Sofya Ulitina, whose compassionate love saves the central character of the novel, Stepan Verkhovensky, from the abyss of Western culture.
15. Berdyaev, *Dostoevsky*, 118.
16. Joanna Hubbs, *Mother Russia: The Feminine Myth in Russian Culture* (Bloomington: Indiana University Press, 1988), 228.
17. F. M. Dostoievsky, *The Diary of a Writer* (London: Cassell, 1949), 340–341.
18. Dostoyevsky, *Crime and Punishment*, 502.
19. Konstantin Mochulsky, *Dostoevsky: His Life and Work* (Princeton: Princeton University Press, 1967), 417.
20. Fyodor Dostoevsky, *The Possessed: A Novel in Three Parts* (London: William Heinemann, 1913), 606. All subsequent citations are from this translation and will be indicated as *P*. Some passages are modified to better reflect the Russian and more modern renderings.
21. Berdyaev, *Dostoevsky*, 112.
22. Sandoz, *Political Apocalypse*, 173.
23. Dostoevsky, *The Brothers Karamazov: A Novel in Four Parts and an Epilogue*, 77–78. Emphasis added.
24. Sandoz, *Political Apocalypse*, 182.
25. Berdyaev, *Dostoevsky*, 126.
26. Dostoevsky, *The Brothers Karamazov: A Novel in Four Parts and an Epilogue*, 80.
27. Sandoz, *Political Apocalypse: A Study of Dostoevsky's Grand Inquisitor*, 181.
28. Berdyaev, *The Russian Idea*, 52.
29. Dostoyevsky, *The Brothers Karamazov: A Novel in Four Parts and an Epilogue*, 78.
30. Berdyaev, *The Russian Idea*, 161.
31. Ivanits, "Dostoevskij's Mar'ja Lebjadkina."
32. Berdyaev, *The Russian Idea*, 132. See also Richard Avramenko, "Bedeviled by Boredom: A Voegelinian Reading of Dostoevsky's *Possessed*," *Humanitas* XVII (2004).

33. Linda Ivanits, *Dostoevsky and the Russian People* (Cambridge: Cambridge University Press, 2008), 112.
34. Hubbs, *Mother Russia: The Feminine Myth in Russian Culture*, 57.
35. Sandoz, *Political Apocalypse*, 29; Hubbs, *Mother Russia: The Feminine Myth in Russian Culture*, 115.
36. Sandoz, *Political Apocalypse*, 28.
37. Cited in Sandoz, *Political Apocalypse*, 59–60.
38. Stefan Zweig, *Three Masters: Balzac, Dickens, Dostoeffsky* (New York: The Viking Press, 1930), 156.
39. Avramenko, "Bedeviled by Boredom," 113.
40. Berdyaev, *Dostoevsky*, 123–124.
41. David Walsh, "Dostoevsky's Discovery of the Christian Foundation of Politics," *Religion and Literature* 19 (1987).
42. Briggs, *How Dostoevsky Portrays Women in His Novels: A Feminist Analysis*, 91.
43. As Father Zosima tells us, "[w]hat is hell? . . . The suffering that comes from the consciousness that one is no longer able to love." Dostoevsky, *The Brothers Karamazov: A Novel in Four Parts and an Epilogue*, 417.
44. Cf. Michael Kochin's chapter in this volume.
45. This communal spirit echoes Christ's Two Great Commandments in Matthew 22:35–40: "You shall love the Lord your God with all your heart and with all your soul and with all your mind. This is the great and first commandment. And a second is like it: You shall love your neighbor as yourself. On these two commandments depend all the Law and the Prophets."

II

Dostoevsky's Political Thought

FIVE

Philosophical Anthropology and Dostoevsky's "Legend of the Grand Inquisitor"

Ellis Sandoz

I.

The political thought of Fyodor Dostoevsky grows out of his opposition to nihilism, atheistic humanism, and socialism in much the same way as the philosophy of Plato grew out of his opposition to the sophists. Indeed, the parallel of Dostoevsky's thought with that of Plato is to be seen in some further aspects of this fundamental opposition. Both the Russian master of the novel and the Hellenic founder of political science confronted adversaries for whom "Man is the measure of all things," and each based his opposition on the principle "God is the Measure," to use Plato's formulation.[1] This declaration, echoing like a thunderclap across more than twenty centuries of history, found consummate expression in the last great work of each writer: the *Laws* and *The Brothers Karamazov*.

To reflect on the political aspects of Dostoevsky's philosophical anthropology and on the problem of good and evil involves recalling the pertinence of anthropology and ethics to political philosophy. Their basic connection is of the utmost simplicity. Insofar as political philosophy is a search (*zetema*) for truth of things political,[2] it is of necessity concerned with man as human and as citizen (*politos*) and with the axiological factors giving order and cohesion to the lives of individuals and communities. The science of man is *anthropology*; and the science of the goods which order human existence is *ethics*.

In a celebrated formula of classical political philosophy, Plato put man at the center of the science of politics: society is man written in large letters (*Republic,* 368 d–e). This formulation, stating what Eric Voegelin calls the "Anthropological Principle,"[3] occurs in what is, after the *Laws,* Plato's most important political dialogue. The substantial identity of the central problems of ethics and politics, of man and society, is thereby postulated. The inquiry of the *Republic* into the nature of Justice (*Dike*) is conducted simultaneously as a political and ethical exploration. Of their interrelationships Eric Voegelin has written:

> The anthropological principle in politics as established by Plato requires that the idea of the perfect polis expresses . . . the nature of man. We must have a systematic understanding of the nature of man if we want to have a systematic political science.

And again: ". . . the substance of society is psyche. Society can destroy a man's soul because the disorder of society is a disease in the psyche of its members."[4] The emphasis in Aristotle is similar. He has divided his treatise on political science into two parts: the *Nicomachean Ethics* and the *Politics.* His philosophical anthropology is given in outline in *Ethics* I.

The centrality of the anthropological problem has not been lost on modern thinkers. Kant, in commenting on the import of his Fourth Question, "What is man?," stated that it encompasses all the other fundamental questions of philosophy. The three prior questions of philosophy in the universal sense (*in sensu cosmico*), that is, "What can I know?" (answered by metaphysics), "What ought I do?" (answered by ethics), "What May I hope?" (answered by religion)—could be reckoned as anthropology, since the first three questions are related to the last.[5]

In French and German positivism, idealism, and materialism, the anthropological question assumed overwhelming proportions. On one hand, French social thought moved from Fourier through Saint-Simon to Comte and the religion of Humanity, the Great Being. On the other hand, the Hegelian Identities opened the way for Feuerbach's anthropological reduction and the final destruction of the idea of man in Marxian sociology. It is in a sense true, as Erich Fromm asserts, that "Marx's concept of socialism follows from his concept of man."[6] At this point Dostoevsky makes his entrance. Beyond him lies the Nietzschean apotheosis of man and the transvaluation of values.

Dostoevsky pitted his conception of man against the anthropology of atheistic humanism. As a young man he wrote: "Man is a mystery. It must be unravelled, and if you give your life to the task, do not think that you wasted it; I devote myself to this mystery because I wish to be a man."[7] He remained true to this task throughout his days and in all his art.

Nowhere has he more profoundly probed the mystery of man and his being than in his "Legend of the Grand Inquisitor." Writing to his friend

A. N. Maikov a decade before he actually came to the creation of his great work, *The Brothers Karamazov,* he spoke of the project as follows: ". . . before I attack it, I shall have to read a whole library of atheistic works by Catholic and Orthodox-Greek writers. Even in the most favourable circumstances, it can't be ready for two years . . . when I have written this last novel, I shall be ready to die, for I shall have uttered therein my whole heart's burden."[8] Eleven years later Dostoevsky supplied brief exegetical comments to Book Five of the novel. The Book, entitled "Pro and Contra," was divided into two installments for its initial appearance in the *Russky Vestnik,* the division being between chapter 4, "Rebellion," and chapter 5, the "Legend of the Grand Inquisitor." With reference to the first installment of "Pro and Contra," Dostoevsky explained: "Its idea . . . is the presentation of extreme blasphemy and of the seeds of the idea of destruction at present in Russia among the young generation that has torn itself away from reality," In this Book, Ivan expresses

> his basic convictions. These convictions form what I consider as the *synthesis* of contemporary Russian anarchism. The denial not of God, but of the meaning of his creation. The whole of socialism sprang up and started with the denial of the meaning of historical actuality, it arrived at the program of destruction and anarchism. The principal anarchists were, in many cases, sincerely convinced men. My hero takes a theme, in my view, an unassailable one: the senselessness of the suffering of children and from it deduces the absurdity of the whole historical actuality. . . . And my hero's blasphemy will be triumphantly refuted in the next (June) number, on which I am working now with fear, trembling and awe, as I consider my task (the refutation of anarchism) a civic exploit.[9]

A month later, speaking specifically of the Legend, Dostoevsky again wrote to Liubimov.

> The day before yesterday I sent to the editorial office of the *Russky Vestnik* the continuation of *The Brothers Karamazov* for the June number (the end of the chapter "Pro and Contra"). In it is finished what *the lips speak proudly and blasphemously.* The modern *denier,* the most vehement one, straightway supports the advice of the devil and asserts that that is a surer way of bringing happiness to mankind than Christ is. For our Russian socialism, stupid, but terrible (for the young are with it)—there is a *warning,* and I think a forcible one. Bread, the Tower of Babel (i.e., the future kingdom of socialism), and the completest overthrow of conscience—that is what the desperate denier and atheist arrives at. The difference only being that our socialists (and they are not only the underground nihilists—you are aware of that) are conscious Jesuits and liars, who will not confess that their idea is the idea of the violation of man's conscience and of the reduction of . . . mankind to the level of a herd of cattle. But my socialist (Ivan Karamazov) is a sincere man who frankly confesses that he agrees with the "Grand Inquisitor's" view of mankind, and that Christ's religion (as it were) has raised man

much higher than man actually stands. The question is forced home: "do you despise or respect mankind, you, its coming saviors?"

And they do all this in the name of the love of mankind, as if to say: "Christ's law is difficult and abstract, and for weak people intolerable"; and instead of the law of liberty and enlightenment they bring the law of chains and subjection by means of bread.[10]

Six months later, in December 1879, Dostoevsky prepared an Introduction to the Legend which he then included in a lecture presented to some students. This introduction, also, contains invaluable hints for the interpretation of the Legend.

An atheist, sick with disbelief, composes in a moment of torment a wild-fantastic poem. . . . The suffering from which the poet is ill has its immediate source in the fact that he, in the fantasy-form of the Grand Inquisitor and his Catholics, has fallen so far away from the old apostolic orthodoxy and view of the world that he knew as a youth and servant of Christ. His Grand Inquisitor is, however, himself really an atheist. The fundamental thought is: Yon spirit, he that caricatures Christianity, the moment he brings it into harmony with the goals of the world, annuls the entire purpose of Christendom and must without any question drive toward absolute disbelief. A second Tower of Babel stands in the place of the high ideals created by Christ. The sublime Christian view of human nature sinks down to the view of an animal herd and, under the banner of Social Love, shows entirely unconcealed its contempt for mankind.[11]

The thematic substance of the Legend, of high interest to political philosophy, clearly emerges from this series of quotations: the ontological character of revelation and the fundamental opposition of the two conceptions of the nature of man; the historical tension which lies between immanent being and the revealed order of a transcendent being; and the political consequences of reducing man to a mere species of animal.

II.

The "Legend of the Grand Inquisitor," a twenty-page chapter in Dostoevsky's last novel, *The Brothers Karamazov* (1879–1880), is almost unanimously agreed to be the greatest masterpiece of his art. Nicholas Berdyaev warned of its "fathomless depth." He viewed Dostoevsky as "the climax of Russian literature" and the Legend as "the high point of Dostoevsky's work and the crown of his dialectic."[12] The art of Dostoevsky has been aptly described as "a Whitmanesque song of himself."[13] In the "Legend" one confronts the grotesque yet magnificent contradiction of rebellion and mystical sublimity and a last agonized hymn of dire prophecy and hopeful hosanna uttered out of the deep of a great soul.

Our intent is to present the central problems of ethics and the anthropology of rebellion as these are raised and resolved in the "Legend." Dostoevsky's thought, of course, does not find expression in abstractions. His politics and philosophy, like his art, are not constricted by the conventional boundary lines which formalize and identify areas of academic endeavor. Nor was his art an art for art's sake. First and last he was a uniquely gifted human being passionately engaged in a no-holds-barred *agon* for existence in truth and freedom insofar as man, being what he is, the world and society, being what they are, and God, being what He is, make this possible. Dostoevsky's existence is emphatically human—his work is anthropocentric, preoccupied with the human condition—not as a curious onlooker, but as a totally committed actor in the drama of human existence. And, ultimately, his work is theocentric: at the center of Dostoevsky's anthropology lies the mystery of man's participation in divine being. As Romano Guardini remarked at the beginning of his study of Dostoevsky's religious thought, whoever attempts to deal with the religious in Dostoevsky's work quickly sees that he has taken for his subject the entire world of the writer.[14] In fact, *all* problems in the work of this novelist find their highest resolution at the level of the spiritual. Because he is a supreme artist, Dostoevsky is not merely a single actor in the drama of human existence under God: he is all of his characters as well; or, all together, they are Dostoevsky. The Karamazov family is engaged in the universal-historical drama of existence. It is the whole family of man, with its light and its dark, its sordid sensuality and pettiness, and its limitless grandeur.[15]

The "Legend of the Grand Inquisitor" is the unwritten poem of the "metaphysical rebel,"[16] Ivan Karamazov, who in a tavern recounts it to his cherubic young brother, Alyosha. The latter is one of Dostoevsky's "whole" men, an accomplished human being, who unlike his brother Ivan, Raskolnikov, and Dostoevsky's other "doubles," has overcome his own "division."[17] The decisive point of the "Legend" is suggested in Alyosha's first reaction: "'But . . . that's absurd!' he cried, flushing. 'Your poem is in praise of Jesus, not in blame of Him—as you meant it to be.'"[18] With this response as our guide, we may now consider the central problems raised and resolved in the Legend.

Christ: The Principle of Active Love

Ivan's poem opens with the reappearance, for a moment, of Christ incarnate. He walks the streets of sixteenth-century Seville. The atmosphere is that of Jesus' triumphal entry into Jerusalem on Palm Sunday. The people all recognize Him; He is the same Christ known through the Gospels. He is the living embodiment of Active Love, as *staretz* Zosima might have said.[19] It is the day after a magnificent *auto-da-fé* which has seen nearly a hundred heretics burned to death at the Grand Inquisitor's direction, for the greater glory of God.[20]

Christ walks in silence. His face shines with love and compassion. The people believe as little children and praise His name. A man blind since birth calls to Him from out of the crowd and, suddenly, he is able to see. The people praise Him and worship His name.

He passes before a door of the great cathedral of Seville, just as a funeral procession bearing the corpse of a seven-year-old girl emerges. The crowd cries to the bereaved mother to ask Christ to raise her. The priest frowns confusedly, but the mother falls at His feet in adoration and implores of Him. In compassion He once again speaks, "Maiden, arise!" The little girl sits up holding the funeral bouquet, refreshed and happy as though waking from a restful sleep. The people feel His burning love as it inundates their souls, and they can but respond by loving Him. They sing "Hosanna!"—*hoshi'ah nna,* Save [us] now, we pray!—and adore Him. He speaks no more throughout the poem.

His identity is established with the people (*narod*) by an act of faith. The communion in God (*sobornost*) of the opening of Ivan's poem is coupled with the kiss placed by Jesus upon the lips of the Grand Inquisitor, which closes the poem in an act of love symbolizing the communalism and personalism of Christian faith. The tension of faith and Christ as the affirmation of the essence of eternal Being Who *is* Love and Freedom and Truth is the "feeling-idea" which dominates the Legend and which makes this piece of writing *itself* the climax of Dostoevsky's Christian metaphysics. Christ demands the free response of man to His truth. Indeed, freedom is the leading theme of the Legend. The experience of faith as the free response of the people of the poem to the person of the Godman is crucial to Dostoevsky's meaning. The negation and rebellion constituting the body of Ivan's poem are bracketed by an affirmation of the reality of transcendent being and an anthropology of its apprehension which are granted the status of "facts." As facts they are to have equal consideration along with the "facts" of the human experience of evil and suffering recounted by Ivan in the conversation preliminary to his recitation of the poem and by the Inquisitor in his meeting with Christ.

The ontological quality of Dostoevsky's faith must be emphasized. Only if faith is conceived as a real experience, as a reciprocal interpretation of man and God, can the Legend be understood. Faith, thus experienced, structures existence, assuages sorrow, appeases suffering, and makes meaningful an otherwise meaningless life.[21] This conception of faith is given splendid expression by Dostoevsky in a sentence about Saint Tikhon Zadonsky, his model for the Elder Zosima: "The most important thing about Tikhon is Tikhon."[22] Likewise, the most important thing about Christ is the *fact* of Christ Himself.[23] In one sense, the fact of revelation is its content.[24] The divine truth, made climax of revelation in Christ, is empirically evinced in the lives of saintly individuals of all ages.

It is the absence of faith, thus strictly understood, from the experience of Ivan which tragically flaws his character and makes him precisely what he is.

The terrible truth of human existence is that human freedom is freedom for both good and evil, as Plato long ago pointed out. The problem of Christianity, the Inquisitor bitterly reminds us in his monologue before Christ, is that the "words of St. Peter—'Thou art the Christ, the Son of the living God'—must burst from the spirit of an unconstrained conscience."[25] Dostoevsky, as he directly tells us on more than one occasion, has gained his faith by an excruciating *Via Crucis,* ranging from the suffocating experience of political imprisonment and exile in Siberia (1849–1859) to epileptic seizure and the torment of personal confrontation with the devil as the indwelling other half of his divided soul. In one of his last issues of his *Diary* he wrote:

> The dolts have ridiculed my obscurantism and the reactionary character of my faith. These fools could not even conceive so strong a denial of God as the one to which I gave expression [in *The Brothers Karamazov*].... The whole book is an answer to *that.* You might search Europe in vain for so powerful an expression of atheism. Thus it is not like a child that I believe in Christ and confess Him. My Hosanna has burst forth from a huge furnace of doubt.[26]

Dostoevsky has made one of the very important discoveries of political philosophy; he has understood the sufferings of mankind to be due to "the fact that man is born a free spiritual creature" and that, being of this nature, he "may prefer to go hungry than to lose his freedom of spirit and be enslaved to material bread."[27] On at least one level of the problem, this is the ultimate refutation of the Grand Inquisitor's "Euclidian" reasoning.

Confessions of Faith

Before turning to the words of the Inquisitor himself, one must be aware of the background of spiritual, or metaphysical, rebellion which Ivan expresses. Camus has noted that God Himself is put on trial in Ivan Karamazov's rebellion. Both His Creation and His Revelation are rejected. Ivan's rebellion begins in outrage and indignation rooted in humanitarian pity for his fellow man, particularly for the guiltless, for children. He reasons, from effect to cause, that their suffering is due to the necessity of suffering in God's Creation in order that man may be permitted a free choice between good and evil, since it is only through free choice of the good that human salvation and the kingdom of God (the "final harmony") can be achieved. To God he opposes the principle of justice and proposes to transform religion into a positivist religion of humanity. All he knows, he says, is that there is suffering where there is no guilt. This is decisive. In a particularly poignant passage, he recounts the most terrifying atrocities perpetrated on children (the innocent) and then almost savagely queries his stricken brother, Alyosha. His question mysteriously transfigures the humanitarian into the man-god charged with judging God and correcting Creation:

> "Imagine that you are creating a fabric of human destiny with the object of making men happy in the end, giving them peace and rest at last, but that it was essential and inevitable to torture to death only one tiny creature—that baby [the one smeared and gorged with its own excrement and forced to spend a cold, frosty, night in a privy by its mother because it would not ask to be taken up at night] beating its breast with its fist, for instance—and to found that edifice on its unavenged tears, would you consent to be the architect on those conditions? Tell me, and tell the truth."
>
> "No, I wouldn't," said Alyosha softly. (I, 250f.)

Here is the problem of theodicy in its most urgent terms, and Dostoevsky's whole being grapples with it.[28] God's creation is rejected and Ivan returns his "entrance ticket" to the eternal harmony that lies beyond it. Reason and justice command this rejection. But, and this is the crucial point, so does the irrational religious consciousness of the humanitarian-socialist-rebel: "I don't want harmony. From love of humanity I don't want it. I would rather remain with my unavenged suffering and unsatisfied indignation, *even if I were wrong.*" As Camus observes, the *even if* is decisive. With it, Ivan becomes a religious founder. He founds the City of Satan and formulates the ideology of his "Legend." He denies Divine will and sets in its place self-will. If there is no God, or even if there is one Whose Creation and Revelation are rejected, then man must become god. And, since a god is a law unto himself, whatever the man-god or superman wills is lawful: hence Ivan's dictum, "All things are lawful."

The anthropology and the political science of atheistic humanism and socialism are presented in the Grand Inquisitor's monologue. What we are told there is cast in the form of a historical prophecy. Without dwelling upon the "prophetic" quality of Dostoevsky's thought, one can but acknowledge that he has given the most profound portrayal of the twentieth century's spiritual rebellion and totalitarian government that has been written. The impact of rebellion upon the psychic and physical being of Ivan himself, as he seeks to live with his "logic" hypostatized into a religious obsession, is equally instructive. His rebellion is not against God but against His Creation. The Gnostic complexion of this rebellion is patent. Personally and concretely, that is, beyond his "fantasy" of theocratic socialism, the issue of "everything is lawful" is parricide: the murder of Fyodor Pavlovitch Karamazov by Smerdyakov, moral Caliban and biological half-brother and spiritual son of Ivan. This "direct attack against nature and procreation," upon a despicable man whose nature is implanted in Ivan's own and keeps him from the God of Alyosha (but who is, nonetheless, his father), drives Ivan mad.[29]

The Grand Inquisitor: The Principle of Negation and Rebellion

Dostoevsky's characterization of the Grand Inquisitor constitutes a complex and almost impenetrably profound anthropology of spiritual disorder.

(1) The possibility of evil goes with freedom. The essence of man is his freedom of conscience in the knowledge of good and evil. According to the verdict of free choice, man can *either* ascend the way of active love through conscience formed by faith in response to revelation and find fulfillment in the perfect freedom and beatitude of Christ as His elect; *or* man can rebel against the prompting of conscience as the purveyor of an absurd mystery built upon "all that is exceptional, vague, and enigmatic," (I, 260) and follow "the spirit of the earth" (I, 258) from the uncertainty, confusion, and suffering of faith through the pride of life, the lust of the flesh, and the lust of the eyes to sin and the rejection of transcendence.

(2) Absolute freedom leads to absolute tyranny. The absolute freedom of rebellious man, claimed in the name of reason in the light of historical experience, is license which perverts the meaning of freedom on principle, enslaves man to his passions, leads him to the anarchy of passionate self-assertion and gratification ending in cannibalism, fratricidal war, the surfeit of self-indulgence which, exacerbated by blasphemy and faithlessness makes man the most miserable of creatures. From this *bellum omnium contra omnes*,[30] there emerges a chastened mankind—the "New Man" of Socialism—purged of its obstreperous elements, and anxious to surrender its freedom in exchange for bread, peace, salved conscience, and the modicum of comfort and self-indulgence which constitutes material happiness. Rebellious man progresses from the tyranny of the libidos to the tyranny of an external power—or, rather, of the *libido dominandi* politically organized.

(3) Men then pass beyond good and evil, for out of the new *anomia* of shattered spiritual and social order emerges the new ethic of absolute submission to absolute power. Everything is without qualification lawful, for the rules, those suffering saviors and men-gods; with the latter's permission everything may be lawful for subject mankind (slave-men)." Oh, they will thank us for allowing them to sin," the Inquisitor raptures. The principle of the earth spirit, of sensuous, gluttonous life, the "strength of the Karamazovs—the strength of the Karamazov baseness" (I, 270), provides the positive orienting force in existence. There is no crime, "hence" no sin, no soul, and no immortality, "hence" no God, no reckoning beyond human happiness conceived in tellurian and utilitarian terms.[31]

(4) But the escape beyond good and evil is, in fact, impossible and is the ultimate lie. The inquisitor's ideology is built upon an acknowledged

lie, which is even more of a lie than he admits. It is a metaphysical swindle. As Ivan's devil jeers in sublime mockery: "He can't bring himself to swindle without a moral sanction. He is so in love with truth—."[32] The hundred thousand elite rule with the knowledge of good and evil, and know that they have rejected Christ and embraced Satan. If men, however, are to be truly beyond good and evil, then neither Satan nor God may exist. And this is precisely the rejection made by Ivan (I, 243). But the ontological status of the soul, even in the absence of faith as a controlling center, gives the lie to this "logical" conclusion." Homeopathetic doses [of faith] perhaps are the strongest," the Devil tells Ivan (II, 302), and no man, not even the Inquisitor or Ivan, can escape the gnawing doubt of reason's conclusions which is the sediment of faith in homeopathic doses. The lie of the Grand Inquisitor is, thus, the lie in the soul, a species of the "true lie" (*alethes pseudos*),[33] the arch lie of human existence: the will of the "I" is the sum total of existentially relevant being *even if* the "Thou" is real. The crux of the matter is as Alyosha says it is: not reason and not experience but a faithless heart and the "lust for power, of filthy earthly gain, of domination" (I, 267). As a type, the man-god is a variety of megalomaniac: a religious fanatic spiritually too weak for faith. In the dreamworld of the superman, everything prohibited in the real world is permitted, and the lie in the soul can be both believed and disbelieved simultaneously. This *nosos* of the soul was first diagnosed on principle by Plato.[34]

Ethical Theory

The problem of good and evil in Dostoevsky is not speculative but existential. The doctrine of Dostoevsky (if he has one) amounts to the classical Christian solution of the problem. Evil is in essence negation, pure negation and denial, the "minus" in existence. Because man cannot bear nothingness, existential evil becomes centered in the Augustinian *amor sui*.[35] But, at bottom, self-love is without content: the man turned radically inward falls into the abyss of his own nothingness. The superman's alternative to this horror is the "moral sanction" of the Inquisitor: the love of self expanded into an anemic love of mankind which forms a humanitarian pity enforced by a lust for power growing, specifically, from the megalomaniac's jealousy of God. Nietzsche's utterance is prototypical: "If there were a god, I could not endure not being he."

Dostoevsky fought his fight, the "Unseen Warfare" of the soul, in the dark depths of human existence. His study of evil in human nature and society, of sin and the devil, of atheism, nihilism, and socialism, is an exhaustive report from the wilderness of life, from the "Underground" as he called it. And *life* is Dostoevsky's preoccupation. His mysticism is predominantly telluric, his love Dionysiac. In the depth of life's horrors and despair he sees a light. Doctrinally, again the answer is classically

Christian: Good is God and all that participates in divine being; and God is revealed in Christ who is, ineffably, love, and freedom, and truth—the unique "higher idea." But the *problem* of good and evil is the real arena of Dostoevsky's striving. Doctrinally, the answer is faith: one maximizes good and minimizes evil through faith. The goal of human endeavor is the eternal harmony, the kingdom of God—conceived apocalyptically and concretely and as personal spiritual beatitude and salvation. The integrity of the human personality is never compromised. But the gulf that separates man from God is the one that divides the finite from the infinite. What, then, for man is the Way to God? The way is faith, and each man must learn for himself what faith is. Here is the stumbling block. The answer is not easy, nor is the Way. It is the *Via Crucis*, the agonizing Way of the Cross, the path of suffering. To come to the Light and make it his own, man must freely choose and accept the proferred love of God through faith. The man who balks and rejects it is the rebel.

Dostoevsky balked and rebelled; he probed rebellion to its limits and, finding it a dead thing dealing only death and destruction, returned to the Way and only Light he had found in all the vast reaches of existential darkness. His song of the Way is not one long Hosanna: it is ribald and blasphemous, as filled with curses as with hallelujahs. But one hears in its dominant resolution the authentic Hymn of Hope of a courageous and authentic man who knew all of life and avoided none of it.

III.

In moving to consider briefly the more general aspects of Dostoevsky's anthropology,[36] it should be emphasized that the marvelous effectiveness of the Legend derives largely from its being the meeting of the God-man and the man-god. Centrally, the Legend is a harrowing adventure in human freedom. The mode of the poem is mythic.[37] It is set at the experiential juncture of time and eternity: *death*. The devout old man of ninety speaks *sub specie mortis,* looking back upon life and forward into the void. Indeed, at one level, he *is* death, destruction, and negation itself. But the tragic *pathos* of the confrontation derives from his being a man and not an impersonal cosmic force. From the perspective of Dostoevsky, man, created in the image and likeness of God, is destined to become the man-god—perfected through faith in Christ and grace after death.

But man in his freedom and Promethean pride can spurn faith and his destiny and proclaim himself transfigured through his own grace into the man-god. "Love yourself through grace," Nietzsche wrote, "then you are no longer in need of your God, and you can act the whole drama of Fall and Redemption to its end in yourself."[38] The Inquisitor is man devoid of faith, hence of hope, and loving no one—neither himself nor his fellow men, nor God. Like Ivan, he has rejected the Creation. But at the root of this rejection lies, not pity for the innocent who suffer, but the rebellious assertion that man has not been created by God, and, therefore, is no dependent being. He is instead lord and master of time and the world—for this is all that truly *is*. Indeed, the arrogance of the Inquisitor reflects the conviction that God has not created man but man has created God. The shadowy figure of the Holy Prisoner is, like Ivan's devil, only a hallucination. In this aspect, the Legend is a study in Feuerbachian theology.

But Dostoevsky goes beyond this. He shows that man's rebellion made in the name of man ends not only by destroying God, but by destroying man as well. Like Marx, the Inquisitor, also, would doubtless refer to the peasants as "troglodytes."[39] Obsessed with power, the man-god loathes not only God in His transcendence but the image of God in existence; for, by Dostoevsky's accounting, the essence of man is his free participation with god in the Creation. The man-god must eradicate this freedom if he is to retain dominion over society and reduce man to the merely human. Man in his freedom is refractory and may challenge authority monopolized in society, just as the man-god has challenged God's authority in being. But, deprived of freedom, man ceases to be man and becomes nothing more than a species—"a herd of cattle" in Dostoevsky's phrase. The de-humanization of man is the first task of the humanist; Dostoevsky called it the creation of the "anthill," the building of the "Tower of Babel." Starting from unlimited freedom, Dostoevsky tell us, the man-god arrives at unlimited despotism.

At the profoundest level, the Legend is an allegory of the cosmic drama of the Creation played out in the history of mankind and the microcosm of the individual soul. At the center of the drama lies the irony of human freedom: the fact of freedom in the nature of man, at once, marks man as God's own and permits him to rebel and assert the claim that he is himself God. "Man was created a rebel," the Grand Inquisitor reminds his Prisoner. This statement points beyond Prometheus to the Beginning itself. The Fall, man's estrangement from God, was the primordial act of rebellion of the creature against the Creator, and, likewise, the primordial act of human freedom. By it man became "like one of us, knowing good and evil," and the Elohim tremble lest man should next eat of the tree of life and challenge the Lord God Himself. By his free act man renounced his dependence and lost the understanding of his creaturely relationship; he asserted for all time his independence and autonomy of will and knowledge. Still withheld from him is the fruit of the tree of life; man must face death and as a result human life becomes a quest for immortality.[40] The Legend is "permeated with burning and fire"[41] as the symbolism of the "flaming sword which turned every way, to guard the way to the tree of life." In this perspective Dostoevsky's assertion that immortality and God are one and the same idea becomes intelligible.[42] The man-god is the primordial rebel who seeks to breach the gates by will and knowledge and, unaided, possess himself of immortality, regain the Paradise he has lost, and establish dominion over the Creation in which the Lord God would then be his Prisoner. The magnificence of Dostoevsky's vision here clearly emerges.

But the man-god's freedom in the search for immortality has derailed because it is infused by prideful rebellion. In the enormity of this pride, and in full knowledge of good and evil, he turns his back upon the way of salvation through grace. A desiccated and diseased soul and the bitterness of defeat are revealed in the withered face of the ancient Cardinal. His rejection of Christ, also, finds its place in the searing symbolism of burning and fire: the pride of the Inquisitor kindles the flames of hell in his own soul. As the conscious accomplice of Satan, "that wise and dread spirit, the spirit of self-destruction and non-existence," he lives the last acrid years of life in hell, sating his pride as tyrant of an earthly hell of his own making, and glimpsing through the suffering of his own wretched soul the smoldering torment of an eternal hell. Yet, there is comfort: through his grace, mankind is with him.

Dostoevsky in the words of Zosima has defined *hell* as "suffering of [or for] the inability to love."[43] The vagaries of rebellion and evil are Legion, but that which freedom seeks as its own is salvation through the ecumenical oneness of Christ Who is Love revealed.[44] The figure of Christ transforms the Legend from a mocking, blasphemous tirade—of keen interest to the political theorist, of course—into a sublime drama of altogether unaccountable power. Dostoevsky means the Legend to be an encounter with the ineffable numen. D. H. Lawrence called it "the fifth Gospel."[45] The confrontation is one with the divine *Logos* Himself. Nicholas Zernov wrote: "The world's literature does not possess any picture of Christ comparable in its power to that given by Dostoevsky...."[46] In the drama of rebellion, the rebel is confronted with the Truth of being. That he can withstand this confrontation and "hold to his idea" is in keeping with Ivan's previous declaration that he would reject the universal harmony, bought through the suffering of the innocent, "even if" he were wrong. So awesome is human freedom!

The tone of the "Legend," however, is not that of the measured grandeur of the Beginning but of the exaltation of the *End*. The prophecy of the Grand Inquisitor is the apocalypse of the end of history, and Dostoevsky's *Notes* for the Legend include the spectacle of the earth vomiting forth the great swarm of locusts heralding the Last Judgment.[47]

Rebellious man perseveres to the End. The apocalyptical arrogance of the Grand Inquisitor represents man, unable to breach the gates of Paradise, undertaking to render mankind captive. God is left in the isolation of His transcendence, and the Creation comes under the dominion of man-god. Not merely men as individuals, but mankind itself stands estranged from the Creator by dupe and design. The spirit of earth has triumphed in the hearts of men; and the Grand Inquisitor at the head of rebellious mankind challenges Christ to render His Judgment against the hundreds of millions who have known no sin (because he has corrected the Creation)—*if He dares!* In the *Notes,* the last word of the Grand Inquisitor reads: "And if there is a single sinner, it is You yourself!"[48] The reign of the Antichrist, thus, reaches its climax.

The familiar theme which underlies this rebellion is that of the gnostic cosmology, introduced into Russia especially by the Bulgarian Bogomils,[49] which conceives the Creation to be the work of Satan. The pattern is confirmed by Ivan's curious affirmation, already noted, that he accepts God but rejects His Creation. The split between transcendent and immanent being is absolute, and God in His transcendence is *deus absconditus:* the Creation is evil and the Christian revelation does not reveal Him. The way to salvation lies through a gnosis, gained by the privileged few, which enables man to overcome the world and save himself. The connection between gnosticism and nihilism, here depicted by Dostoevsky, has been confirmed by modern scholarship.[50] The general configuration entails the anarchistic rejection of all authority, the destruction of the powers which order social and individual existence, and then the reorganization of the world in accordance with the "truth" as this has been gained through the gnostic illumination. The varieties are infinite and Dostoevsky was well acquainted with some of them, not only in the guise of political and social revolutionism, but also through various Russian sectarian movements, particularly the Khlysty and Skoptsy which he studied in connection with the writing of *The Brothers Karamazov.*[51] The idea that the Roman Catholic Church would become the vehicle for this massive disciplined gnostic rebellion is perhaps drawn from Comte, where the notion is well developed, rather than from Dostoevsky's well-known aversion to Catholicism.[52]

The Legend in its entirety has been considered by some to be an anarchistic manifesto.[53] Any discussion of this aspect of the work must be cautious not to misread Dostoevsky. While we cannot enter into the problem on this occasion, it must be said that, insofar as Dostoevsky is directly concerned here about problems of social order, he is concerned because of man's relation to the order of transcendent being. With respect to any authoritarian apparatus, sacerdotal or political or totalitarian, which intervenes between man and the divine, Dostoevsky affirms the inviolability of human freedom and the autonomy of the individual person under God. To authoritarians, this may well be anarchism; but whether Dostoevsky was a political anarchist or an "embattled reactionary ideologue"[54] is not to be proved from the Legend because the questions themselves are inapposite. The overall issue, however, is a real one, the solution of which turns on the problem of differentiation in Dostoevsky's thought.

The Legend resolves the central paradox of existence in such a way that Ivan and Alyosha (not to mention scores of interpreters over the last eighty years) can draw diametrically opposed conclusions from it. Ivan, as its ostensible author, has intended it as an incontrovertible indictment of the human condition, of Christianity as the foundation of the social and spiritual order,[55] and as a refutation of the claim of Christ sufficient to make Him superfluous because He is irrelevant to man and life as they truly are and He only exacerbates human misery.

The power of this attack has been emphasized. In Ivan and his poem, however, there is a noteworthy element of playful suspense. One student of Dostoevsky has observed that Ivan on his own authority never utters his most famous slogan, which ends in the words ". . . all things are lawful." The sudden smile which plays across his face after the Inquisitor's "*Dixi*," explained as the indication of incipient epilepsy, suggests aesthetic distance as well. But there is also the denial, in the face of Alyosha's outburst, of the seriousness of the Legend: it is just the stupid poem of a stupid student; in the interview with the devil, Ivan is "ashamed" of the Legend and forbids the devil to speak of it. In the *Notes* to the Legend, the notion of a suspension of judgment, a wandering between doubt and faith is indicated, rather than the rabid atheism of the Inquisitor himself: it is all only a "trial balloon," Ivan says.[56] The Legend expresses the "furnace of doubt" and the most powerful argument which Dostoevsky could conceive for the thoroughgoing atheist. But his hero has been kept back a little distance from the plunge into the abyss. There is also in Ivan's attitude toward the Legend the suggestion of a similar attitude on the part of the Christ of the Legend toward the Creation: perhaps it will not work out, perhaps man *is* too weak, it is all a cosmic experiment, another "trial balloon."

D. H Lawrence seized upon this element when he explained the meaning of the *kiss* placed by the Holy Prisoner on the lips of the Inquisitor: "Jesus kisses the Inquisitor: Thank you, you are right, wise old man." "Let them be glad they've found the truth again."[57] The ambivalence of Ivan gives us the key to his symbolic function in the novel: he is the representative of the *intelligentsia* of the age, the "wanderer" (*skitaletz*) of whom Dostoevsky spoke so fully in his "Pushkin Speech" and in the apology directed to Professor A. D. Gradovsky. On the part of Dostoevsky this is, itself, a clever play with symbols. The New Man of Russia has been subtly identified with the sectarians, the extremists of the *Raskol'* called the *Stranniki* or "Wanderers."[58] The gnostic connection is underscored.

In the mind of Alyosha, on the other hand, the Legend is a hymn of praise to the humiliated Savior Who suffered in silence before His accusers and Pontius Pilate and suffers throughout time in silence before those who rebel and blaspheme. The intent of Dostoevsky here is marvelously intricate and subtle. At the center, however, is Russia's "Word"—the long awaited revelation "to the world [of] her own Russian Christ, whom as yet the peoples know not, and who is rooted in our native Orthodox faith."[59] In the Legend Dostoevsky has undertaken to utter the "Word." Revealed in the Christ of the Legend is the Russian Christ as mediated by contemplatives from the time of Boris and Gleb. It is the kenotic Christ of self-humiliation, suffering, love, humility and voluntary sacrificial death; it is the Christ of the hesychasts, of the *Philokalia* and the *Unseen Warfare,* whose life is the transfiguration wrought through mystical silence in constant prayer. At a slightly different level, the Christ of the Legend is Russia herself, the "God-bearing people," the true "Holy Russia" of Dostoevsky's meditations, whose faith is perfected through the centuries of suffering in silence and humility and who now must face the last great antagonist, Leviathan and the Antichrist himself.[60]

The secret is that Christ *is* Truth. There is no "other" Truth which can oppose Him: the gnostic delusion lies precisely here, and Alyosha is no gnostic even if Ivan may be.[61] The rebellion of the man-god is a grotesque variation on the theme of the central constitutive fact of the *conditio humana:* the Fall of man. And it was to redeem fallen man that Christ, the Incarnate Word, entered history. Without the Fall and the fact of *sin* there would be no need for Christ and for Redemption. The Inquisitor's effort to abolish sin, like all of that kind, is a covert existential weapon for the abolition of Christ. But however rebellious and deluded man may become, no amount of empirical defection from the order of being can touch the truth of being itself.[62] It is this ontological perspective which makes so meaningful the kiss of Jesus. To the man of faith, to Alyosha for whom faith is existentially real, it is the *philema agapes* of the Sovereign God-man who is Love, who taught men to love their enemies, and prayed from the Cross for the forgiveness of His murderers "for they know not what they do." The kiss is that prayer again. "Oh, the Crucifix is a terrible argument!" the Inquisitor is made to exclaim in the *Notes* to the Legend.[63] Yet it is the irreducible paradox and infuriating dysteleology of the Crucifixion which, nonetheless, remains the final argument of the Legend. Inexplicable as is the mystery of the Crucifixion and Atonement, so also inexplicable is the mystery of suffering and of human rebellion. But that these things serve the inscrutable purpose of Divine Providence is not within the faithful heart—neither of a Job nor of a Dostoevsky—to deny. In a Russian folk legend, Christ kisses Judas after his betrayal: in the universal-historical drama of salvation under God, both the betrayer-rebel and the Savior have essential roles to play.[64]

The trans-historical aspect of the Legend is, however, not to be forgotten. The eschatological hardness of Christ also finds expression in the kiss as the wrath of God. Here is no sentimental, simpering Christ as some have supposed. For the Love of the Savior in no way impairs His sovereign authority in being: beyond the grave, at the End of time, men shall be Judged with a Judgment that is not their own. The kiss in the sense is the seal of impending certain destruction set upon the lips of the prophet of Satan by the righteous God. It is the Kiss of Death, not, of course, in the

Rabbinical tradition of the *bi-n shikah*, but in the meaning of the *pneúmati toú stómatos autoú* of the New Testament prophecy of the End. "Then will be revealed the lawless one whom the Lord will consume with the breath of His mouth and annul by the appearing of His Coming."[65] At the *Parousía* the vain pretense of the Antichrist will be played out.—*If*, indeed, there be an End! The kiss that burns on the lips of the Inquisitor, the shudder that shakes his frame, these are consequences of the encounter with infinite Love Who is also the Omnipotent Sovereign. He has met both the Grace of Salvation and the inexorable power of doom to the iniquitous in that most intimate expression of the existential Truth in Christ. Hence the final words of the faithless and rebellious can only be: "Go and come no more . . . come not at all, never, never. . . ." And he clings to his idea.

If the Grand Inquisitor has spoken *sub specie mortis*, Dostoevsky has spoken *sub specie aeternitatis*. His Legend points toward eternity as the destiny of man. Through trenchant parody and caricature he constructs a devastating refutation of the inflated and psychically diseased superman of all the ages of history.[66] His concern is with the spiritual crisis of our time and its metaphysical danger to man. In a uniquely powerful way, Dostoevsky has affirmed that the life of man in society is not merely life in the world, but that man in society participates also in the order of transcendent being. Mankind is, through his work, once again warned that a diseased social order can destroy the specifically human in the men who are its citizens, and that, after this initial destruction, the wholesale slaughter of man by man in the name of "truth" become ineluctable. His warning is one our age may ponder well.

NOTES

Originally published as Ellis Sandoz, "Philosophical Anthropology and Dostoevsky's 'Legend of the Grand Inquisitor,'" *The Review of Politics* 26 (1964). Reprinted with permission.

    1. "No it is God who is, for you and me, of a truth the 'measurement of all things,' much more truly than, as they say, 'man.' So he who would be loved by such a being must himself become such to the utmost of his might, and so, by this argument, he that is temperate among us is loved by God, for he is like God, whereas he that is not temperate is unlike God and at variance with him; so also it is with the unjust, and the same rule holds in all else." Plato, *The Laws* (London: Dent, 1960), 716 c–d, 100f. For a discussion of this opposition, see Werner Jaeger, *Humanism and Theology* (Milwaukee: Marquette University Press, 1943), passim.

    2. Leo Strauss, *What Is Political Philosophy?* (Glencoe, IL,: Free Press, 1959), 10ff.

    3. Eric Voegelin, *Order and History, 3 vols.* (Baton Rouge: Louisiana State University, 1956–1957), III, 69.

    4. Voegelin, *Order and History, 3 vols.*, III, 296 and 69.

    5. From Kant's *Handbook* to the lectures in logic, quoted by Martin Buber in Martin Buber, *Between Man and Man* (New York: Macmillan, 1965), 142.

    6. Erich Fromm, "Introduction" in *Marx's Concept of Man* (New York: F. Ungar Publishing Company, 1961), 58.

7. Avrahm Yarmolinsky, *Dostoevsky, His Life and Art* (New York: Criterion Books, 1960), 28.

8. Letter to A. N. Maikov, December 11, 1868, from Florence, in Fyodor Dostoevsky, *Letters of Fyodor Michailovitch Dostoevsky to his Family and Friends* (New York: The Macmillan Company, 1961), 157f. Hereafter this book will be cited *Letters* (Mayne).

9. Letter to N. A. Liubimov, Associate Editor of the *Russky Vestnik*, May 10, 1879, from Staria Roussa, in "Dostoevsky on *The Brothers Karamazov*," trans. S. S. Koteliansky, in the *New Criterion* IV (1926), 552f.

10. Letter June 11, 1879, *ibid.*, 554f.

11. Translated from W. Komarowitsch, *Die Urgestalt der Brueder Karamasoff: Dostojewskis Quellen, Entwuerfe und Fragmente* (München: R. Piper, 1928), 540f.

12. Nikolai Berdyaev, *Dostoevsky* (New York: Meridian Books, 1957), 210, 30, and 188. Dostoevsky himself is said to have regarded the Legend as the culminating point of his artistic life. See Komarowitsch, *Die Urgestalt der Brueder Karamasoff: Dostojewskis Quellen, Entwuerfe und Fragmente*, ix.

13. Avrahm Yarmolinsky, *Dostoievsky: A Study in his Ideology* (New York: Publisher Unknown, 1921), 7.

14. Romano Guardini, *Religioese Gestalten in Dostojewskijs Werk* (München: Kösel, 1951), 7.

15. Guardini, *Religioese Gestalten in Dostojewskijs Werk*, 235f.

16. Albert Camus, *The Rebel: An Essay on Man in Revolt* (New York: Vintage Books, 1958), 55ff.

17. Berdyaev, *Dostoevsky*, 120.

18. F. M. Dostoyevsky, *The Brothers Karamazov* (J. M. Dent, 1927), I, 267. Further references to this novel are to this edition and are given in the text by volume and page numbers, designated by Roman and Arabic numerals, respectively.

19. The figure of Elder Zosima is, like all of Dostoevsky's characters, a composite. He is based in the main on Saint Tikhon Zadonsky (1724–1783). The idea of "Active Love," the central preachment of Zosima, is taken directly from Tikhon. See Nadejda Gorodetzky, *Saint Tikhon Zadonsky, Inspirer of Dostoevsky* (London: S.P.C.K., 1951), vii, 181ff. and 186; see, also, Dostoevsky's letter to A. N. Maikov, March 25, 1870, from Dresden, in *Letters* (Mayne), pp. 190f. The name *Zosima* probably was taken from Saint Zosima, one of the two founders of the great monastery of Solovki in the fifteenth century. For understanding the highly detailed symbolism pervading *The Brothers Karamazov* (but which we cannot enter into here), the connection of the Solovki monastery with the Schismatics is of significance. See Serge Bolshakoff, *Russian Nonconformity: The Story of "Unofficial" Religion in Russia* (Philadelphia: Westminster Press, 1950), 70. Because of the limited space here available to us, it is the more important to emphasize the significance of Tikhon Zadonsky for the views of Dostoevsky, especially for his Augustinianism and his anthropology—both of which receive attention in this paper. On this last, some useful hints are to be found in G. P. Fedotov, *A Treasury of Russian Spirituality* (New York: Sheed & Ward, 1948), esp. 182 and 234f.

20. This phrase in Latin occurs in Fyodor Dostoyevsky, *The Diary of a Writer* (New York: C. Scribner's Sons, 1949), I, 261 March, 1876, ii, 1, in the context of a discussion of Schiller's *Don Carlos* and the Grand Inquisitor. The connection of Schiller's drama to the Legend is discussed Robert Payne, *Dostoevsky: A Human Portrait* (New York: Knopf, 1961), 375ff. The sources of the Legend are extraordinarily varied and complex; cf. Komarowitsch, *op. cit.*, and Ralph E. Matlaw, *The Brothers Karamazov: Novelistic Technique* (The Hague: Mouton, 1957), 14. The critical literature is enormous.

21. This conception of faith is to be found in Rudolph Otto, *The Idea of the Holy: An Inquiry into the Non-rational Factor in the Idea of the Divine and its Relation to the Rational* (New York: Oxford University Press, 1958), 56f., 77ff., 172f. and passim.

22. Quoted in Gorodetzky, 193.

23. For Dostoevsky's view of Christ see Nicholas Zernov, *Three Russian Prophets: Khomiakov, Dostoevsky, Soloviev* (London: S.C.M. Press, 1944), 106ff. The significance of Vladimir Solovyov for Dostoevsky's conception of Christ and the God-man and man-

god relationship can scarcely be exaggerated. Cf. Solovyov, *A Solovyov Anthology* (London: S.C.M. Press, 1950), 35ff; also, Vladimir Seduro, *Dostoyevski in Russian Literary Criticism, 1846–1956* (New York: Columbia University Press, 1957), 310f. The personal relationship of Solovyov and Dostoevsky is set forth in Edward Hallett Carr, *Dostoevsky (1821–1881): A New Biography* (Boston: Houghton Mifflin, 1931), 277ff. Solovyov is particularly important for understanding the gnosticism of Dostoevsky.

24. For this view of revelation, see Eric Voegelin, *The New Science of Politics: An Introduction* (Chicago: University of Chicago Press, 1952), 78; and H. Richard Niebuhr, *The Meaning of Revelation* (New York: Macmillan, 1941), ch. iii.

25. Berdyaev, *Dostoevsky*, 80.

26. Quoted in Henri de Lubac, *The Drama of Atheistic Humanism* (Cleveland: World Publishing Company, 1949), 180.

27. Berdyaev, *Dostoevsky*, 144.

28. The problem of theodicy in Ivan's presentation of it is, in fact, not so "unassailable" as Dostoevsky believed it to be. See the remarks on the problem in Eric Voegelin, *Order and History, Volume 2: The World of the Polis* (Baton Rouge: Louisiana State University Press, 1957), 255.

29. Camus, *The Rebel: An Essay on Man in Revolt*, 59n.

30. Cf. Thomas Hobbes, *Leviathan*, ch. xiii.

31. Cf. the discussion of "No morality without Immortality" in Dostoevsky by a contemporary theologian, Paul Ramsey, "No Morality without Immortality: Dostoevski and the Meaning of Atheism," *The Journal of Religion* 36 (1956), 90–108.

32. *Brothers Karamazov*, Bk. XI, ch. ix (II, 307).

33. *Republic*, 382 a–b.

34. *Republic*, 572e–576b.

35. Fedotov, *A Treasury of Russian Spirituality*, 182, wrote: Through Tikhon the "fundamental ideas of St. Augustine now made their first entrance into Orthodox theology."

36. The best discussion of Dostoevsky's anthropology I have seen is H. E. Strakosch, "Dostoevsky and the Man-God," *Dublin Review* 22 (1955). Its principal deficiency derives from the attempt to force Dostoevsky into the mold of Neo-Scholasticism. See, also, Andrew Hacker, "Dostoevsky's Disciples: Man and Sheep in Political Theory," *The Journal of Politics* 17 (1955), 597ff.

37. The mythopoeic character of Dostoevsky's art, and the Legend in particular, which can only be mentioned here, supplies the basis for the interpretation. See Matlaw, *The Brothers Karamazov: Novelistic Technique*, 20; Renato Poggioli, "Dostoevski, or Reality and Myth" in *The Phoenix and the Spider: A Book of Essays about Some Russian Writers and Their View of the Self*, ed. Renato Poggioli (Cambridge: Harvard University Press, 1957), 29ff; also Vyaacheslav Ivanov, *Freedom and the Tragic Life* (New York: Noonday, 1952). Ivanov's study, however, for all its ingenuity and great value for the problem of the myth in Dostoevsky, is vitiated by poetic extravagance.

38. Nietzsche, *Morgenroethe*, Sec. 79.

39. Cf. Evgenii Lampert, *Studies in Rebellion* (London: Routledge and K. Paul, 1957), 142.

40. *Genesis 3*. Cf. Gerhard von Rad, *Genesis: A Commentary* (Philadelphia: Westminster Press, 1961), 83ff. and 94.

41. Matlaw, *The Brothers Karamazov: Novelistic Technique*, 32.

42. *Genesis* 3:42. See Letter to N. L. Osmidov, February 18, 1878, from Petersburg, in *Letters* (Mayne), p. 234.

43. I, 334.

44. Ivanov, *Freedom and the Tragic Life*, 140f.

45. Quoted in Payne, *Dostoevsky: A Human Portrait*, 363. The Inquisitor's argument has been examined from the viewpoint of political theory by Neal Riemer, "Some Reflections on the Grand Inquisitor and Modern Democratic Theory," *Ethics* 67 (1957), 249–256.

46. Zernov, *Three Russian Prophets: Khomiakov, Dostoevsky, Soloviev*, 108.

47. *Revelation* 9:3. See Komarowitsch, *Die Urgestalt der Brueder Karamasoff: Dostojewskis Quellen, Entwuerfe und Fragmente*, 515.

48. Komarowitsch, *Die Urgestalt der Brueder Karamasoff: Dostojewskis Quellen, Entwuerfe und Fragmente*, 515, 539.

49. See P. N. Miliukov, *Outlines of Russian Culture* (Philadelphia: University of Pennsylvania Press, 1942), II, 3–5. Also, F. J. Powicke, "Bogomils," *Hastings Encyclopaedia of Religion and Ethics*, 12 volumes (New York, 1928), II, 784.

50. See, in particular, Hans Jonas, "Gnosticism and Modern Nihilism," *Social Research* 19 (1952), and Hans Jonas, *The Gnostic Religion: The Message of the Alien God and the Beginnings of Christianity* (Boston: Beacon Press, 1958), passim and 46. Also, Voegelin, *The New Science of Politics: An Introduction*, 110ff; Lampert, *Studies in Rebellion*, esp. 137, 155ff.; and Nikolas Berdyaev, *The Russian Idea* (London: Geoffrey Bles & The Centenary Press, 1947), 148ff. and passim.

51. See Letter to Maikov, December 11, 1868, from Florence, in *Letters* (Mayne), p. 158; also Letter to Maikov, March 25, 1870, from Dresden, *ibid.*, p. 190. The Khlysty, Stundists, and sectarians generally were frequently discussed or alluded to in the *Diary of a Writer*.

52. Cf. Auguste Comte, *Cours de philosophie positive* (Paris: Bachelier, 1841), V, 343f. Dostoevsky had his introduction to philosophy, especially to Hegel, Feuerbach, and Comte, from Vissarion G. Belinsky. See T. G. Masaryk, *The Spirit of Russia: Studies in History, Literature and Philosophy* (London: G. Allen & Unwin, 1955), I, 334ff., for a discussion of Belinsky's intellectual development and relationship to Dostoevsky; also the excellent discussion by Lampert, *Studies in Rebellion*, 46–108. For Dostoevsky's description of his relationship to Belinsky, see the first issue of *Diary of a Writer* (*Grazhdanin* No. 1, 1873). I see no reason for supposing, as is frequently done, that Dostoevsky was not informed about and well read in contemporary thought and affairs. In any event, he certainly was aware of Feuerbach and Comte, not to go farther.

53. Cf. Berdyaev, *Dostoevsky*, *passim*.

54. Philip Rahv, "The Legend of the Grand Inquisitor," *Partisan Review* 21 (1954), 250. T. G. Masaryk has hinted that Dostoevsky portrayed his friend and admirer K. P. Pobedonostsev, *Ober-Procurator* of the Holy Synod, in his Grand Inquisitor!

55. It is to be remarked that neither in the Legend nor elsewhere does Dostoevsky debate the question whether Christianity is the foundation of the social and political order. That is taken as a self-evident or "axiomatic," as he would say. Dostoevsky was profoundly convinced that Christianity was "the foundation" from the age of eighteen onward. The shorthand expression, "the foundation," runs through his publicist writings like a thread. Cf. letter to his brother Michael, January 1, 1840, from Petersburg, in *Letters* (Mayne), p. 13. Dostoevsky's fullest statement of his own views on this subject is to be found in the penultimate issue of the *Diary* (August, 1880; ch. iii), II, 981ff.

56. See Komarowitsch, *Die Urgestalt der Brueder Karamasoff: Dostojewskis Quellen, Entwuerfe und Fragmente*, 538.

57. D. H. Lawrence, "The Grand Inquisitor" in *Selected Literary Criticism*, ed. E. Beal (New York: Viking Press, 1956), 241. The "play" element here is of significance for the understanding of the Legend as myth. See Johan Huizinga, *Homo ludens* (London: Routledge and Kegan Paul, 1949).

58. See the *Diary* for August, 1880, *passim*. Dostoevsky makes the implicit connection explicit by characterizing the "new Russian" of "the future" as a peasant sectarian of the time of Tsar Paul I. The reference is to Conrad Selivanov, "Christ Peter III" of the *castrati* Skoptsy. See Letter to Maikov, March 25, 1870, from Dresden in *Letters* (Mayne), p. 191. The "Wanderers" of the Schismatics are the Beguni for whom the state and church are in Antichrist's power and the Orthodox Church is Satan's prophet. The Bogomil-Manichaean duality is pronounced with the Beguni and even more so with the Khlysty and Skoptsy. See A. von Stromberg, "Russian Sects," *Hastings Encyclopaedia of Religion and Ethics*, XI, 338. For the sources of the Russian sectarian movements see the detailed study of Karl Konrad Grass, *Die Russischen Sekten* (Leipzig: Druck von C. Mattiesen: J. C. Hinrichs, 1907–1914), I, 588ff. The Bogomil relationship

is discussed *ibid.* 626ff. and the gnostic character of the movements (particularly of the Khlysty) at *ibid.*, 636–648. A study of our contemporaries, the Soviet "New Men," in light of Dostoevsky, might prove rewarding.

59. Letter to Strachov, March 18, 1869, from Florence, in *Letters* (Mayne), p. 175.

60. Cf. Fedotov, *A Treasury of Russian Spirituality* for this account of the Russian Christ. Also, Zernov, *Three Russian Prophets: Khomiakov, Dostoevsky, Soloviev* and Nicolas Zernov, *Eastern Christendom: A Study of the Origin and Development of the Eastern Orthodox Church* (New York: Putnam, 1961).

61. Dimitri Merejkowsky has made much of the "two truths"; see Dmitry Sergeyevich Merezhkovsky, *Tolstoi as Man and Artist, with an Essay on Dostoïevski* (New York: G. P. Putnam's Sons, 1902), 289ff.

62. Cf. Voegelin, *Order and History*, I, 464f.

63. See Komarowitsch, *Die Urgestalt der Brueder Karamasoff: Dostojewskis Quellen, Entwuerfe und Fragmente*, 545.

64. Cf. Eric Voegelin, "Bakunin's Confession," *The Journal of Politics* 8 (1946), 30.

65. Second Thessalonians 2:8. This is the only place in the New Testament where it is said that Christ destroys Satan with the "Breath of His mouth." Cf. Isaiah 11:4 and Job 4:8–9.

66. On the technique of caricature in Dostoevsky see the excellent study by Joseph Frank, "Nihilism and 'Notes from Underground,'" *The Sewanee Review* 69 (1961).

SIX

Ugliness, Emptiness, and Boredom

Dostoevsky on the Secular Humanist Social Religion

Ethan Alexander-Davey

INTRODUCTION

A generation ago, Ellis Sandoz presented F. M. Dostoevsky's prescient analysis of totalitarian communism in the "Legend of the Grand Inquisitor." Sandoz's interpretation of Dostoevsky's political thought could scarcely have been more timely in a period when America, having engaged one totalitarian monster in a fantastically bloody duel to the death, found itself in a protracted cold war, always on the verge of nuclear annihilation, with another. But the corpus of Dostoevsky, and indeed that of other conservative Russian thinkers, provides, arguably, a no less prescient account of what some might consider a current threat to civilization, that is, the ideology of twenty-first-century global liberal democratic elites and their program for transforming humanity and the world. Russian conservatives such as Dostoevsky, together with conservatives of other nationalities, saw socialism and liberalism (democratic or bourgeois capitalism) as two heads of the same dragon.[1] Offered the choice between one or the other head of this irreligious dragon, Dostoevsky would accept neither, and would demand a third way. Russian conservative alternatives to liberalism and socialism will seem impractical to inhabitants of the twenty-first-century world. To the socialist or liberal cosmopolite in particular, they will seem ghastly. But in this era of global social and economic crises, one must be allowed to waive such considerations and seek insight even in heretofore forbidden places.

The Russian conservative critique of democratic capitalism itself—and capitalism's association in the Russian conservative mind—with totalitarian socialism, have been noticed by Western scholars but never taken seriously.[2] Outwardly, these two "political religions" look and sound very different.[3] The totalitarian socialist is a textbook Gnostic psychopath. As Ellis Sandoz notes, the words of Dostoevsky's anti-hero Peter Verkhovensky in *Demons* —"They shout 'a hundred million heads'; that may be only a metaphor, but why be afraid of it? . . . We believe our program is correct; that is the reason we have decided on blood"—are echoed by Lenin—"Why should we be squeamish about the sacrifices to our righteous cause? . . . It does not matter if three quarters of mankind is destroyed; all that counts is that ultimately the last quarter should become Communist."[4] It is impossible to read such words and not exclaim: "Aha!" The message bursts forth from the mouth of the communist head of the dragon in a terrifying blaze of fire; its opponents are quickly alerted to the peril they face. But there is no "aha!" moment in the other case. The liberal head of the dragon speaks in much more moderate tones. It speaks of gradualism, reform by legislation and persuasion, rather than sudden and repeated applications of brute force, which, as the communist head of the dragon readily acknowledges, will leave piles of corpses in their wake. The liberal head of the dragon does not breathe fire; it breathes warm air on its victims, which grows progressively warmer over a long space of time, such that when one finally realizes one is being cooked, it is already too late. The approaches are different, but the general assumptions about human nature, and the *telos* are much the same for both. As the Russian conservatives show us, both ideologies begin with a nakedly materialistic and individualistic philosophical anthropology, and both aim at a transformation of humanity that will bring maximal individual autonomy, global harmony and a high level of material well-being to all.

The Russian conservative critique of the ideologies of earthly salvation has two facets: First, in either formulation, the project cannot succeed, and, on the road to its imaginary heaven on earth, it will destroy, perhaps irreparably, much that is good in the world. Second, even if the goal could be achieved, the result would be profoundly ugly, miserable and boring. The Russian conservative alternative to a globally integrated, uniformly satiated humanity is a world divided into distinct nations, understood as cultural organisms composed of diverse social classes and regions, tied together by a common national spirit and common customs. It is a world in which sovereign nations and local communities restrain the mass movement of capital and labor, both within their borders and across national boundaries, for the sake of preserving difference, for the sake of protecting the spiritual health and beauty of particular communities from the homogenizing and spiritually deadening effects of secular mass education and materialistic social reorganization of the state-socialist or market capitalist variety. Other Russian conservatives had something to say about the institutions necessary for the promotion of this vision. Dostoevsky, however, was, on the whole, uninterested in such questions.[5] As Berdyaev observes, for Dostoevsky "the human spirit alone exists, and in that alone is the writer interested."[6] Dostoevsky considers all social problems traceable to problems of the human spirit, and it is only at that level, the level of the individual human soul, that he seeks solutions.

Fundamentally, Dostoevsky is a theocentric thinker. For him the spiritual dimension of the human being is primary, the material secondary, and this hierarchy of the spiritual over the material must extend in some manner to all aspects of human life. The reversal of this hierarchy produces unbalanced human beings, obsessed with material satisfactions that do not satisfy, afflicted by loneliness and boredom, bemused by their own banality, and at times, driven by their desperation to destructive behavior. A society composed of such individuals will be devoid of beauty and greatness in religion, art and politics, sapped of internal strength for necessary common exploits and fated to follow the liberal path of a slow slide towards collapse and dissolution, or the totalitarian socialist path, which begins with mass bloodshed and ends with universal slavery and mediocrity. The focus here is on Dostoevsky's critique of the liberal path, since that seems more relevant in the twenty-first century, but as the two paths are connected in Dostoevsky's writing, it is necessary to note the points at which they converge. Dostoevsky's alternative sociopolitical vision is one of messianic and apocalyptic grandeur. Russia, he thought, would make Christ's kingdom come, saving all mankind with her own Orthodox recipe for human brotherhood. Be that as it may, Dostoevsky had enough sense to express doubts about the feasibility of this vision. For example, in one entry of his *Diary of a Writer*, after describing this great fellowship of mankind that Russia was to bring about, Dostoevsky says playfully, "However, did I actually want to convince anyone?—It was a joke."[7] Therefore, it is reasonable to consider a less grandiose, less apocalyptic alternative socio-political vision, an outline of which emerges from Dostoevsky's various observations on the human spirit and social relations in Russia. This Russian conservative alternative to liberalism and socialism is national Christian fellowship, a uniting of the individual members and classes of Russian society through recognition of their common "national treasure," that is, Russia's Orthodox Christian heritage.

OF BEAUTY AND TOIL

With his observations on life in Western Europe, and his analysis of materialist political thought, Dostoevsky, consummate psychologist that he was, gives us the view of the individual and his relations to those close to him. His most concise statement of his own philosophical anthropology is found in a letter to a subscriber to his *Diary of a Writer* quoted at length below. Nineteenth-century socialist doctrines are the main target in this passage, but Dostoevsky's arguments are certainly relevant to twenty-first-century welfare state capitalism, and the ideology of global politico-economic development as well. Dostoevsky asserts that from the materialist point of view, social ills have none but material causes:

> Command then that, henceforth, the earth bring forth without toil, instruct people in such science or instruct them in such an order, that their lives should henceforth be provided for. Is it possible not to believe that the greatest vices and misfortunes of man resulted from hunger, cold, poverty, and from the impossible struggle for existence?
> Here is the first idea which was posed by the evil spirit to Christ. It is difficult to correct him. Contemporary *socialism* in Europe, even our own, is completely separated from Christ; it is concerned almost completely about *bread*; it looks to science and declares that the cause of all man's miseries is poverty alone, the struggle for existence, the "environment tangle."
> To this Christ answered: "Man does not live by bread alone" –that is, spoke the axiom of the spiritual origin of man. The idea of the devil could be suitable only to a man-brute; Christ knew that it was not bread alone that would give man life. If, furthermore, there is no spiritual life, no ideal of Beauty, then man will pine away (*zatoskovat'*), die, lose his mind, kill himself or give himself over to pagan fantasies. But since Christ, in Himself and in His Word, is the ideal of Beauty, he decided: it is better to inspire man's soul with the ideal of Beauty; possessing it in their souls, all men become brothers and then, finally, working for each other, they also become prosperous. But give them bread and from boredom they will become enemies of one another.[8]

The key line in the passage of course belongs to Christ: "Man does not live by bread alone." Man cannot be satisfied by material security and comfort alone. There are deeper spiritual needs. If these are ignored, if these are left out of the "social formula for human well-being," then individual, society, state and international order are undone.

Dostoevsky names two spiritual needs in the passage above: toil and an ideal of beauty. By toil as a human need, Dostoevsky does not mean merely "having an occupation," although that is one component of it. The other component is suffering. Suffering teaches man lessons that he is loath to learn, the lesson that material gratification is not primary, and the lesson of compassion. For Dostoevsky, suffering, whether it be from spiritual or material privation, is perhaps, more than anything else, the thing that causes man to seek fellowship with others of his kind. If one removes the possibility of physical and psychological suffering, then one also eliminates a powerful impetus toward brotherhood. The ideal of beauty that Dostoevsky posits as a human need is almost always a social one. It is a vision of perfect Christian brotherhood, binding men to each other through their communion with Christ the Savior, and the treasures of their native soil. This will be addressed in greater detail at the end, but first it is appropriate to consider what, in Dostoevsky's view, happens to human beings when toil and beauty, thus understood, are taken away from them. As is asserted above, they become brutes, they pine (*zatoskovat'*), they lose their minds, they destroy themselves, or turn to pagan fantasies. These are the symptoms he observes in Westerners, and in the Russians who inhabited Russia's most Westernized city, St. Petersburg. These are the basic parameters of the psychopathology he explores time and again in his novels. Two of Dostoevsky's works in particular, *Winter Notes on Summer Impressions* and *Notes from Underground*, together with selections from *Diary of a Writer*, provide a wealth of material for an examination of some of the variety of forms this general pathology may take.

ATOMIZATION, ALIENATION AND MISERY IN THE CRYSTAL PALACE

Winter Notes on Summer Impressions contains Dostoevsky's observations and reflections on the social and spiritual conditions in England and France. Presenting these impressions of the West in a satirical tone, Dostoevsky focuses almost exclusively on scenes of the grotesque and the banal. But as is already apparent, these ills are, for Dostoevsky, not aberrations, but symptoms of a society whose spiritual core is rotten. English and French society lack a genuine ideal of beauty to unite their members, and thus also lack any real sense of community. The Crystal Palace—a gargantuan structure of cast iron and glass built for London's World's Fair of 1851 to demonstrate the achievements of modern British industry—comes to symbolize for Dostoevsky the malignancy of a Western social ideal that is outwardly awe-inspiring but ultimately hollow.[9] Dostoevsky describes his first impressions from the Crystal Palace as follows:

> Can this be, in fact, the accomplished ideal?—you think;—is this here not the end? Is this not, in fact, the "one fold"? Will one not have to accept this, in fact, as the whole truth and go silent once for all? It's all so majestic, triumphant and proud that it begins to take your breath away. You look at these hundreds of thousands, at these millions of people, obediently flowing hither from all over the globe . . . and you feel that here something has been accomplished once for all, accomplished and ended. It's some kind of Biblical illustration, some kind of prophecy from the Apocalypse fulfilled before your eyes. You feel that much steadfast spiritual resistance and negation will be needed so as not to surrender, not to submit to the impression, not to bow down to the fact and deify Baal, not to accept what exists as your own ideal.[10]

Suffusing his reflections here with religious imagery, Dostoevsky presents the Crystal Palace as a sort of Supreme Temple of the new secular religion, with its technical marvels promising prosperity to all, solutions to all the world's ills, an end to violence, pain and suffering. The "one fold" to which he refers above is the *edino stado* from the Old Church Slavonic translation of John 10:16, "And other sheep I have, which are not of this fold: them also must I bring and they shall hear my voice; and there shall be one fold, *and* one shepherd." Millions from throughout the world, all desiring fulfillment of the aforementioned promises, have come to see the new temple, to bow before the new shepherd, who is none other than Baal, and to enter his fold. The spectacle fills one with such awe, one can scarcely argue with it, scarcely resist its temptations. Yet, Dostoevsky shows us, if one looks at the results of a society that deifies Baal in this fashion, one sees very clearly that the Crystal Palace is the temple of a false religion.

According to Dostoevsky, the symptoms of spiritual gangrene manifest themselves in all orders of Western society, from the urban working class to the bourgeoisie, to the clergy and the rich, to merchants and nobles. In *Winter Notes,* we find an account of how the English working class spent its disposable income. On Saturday nights, Dostoevsky writes,

> half a million working men and women and their children spill like the ocean all over town . . . and eat and drink like beasts enough for a whole week. They bring their weekly savings, all that was earned through hard work and cursing. . . . People mass in the open taverns and the streets. There they eat and drink. The beer houses are decorated like palaces. Everyone is drunk, but without joy, rather gloomily and heavily, and everyone is somehow strangely silent. Only curses and bloody brawls break that suspicious and oppressively sad silence. . . . All are in a hurry to get so drunk that they lose consciousness . . . wives in no way lag behind their husbands and all get drunk together, while children crawl and run about among them.[11]

The working class does not engage in such drunken joylessness alone, however. As Dostoevsky describes the English urban scene, members of all classes mingle together: "The drunken tramp jostles amid this terrible crowd, even the titled rich man walks in here."[12] While the beggars and tramps of all ages shuffle amid the working class mob, the rich stealthily make their way to the casinos and brothels. Members of the clergy play no direct role in this grim Bacchanalia, but, on the other hand, they do little to combat it. In reference to Anglican bishops and ministers he writes:

> These professors of religion, who carry their conviction to the point of obtuseness, have one sort of amusement: it is missionary work. They travel all over the earth, penetrate deep into Africa to convert one sav-

age, and forget the million savages in London, because these have nothing to pay them with.[13]

What emerges here is a picture of society whose members mingle with each other across class boundaries, but have no sense of community at all. It is a deeply atomized and materialistic society whose members take no joy in each other's company. The description of the Anglican church is most damning, especially from Dostoevsky's point of view, because Christianity is supposed to provide the ideal of beauty, the model of brotherly love upon which a genuine organic community might be built. In contrast, the bishops and ministers of the Church of England show little interest in the condition of their neighbors, whom Christ commanded them to love. They focus their missionary work on people far away with whom they have no connection.[14] They are, one could say, spiritual cosmopolitans.

In such an environment, it is not to be doubted that many people may become alienated and turn to extremes. As Dostoevsky puts it:

> We are surprised at the stupidity which leads people to become shakers and tramps, and fail to hit upon the fact that what we have here is a separation from our social formula, an obstinate and unconscious separation; an instinctive separation at any cost, in order to achieve salvation.... This is the last desperate attempt to huddle together and form one's own heap, one's own mass, and to separate from everything, from the very image of man if need be, only to be oneself, only not to be with us....[15]

The social formula of Western societies, argues Dostoevsky, yields the atomization and alienation that gives rise to sectarian extremism, and socialism. The most alienated will thus seek some way to reverse their condition, and the solution that presents itself is to join with others in an "ant hill." The anthill is, of course, Dostoevsky's symbol for socialist utopia. Ultimately the anthill is a dead end; it cannot satisfy the spiritual hunger of human beings. But the spiritual vacuity of Western liberalism nevertheless pushes people to "turn into an ant hill—if only to settle down without having to devour each other—the alternative is to turn into cannibals."[16] Because human beings have a need to "live in some sort of harmony with each other," conditions of extreme individualism push the most alienated segments of the population to seek the opposite extreme, some form of totalitarian socialism.

The pathologies observable in English society in particular, and the West in general, Dostoevsky argues, have a direct connection to the social formula these societies collectively embrace. Theirs is an exclusively materialistic ideal of maximal physical satisfaction and comfort for the individual, which for Dostoevsky is symbolized by the Crystal Palace. The Crystal Palace is the new Tower of Babel, where pilgrims come to bow down and worship Baal.[17] The Saturday night grim Bacchanalia is the new Sabbath, at which, as we have seen, grisly rituals entirely appropriate to Baal-worship are performed.

THE BANALITY OF THE BOURGEOISIE

The Crystal Palace ideal, which infects all segments of Western society, arose from a particular class, the bourgeoisie. This is one of the main themes in the Dostoevsky's chapters on France. Dostoevsky finds Paris different from London in this respect, that in the French capital, the warts and cankers on the body politic that would alert any observer to the underlying spiritual disease are well hidden. The beggars and tramps are kept out of sight. The epidemic of marital infidelity in Parisian bourgeois families remains a dirty secret, which everyone knows, but no one acknowledges publicly. The bourgeois knows that his newspapers would print anything for a bribe, that he is paying high taxes to support the police spies of his national security state, but he will not admit any of this, because

> otherwise people might perhaps think that the ideal has not been reached yet, that Paris is not yet heaven on earth, that something could perhaps still be wished for, that therefore the bourgeois himself is not quite satisfied with the order he stands behind and which he tries to force on everyone, that the fabric of society has rips which must be mended.[18]

The bourgeois is not so well satisfied with the new order shaped primarily by his class, *le tiers etat*, but he believes so strongly, adopting the phrase of Sieyes, that *le tiers etat c'est tout*, that he is the highest achievement of humanity, that he seeks to impose his way of life on the rest of his country and the world.

The missionary spirit of the bourgeoisie is especially pernicious because precisely this class is most afflicted by the spiritual disease of Western materialism. Dostoevsky's description of their measure of personal success and self-worth is telling:

> To amass a fortune and possess as many things as possible—this has become the main moral code, the Catechism of the Parisian. The same thing happened in the old days too, but now—now it has, so to speak, a sort of sacramental aspect. In the old days something was acknowledged besides money, so that a man with no money but possessing other qualities could expect some kind of esteem; but now—nothing doing.[19]

The new social dogma, the new religion which the bourgeoisie has created for itself and seeks to impose on the rest of society, is that the primary goal of life is to acquire money and things. The worth of a man is to be measured by the quantity of his money and the quality of his material possessions and comforts. The bourgeois believes this doctrine, and practices it. But his dissatisfaction with this doctrine and practice is apparent to the outside observer. Dostoevsky notes that although the Parisian bourgeois preaches and practices a sort of enlightened selfishness, he desires to see the opposite of this when he attends the theatre: "The bourgeois is passionately fond of stunning high-mindedness. On the stage he must have nothing but people completely disinterested in money. Gustave must shine by the light of high-mindedness alone and the bourgeois sheds tears of tender emotion."[20] The bourgeois can allow himself to experience high-mindedness and self sacrifice, but only vicariously. But he wishes to experience these feelings nonetheless, an indication of the falseness of his way of life with which he is unable or unwilling to come to terms.

Bourgeois acquisitiveness might not lead every member of *le tiers etat* to become a great exploiter of men. But in Dostoevsky's view, it does prevent the greater part of Western mankind from becoming good citizens. The cares and aspirations of the French bourgeois are petty and banal. To social and political problems he is more or less indifferent.[21] The crowning achievement of life for an average Parisian bourgeois is to be able upon retirement to enjoy two things: *"voir le mer"* and *"se rouler dans l'herbe"* (to see the ocean and to roll in the grass). If the retired bourgeois cannot not find a place by the sea, he can at least acquire a little plot upon which to build his retirement cottage: "Let it all be on the most microscopic scale, no matter—the bourgeois is childishly, touchingly delighted: *'mon arbre, mon mur'* [my tree, my wall] he constantly repeats to himself and to all his guests and never thereafter ceases from repeating it. . . ."[22] In this too we see the realization of the ideal of the Crystal Palace: the small individual freeholder alone on his tidy, comfortable plot, separated by walls (*mon mur*) from his neighbors and from the rest of his countrymen and whatever cares they might have.

BOREDOM IN THE CRYSTAL PALACE

The foregoing paragraphs have focused on the pathologies visible in societies lacking a common ideal of beauty. We now turn to the consequences of depriving men of toil. This was a condition experienced only by a small number of men in Dostoevsky's time, and perhaps even fewer in earlier ages. A whole society lacking toil was something that had to be imagined. As Dostoevsky notes in the letter quoted above, men without toil will become bored, and in their boredom, they might well become enemies. Dostoevsky returns to this theme in *Notes from Underground* and, as Avramenko argues, in *The Possessed*.[23] In *Notes from Underground* the narrator refutes the argument of nineteenth-century socialists, which twenty-first-century social democrats continue to assert, that by providing all with food and a place to live, that is, eliminating the suffering associated with material poverty and the necessity of toil, one may eliminate most other social ills. Provide people with sustenance and security, and they will no longer feel that they have nothing to lose. They will govern themselves so as to protect these advantages. The underground man pours scorn upon this thesis:

> Who was it who first declared, who first proclaimed, that a man does evil things only because he does not know his real interests, and if one could enlighten him and open his eyes to his own best and normal interests, man would at once cease to do evil things and at once become kind and noble . . . ? Oh, what a baby! Oh, what a pure innocent child![24]

Of course, for the underground man, the idea of advantage so understood is flawed. When the liberal or socialist thinks of advantage, he has in mind chiefly considerations of material sustenance and security. But as we know, from Dostoevsky's point of view, these things by themselves cannot satisfy. "Advantage" and "interest" being thus understood, he asks "when in all these thousands of years have men acted solely in their own interests? . . . Can you undertake to define exactly in what a man's advantage consists? What if it so happens that a man's advantage *sometimes* not only can, but must consist in desiring in a certain case not what is good but what is bad for him?"[25]

Dostoevsky's assertion here, voiced by the underground man, is that if man is granted material security, even a high degree of luxury, and nothing else to occupy his life, he may well turn to evil and destruction out of sheer boredom. "They say," he remarks, "that Cleopatra (excuse my taking an example from Roman history) liked to stick golden pins into the breasts of her slaves, and took pleasure in their screams and writhings."[26] It is obvious that she did not impale her servants because of an insufficiency of wealth, luxury or power. The underground man further insists that barbarism, lack of modern enlightenment, also has nothing to do with it. If on the basis of a new political economy, the whole world, or a large part of it, could be transformed into a Crystal Palace, with peace and plenty for all, he says, this would not necessarily be a desirable outcome:

> Suppose new economic relations will arise, totally ready-made and also calculated with mathematical exactness, so that in one instant all sorts of questions will disappear, because all sorts of answers to them will have been found. Then the Crystal Palace will be built. . . . Of course, it is quite impossible . . . to guarantee that it won't be terribly boring. . . . Of course, boredom leads to every possible kind of ingenuity. After all, it is out of boredom that pins get stuck into people. . . . Really I shall not be in the least surprised if, for example, some gentleman with an ignoble, or rather with a retrograde and mocking physiog-

nomy, springs up suddenly out of nowhere, puts his arms akimbo and says to all of us, "Come on, gentlemen, why shouldn't we get rid of all this reasonableness with one kick, just so as to send all these logarithms to the devil and be able to live our own lives according to our own foolish will?"[27]

Provided with all the necessities of life and deprived of toil, human beings may well turn to destruction and even sadism out of sheer boredom. Compared to such a placid and unchallenging existence, a life of following mere caprice seems to have at least the potential of being interesting.

One must not be taken in by all the pronouncements of this hermit, who lives in seclusion only to avoid subjection to the will of others. The ostensible affirmation in the first part of *Notes* of the ideal of total freedom to follow one's own arbitrary will to any length is ultimately rejected by the narrator himself.[28] Like the gentleman with the retrograde and mocking countenance, the narrator mocks the uninspiring ideal of the social democrat: "I will not accept as the crown of my desires a block of housing with apartments for poor residents." But it is only with this tiresome ideal that the existential freedom of the mousehole favorably compares. "Give me another ideal," he says, "show me something better, and I shall follow." Later, having asserted the advantages of his spiteful existence, he admits that he is lying: "Ach, but you see I'm lying here. I lie because I know just as twice two [equals four] that the mousehole is not at all better, but that it is for something other, something entirely other, which I thirst, but which I shall never find! To the devil with the mousehole!"[29] With neither toil nor an ideal of beauty to nourish his soul, the mouse man can only stew in his own bile. There is little doubt that this voice "from under the floor" expresses Dostoevsky's view of the potential consequences of mass boredom.

Indeed, boredom may help to explain a great deal of the pathological behavior in this world of ours, much of it earnestly striving toward the ideal of the Crystal Palace, from the mass destruction caused by well-fed, jobless urban rioters, to terrorist bombings perpetrated by the sons and daughters of well-to-do Middle Eastern doctors and lawyers. The provision of material sustenance and security to all, in whatever degree, does not satisfy the soul's need for beauty and toil. An order that provides the former but not the latter cannot stand on its own "reasonableness." To the bored soul, starved of beauty and toil, the very reasonableness of the Crystal Palace is an insult; by declaring itself the height of reasonableness, it asks the miserable mob to rise up and destroy it.

RULE BY THE WORST MEN: MILLIONAIRES AND THE LIBERAL INTELLIGENTSIA

In *Diary of a Writer*, Dostoevsky revisits many of the above observations and insights. Most of the numbers of the *Diary* focus on Russian affairs, but as any reader of the *Diary* will understand, Dostoevsky styled himself a prophet not just for Russia, but for humanity as a whole. He thought that Russia contained within herself the solutions to global problems. The critique of Russian liberalism and Russian political-economic development was for him a critique that had universal significance. In the *Diary* one finds some of Dostoevsky's most penetrating criticisms of the materialist social formula of the West, and of the classes that advance it—namely, the merchant class (the bourgeoisie) and the liberal intelligentsia. Though he sometimes resists the idea in favor of a more classless egalitarian vision, Dostoevsky generally argues that political communities, and larger, more universal political projects, cannot survive absent a group of "best men" to lead them. Russia would need best men to lead the effort to repair the rift between the Europeanized upper crust of the Russian nation and the peasant majority in such a way that the philosophical and technical learning of the former could be combined with the religiosity and rootedness of the latter. It is from such a synthesis that the social pathologies of single-minded materialism might be avoided, without abandoning the advantages of modern technology.[30] Europe in general, and perhaps the rest of the world, needs to develop a similar synthesis, for which Russia could provide a model.

The emergent leading classes of Russia in Dostoevsky's day were not suitable as "best men" because they themselves were the most materialistic and rootless members of society. If allowed to impose their enlightenment and their ways on everyone else, they would only instill corruption. As Dostoevsky notes, until recent times, the business class (merchants) could have made no pretense about themselves being the best men. In pre-Petrine Russia, and old Europe, the "best men always elaborated for themselves a rather harmonious code of valor and honor" which, despite being at times "greatly at variance with the ideals of the people" nevertheless obligated each of them "to give his life for his fatherland whenever such a sacrifice was required of him, and he did actually die as a matter of duty and honor 'since otherwise great dishonor would be cast upon my family.'" Peter I imposed significant changes on this class, adding many new families to their number. But though the reforms increased the distance between nobility and people, still the best men were required to serve.[31]

Merchants had never been considered best men: "Our former merchant, notwithstanding the role which everywhere in Europe capital and the millionaires have played, in Russia, comparatively speaking, occupied a rather insignificant place in the social hierarchy." However, by the middle of the nineteenth century, these merchant millionaires had risen to prominence. Dostoevsky, it should be noted, does not condemn all merchants; the majority of them, he says, are not corrupted by wealth. Instead, he singles out the richest of them: "The richer the former merchant grew, the worse he became. Essentially, he was nothing but a peasant—merely a corrupted peasant."[32] It is this class of millionaires that, with some notable exceptions, was most morally "detached from the people.... And never have the people been in a worse bondage than in the factories owned by some of these gentlemen!"[33] Whereas historically all Russian people had been rooted in their native soil, connected to one another through their Orthodox heritage, their common worship of God, the newly rich Russian had abandoned this God: "This former merchant worshipped his million as God: in his view the million was everything; the million extricated him out of nothingness and gave him importance."[34] Merchants of this type are, it is no surprise, utterly without shame: "There prevailed the conviction which assumed the form of an axiom: 'With money I can buy everything, every distinction, every valor; I can bribe everybody and can bail myself out of everything.'"[35] For the corrupted, rootless merchant, money is God, and therefore, all is permitted.

In more recent times, continues Dostoevsky, the limits on the activity of the millionaire merchant had been removed. He rose in wealth, influence and social prestige. Now "he becomes more and more wholeheartedly convinced that he is 'the best' man on earth, in lieu of all the former ones. But the pending calamity is not that he entertains such nonsense, but the fact that others also, it would seem ... begin to reason in the same way."[36] As the millionaire merchants increase their power and transform the whole world into their global "market," the common people were in danger not only of being exploited, but of being corrupted. The innocent peasants, the people still connected to Russia, to the God of the Orthodox Church, and to each other, are left without protection: "What are they going to set against the monster of materialism, in the guise of the gold bag, marching on them?—Their misery? Their rags?"[37]

The millionaires are some of the worst men; they therefore must not be permitted to be leaders. On the contrary, other leaders are needed to restrain *them*. The other group that, according to Dostoevsky, has no right to lead was the liberal intelligentsia. Motivated by abstract ideals, these men are detached from their native soil, and have no sympathy for any particular people, least of all their own. In a reply to the Russian liberal Granovsky, Dostoevsky refutes the claim that Russian liberals are, and had been, appropriately civic-minded. They claim, he says, to have been the most ardent advocates for the abolition of serfdom. Dostoevsky replies:

> The point is in fact they hated serfdom not for the sake of the Russian peasant who worked for them and fed them, and whom they, among others, oppressed ... who prevented them from simply liberating their peasants with land [?] ... Why these gentlemen acted even in a simpler manner: they pledged, sold or exchanged ... their peasants, and having thus raised money, they went to Paris and financed there the publication of French radical newspapers and magazines for the salvation of all mankind, and not just the Russian peasant.
>
> You assure us that sorrow for the peasant serf devoured all of them. Not really for the peasant serf, but abstract sorrow about slavery prevailing in mankind. "This shouldn't be! This is unenlightened. Let's have *Liberte, Egalite et Fraternite!*"[38]

As Joseph Frank notes, one of the specific targets of this general attack on the liberal intelligentsia was the Russian social democrat and absentee landlord Alexander Herzen, who had used income from his Russian estate to help finance the publication of a newspaper by the French socialist Proudhon.[39] For Dostoevsky, the Russian liberal intelligentsia are rootless, sentimental wanderers whose abstract, enlightened sympathy for mankind makes them callous and disloyal to members of their own nation, specifically, to the peasants with whose plight they claim to be concerned. The Russian liberals are no better than the Anglican ministers whom Dostoevsky excoriates in *Winter Notes on Summer Impressions* for pursuing missionary work in Africa instead of tending to the needs, spiritual and material, of the poor and miserable in their own country. Sympathy for humanity, outrage at inequality in the abstract, prevents one from performing one's proper duty as a Christian, to love and serve one's own neighbors.

For the twenty-first-century Anglophone world, the following analogy suggests itself. The Russian liberal intelligentsia, as Dostoevsky portrays it, is not unlike the rich editorial writers for the *New York Times* or the *Guardian* who despise their own materially humble working class and rural dwellers for their xenophobia, religion, guns, hunting, and patriotism and use their papers to advocate humanitarian military interventions and increases in foreign aid to end poverty and human rights abuses abroad (knowing that the poor will do the actual fighting and foot part of the bill with their taxes). The members of a liberal intelligentsia are detached from their own people, indeed from all people, and view the world as a sphere of chaos which is at odds with their abstract rational ideals. Abstract sympathy for humanity relieves the liberal of feelings of duty towards his actual neighbors.

BE GOOD BECAUSE IT IS IN YOUR OWN INTEREST (*FRATERNITE, OU LA MORT!*)

For Dostoevsky, the oligarchic businessmen and the liberal intelligentsia are the last people who should become leaders, either of nations or of any international political effort. From his point of view, then, it is no coincidence that the liberal social formula, though it provides ideological cover for the businessman who worships his million, is incapable of inspiring genuine civic feeling, at least not by itself. Liberal and socialist appeals for civic responsibility are always rooted in the idea of individual material self-interest. To the extent that the Crystal Palace is a community, it is a community of individuals seeking to maximize their security, comfort, and enjoyment. Dostoevsky's response to this: "Just try to cement men into a civic society with the sole aim of 'saving their hides'! You will derive nothing but the moral formula: '*Chacun pour soi et Dieu pour tous.*'"[40] It is this formula that Dostoevsky finds most disturbing. Abstract notions of placeless and soulless solidarity—the ideal of saving one's hide—provide the recipe for the most egregious violation of the Biblical injunction to love one's neighbor." Dostoevsky is adamant on this point:

> "The saving of hides" is the most impotent and lowest of all ideas uniting mankind. This is the beginning of the end, a premonition of the end. People pretend to stick together, but at the same time they are on a sharp look-out for the first moment of danger, ready to disperse. And what, in this case, can an "institution," as such, save? If there be brethren, there will be brotherhood. If there are no brethren, no "institution" will ever produce brotherhood. What is the sense of establishing an "institution" and inscribing on it: *Liberte, Egalite, Fraternite!* You will get no sense at all out of such an "institution," and so it will become necessary, quite inevitably, to add to these three constituent words, three new ones: "*ou la mort,*" "*fraternite ou la mort,*" and brethren will start chopping off the heads of their brethren in order to achieve brotherhood through "the civic institution."[41]

The actual Russian phrase I have translated as "saving their hides" is *spasti zhivotishki*—"to save their bellies," which is especially appropriate in view of Dostoevsky's frequent allusions to the words of Christ, that "man does not live by bread alone." A genuine community does not arise from a mass of individuals who are concerned, first and foremost, "to save their bellies," or, as we are more accustomed to say in English, to save their own hides. When a civic doctrine starts from this premise, it can only fail to inspire the depth of civic commitment for which liberal intellectuals hope. The millionaire businessman may fancy this doctrine because it permits him to think his steadfast efforts to save his own hide will trickle down and save the hides of others. But when this does not happen, and everyone saves his own hide at the expense of others, the true believer in the doctrine becomes desperate: "*fraternite, ou la mort!*"

Here is the impetus for a reign of terror, the origin of the totalitarian temptation to which the liberal and socialist doctrinaires are vulnerable. This is how Dostoevsky understood the failure of the French revolution, and how he thought such failure could be repeated in Russia. The horrors of the twentieth century have, one hopes, inoculated most liberals and socialists against this totalitarian temptation. Yet, though we appear safe for the moment from that particular danger, a world being dragged more gradually toward the ideal of the Crystal Palace by the global billionaire and the cosmopolitan liberal intelligentsia produces monsters enough as it is.

Dostoevsky's insights on a humanity conquered by the materialist monster show us the origin of such socio-economic phenomena as the devil-may-care, drug-addled, whoring gamblers and gangsters of American high finance who lately blew up the global economy, and will likely blow it up again before long. He helps us to understand why the rootless billionaires will skin others to save their own skins, and why large numbers of the idle, public-assistance-collecting poor save them the trouble by developing addictions to methamphetamine and burning their own skins off. Those who are deprived of beauty and toil will pine away, ruin themselves and others, lose their minds and lose their humanity.

A DOSTOEVSKIAN SOLUTION?

Whether or not one agrees with Dostoevsky's critique of liberalism and socialism both in the West and in Russia, one must admit that his depictions of their failings are vivid, concrete, psychologically deep and imaginative. The same cannot be said, unfortunately, for Dostoevsky's ideas on the Russian alternative to materialistic social doctrines and practices. One finds in Dostoevsky's corpus almost no descriptions or even literary depictions of communities made whole, or that might be made so, by beauty and toil. The most one finds are scattered instances of individuals, usually individual peasants, manifesting Christian virtues. It is often thought that Dostoevsky saw the Russian peasant commune (*obshchina* or *artel'*) as a model for social organization. But Dostoevsky never actually describes the peasant commune either in a historical, sociological, or even in a literary way.[42] It is clear that Dostoevsky saw a need for a new class of best men, rooted in national traditions, to heal the rift between Russia's upper crust and the peasant masses, and to, if not end, then at least ameliorate the exploitation of the latter by the former. But no such exemplary men, neither literary creations nor historical figures, ever appear in his novels or his journalistic writing. Konstantin Leontiev, a contempory of Dostoevsky, notes with frustration that while Dostoevsky declares in *The Adolescent* that Russia needs a strong and honest nobility, all the main noblemen who appear in the book are depicted as "broken, spineless, and all but mad."[43] On the whole, Dostoevsky's positive formulations, at least when compared to his social criticism, are vague, abstract and insufficiently elaborated, and thus bound to disappoint. It is worthwhile, nonetheless, to lay them out.

The key ideas of Dostoevsky's solution are rootedness and moral self-betterment. Indeed, one sees in Dostoevsky's writings that the return to one's cultural roots is typically the route to moral self-betterment. In a piece in his *Diary* on the Nechaev affair, Dostoevsky imputes the destructiveness of Russia's radical socialist youth to their rootlessness. "Very often," he writes, "I stop to think, and I am now asking myself: what kind of impressions do our contemporaneous youth mostly derive from their childhood?"[44] The impressions these children of privilege derive from their upbringing, he says, inspired in them contempt for their fatherland and Orthodoxy:

> If the word "fatherland" has been pronounced in their presence not otherwise than with a derisive expression; if for the cause of Russia all those who have been bringing them up have maintained contempt or indifference; if the most magnanimous among the fathers and the educators have kept talking about "cosmopolitan" ideas; if, even in their childhood, their nurses have been dismissed because, over their cradles, they—those nurses—said the prayer "mother of God"—tell me: what may one demand from these children . . . ?[45]

Exposed to constant negation of their own heritage, and offered nothing but the vaguest, most inchoate cosmopolitan dreams of the brotherhood of man, how could they become anything other than nihilists? Having learned to despise the manifestations of beauty that Russia had to offer, these children of liberal nobility and gentry could not grow into an elite capable of leading Russia toward regeneration.

Reflecting upon his own youthful radicalism as a member of the Petrashevsky circle, Dostoevsky claims to have been saved from socialism and nihilism ultimately by his more pious and patriotic upbringing:

> And yet I was, perhaps, one of those (again, I am speaking only about myself) to whom the return to the popular root, the understanding of the Russian soul, the recognition of the people's spirit, has been made particularly easy. I am descended from a pious Russian family. As far as I can remember myself, I recall my parents' love for me. We, and our family, have known the gospel almost ever since our earliest childhood. I was only ten when I already knew virtually all the principal episodes in Russian history from Karamzin whom, in the evenings, father used to read aloud to us. Every visit to the Kremlin and the Moscow cathedrals was, to me, something solemn.[46]

The experience of his childhood, early knowledge of the Gospel and the history of his fatherland, reverence for the stories and symbols of both eased Dostoevsky's spiritual homecoming after his dangerous flirtation with socialism and the West. Those radical youth of the present, had they been afforded such an upbringing, would not be so irrecoverable now.

A telling inconsistency in Dostoevsky's understanding of rootedness should not escape our notice here. Dostoevsky describes his homecoming as a "return to the popular root" (*narodnyi koren'*). As Berdyaev correctly observes, when Dostoevsky speaks of "the people" (*narod*) he always means *plebs* and not *natio*.[47] After his period of exile, Dostoevsky imagined he had once again entered into communion with the authentic Russian spirit preserved in the Russian *plebs*. This, he said shortly after the Edict of Emancipation (1861), was the only way for the Russian intelligentsia to become rooted; they could either come to know the common people and commune with that purer spirit they had preserved or remain "mental proletarians, people without any soil under their feet, international mediocrities" or "young people wearing excellent gloves whose minds wander in eternal gloom, and whose hearts desire only money."[48] But in this case, the moral and historical imagination of a nobleman, N. M. Karamzin, and the political and religious monuments of great Muscovite princes, tsars, patriarchs and bishops appear to be the emblems of that authentic Russian spirit, to which Dostoevsky returned, not to mention his family Bible, probably gilt and illustrated, which illiterate serfs could not read. Though the acknowledgement appears accidental here, possession of high culture, *national* culture, and not just plebeian culture, seems essential if the upper classes are to become enrooted once again.

Dostoevsky usually presents the common people as the only true bearers of Russia's sacred traditions and Christian spirit, with which the upper crust of the Russian nation had lost touch. They, he claims, are the most rooted, more so than even the Slavophil portion of the Russian intelligentsia. Therefore it is from the common people that Russia's upper classes have the most to learn:

> And yet our people know their Christ God—perhaps even better than we, although they did not attend school. They know, because throughout many a century they have endured much suffering, and in their sorrow, from the beginning and up to our time, they have been accustomed to hear about this Christ God of theirs, from their saints who labored for the people and to defend the Russian soil—sacrificing their lives; from those very saints whom they have revered up to the present day, remembering their names and praying at their graves.[49]

Though illiterate, the common people are rooted in Orthodoxy and the fatherland by experience and ritual. Their physical suffering makes them more receptive to Christ. Their ritual veneration of Russian saints who toiled for their benefit and defended their home soil from invaders reinforced their communion with Christ, and their attachment to the fatherland. As always, however, Dostoevsky is interested primarily in the "spirit" supposedly preserved in the common people, which he sees as some sort of general, abstract inclination toward brotherhood, not in their actual religious rituals or other communal practices, not in their stories. Should the educated classes re-learn to commune with Christ and experience rootedness in the same way as the serfs? How is their return to the native root to be brought to pass? If Dostoevsky is unclear on the question of what precisely the "popular spirit" is, he is hopelessly vague on the question of how the members of the uprooted classes are to acquire it.

There is an additional problem, and this one Dostoevsky addresses more directly: by and large, the Russian serf, however deeply ingrained his Orthodoxy and rootedness in the soil, was too often a source of embarrassment for the educated classes. The proclivity of so many of the common people for drunkenness and loutish behavior seemed to give the lie to the populist story of the pious and patriotic *muzhik*. So much drunkenness, superstition and loutishness being in evidence among the peasants, one could hardly expect the upper classes to see them as anything but mere cattle, the change in their legal status by the Tsar's Edict of Emancipation notwithstanding, much less as the bearers of an authentic Orthodox Russian spirit which they ought to embrace. As has been shown above, Dostoevsky was certain that neither liberalism, the doctrine of "every man for himself" nor socialism, the doctrine of "class struggle," could produce the sort of community in which citizens would care for one another. Making the serfs free and equal persons under the law, or mandating socialist wealth transfers, would not create a community. Both liberalism and socialism are fundamentally flawed, because at the foundation of each doctrine is the fatal assumption that community can arise merely from the desire of free and equal individual human beings to save their own hides. If the upper classes are to see the Russian serfs as something other than beasts, cattle to be bought and sold, and the serfs to see their former owners as fellow citizens and not exploiters, then each part of the nation would have to learn to see the other not as culturally unencumbered, free, equal, and rights-bearing human beings, but as fellow Russians and fellow Christians.

As the more rootless and more powerful portion of the nation, it was the educated classes who first needed to remove the beam from their eye. In *Diary of a Writer,* Dostoevsky recounts in a very personal way how his own sympathy for the Russian *muzhik* developed. The story, "The Peasant Marei," is delivered with considerable literary skill, and so, the effect of it cannot really be appreciated unless it is read in full. A brief summary will have to suffice here. Dostoevsky begins by reminiscing about his time in Siberia among other convicts. The peasant criminals, he recalls, could be shockingly bestial. After witnessing a group of peasants beat another peasant nearly to death, he had retreated to his prison bunk, and begun to meditate upon his experiences in the forced labor camp. While going over the last four years of his penal servitude in his mind, he had hit upon a memory from childhood, a chance encounter with a peasant of his father's estate. A child of nine at the time, while playing at the edge of the forest he had thought he heard someone cry "a wolf's running." In terror, he had run screaming in the direction of a peasant he had seen earlier plowing the field. The peasant Marei had stopped what he was doing and calmed Dostoevsky as if the boy had been his own child: "It's all right, Christ be with you. Cross yourself." When Marei had finally convinced the nine-year-old Dostoevsky that there was no wolf and calmed him, he had sent him on his way: "'Well, go on then! And I'll be watching after you! I'll surely not let the wolf get you!'—He added with that the same motherly smile—'Well, Christ be with you. Go on, then!'—And he crossed me with his hand and then crossed himself."[50]

Dostoevsky claims that this reminiscence, forcing itself onto his mind when it did, had had a transformative effect upon him:

> The meeting was a solitary one, in a vacant field, and only God, maybe, perceived from above what a profound and enlightened human sentiment, what delicate, almost womanly, tenderness, may fill the heart of some coarse, bestially ignorant Russian peasant serf, who, in those days, did not expect, nay, had no forebodings about his freedom. . . .[51]

It is clear what Dostoevsky considers to be the origin of this peasant's enlightenment. In attempting to calm the boy, his instinct was to tell him to cross himself. His last act before little Dostoevsky went on his way was to cross the boy, and then cross himself. Here was that Orthodox piety preserved in the common people, those closest to their native soil. In the light of this reminiscence, looking upon the peasants who shared the labor camp with him, continues Dostoevsky, "I suddenly felt that I could behold these unfortunate men with a wholly different outlook."[52]

The solution to the problem of social organization, then, lies in the conversion of individuals to Christ, in their becoming more perfect Christians, and in recognizing one another as Christians as Dostoevsky himself had done thanks to his experience with pious and patriotic peasants rooted firmly in their native soil. The gulf between classes would be narrowed by all of them becoming, not more liberal, but more Orthodox. Dostoevsky greeted the legal emancipation of serfs with jubilation. But a change in formal legal arrangements, he was certain, did not mean a change in the souls of men. So Dostoevsky declares in a polemic with the liberal Granovsky, who doubted the power of Christian moral self-betterment, insisting that "progress" was more "dependent upon social institutions." Referring to one of the unsympathetic serf-owning families depicted in Gogol's *Dead Souls*, Dostoevsky replies:

> Had Korobochka become, or could she have become, a *true*, perfect Christian, there would have been no serfdom on her estate at all. . . . She would have been their mother, a real mother. . . . The former mistress and the former slave would have vanished like mist in the rays of sun, and altogether new human beings would have come into

existence, and quite new, hitherto unheard-of relations would have ensued between them.[53]

The problem with Granovsky and other liberals is that they seek to create a civic ideal and social institutions independently of Christian truth and the native traditions of the Russian people. They, like Western Europeans, seek ingenious institutions that will make men good mechanically by acting upon their individual self-interest. Dostoevsky insists that social organization cannot be improved without reaching men's individual souls, and that souls cannot be reached without religion:

> Whence can the ideal of civic organization in human society be derived? . . . You will see that it is solely the product of moral self betterment of individual entities. . . . In the origin of every people, of every nationality, the moral idea invariably preceded the origination of the nationality itself, *since the former created the latter*. The moral idea always emanated from mystical ideas, and the conviction that man is eternal, that he is not a mere earthly animal, but that he is tied to other worlds and eternity. Invariably and everywhere these beliefs assumed the form of religion, the form of the confession of the new idea. And just as soon as a new religion came into being, a new civic nationality came into existence.[54]

At the origin of all nations, Dostoevsky asserts, is the coalescing of human groups around certain religious ideas. As these religious ideas, eventually formulated into a particular confession, are the basis of the original unity, civic ideals and institutions must be built on that same foundation. In short, religion is and must remain the foundation of community.

Liberals and socialists alike err in their most basic assumptions about what draws human beings together in communities, and what makes them care for one another. Social doctrines that appeal to individual self-interest only turn the individual back upon himself and away from his community. Human beings are attracted to one another by a desire to preserve common treasures, common ideals and emblems of beauty.

> To preserve the acquired spiritual treasure, men are forthwith attracted to each other, and only then do they zealously and anxiously, "working beside each other, one for the other, one with the other" . . . begin to investigate how they should organize so as to preserve the treasure without losing any part of it; how to find such a *civic* formula of common existence as would help them promote throughout the world the acquired moral treasure in its full glory.[55]

One wishes Dostoevsky had paused here and elaborated his thought. It is precisely in this sort of common endeavor, it seems, here only vaguely and abstractly delineated, that the human need for beauty and toil can be fulfilled. The essence of the social bond, as Dostoevsky describes it here, is common ideals and emblems of beauty, the treasures of one's native religion and native soil. For the sake of their preservation and promotion, men can be drawn out of their self-absorption and boredom and be inspired to toil zealously beside, for, and with one another.

CONCLUSIONS

Dostoevsky offers a profound critique of the Western religions of physical well-being, liberalism and socialism, as organizing principles for nations and for humanity as a whole. The implementation of this materialistic program to save the world, he argues, can only act as a solvent on existing organic communities, and can scarcely create new communities in their place. It must deprive many people throughout the world of their spiritual needs for community and beauty and thereby generate a variety of social pathologies. The new world it produces can only be less colorful, less vibrant, and less interesting. For this reason, Dostoevsky and other Russian conservatives lay out an alternative path for their nation, and other nations, predicated on the preservation and promotion of particular native treasures.

It ought perhaps to be stated directly, that unlike other enemies of capitalism Dostoevsky never expresses any desire to see the bourgeoisie "liquidated as a class." Rather, he insists that bourgeois thinkers are not equipped to provide a vision for life throughout the world, and therefore must not be allowed to define "development" goals for everyone else, must not be permitted to lead, at all events. Vast numbers of people of the capitalist or socialist mindset might be entirely decent people, and nothing ought to prevent them from performing useful labor in their several capacities for the communities they inhabit. But their socio-political philosophy is irredeemable. The various bourgeois and socialist types that Dostoevsky describes, the ordinary shopkeeper with his petty aspirations, the shameless millionaire, the liberal intellectual with his abstract sympathy for mankind and aloofness toward those close to him must not be writ large, as Plato puts it (*Republic*, 368 c–d). If there is to be any role for these persons—and for merchants and other producers there will always be a role—it is to be subordinate. Neither private capitalists nor state socialists should be allowed to have undue influence on the organization of political communities, much less be permitted to lead them. They must operate within communities whose ideals are defined by others, namely, by culturally rooted national elites who have sufficient vision to understand, that for political communities to truly flourish, they must toil together, and have common ideals and emblems of beauty to unite their individual members and nourish their spirits.

NOTES

1. As Nicolai Berdiaev indicates, this animus for socialism and "middle class civilization" together, seen as different versions of the same irreligious culture, was not unique to nineteenth-century Russian intellectuals. Nineteenth-century Frenchmen such as Barbey d'Aurevilly, Villiers de l'Isle-Adam, Huysmans, Leon Bloy, and Germans such as Nietzsche "were no less wounded by the spectacle of contemporary European civilization than were Dostoyevsky and [Konstantin] Leontyev." But "it so happened that Russians felt it more keenly than anybody else" (Nikolai Berdyaev, *Dostoevsky* (New York: Meridian Books, 1957), 176).
2. See Wayne Dowler, *Dostoevsky, Grigor'ev, and Native Soil Conservatism* (Toronto: University of Toronto Press, 1982).
3. The term "political religion" belongs to Eric Voegelin. Voegelin argued that "the Christian apocalypse of the empire and the symbolism of the late Middle Ages form the historical basis for the apocalyptic dynamics in modern political religions." The "three empires" of Marx's theory of history, the "Third Reich of National Socialism," and the "fascist third Rome" all mimicked Joachim of Fiore's historicization of the Christian Apocalypse. But in the modern political religions "the end realm is no longer a transcendent community of the spirit but an earthly community of perfected humanity." Voegelin also regarded progressive liberalism as a political religion of this type. One could see this in Kant's "view of history in which the rational and enlightened person climbs to ever-higher stages of perfection . . . until, finally he moves forward to the repression-free, cosmopolitan community with a suitable leader." Moreover, communism, Voegelin argued, should be thought of as liberalism's radical cousin: "If liberalism is understood as the immanent salvation of man and society, communism is certainly its most radical expression; it is an evolution that was already anticipated by John Stuart Mill's faith in the ultimate advent of communism for mankind." See Eric Voegelin, *Modernity without Restraint* (Columbia: University of Missouri Press, 2000), 51, 52, 60–61, 230–31. Indeed, Dostoevsky and other Russian conservatives saw bourgeois liberalism and communism in much the same way, as false, substitute religions, that "immanentize the eschaton" in Voegelin's famous phrase (Eric Voegelin, *The New Science of Politics: An Introduction* (Chicago: University of Chicago Press, 1987), 120). Of course, Dostoevsky's own social doctrine in its full-blown form is no less apocalyptic, no less an immanentization of the eschaton.
4. Ellis Sandoz, *Political Apocalypse: A Study of Dostoevsky's Grand Inquisitor* (Wilmington, DE: ISI Books, 2000), 22.
5. There is, however, the intriguing dialogue on theocratic government in Book II, chapter 5 of *Brothers Karamazov*. Starets Zosima and two other clerics discuss Ivan Karamazov's article on how the Church should absorb the state and govern not "mechanistically" but by appealing to the Christian conscience of its citizens. I do not consider this here, as it is not clear whether Dostoevsky meant for Ivan's proposal to be taken as his own. He expressed his other views quite forthrightly in *Diary of a Writer*, but the idea of an institutional theocracy only appeared in his novel. See Fyodor Dostoevsky, *The Karamazov Brothers* (Oxford: Oxford University Press, 1994), 75–84, PSS: 14, 55–63.

A note on translations: for the reader's convenience I cite popular, easy-to-find English editions of Dostoevsky's works, but in many instances I have corrected them to bring them closer to the original Russian in the Fyodor Dostoevsky, *Polnoe sobranie sochinenii v tridtsati tomakh* (Leningrad: Nauka, 1972b), hereafter PSS, followed by volume, page number. I have found translators sometimes tone down Dostoevsky's language, or otherwise make odd and unnecessary changes to his texts.

6. Berdyaev, *Dostoevsky*, 40.
7. Fyodor Dostoyevsky, *The Diary of a Writer* (New York: C. Scribner's Sons, 1949), 582, PSS: 23, 25.

8. Quoted in Sandoz, *Political Apocalypse: A Study of Dostoevsky's Grand Inquisitor*, 150–151. The Russian *zatoskovat'* is difficult to translate, but "to feel deep melancholy, loneliness, or boredom" is the sense of it.

9. Joseph Frank, *Dostoevsky: The Stir of Liberation, 1860–1865* (Princeton: Princeton University Press, 1986), 238–242.

10. Fyodor Dostoyevsky, *Winter Notes on Summer Impressions* (Surrey, England: Oneworld Classics, 2008), 50, PSS: 5, 69–70.

11. Dostoyevsky, *Winter Notes*, 52, PSS: 5, 70.

12. Dostoyevsky, *Winter Notes*, 52, PSS: 5, 71.

13. Dostoyevsky, *Winter Notes*, 57, PSS: 5, 73.

14. This, notes Berdyaev, is an important and recurring theme in Dostoyevsky's work: "Dostoyevsky taught the religion of love for one's neighbour, and he denounced the falsity of . . . disinterestedness in favour of some far-away end . . . [T]here is a 'far-away' principle, it is God—and he tells us to love our neighbour" (Berdyaev, *Dostoevsky*, 99).

15. Dostoyevsky, *Winter Notes*, 53, PSS: 5, 71.

16. Dostoyevsky, *Winter Notes*, 53, PSS: 5, 69.

17. Dostoyevsky, *Winter Notes*, 50–51, PSS: 5, 70.

18. Dostoyevsky, *Winter Notes*, 60, PSS: 5, 77.

19. Dostoyevsky, *Winter Notes*, 62, PSS: 5, 78.

20. Dostoyevsky, *Winter Notes*, 64, PSS: 5, 77.

21. Dostoyevsky, *Winter Notes*, 80, PSS: 5, 86.

22. Dostoyevsky, *Winter Notes*, 98, PSS: 5, 95.

23. See Richard Avramenko, "Bedeviled by Boredom: A Voegelinian Reading of Dostoevsky's *Possessed*," *Humanitas* XVII (2004).

24. Fyodor Dostoyevsky, *Notes from the Underground. The Double* (Baltimore: Penguin Books, 1972a), 29, PSS: 5, 110. In this and in the following passages, Dostoyevsky was reacting specifically to the materialist determinism of Chernychevsky in *What Is to be Done?* and the attempt of Fourier to tabulate mathematically all the passions of mankind and construct a "model social order" on that basis (see Frank, *Dostoevsky: The Stir of Liberation, 1860–1865*, 320–326).

25. Dostoyevsky, *Notes from the Underground. The Double*, 29, PSS: 5, 110.

26. Dostoyevsky, *Notes from the Underground. The Double*, 32, PSS: 5, 112.

27. Dostoyevsky, *Notes from the Underground. The Double*, 33, PSS: 5, 113.

28. See Frank, *Dostoevsky: The Stir of Liberation, 1860–1865*, 328–331. The correct title of this work, as many have noted, is *Zapiski iz podpol'ya*, "Notes from under the floor" or "Notes from a mousehole."

29. Dostoyevsky, *Notes from the Underground. The Double*, 42–43, PSS: 5, 120–121.

30. See Dowler, *Dostoevsky, Grigor'ev, and Native Soil Conservatism*.

31. Dostoyevsky, *The Diary of a Writer*, 481, PSS: 23, 154.

32. Dostoyevsky, *The Diary of a Writer*, 484, PSS: 23, 157.

33. One wishes Dostoevsky had elaborated on these exceptions. He wanted a natural aristocracy of conservative intelligentsia, and existing virtuous nobles and merchants, open to anyone with proven talent from any class. Many of the merchants were patriotic, supported his own endeavors, did charity, built churches, etc. See Dowler, *Dostoevsky, Grigor'ev, and Native Soil Conservatism*, 37.

34. Dostoyevsky, *The Diary of a Writer*, 485, PSS: 23, 158.

35. Dostoyevsky, *The Diary of a Writer*, 486, PSS: 23, 158. This is the theme of both *Crime and Punishment* and *The Adolescent*—both stories centering on a young man of the new generation dreaming of becoming either a Napoleon or a Rothschild.

36. Dostoyevsky, *The Diary of a Writer*, 486, PSS: 23, 159.

37. Dostoyevsky, *The Diary of a Writer*, 488, PSS: 23, 160.

38. Dostoyevsky, *The Diary of a Writer*, 992–993, PSS: 26, 158.

39. Joseph Frank, *Dostoevsky: The Mantle of the Prophet, 1871–1881* (Princeton: Princeton University Press, 2002), 544. As Frank also notes, one can see in Dostoyevsky's attack a possible allusion to the title character of Ivan Turgenev's *Rudin*, who, having

fled his homeland, dies "heroically" in the barricade in Paris in 1848. Dostoevsky made no secret of his dislike of the liberal Turgenev, who had, in Dostoevsky's view, abandoned his fatherland for Baden Baden.

40. "Every man for himself, and God for all" (Dostoyevsky, *The Diary of a Writer*, 1000, PSS: 26, 164–165).

41. Dostoyevsky, *The Diary of a Writer*, 1002, PSS: 26, 167.

42. With this exception: He refers to another writer's description of a meeting of a peasant commune in the play *Pit' do dna—ne vidat' dobra* (Drink to the bottom—see no good) as follows: "This meeting is all that is left of the firm and cornerstone foundations of the Russian people, their main traditional link and their main future hope." But the reader is left in the dark as to what, practically, Russians are to make of this ancient tradition. See Dostoyevsky, *The Diary of a Writer*, 112, PSS: 21, 100.

43. K. N. Leontiev, *Khram I Tserkov'* (Moskva: Izdatel'stvo, 2003), 386–387.

44. Dostoyevsky, *The Diary of a Writer*, 152, PSS: 21, 134.

45. Dostoyevsky, *The Diary of a Writer*, 153, PSS: 21, 135.

46. Dostoyevsky, *The Diary of a Writer*, 152, PSS: 21, 134.

47. Berdyaev, *Dostoyevsky*, 167.

48. Quoted in "Dostoyevsky as a Journalist" in Ivan Ilyin, *Sobranie sochinenii v desyati tomax* (Moskva: Russkaya kniga, 1997), t. 6, kn. 3, 357.

49. Dostoyevsky, *The Diary of a Writer*, 286, PSS: 22, 113.

50. Dostoyevsky, *The Diary of a Writer*, 209, PSS: 22, 48. Marei is probably the most memorable of Dostoyevsky's saintly peasants. Ivan Ilyin in his lecture "Dostoyevsky as a Journalist" lists all the other instances of peasant saintliness documented by the author in his occasional writings: Ilyin, *Sobranie sochinenii v desyati tomax*, t. 6, kn. 3, 361–362.

51. Dostoyevsky, *The Diary of a Writer*, 210, PSS: 22, 49.

52. Dostoyevsky, *The Diary of a Writer*, 210, PSS: 22, 49.

53. Dostoyevsky, *The Diary of a Writer*, 997–998, PSS: 26, 162–163.

54. Dostoyevsky, *The Diary of a Writer*, 1000–1001, PSS: 26, 165.

55. Dostoyevsky, *The Diary of a Writer*, 1001, PSS: 26, 165.

SEVEN

Between Compassion and Misanthropy

On Moral Reasoning in Fyodor Dostoevsky's Crime and Punishment

Khalil M. Habib

INTRODUCTION

Fyodor Dostoevsky's *Crime and Punishment* has earned its place among world literature's greatest psychological masterpieces for the subtlety of its insights into the human soul and the conditions that lead tormented individuals to seek God and redemption in a fallen world. Set in St. Petersburg in the nineteenth century during Russia's uneasy transition to the modern age, the novel takes place during a period of great upheaval in Russian life. Central to the novel is Rodion Romanovich Raskolnikov, a poverty-stricken student who, seeing his impoverished family sacrificing for him, resolves to end his financial troubles by murdering a cruel and unsympathetic pawnbroker, an old woman he believes to be a parasite on society. Raskolnikov vacillates between two theoretical justifications for his plot. The first grows out of the various socialist principles taking hold in Russia at the time. The grinding poverty of the masses in Russia, coupled with a growing dissolution with the aristocracy and serfdom, pushed many to read and espouse the thought of writers such as Proudhon and Fourier.[1] The second, believing himself a great man, a kind of Napoleon exempt from traditional moral considerations, Raskolnikov justifies his murder by theorizing that violence purifies those who, like himself, are strong-willed and beyond good and evil. This theory, we learn, is informed by principles foreign to the Russian people, such as Bentham's utilitarianism or even later what would be synthesized by Nietzsche in his doctrine of the will to power.[2] Pursued by a clever detective and haunted by guilt, Raskolnikov's conscience torments him until he finds reprieve from his torment in the redemptive love he receives from a prostitute, Sonia Semyonovna Marmelodova.

While the story is straightforward, understanding Raskolnikov's motives is no easy task. If we trace the twists and turns of Raskolnikov's self-justifications and motives, we shall see that he did not fully understand (or reveal) his own complex motivations until he finally confesses to Sonia. Throughout the novel Raskolnikov equivocates between a deep sympathy for the suffering of humanity and a cold disdain for his fellow human beings. Dostoevsky scholars recognize well this "schism" in Raskolnikov's personality—his name, after all, points directly at this.[3] The Russian root of his name, *raskol'nik*, means schism and probably, as Ellis Sandoz hints, points to the Great Schism of 1054 when the Christian church split into the Eastern Orthodox and the Roman Catholic.[4] It is this schism that lies at the heart of Raskolnikov's own psychological torment. To understand Raskolnikov, one must recognize that Dostoevsky is pointing to this vacillation between East and West in both Raskolnikov and Russia herself. Just as Raskolnikov vacillates between a great compassion for his fellow Russians on the one hand, and a cold, misanthropic disdain for them on the other, so vacillates the Russian collective consciousness.

It is at the end of a long and painful process that Raskolnikov realizes that the Western, so-called humanitarian justifications cannot justify the crime for a properly thinking human being. As he confesses to Sonia, he killed for one reason only: to test the strength of his own will and reason and to see for himself whether or not he was an extraordinary man, a man beyond good and evil. He wanted to know if he could kill with a clear conscience and therewith have the right to take a human life. It is as if he wanted to test Saint Paul's claim that there is a moral law written across the heart of every human being, in which "their conscience testifying with them, and their thoughts among themselves accusing or else excusing them" (*Romans* 2:15). In short, whereas most readers understand Raskolnikov's split personality, that is, his struggles with his conscience, as either symbolic of the East-West split in Russia's history, or as Raskolnikov himself splitting away from his Russian roots, I would like to add another possibility. Raskolnikov is not just splitting from Russia, or from Europe, or from the church (either Greek or Latin), but from humanity itself. Raskolnikov's effort is to extract himself from sharing in the suffering of all humanity to a position above all this. In short, Raskolnikov vacillates between compassion and misanthropy.

This is not to say, however, that Raskolnikov's social and economic justifications for murder do not serve an important purpose. For one, such rationalizations allow those who cannot understand the depths of evil to dismiss crimes in a way that least disturbs them. Although unpleasant and difficult, it is easier to accept murder in the name of financial necessity or with the casuistry of utilitarianism and greater social happiness than it is to accept the idea that someone would kill for the sheer pleasure of doing so or to test his own strength and independence. The latter is simply too unsettling; it lacks sufficient cause or justification. Raskolnikov killed because he hoped to enjoy the triumph of his will over his victim while affirming his place among history's extraordinary individuals who, in his mind, have a right to transgress the moral restraints that govern the actions and lives of ordinary human beings. It is easy to see, on the basis of this psychology, why Nietzsche considers Dostoevsky one of the greatest psychologists who ever wrote.[5] Finally, the material and utilitarian justifications for killing the pawnbroker—that is, poverty is the reason and that one small crime can benefit society—allow Dostoevsky to stop along the way to offer a critique of the new wave of utilitarianism sweeping across Russia in an age when throne and altar are nearly moribund. We shall trace the twists and turns of Raskolnikov's mind as presented and developed in the novel until we finally reach the moment of his confession to Sonia and his own realization of his motives.

SETTING THE STAGE

The novel begins in St. Petersburg with Raskolnikov hopelessly in debt to his landlady. He slips out of his tiny garret unnoticed and wanders around the squalor of his neighborhood, passing drunks and prostitutes along the stinking streets. He is troubled, and his mind is in turmoil. He is clearly conflicted by an unspoken idea. Deep in reverie and contemptuous of his surroundings, he loses himself in his muddled thoughts as he wanders aimlessly through the dark streets. Eventually, he approaches his destination, the house of Alyona Ivanovna, the elderly and repulsive pawnbroker, to rehearse his future deed: he has hatched a plan to murder her, thereby ending, in one stroke, his financial troubles. Both the victim and the idea of the crime disgust him, but he resolves to continue, pawning an old watch for a pittance. He then enters a tavern for a drink.

The tavern is a microcosm of life in St. Petersburg, Russia, and the "new" modern world. The city is a scene of bleak poverty, and the tavern is frequented by hard-working laborers and the unemployed. Deep suspicion of one's fellows and their motives reflects the breakdown of trust within this society. Dostoevsky depicts here a troubling scene of the general struggle against sin and social and political marginalization in a fallen world, where life offers little economic and political opportunity.

Russia, it seems, is as poor as Raskolnikov, both materially and spiritually. It is here, in this pub, as he comes into contact with the human misery around him, that Dostoevsky accentuates the social-humanitarian motivation that inform some of Raskolnikov's sensibilities.

At the tavern, it does not take long to discover that fashionable social and moral theories from Europe, in particular England, are being introduced and applied to Russian society. During a conversation with Raskolnikov, Marmeladov, a drunken government clerk, describes applying for a loan he knows he cannot repay, and understands that his failure to secure a loan is in accord with "modern" ideas. Marmeladov proudly quotes Mr. Lebeziatnikov, a progressive, "who keeps up with modern ideas," saying, "that compassion nowadays is forbidden by science itself, and that that's what is done now in England, where there is political economy."[6] Joseph Frank, writing about this scene, points out that "Raskolnikov's own reasoning [for murdering the pawnbroker] is based on exactly the same Utilitarian notions of 'political economy,' which exclude any feeling of compassion for the 'useless' individual marked out as the sacrificial victim."[7] Although there are deeper reasons that contribute to Raskolnikov's fateful transgression, it is clear that Western social theories and progressivism have arrived in St. Petersburg and are integral to the theme of the novel.

Over the course of their drunken conversation, Marmeladov tells Raskolnikov that he was fired from his position because of his drinking. As a result, Marmeladov's young daughter Sonia is forced into prostitution to support the family. To make matters worse, five days earlier Marmeladov absconded with his family's money for a five-day drinking binge. Afraid to go home and face his wife, Katerina Ivanovna, he hides in the tavern drinking.

What is important in this encounter is that Marmeladov, a lost Russian soul, makes frequent references to scripture. He refers to Sonia, his daughter from a previous marriage, as his "daughter who gave herself for the cross" (CP 24), connecting her to the Savior. On closer inspection, however, Marmeladov's Christianity is questionable. While unwilling to suffer hard work or to give up drinking, he suffers under the weight of his sin and consoles himself in his belief that God will forgive Sonia and his whole family on Judgment Day. The others in the tavern laugh and mock him, as they see through his self-serving rationalizations. His supposed faith in God's Grace allows him to abnegate responsibility and "to find sympathy and feeling in drink" (15). As he explains to Raskolnikov, "I drink so that I may suffer twice as much [as my family]!" (15). Amidst the laugher and ridicule heaped upon him in the tavern, Marmeladov declares that he does not seek pity, but only to be a martyr:

> "To be pitied! Why am I to be pitied?" Marmeladov suddenly declaimed, standing up with his arms outstretched [as though on a cross].

"Why am I to be pitied, you say? Yes! There's nothing to pity me for! I ought to be crucified, crucified on a cross, not pitied! Crucify me, oh judge, crucify me but pity me! And then I will go to myself to be crucified, for it's not merry-making I seek but tears and tribulation!" (22).

The Christian overtones framing the encounter continue when Marmeladov takes Raskolnikov to his home to witness the deplorable conditions of his family's life. Furious at his having stolen their money, his wife seizes Marmeladov by the hair and beats him in front of Raskolnikov. Fulfilling his self-appointed role as martyr, Marmeladov cries out in pain, "And this is a consolation to me! This does not hurt me, but is a positive con-so-la-tion . . . sir" (26). He takes comfort and pleasure in being beating by his wife; his suffering consoles him and offers an inkling of meaning to his wretched life. Yet, despite all this, Dostoevsky's point is clear: the pretense to martyrdom leads Marmelodov neither to God nor to salvation but to harm for both his family and himself, sinking them all deeper into urban Russian nihilism. The men of Russia, it seems, have lost their way. Marmeladov's suffering and self-pity are a sham and only afford him a psychological crutch to continue his degenerate existence. Yet amidst this reprobate's world, Dostoevsky introduces his reader to Sonia, whose role as conciliatory emerges as the novel unfolds.

The scene proceeds with Raskolnikov who, although in dire need of money himself, quietly leaves a few coins on the windowsill for the family. As is usually the case, immediately after this selfless act of charity, he regrets it and abuses himself over the "lapse." His initial sympathy for the family transforms into cold disdain and misanthropy. Once outside, Raskolnikov mocks Marmeladov and ridicules him and his wife for forcing Sonia into prostitution. His pride immediately extinguishes the compassion awakened by Marmeladov and his family, as he laughs malignantly, congratulating himself: "They would all be without a crust tomorrow except for my money!" (22). Rather than sharing the suffering of the family, he writes them off as happy scoundrels profiting from Sonia's degradation, as if the whole family had chosen their life of abject poverty. The pendulum then completes its swing and Raskolnikov dismisses all of humanity as beneath him. Yet suddenly and almost manically, Raskolnikov questions his contempt for humankind, aroused by a new thought: "What if man is not really a scoundrel, man in general, I mean, the whole race of mankind—then all the rest is prejudice, simply artificial terrors and there are no barriers and it's all as it should be" (27).

This episode reveals Raskolnikov's general pattern of behavior: as soon as his compassion is enkindled, he quickly isolates and detaches himself in his misanthropy. The pattern repeats itself through the novel: he is continually torn between a sense of his own superiority over others and his nagging conscience and love for his Russian brethren. It is as though he is two personalities: murderous yet sympathetic, depressed yet hopeful, calculating yet empathetic. In short, the hubris of his intellectualism is in conflict with his heart and conscience. The former opens the way to murder and self-absorption, whereas the latter enkindles his spirit and clears a path home from the nihilism, isolation, and the anguish of Western rationalism and individualism, just as the vacillation between compassion and misanthropy mirrors Russia's own vacillation between East and West.

The schism revealed in the presence of the Marmeladov family repeats itself in relation to Raskolnikov's own family. The following day Raskolnikov receives a letter from his mother informing him that his sister Dounia is engaged to a successful lawyer named Pyotr Luzhin. If Raskolnikov is going to reject his own compassion for others, he must also reject all compassionate acts directed at him and his family. Assuming that his sister is sacrificing herself by marrying Luzhin for Raskolnikov's sake, his misanthropy surfaces unmistakably:

> Why is [Dounia] consenting then? What's the point of it? What's the answer? It's clear enough: for herself, for her comfort, to save her life she would not sell herself, but for someone else she is doing it! For one she loves, for one she adores, she will sell herself! She will sell everything! . . . It's as clear as daylight. It's clear that Rodion Romanovitch Raskolnikov is the central figure in the business, and no one else. . . . Oh, loving, over-partial hearts! (42).

Too detached from the complexities of love and the duties that link people together, he fails to consider that she might be marrying Luzhin to better her own life and their mother's. His misanthropy blinds him to the fact that human life itself, both in its biological necessity and its moral dimensions, requires that individuals form an attachment to others; that they sacrifice some liberty and spiritual autonomy for shared compassion and charity. Such an idea is repugnant to Raskolnikov precisely because he has split himself from this realm of humanity.

It is thus that Raskolnikov resolves to stop their wedding even if it means the end of his own existence: "I won't have your sacrifice, Dounia, I won't have it, mother! It shall not be, so long as I am alive, it shall not, it shall not! I won't accept it!" (43). In Raskolnikov's imagination, his sister is dragging him into the pitiful condition of compassion, and in so doing is degrading him to the level of the drunken Marmeladov—who is completely dependent on the sacrifices of his poor daughter, Sonia. Raskolnikov will not prostitute Dounia. He is too proud for others to make sacrifices for him. He is superior to the Marmeladovs, and to Luzhin, the successful lawyer whom he clearly resents and mocks as a "rational" and "sensible business man . . . one who has a fortune . . . a man who shares the ideas of our most rising generation" (39). He does not want to be confused with these lowlifes. He loses himself once again in thought:

"'never such a marriage while I am alive and Mr. Luzhin be damned! The thing is perfectly clear,' he muttered to himself, with a malignant smile anticipating the triumph of his decision" (39).[8]

His indignation over the news of his sister reminds him of his plan to kill the pawnbroker. Dostoevsky's language is very telling:

> He gave a sudden start; another thought, that he had had yesterday [of murdering the pawnbroker], slipped back into his mind. But he did not start at the thought recurring to him, for he knew, he had *felt beforehand*, that it must come back, he was expecting it; besides it was not only yesterday's thought. The difference was that a month ago, yesterday even, the thought was a mere dream: but now . . . now it appeared not a dream at all, it had taken a new menacing and quite familiar shape, and he suddenly became aware of this himself. . . . He felt a hammering in his head, and there was a darkness before his eyes (44).

Whereas the plan was originally hatched out of his utilitarian calculus, that is, out of the need for money, the necessity of the murder comes fully to light. To free himself from compassion, he *must* kill the pawnbroker. As Raskolnikov puts it, keeping himself above humanity requires that he "check [his] spontaneous outflow of pity, and with a 'malignant laugh' he ponders the infinite capacity of mankind to adapt itself to the most degrading circumstances."[9] The idea of killing the old pawnbroker and forcibly swinging the pendulum to misanthropy is no longer a dream.

THE MISANTHROPIC DREAMWORLD

The following day, after a few drinks, Raskolnikov falls asleep and dreams of his childhood, where he is about seven years old, on a walk with his father to visit his grandmother's grave. A large, drunken crowd is assembled near the graveyard just outside a tavern, very much like the one he has recently been frequenting. On their way from visiting his grandmother's grave, they walk by the tavern and witness a loud group of drunken peasants beating an old horse to death and delighting in their cruelty. Attached to this old, helpless mare is a rickety cart laden with casks of wine and heavy goods. Suddenly a large, drunken peasant runs out of the tavern shouting, "Get in, get in!" leaping into the cart. "I'll take you all, get in!" The peasants pile into the cart, laughing and making jokes. "Get in, all get in," cries the driver of the cart, "she will draw you all. I'll beat her to death!" (56–57), and he beats the horse. The old horse is unable to pull the weight of the village, but the driver continues to beat it. He whips the horse in the face and eventually bludgeons it to death with a thick crowbar. The peasants laugh and crack nuts as the horse falls dead on the ground. Someone in the crowd shouts, "No mistake about it, you are not a Christian" to the man brandishing the bar that killed the horse (59). A young boy, who is clearly Raskolnikov as a child, cries out against the senseless act and asks, "Father! Why did they . . . kill . . . the poor horse!" (59).

At this moment, just as the peasants are declared unchristian, Raskolnikov awakes, soaked in sweat and stricken with horror. He immediately connects the horrifying dream to his idea of murdering the pawnbroker. "Good God!" he wonders, "can it be, can it be, that I shall really take an axe, that I shall strike her on the head, split her skull open . . . ?" (59). Disgusted with himself and believing himself possessed with some devilment, he renounces his plan and wonders, "Why am I going on like this? I knew that I could never bring myself to it, so why have I been torturing myself? Yesterday I realized completely that I could never bear to do it. . . . Why am I going over it again, then?" His thoughts run on, "As I came down the stairs yesterday, I said to myself that it was base, loathsome, vile . . . the very thought of it made me feel sick and filled me with horror" (59–60). What is interesting is that the horrors of the dream—of the obvious pull to the secular West—is that the schism is, at least momentarily, mended through prayer. Raskolnikov prays and, for the moment and temporarily, feels liberated from the "burden that had so long been weighing upon him, and all at once there was a sense of relief and peace in his soul" (60). The return to childhood, to his Russian, Christian origins, and the ensuing momentary inner peace, is brief but significant, as it hints at his struggle to free himself from his Christian conscience.

Raskolnikov's reaction to the brutal death of the old horse in his dream reveals a buried Russian with a capacity for compassion and the turmoil fighting within his conscience, as he struggles to suppress his spontaneous moral sensibilities. On the one hand, the little child still exists in the depths of Raskolnikov's soul; on the other hand, there is the grown Raskolnikov whose social-humanitarian and Utilitarian notions cause him to behave exactly like the drunken villager who killed the "useless" old mare in his dream. His despair is painful. The agonizing conflict between his Russian moral conscience and his "rational" theory must be resolved. At this moment of crisis, he manages to suppress the rational, utilitarian man and reawaken the more innocent child's sensibilities. For the moment, he (mistakenly) believes that he has overcome his desire to kill.

THE OMEN

But Raskolnikov does eventually murder the pawnbroker. The question must arise, what makes him kill in spite of his obvious disgust with himself and horror at the thought of committing murder? Immediately after the dream, Raskolnikov strolls through the Haymarket where he overhears the pawnbroker's sister Lizaveta reveal that the pawnbroker will be alone the following day, providing him with a prime opportunity to murder her. Upon learning of this opportunity, Raskolnikov suddenly feels he has surrendered his free will to forces greater than himself, that his whole being had "no more freedom of thought, no will, and that everything was suddenly and irrevocably decided" (62). He interprets this chance opportunity to kill the old pawnbroker as some miraculous omen. He was superstitiously impressed by this circumstance, which . . . "always seemed to him afterwards the predestined turning-point of his fate" (60).

This sense of determinism, of being a unique and chosen participant in a higher history, allows him to avoid responsibility for the crime, while his pride conspires against his moral sensibilities by fooling him into thinking he is an instrument of fate and that his actions are justified and full of cosmic significance and meaning. "Fate thus takes a hand, but it is fate acting on a pathological psychic predisposition to kill conditioned by [the] ideological self-intoxication" of utilitarian theory.[10] With the cosmos now endorsing his actions, Raskolnikov moves closer to what he holds to be his fateful deed. The fact that he cannot allow himself to believe he is acting voluntarily reveals his deep ambivalence about the crime. Unable to clearly reason his way through his motivations, he surrenders his reason to his twisted sense of destiny. His "rational" justifications tell him one thing, his heart tells him another. His Western rational calculus divorces him of responsibility—especially of responsibility to other, unique and suffering individuals. His rationalizations are in conflict with his conscience, which he persistently struggles to suppress upon the slightest sign of compassion and self-doubt.

On seeing Lizaveta in the Haymarket, Raskolnikov recalls the first time he had met her sister, the old pawnbroker Alyona Ivanovna. As he replays that meeting in his mind, we learn how Raskolnikov first developed the idea of the murder. He visited her one day to pawn off his father's old silver watch and a little gold ring his sister had given him as a parting gift. Indignant at his poverty and resentful of having to sell his gifts, he projected an immediate and insurmountable repulsion onto the old woman. After the transaction, he stopped in a tavern. There, sipping his tea, he sank deep into thought. "A strange idea was pecking at his brain like a chicken in the egg, and very, very much absorbed him" (63). That idea, the subject of his essay "On Crime" and about which we learn later in the novel, is that murder is justified by a higher social good.

Sitting almost beside him at a table nearby was a young student, whom he did not know, and with him a young officer. The student, for Dostoevsky, serves as a mirror for Raskolnikov. It is as if Raskolnikov is listening to himself speak. This "other self," this interlocutor, however, fails to serve as the voice of conscience. The two-in-one conversation with one's self, which Hannah Arendt describes as both representative of the thinking process and the conscience, does nothing to awaken Raskolnikov's self-aware conscience.[11] Instead, the mirror goads him on. He hears the student give his companion the pawnbroker's address: "This of itself seemed strange to Raskolnikov; he has just come from her . . . of course it was a chance, but he could not shake off a very extraordinary impression, and here someone seemed to be speaking expressly *for him*" (64). The student narrates various details about the pawnbroker's life, describing how spiteful Alyona Ivanovna is, how if someone were only a day late with payments, the pledge is lost, and how the old lady had left her sweet sister, Lizaveta, entirely out of her will. As the student tells it, "All the money is left to a monastery" while her sister is reduced to rags (64).

The student then adds how killing Alyona Ivanovna and distributing her money to help the poor could easily be excused by a simple utilitarian calculus:

> [L]ook here; on one side we have a stupid, senseless, worthless, spiteful, ailing, horrid old woman . . . on the other side, fresh young lives thrown away for want of help and by thousands, on every side! A hundred thousand good deeds could be done and helped, on that old woman's money which will be buried in a monastery! Hundreds, thousands perhaps, might be set on the right path; dozens of families saved from destitution, from ruin, from vice . . . and all with her money. Kill her, take her money and with the help of it devote oneself to the service of humanity and the good of all . . . would not one tiny crime be wiped out by thousands of good deeds? For one life thousands would be saved from corruption and decay. One death, and a hundred lives in exchanged—it's simple arithmetic! (65–66).

The young student's low estimation of the old pawnbroker's life reflects the "simple arithmetic" of utilitarianism and Raskolnikov's own thoughts at the moment. According to the general empirical view of utilitarianism, right and wrong action are determined by weighing the negatives of an action against its benefits. Or, put otherwise, Utilitarianism holds that we ought to pursue the greatest good for the greatest number of people. Hence, if one person has to die to save a thousand, that one death is justified. And in this tavern, the young student is actually suggesting that killing Alyona Ivanovna could be justified by the positive benefits her money will bestow on a greater number of people. In response, the student's friend remarks, "Of course she does not deserve to live, but there it is, it's nature." "Oh, well, brother," objects the students, "but we have to correct and direct nature but for that, there would never have been a single great man" (66).

The officer, the voice of law, responds by asking the student whether or not he himself would kill her. The student admits that he could not kill her, to which the officer says, "If you would not do it yourself, there's no justice about it!"(66). In other words, a theory is no theory if it cannot be put into practice by the person espousing it. Justice requires action, not intentions. The student's admitted inability to follow through on his theory provides here Dostoevsky's view that utilitarianism can flatter ordinary men into thinking they are extraordinary and historic figures, who, through their Western brand of reasoning, can justify even murder through an abstract and "simple" arithmetical equation. What's important in this scene is that the theory expressed by this student is the same as the one Raskolnikov has been pondering to justify one horrendous crime for the service of humanity. While Dostoevsky may be indicating how widespread utilitarianism was among young students and intellectuals in Russia at this time, the scene serves as a catalyst for Raskolnikov to act on his theory. By the end of the conversation, Raskolnikov is violently agitated: "Why had he happened to hear such a discussion and such ideas at the very moment when his own brain was just conceiving . . . *the very same ideas?*" (66). To his mind, this is no mere coincidence but a sign. Indeed, "The traces of superstition remained in him long after, and were almost ineradicable. And in all this he was always afterwards disposed to see something strange and mysterious, as it were, the presence of some peculiar influence" (63). His belief that he is an instrument of fate is tied to his pride, and the belief that he is superior to other human beings convinces him that it is his destiny to kill Alyona Ivanovna. Although Raskolnikov's young foil can discuss the same theory, it is Raskolnikov, he tells himself, who can make the theory manifest. He is the extraordinary man. He is the hero in an age of mediocrity who can bring humanitarian reasoning to bear and really fulfill the destiny of Russian compassion. He is now ready and able to perform the grisly axe murder. It is meeting his weaker self in the mirror, so to speak, that pushes Raskolnikov into action.

"ON CRIME"

It is through Raskolnikov's article, "On Crime," that Dostoevsky sheds light on the reasoning behind what he regards as Raskolnikov's twisted self-understanding and demented view of his place in the world. It is important to note that Dostoevsky reveals the content of the article in a conversation between Raskolnikov and the criminal investigator, Porfiry Petrovitch. Petrovich is every bit the psychologist, and the article, like the whole novel itself, is a foray into the psychopathology of modern Western reasoning. Moreover, the conversation takes place in Petrovitch's apartment with Razumikhin, Raskolnikov's reasonable friend present. After a brief and awkward exchange of pleasantries, the conversation turns to a discussion about socialism and crime.

Razumikhin is the first to speak. He argues against the popular theories about socialism and fears that this new social science dangerously ignores, rejects, or perverts the lessons of history—that is, a community's shared culture, history, and social experience, and development. This new "science" of socialism, he argues, offers nothing but abstract theories as an alternative to the lessons of the past. Socialists, he argues, naively assume that if society is properly organized by some enlightened social engineer, "all crime will cease at once, since there will be nothing to protest against and all men will become righteous in one instant" (260). Razumikhin accuses these radical political idealists of ignoring human nature. According to him, human nature is "excluded, it's not supposed to exist," for nature would place a limit on utopian dreams and any effort at central planning. Utopian social engineering is irrational in theory and practice, he contends, for it attempts to control the complexity of mankind and can only do so by rejecting or ignoring human nature and breaking with the social continuum of shared experience. "What they want . . . smells of death . . . at least [it is] not alive, has no will, is servile and won't revolt! And it comes in the end to their reducing everything to the building of walls and the planning of rooms and passages in a phalanstery!" (260). Razumikhin's critique of the false assumptions and scientific pretenses of the tyranny of utopian social engineering anticipate Karl Popper's view that "[a]ny social science which does not teach the impossibility of rational social construction is entirely blind to the most important facts of social life, and must overlook the only social laws of real validity and of real importance. Social sciences seeking to provide a background for social engineering cannot, therefore, be true descriptions of social facts. They are impossible in themselves."[12] In short, we hear from Razumikhin a well-grounded, well-argued rejection of socialist theories in favor of the reasonable traditions passed down through history, grounded in local practices, local leadership, and local judgment. For Razumikhin, the new social science is informed by a vision of the good society that fails to "recognize that humanity, developing by a historical living process, will become at last a normal society, but [the social engineers] believe that a social system that has come out of some mathematical brain is going to organize all humanity at once and make it just and sinless in an instant, quicker than any living process!" (260). Hence, he explains, socialist intellectuals deride history and dismiss it as an ugly stupidity. Razumikhin believes in a process whereby humanity, and not only a few anointed individuals, collectively lead civilization to what he calls a "normal society." This society is characterized by the ebb and flow of a spontaneous organic community.

By contrast, Raskolnikov's theory points to extraordinary individuals as the true creators of community. Like Machiavelli before him, he views humanity in scientific terms whereby the masses are mere materials to be molded and shaped by founders who are, like science, beyond good and evil (265). Accordingly, he claims that there is a law of nature that can be known to mankind that bifurcates humanity into two types—extraordinary and ordinary individuals. "On Crime" defines what it means to be extraordinary and justifies why these rare types, such as Napoleon, have a perfect right to overstep the traditional boundaries of morality and lawful behavior. An extraordinary man, explains Raskolnikov, has "an inner right to decide in his own conscience to overstep" and transgress the moral law for the benefit of the whole of humanity (264). This claim, which would have been obvious to Dostoevsky's intended audience, is a direct rejection of the Christian understanding of the conscience as articulated in Saint Paul's letter to the Romans. Yet, to clarify his point, Raskolnikov maintains that "if the scientific discoveries of Kepler and Newton could not have been made known to the general public except by sacrificing the lives of one, a dozen, a hundred, or more men, Newton would have had the right, would indeed have been in duty bound . . . to eliminate the dozen or the hundred men for the sake of making his discoveries known to the whole of humanity" (263).

Whereas Razumikhin denies the possibility that any one individual could organize all humanity at once, Raskolnikov maintains, like Machiavelli, that the greatest legislators and leaders of men, "such as Lycurgus, Solon, Mahomet, Napoleon, and so on, were all without exception criminals" who, through the strength of their own will and reason, were able to establish a new law by transgressing "the ancient one, handed down from their ancestors and held sacred by the people" (264).[13] And, he adds, "they did not stop short at bloodshed either, if that bloodshed—often of innocent persons fighting bravely in defense of ancient law—were of use to their cause" (264). Raskolnikov attributes a desire to be distinct from the common man to the motives of these extraordinary men, reading into their actions his own misanthropy. Without criminality, he claims, "it's hard for them to get out of the common rut; and to remain in the common rut is what they can't submit to, from their very nature again, and to my mind they ought not, indeed, submit to it" (264).

Elaborating on his thesis, Raskolnikov argues that humanity is generally "divided by a law of nature into two categories, inferior (ordinary), that is . . . material that serves only to reproduce its kind, and men who have the gift or the talent to utter *a new word*" (264). The inferior types are, generally, conservative and law-abiding. They live under laws they did not create and expect to be controlled by their leaders. That is their temperament, he says, and there is nothing degrading to them in their meekness. By contrast, the superior types are destroyers of the old traditions. They transgress the traditional laws and obliterate the present for the sake of a better future: "If such a one is forced for the sake of his idea to step over a corpse or wade through blood, he can, I maintain, find within himself, in his conscience, a sanction for wading through blood—that depends on the idea and its dimensions" (264). These extraordinary criminals—those individuals who can extract themselves from humanity and the laws and tradition bound up with their communities, can use this power to dehumanize the masses and delegitimize their right to exist. Once the old has been abolished and the new has been established, the masses "set these criminals on a pedestal in the next generation and worship them" (265). The ordinary mass of humanity lives in the present; the extraordinary man lives in the future: "The first preserve the world and people in it, the second move the world and lead it to its goal" (265). For Raskolnikov, the vast mass of human beings, whom he holds in contempt, is "mere material, and only exists in order by some great effort . . . to bring into the world at last perhaps one man out of a thousand with a spark of independence" (267).

Razumikhin finds it difficult to believe that Raskolnikov genuinely holds such views. What disturbs the psychologist Petrovitch, however, is Raskolnikov's view that some individuals believe they have a right to kill in the name of a higher social good. Are these extraordinary souls, asks the investigator, beyond the reproach of their own conscience? "Why do you care about that?" snaps Raskolnikov who, up until this moment, had been elaborating on his theory rather calmly. Why this reaction to Petrovitch's query regarding the conscience and religion? Raskolnikov's response is revealing, and redolent of precisely Arendt's view of the relationship between thinking and moral considerations: "*If* he has a conscience," Raskolnikov maintains, then "he will suffer for his mistake" (emphasis added, 268). Raskolnikov admits to giving considerable thought to the "psychology of a criminal before and after the crime," and concludes that "the perpetration of a crime is always accompanied by illness" (262).

A clue to what Raskolnikov means by "a crime is always accompanied by illness" is revealed in several scenes in the novel and in his essay "On Crime," that center on the status of the conscience. During the moments leading up to his final preparations for the murder, for instance, Raskolnikov convinces himself that ordinary criminals suffer from "a failure of will and reasoning power" brought on by the pang of the criminal's conscience, which gives them away in their erratic actions (71). By contrast, "extraordinary" individuals, as he elaborates in his article, are immune from their consciences because they have a moral right to transgress the existing laws. In a scene the day following the murder, however, the "illness" of losing his reason to the witness of his own conscience starts to manifest itself in Raskolnikov's mind, calling into question his status as an extraordinary man. In his frightful state, he continually asks himself, "My God! . . . What's the matter with me?" and later, "Surely it isn't beginning already! Surely it isn't my punishment coming upon me?" (91). All his faculties, even memory, and the simplest power of reflection, begin to fail him. Could it be the judgment of his agonizing conscience? Upon reflecting on the consequences of his actions and his reaction to his crime, he concludes, "it is!" (91). Raskolnikov wants to know whether or not the conscience is a sign of God's witness or just an artificial voice of guilt punishing the mind of a weak soul. Whichever the case, it is important to note that when the conversation does start—the conversation that *is* the conscience—it is as if Raskolnikov's interlocutor is God himself. In other words, there's a different kind of thinking that undergirds a healthy consciousness.

THE CONFESSION AND MOMENT OF TRUTH

When the internal conversation, that is, when the moral reasoning gets underway, Raskolnikov can only reject the utilitarian moral justification for the murder he committed; he refuses the notion that he acted in response to perceived social ills. As he finally confesses to Sonia, when he really starts to think it becomes clear that his deepest motive in killing the old pawnbroker "was to test (unsuccessfully) whether he could overcome his Christian conscience" and to see whether or not he was in truth a great man beyond good and evil, and so possessed the "right" to kill.[14] Here is how Raskolnikov explains his motivations to Sonia:

> If I worried myself all those days, wondering whether Napoleon would have done it or not, I felt clearly of course that I wasn't Napoleon. I had to endure all the agony of that battle of ideas, Sonia, and I longed to throw it off: I wanted to murder without casuistry, to murder for my own sake, for myself alone! I didn't want to lie about it even to myself. It wasn't to help my mother I did the murder—that's nonsense—I didn't do the murder to gain wealth and power and to become a benefactor of mankind. Nonsense! I simply did it; I did the murder for myself, for myself alone. . . . I wanted to find out then and quickly whether I was a louse like everybody else or a man. Whether I can step over barriers or not, whether I dare stoop to pick up or not . . . whether or not I had the *right* . . . to kill (424).

Raskolnikov, in the redemptive company of Sonia, returns to his religious, Russian roots, confessing to her that he was possessed by evil: "I know myself that it was the devil leading me. . . . I used to lie there in the dark and all this became clear to me . . . it [was] a temptation of the devil" (424). The language itself that he chooses ("devil," "darkness") reverts to his religious instincts. His vain and criminal ambition is in conflict with his Christian conscience. He is, by the end of the novel, convinced that his utilitarian principles were founded on the sin of pride, seducing him into believing that he was above humanity and the pang of his own conscience, and that he belonged to his imagined category of extraordinary men. The idea to kill for no other reason than to test whether or not he was beyond good and evil incubated in his mind, took root there as a youthful Napoleonic fantasy, and transformed into action when he could no longer restrain it. The casuistry of utilitarian logic disguised his sadistic and narcissistic motives, even to himself. His self-indulgent fantasy initially took the form of a grand social ideology in order to bury his moral sensibilities, raise him up to the illusion of superiority, while at the same time dehumanizing and delegitimizing the pawnbroker's life.

Whereas the young student in the tavern recognizes that he is not up to the task—but enjoys indulging his vanity in temporarily thinking that he is—Raskolnikov's pride tricks him into thinking he is an "extraordinary" elite, beyond ordinary morality. This helps to explain his earlier continuous inner struggle to suppress any feelings of compassion and pity "in order to bring about a humanitarian and morally beneficent end."[15]

CONCLUSION

Raskolnikov's disdain for "ordinary" people points to his own false sense of superiority and, especially, the misanthropy bound up with thoughtlessness. It also clouds his judgment through pride, allowing him to misidentify himself as one of these "extraordinary" men. Almost immediately after committing the crime he feels remorse and is haunted by the faint voice of his conscience, which he is no longer able to suppress by utilitarian logic. In spite of his many attempts, his futile attempt to hang his actions on the lofty idea of determinism necessarily conflicts with his moral sentiments, as his conscience is too much a part of him to completely suppress. What occurs in the scenes we have examined "illustrates the manner in which Raskolnikov's ideas have been affecting his personality, and they cast an important light on what has been taking place within him emotively ever since he fell under their influence."[16]

In the end, Raskolnikov's effort to extract himself from humanity by including himself among the world's "extraordinary" leaders and founders resulted only in two murders and an inner life of isolation and psychological soliloquy. Unlike the fabled founders of new civilizations, his experiment produced no new order. No great new world emerged to replace the old Russian Christian one he had inherited and grown up in. Just as utilitarianism had flattered the young student in the tavern into thinking he could benefit all of society by committing one small crime, Raskolnikov, too, is duped by his own pride and by the simplistic and beguiling allure of an abstract theory. And so Raskolnikov begins his exile, but not in soliloquy—finding his conscience, he is in steady and healthy conversation not just with himself, but with Sonia, the bearer of redemptive love. It is only with the awakening of moral and religious reasoning and conversation with Sonia, not the abstract and solipsistic reasoning of Western utilitarianism, that he finds a reawakened appreciation and understanding of his limits, his conscience, and God.

NOTES

1. Dostoevsky's own involvement with "Western" socialism is well documented. See Joseph Frank, *Dostoevsky: A Writer in His Time* (Princeton: Princeton University Press, 2009); Ellis Sandoz, *Political Apocalypse: A Study of Dostoevsky's Grand Inquisitor*

(Baton Rouge: Louisiana State University Press, 1971). For more on socialism and Russia, see Joseph Frank, "Dostoevsky: The Encounter with Europe," *Russian Review* 22 (1963); Liza Knapp, *Dostoevsky as Reformer: The Petrashevsky Case* (Ann Arbor, MI: Ardis Publishers, 1987); Irving Howe, "Dostoevsky: The Politics of Salvation," *The Kenyon Review* 17 (1955).

2. This is also the central theme of Dostoevsky's *Adolescent*. For more on the relationship between Dostoevsky and Nietzsche, see James M. Curtis, "Shestov's Use of Nietzsche in His Interpretation of Tolstoy and Dostoevsky," *Texas Studies in Literature and Language* 17 (1975); Rene Girard, "Superman in the Underground: Strategies of Madness—Nietzsche, Wagner, and Dostoevsky," *MLN* 91 (1976); Janko Lavrin, "A Note on Nietzsche and Dostoevsky," *Russian Review* 28 (1969).

3. Victor Terras, *Reading Dostoevsky* (Madison: University of Wisconsin Press, 1998); Antony Johae, "Towards an Iconography of *Crime and Punishment*," in *Dostoevsky and the Christian Tradition*, ed. George Pattison and Diane Jenning Thompson (Cambridge: Cambridge University Press, 2001).

4. Ellis Sandoz, *Political Apocalypse: A Study of Dostoevsky's Grand Inquisitor* (Wilmington, DE: ISI Books, 2000), 204.

5. Friedrich Nietzsche, *Twilight of the Idols with the Antichrist and Ecce Homo* (London: Wordsworth Editions Limited, 2007), 77.

6. Fyodor Dostoevsky, *Crime and Punishment* (New York: P. F. Collier & Son Company, 1917), 22. All reference hereafter will be in-text and refer to this translation.

7. Frank, *Dostoevsky: A Writer in His Time*, 486–487.

8. The letter ends with Raskolnikov's mother asking him if he still believes in God and prays (38). Her concern underscores the intellectual climate in which the novel takes place. She explicitly fears that Raskolnikov may have broken with his faith and has adopted the fashionable atheism sweeping over the young generation of Russians.

9. Frank, *Dostoevsky: A Writer in His Time*, 488.

10. Frank, *Dostoevsky: A Writer in His Time*, 491.

11. Hannah Arendt, "Thinking and Moral Considerations," *Social Research* 38 (1971).

12. Karl Popper, *The Poverty of Historicism* (New York: Routledge Classics, 2010), 43.

13. Raskolnikov's essay "On Crime" bears a striking resemblance to chapter 9 of the *Prince*, in which Machiavelli divides all of humanity into the "people" and the "great." In chapter 6 of the same book, Machiavelli argues that genuine founders, such as Moses, Cyrus, Theseus, and Romulus, forge new modes and orders (peoples and fatherlands) by viewing the "people" as mere matter to be given political ends and direction, not by a teleological nature or providence, but through the will and imagination of an extraordinary founder who forms a new order by breaking with tradition and forming an entirely new political order, a theme that runs throughout Raskolnikov's essay "On Crime."

14. Frank, *Dostoevsky: A Writer in His Time*, xvi. Frank argues that Raskolnikov wanted to test himself and to see whether or not he had a right to commit a crime in order to benefit society. Yet, Raskolnikov's confession to Sonia seems to reject this possibility, as he tells Sonia that such considerations were not the real reasons behind his decision to kill.

15. Frank, *Dostoevsky: A Writer in His Time*, 489.

16. Frank, *Dostoevsky: A Writer in His Time*, 489.

EIGHT

Freedom from Freedom

On the Metaphysics of Liberty in Dostoevsky's Crime and Punishment

Richard Avramenko

INTRODUCTION

In his masterful book on Dostoevsky, Nicholas Berdyaev writes that "for Dostoievsky the theme of man and his destiny is in the first place the theme of freedom, that freedom is the centre of his conception of the world, that his hidden pathos is a pathos of freedom."[1] For most readers of Dostoevsky's work, this point is not overlooked. From his first novel, *Poor Folk*, to his magnum opus, *The Brothers Karamazov*, freedom is a central theme. Less obvious, however, is the evolution of his understanding of freedom. If freedom was a central theme in his early, pre-Siberian work (i.e., during his days as a secular, socialistic, revolutionary), it is not the same freedom we find in his mature works. Typically, the evolution of Dostoevsky's thought is tracked through his religious awakening, an awakening he himself recounts in his *Diary of a Writer*.[2] The problem with this view, however, is that Dostoevsky's commitment to freedom was constant, regardless of his religious convictions; it was central to his thought before and after his religious awakening.

The central purpose of this chapter is to call attention to two divergent visions of freedom in Dostoevsky's work. There is, on the one hand, a freedom that readily tracks onto the debates with which political theorists are familiar—the debates framed by Isaiah Berlin's famous essay, "Two Concepts of Liberty," and, more recently, in the liberal/republican debates about liberty.³ This is the freedom for which Dostoevsky advocated as a young man, wrote about in *Poor Folk* and *The Double*, and pursued as a member of the Petrashevsky Circle.⁴ This understanding of freedom, whether we understand it as negative or positive, or divide these into individual and political as has recently been envisioned, liberty in this sense pertains to control.⁵ It pertains to who controls whom and/or how well one controls oneself. As a matter of control, this understanding of liberty is empirical: it speaks to empirics, empire, imperialism, experiments. It is bound up with what the Greeks call the *peras*, the limited, the bounded, the finite, the divisible. Empirical liberty creates boundaries and limits between both individuals and individuals and the *civitas*. It is inseparable from what Martin Heidegger calls Western metaphysics.⁶

There is, on the other hand, another kind of freedom present in Dostoevsky's thought. This freedom, it will be suggested, stands over and against the metaphysics of liberty that Dostoevsky regards as dominant in Western Europe. It is a sort of freedom from this freedom. This claim, however, can only be provisional because Dostoevsky himself uses no such language. As a medium, the novel rarely affords the kind of precision normally needed for making such a claim. The novelist's craft, as Michael Kochin artfully describes, is more blood and demons than *logos* and syllogism.⁷ As such, the exploration of Dostoevsky's vision of nonmetaphysical freedom requires the imposition of language on a phenomenon itself unreceptive of language. It requires, as it were, a sifting and sorting of blood and spirit. What follows, then, is a sifting and sorting of Dostoevsky's *Crime and Punishment*—a sifting and sorting that yields the provisional language of approximate freedom and proximate freedom.

APPROXIMATE FREEDOM

Crime and Punishment (*Prestupleniye i Nakazaniye*), like the *Notes from the Underground,* features an anti-hero, Rodion Romanevich Raskolnikov, a twenty-three-year-old student from a minor noble family. Shackled by poverty, Raskolnikov has been forced to leave his study of law. For several months he aimlessly wanders the streets of Petersburg contemplating his *idea*. He is hungry, dressed in rags and forced to pawn his last few possessions to Alyona Ivanova, an old woman money-lender. Being shackled by poverty is a recurring theme in the beginning of the novel. Probably ill from hunger, Raskolnikov ambles among prostitutes and stinking pubs filled with men drinking away their last kopeck; he comes across a drunken young girl about to be raped. In one of the stinking pubs, he comes across Marmeladov, a father of four children who has lost his job as a civil servant because of habitual drinking. And key to these recurring encounters, he meets Marmeladov's oldest daughter (his only child from his first wife), Sonia, an eighteen-year-old girl who has become a prostitute to support her step-mother and three half-siblings. In short, the novel is rife with people enslaved to poverty.

The shackles of poverty strike Raskolnikov both physically and psychologically. It stings him most deeply when he receives a letter from his mother informing him that his sister is going to be married to a "self-made" man who will help the family financially after the wedding. Raskolnikov considers his sister's choice to be the same as Sonia's—a form of prostitution. Delirious, he walks through the Hay Market thinking that the only thing he can do is carry out his plan—kill the usurer and take her money, thereby liberating himself, his mother and sister, Sonia, and anybody else he can help with the money. At the Hay Market, as if by fate, he overhears a conversation between a man and Lisaveta, the money-lender's handicapped sister. He discovers she has a rendezvous at that same place the very next evening. The perfect opportunity to carry out his plan presents itself.

He goes into a pub and sits mulling over his plan when he eavesdrops on another conversation, this time between an officer and a young student about his age. They are discussing Alyona Ivanova and Lisaveta. Raskolnikov is surprised that they are talking about this pair particularly because he has just come from their place. He listens half-interested until the young student says, "I'd gladly murder that damned old woman and rob her of all she has, and that, I assure you, without the slightest compunction." Raskolnikov gives a start and listens more intently. The student presents the first iteration of what I am calling approximate freedom:

> I was joking of course, but look here; on the one side we have a stupid, senseless, worthless, spiteful, ailing, horrid old woman, not simply useless but doing actual mischief, who has not an idea what she is living for herself, and who will die in a day or two in any case. . . . On the other side, fresh young lives thrown away for want of help and by thousands, on every side! A hundred thousand good deeds could be done and helped, on that old woman's money which will be buried in a monastery! Hundreds, thousands perhaps, might be set on the right path; dozens of family saved from destitution, from ruin, from vice, from the Lock hospitals—and all with her money. Kill her, take her money and with the help of it devote oneself to the service of humanity and the good of all. What do you think, would not one tiny crime be wiped out by thousands of good deeds? For one life thousands would be saved from corruption and decay. One death, and a hundred thousand lives in exchange—it's simple arithmetic? Besides, what value has the life of that sickly, stupid, ill-natured old woman in the balance of existence?[8]

In short, the student outlines the kind of freedom against which Dostoevsky is fighting. It is the kind of freedom that besets the Underground Man—he inherits enough money to retire from his position in the civil service. His "liberation," he discovers, only makes sense insofar is human life is measurable in economic terms, or can be made measurable and reduced to "a simple sum in arithmetic." For Dostoevsky, the Euclidean world of the Westernizers, the socialists, the atheists, or howsoever he characterizes them, any such "liberating" actions can be justified if human existence is merely a matter of a simple sum in arithmetic. Such calculations of freedom, however, are abstract and overlook what is most proximate. In this case, the calculation overlooks the tangible, corporeal, actual fact that a human being must be killed for the sake of the liberty of others. These abstract calculations of freedom, it seems, are incompatible with the kind of freedom Dostoevsky has in mind. They are the progeny of Western metaphysics. They approximate freedom, but they are not freedom.

The army officer's response to the student can be taken as Dostoevsky's response to such an assertion, albeit short and simple (which Dostoevsky never is). He reminds the student, "there it is, it's [human] nature" (CP 66). The student, however, rejects this and pushes the case for approximate freedom: "Oh well, brother, but we have to correct and direct this nature, and but for that, we would drown in an ocean of prejudice" (CP 65). What he fails to say is that this form of freedom usually requires extensive re-education, usually in Siberia or another sort of concentration camp. Raskolnikov, however, does not bother to listen to the end of the conversation where the officer asks the student if he would kill the woman himself and is told, "Of course not! I was only arguing the justice of it. It's nothing to do with me" (66). Instead Raskolnikov thinks that it was a stroke of fate that he should happen to hear the expression of the very ideas that were stirring in his own mind. The conversation makes him believe that it was "as though there had really been in it something preordained, some guiding hint" (66).

The action that follows this argument is not a secret. Raskolnikov carries out his plan. He acts on this idea of freedom and buries a hatchet in the old woman's forehead the next evening. He pre-planned the whole murder, employing reason and logic the whole time, and, as far as murders can be successful, he was successful. The murder was marked by a series of coincidences, including the arrival of Lisaveta, who, in payment for her bad timing, also received a hatchet in her forehead. Raskolnikov leaves the scene, quite miraculously, without being detected. He takes with him all the monies and goods he could find and returns to his flat. After this great moment of liberation, we are told, he feels "more dead than alive" (CP 87).

What is interesting is that before the murder, while contemplating the crime, Raskolnikov's state of mind is described as follows: he was "like a man condemned to death. He thought of nothing and was incapable of thinking; but he felt suddenly in his whole being that he had no more freedom of thought, no will, and that everything was suddenly and irrevocably decided" (CP 62). He was completely taken by the *idea of action* and unable to think. Dostoevsky's point is clear: the attachment to abstract political ideas removes one from the here and now. It prevents one from the sort of thinking that either cares about or even can foresee the moral implications of one's actions in one's immediate, proximate world. Raskolnikov, for instance, acts in accordance with the computations of his idea. He made up his mind to act on his idea, and to follow the rules of fair play, which, in this case, follow the rules of arithmetic. What he misses, however, is that these rules that guide his vision of freedom are, at best, an imperfect fit for human beings *qua* human beings. This point is not lost on Razumikhin. As he puts it,

> The phalanstery is ready, indeed, but your human nature is not ready for the phalanstery—it wants life, it hasn't completed it's vital process, it's too soon for the graveyard! You can't skip over nature by logic. Logic presupposes three possibilities but there are millions! Cut away a million, and reduce it all to the question of comfort! That's the easiest solution of the problem! It's seductively clear and you mustn't think about it. That's the great thing, you mustn't think! The whole secret of life in two pages of print! (260).

There are, however, other characters in the novel who recognize the fallacy of the doctrine, but Raskolnikov ignores them. He is certain that his plan, that his idea for freedom, is correct and that all he need do is act rationally and according to mathematical prescriptions. He is positive that once the obstacle of human nature has been overcome he will be able to bring freedom to many others, and to carry out the "thousands of good deeds."

Dostoevksy's objection to this reasoning surfaces when Raskolnikov begins wrestling with his conscience. The conscience, for Dostoevsky, is the part of our humanity that resides beneath the liminality of reason. It is thus when his conscience obtrudes that Raskolnikov is reminded that the whole of human life is not as simple as 2+2, as the Underground Man would say. But not to be swayed by the unfreedom of compunctions, moral considerations or other such irrational thoughts, he vows:

> "Enough," he pronounced resolutely and triumphantly. "I've done with fancies, imaginary terrors and phantoms! Life is real! Haven't I lived just now? My life has not yet died with that old woman! The Kingdom of Heaven to her—and now enough, madam, leave me in peace! Now for the reign of reason and light . . . and of will, and of strength . . . and now we will see! We will try our strength!" he added defiantly, as though challenging some power of darkness. "And I was ready to consent to live in a square of space!" (CP 191)

His actions, he holds, are appropriate, and he need not answer questions concerning them. All he must do is maintain his logical stance and he will acquire "freedom and power—and above all power. Over all the trembling creation and all the antheap. . . . That's the goal" (336). Of course, later Raskolnikov confesses, but not before he reasons through all of the arguments in favor of this kind of freedom.

It is not by accident that the pub in which the idea of killing the old woman is first expressed is called the "Crystal Palace."[9] The Crystal Palace is a recurring symbol for Dostoevsky. It first appears in his *Winter Notes on Summer Impressions*, which is a journalistic account of his trip to London's Universal Exhibition of 1862. It was during this exhibition that he visited the famed Crystal Palace on Sydenham Hill. In his recollection of the visit he says that upon the sight of the Palace, he felt "frightened and oppressed at this Universal Exhibition by the impression of finality, profound triumph, the impression of a 'complete truth' that permits no argument."[10] He considered the exhibition a demonstration of the freedom of the "rational thinkers," as the Underground Man would call them. For Dostoevsky the sight provoked a "terrible force" and made him "feel as if something has been achieved here, that there is victory and triumph." His description is poignant:

> Can this, you think, in fact be the final accomplishment of an ideal state of things? Is this the end by any chance? Perhaps this really is the "one fold?" Perhaps we shall really have to accept this as the whole truth and cease from all movement thereafter? . . . People have come with only one thought in mind, quietly, stubbornly milling around in this colossal place and you feel that something final has been accomplished here—accomplished and completed. It is a Biblical sight, some prophecy out of the Apocalypse being fulfilled before your very eyes. You feel that a rich and ancient tradition of denial and protest is needed in order not to yield, not to succumb to impression, not to bow down in worship of fact, and not to idolize Baal, that is, not to take the actual for the ideal. . . .[11]

In a part of *Notes from the House of the Dead* not included in the original publication, Dostoevsky reiterates his fears:

> What is bread! People eat bread in order to live, but this is not life! Go ahead now, build a palace. Outfit it with marble, pictures, gold, heavenly birds, hanging gardens, whatever you can think of . . . and enter it. Indeed, perhaps you would never want to leave it! Perhaps in fact you really would not leave it! Everything is here! What more could you ask for! But then, a trifle: your palace is encircled by a fence and you are told—it's all yours, enjoy yourself! Only you must not step from here! Well, you may rest assured that at this moment you will want to abandon your heaven and vault over the fence. What is more, all this luxury, all this comfort only serves to increase your suffering. You grow offended over just this luxury.[12]

The Palace—the great symbol of freedom—espouses a kind of heaven on earth but in the end becomes a prison when people are told a) they must enter, and b) that they must remain. In other words, freedom understood as bread and material well-being for everybody, i.e., as liberation from poverty and suffering, is a "lofty and beautiful" ideal, but it can harbor individuals if and only if we overlook the proximal character of freedom. Approximate freedom, by abstracting the individual, demands that individuals forego their proximate freedom. The Crystal Palace thus becomes a prison.[13] And it is in a pub called the Crystal Palace that Raskolnikov's abstract idea of freedom becomes a reality.

Dostoevsky's protest is not against the Crystal Palace and the alleviation of physical suffering *per se*, but against the expectation that humans must, because they are rational beings, accept that which the technological marvel symbolizes—the utopian world where the oppression of hunger, suffering, and poverty are abolished. He is rebelling against the doctrine that man, insofar as he is progressive and enlightened, must, because of abstract "laws of nature . . . behave according to the laws of reason and science."[14] For Dostoevsky, it is not abstract, unearthed, incorporeal, dislocated freedom that speaks most loudly to the human heart. There is, on the contrary, a kind of freedom that is contrary to "advantage." This freedom, prima facie, runs against one's advantage and interest. As Dostoevsky puts it, "Who has ever, in all these millennia, seen men acting solely for the sake of advantage?"[15] There is more to life than mere advantage. While it may be to our advantage to release humanity from the unfreedom of poverty, Raskolnikov is clever enough to realize that this is the basest of the rationalizations and might very well amount to little more than murder and robbery. He therefore has a more elaborate rendition of this theme.

Before he was forced to leave the university, Raskolnikov wrote an article called "On Crime." In this article he contends that the perpetration of a crime is always accompanied by an illness. This was an original idea, he is told by Porfiry, the Chief Inspector of the police, but not the most interesting part of his argument. The most interesting claim is that

> there are certain persons who can . . . that is, not precisely are able to, but have a perfect right to commit breaches of morality and crimes, and that the law is not for them . . . [A]ll men are divided into "ordinary" and "extraordinary." Ordinary men have to live in submission, have no right to transgress the law, because, don't you see, they are ordinary. But extraordinary men have a right to commit any crime and to transgress the law in any way, just because they are extraordinary (CP 262–263).

Raskolnikov admits that this is his argument, but completes the claim by adding that

> I don't contend that extraordinary people are always bound to commit breaches of morals, as you call it. In fact, I doubt whether such an argument could be published. I simply hinted that an "extraordinary" man has a right . . . that is not an official right, but an inner right to

decide in his own conscience to overstep . . . certain obstacles, and only in case it is essential for the practical fulfillment of his idea (sometimes of benefit to the whole of humanity) (CP 263).

His idea is elaborate, and he takes the time to explain it. He tells the inspector that if, for example, the discoveries of great men, such as Newton and Kepler, could not be made public because of the probability of persecution, these "extraordinary" men would have the right, or more accurately, be duty-bound "to *eliminate* the dozen or the hundred men for the sake of making his discoveries known to the whole of humanity" (CP 263). These extraordinary men would not have the right to murder and steal indiscriminately, but they would be free to transgress the ancient laws held sacred by the ordinary people. This, he says, has always been so—one need only look at the Lycurguses, Solons, Mahomets and Napoleons as examples of great men forced to shed blood to spread their new ideas. Raskolnikov continues:

> The crimes of these men are of course relative and varied; for the most part they seek in very varied ways the destruction of the present for the sake of the better [future]. But if such a one is forced for the sake of his idea to step over a corpse or wade through blood, he can, I maintain, find within himself, in his conscience, a sanction for wading through blood—that depends on the idea and its dimensions, note that. . . . The first category is always the man of the present, the second the man of the future (CP 264–265).

His theory, he assures his listeners, is not as dangerous as it sounds because the canaille seldom recognizes the extraordinary man's right to step over these obstacles and thus, in the rare instances an extraordinary figure appears on earth, he is more often than not hanged or beheaded.

Porfiry is the first to raise an objection to this idea. First he says a misunderstanding could arise from a member of the first category who incorrectly imagines himself to belong to the other category and thus begin eliminating varied obstacles. Second, he asks Raskolnikov, is it not somewhat disturbing to think that there might be a great many people who have this right to murder other people? Raskolnikov explains that, in the first case, it is a mistake that could only be made by one who is of the ordinary category, and given this, he would never get far. Such men may occasionally get carried away by their ideas and it may be necessary to administer a thrashing now and then, but usually such a thing would be superfluous because, being what they are, they will thrash themselves and "impose various public acts of penance upon themselves with a beautiful and edifying effect; in short, you've nothing to be uneasy about. . . . It's a law of nature" (CP 266).

This doctrine, even after the objections are made, does not satisfy Razumikhin. The argument is neither new nor proper. In fact, he says, it's a position that we've read and heard a thousand times already; but what is really *original* in all this, and is exclusively your own, to my horror, is that you sanction bloodshed *in the name of conscience,* and, excuse my saying so, with such fanaticism. . . . That, I take it, is the point of your article. But the sanction of bloodshed *by conscience* is to my mind . . . more terrible than the official, legal sanation of bloodshed (CP 267).

Dostoevsky's objection to Raskolnikov's idea lies in the fact that a human being, insofar as human beings are human, cannot possibly carry out such a plan without a troubled conscience, even only part of the way that Raskolnikov suggests an extraordinary man ought to go. Quite obviously, Dostoevsky is rejecting Nietzsche's idea of the *Übermensch,* or, as it is in Russian, the *chelovekobog*—the man-God. Above all, he is rejecting the desirability of any human being abstracting himself from his proximate world. For Raskolnikov's vision of freedom to come to fruition, he must cut himself off from the flock, so to speak. Dostoevsky's rejection of this idea is in the first place couched in theistic terms. To approximate oneself is to reject the organic whole that is the world given by God. For Dostoevsky, this is not merely a matter of one choice against another. Instead, rejecting the organic world bound up with Orthodox Christianity requires a wholly distinct consciousness. Ivanov describes this distinction well: faith in God and the rejection of God "are not simply two different conceptions of the world, but two essentially different worlds of the spirit, existing side by side, like an Earth and a counter-Earth, each fully living in its own orbit of activity."[16] Self-deification is thus the affirmation of absolute unhumanness; it denies man the ideal of the divine and of immortality. As Berdyaev understands this point in Dostoevsky's work, "to deny immortality is to deny the existence both of good and evil."[17] To subscribe to this kind of liberty is to remove oneself from the limited, the local, the proximate character of the human world. It is to reject one of the oldest insights about the human condition: It is not good for man to be alone.

Thus Raskolnikov's third rationalization is directly related to the aforementioned deification of man. While discussing "On Crime" and the idea of the extraordinary and ordinary man, Porfiry asks if, perhaps, because of "some worldly difficulties and hardship or for some service to humanity—to overstep obstacles? . . . For instance, to rob and murder?" (CP 269). The question contains the central idea against which Dostoevsky is arguing. The Russian for "to overstep" is *prestupat*. This is noteworthy because the word for crime is nearly the same: *prestupleniye*—an overstepping. Knowing this makes the statement that the extraordinary man has a right to "permit his conscience to *step over* certain obstacles" much more meaningful. If one has a conscience at all, then committing a crime must necessarily be done by *permitting* the conscience to ignore the moral considerations of one's actions; one must ignore the "humanness" of conscience. Indeed, to "step over" is to renounce human being and all that is associated with it, such as the possibility of error and limitations. In other words, to step over is in the first place a primordial act of pride, from the Christian point of view, or hubris is one's sympathies are more classical. In Dostoevsky's world, this pride is not only a stepping over, but a stepping out of proximal human relations. It is closing oneself off from the suffering of others; it is, as Kirilov in *The Possessed* demonstrates, not a divine ascension, but a bestial descent.[18]

Razumikhin recognizes this as the central point of the kind of freedom espoused by Raskolnikov. The problem is that it is incompatible with the very nature of human beings, and thus to achieve it people must strive "not to be themselves, to be as unlike themselves as they can. That's what they regard as the highest point of progress" (CP 202). Progress and approximate freedom, he is saying, are entangled with the idea of remaking man—remaking him such that he exceeds the sorry creature that God put on the earth. It aims to remake man such that he is sufficiently separated from others that he need not suffer their real, corporeal, pain. The murderer of God, armed with approximate freedom, steps over the obstacles or limits imposed by the conventional moral codes normally held near and dear. When God is murdered, the obstacle is removed. For Raskolnikov and a world possessed by this notion of freedom, the obstacle is proximal humanity; the solution is approximation.

PROXIMATE FREEDOM

If Raskolnikov is imprisoned in the Crystal Palace of approximate freedom, it is from Sonia that he might be brought back to proximate freedom. Late in the novel, after struggling with his conscience, Raskolnikov asks Sonia to engage in a thought experiment with him. He asks her, given that she is permitted to make a choice between the life of the debaucherous Luzhin and Mrs. Marmeladov, which of the two must die? The question is asked in such a way that there is no alternative—one of them must die. Her answer might well be Dostoevsky's first response to the arguments in favor of approximate freedom. She says:

> But I can't know Divine Providence. . . . And why do you ask what can't be answered? What's the use of such foolish questions? How could it happen that it should depend on my decision—who has made me a judge to decide who is to live and who is not to live? (CP 413)

Raskolnikov can only answer these questions insofar as holds himself to be an extraordinary man—a man abstracted from the rest of humanity. However, after Sonia's response Raskolnikov mutters, "Oh, if the Divine Providence is to be mixed up in it, there is no doing anything" (413). For Raskolnikov, however, God is *not* dragged into it. God is dead. The only question is whether or not Raskolnikov can will himself to step over the corpse; it is not a problem of whether making such a decision is permitted, but whether *he* is the one to step over the line. Wrestling with this problem, Raskolnikov admits that he "wanted to be a Napoleon" (CP 420). As he puts it in more detail:

> Power is only vouchsafed to the man who dares to stoop and pick it up. There is only one thing, one thing needful: one has only to dare! Then for the first time in my life an idea took shape in my mind which no one had ever thought of before me, no one! I saw clear as daylight how strange it is that not a single person living in this mad world has had the daring to go straight for it all and send it flying to the devil! I . . . I wanted *to have the daring* . . . and I killed her. I only wanted to have the daring, Sonia! That was the whole cause of it! (CP 423–424)

This admission is central for understanding Dostoevsky's idea of freedom. It demonstrates that Raskolnikov, by not dragging God into the question, is free to act on the dictum *"tout est permis."* He is free to make the decision Sonia refuses to make. As a man-God, he can decide who lives and who dies. Yet, for Dostoevsky, the freedom Raskolnikov gains from the abstract murder of God is nothing more than the freedom to step over (*prestupat*) and commit crimes (*prestupleniye*). The logical end of the Underground Man's "2+2=4" is therefore crime. Nothing more and nothing less. Freedom becomes tyranny, an old woman has a hatchet in her forehead, and the world is no closer to the abstract, universal freedom at which Raskolnikov's idea aims.

After the murder Raskolnikov recognizes the possibility of error. He confesses to Sonia:

> "I wanted to find out then and quickly whether I was a louse like everybody else or a man. Whether I can step over barriers or not, whether I dare stoop to pick up or not, whether I am a trembling creature or whether I have the *right* . . ."

> "To kill? Have the right to kill?" Sonia clasped her hands.

> "I want to prove one thing only, that the devil led me on then and he has shown me since that I had not the right to take that path, because I am just such a louse as all the rest" (CP 425).

This confession, however, stems not from the recognition that the idea is intrinsically wrong. Instead, Raskolnikov is merely concluding that the form was flawed—that he was not the one to step over. The error, he says, was that his act was not "picturesque, not aesthetically attractive" (CP 528) and later, about the other Napoleons, "those men succeeded and so *they were right*, and I didn't, and so I had no right to have taken that step" (CP 552).

For Dostoevsky, however, it is not the form that is being rejected— that hatchets in the forehead are too crude—but the very foundation of the *idea*. His objection, as is often the case in Dostoevsky's work, comes from the supposedly lowest members of the community: drunks, buffoons, lunatics. In *Crime and Punishment*, this voice is given to the prostitute, Sonia. Still thinking it to be a question of aesthetics, Raskolnikov asks her, "Haven't you done the same? You, too, have stepped over . . . have had the strength to step over—you have laid hands on yourself, you have destroyed a life . . . your own (it's all the same)" (CP 335). Sonia's prostitution, however, is not the same thing. She has freely given her *own* life for the sake of others. The murder of the old woman does not amount to the same thing as Sonia's sacrifice, which is an obvious allusion to Christ's sacrifice. For Dostoevsky, the kind of suffering and self-sacrifice demonstrated by Sonia are the very source of proximate freedom. By following in the footsteps of Christ—not by deciding who should live and die—but through every act of self-sacrifice, Sonia paves the way to proximate freedom. Similarly, Raskolnikov's sister says of her decision to marry Luzhin, "If I ruin any one, it is only myself. . . . I am not committing a murder" (235). She too is willing to give herself freely for the sake of others, but in this case, not with the grand scheme of freeing all mankind once and for all. There is nothing abstract, nothing approximate in her actions. She simply wants to help her mother and brother—people near and dear to her. From the vantage of the metaphysics of freedom, she is not free. Yet, her actions are freeing.

Dunya Raskolnikov's sacrifice, however, is somewhat different than Sonia's. Sonia has indeed damned herself, if not in the afterlife, then in the here and now. She is a pariah from the so-called proper circles, and people treat her with disdain. Despite this, she maintains the human relationships, based on love, between herself, her step-mother, her step-siblings, and in many ways, between herself and Raskolnikov. She is alienated but not alone. Her sacrifice parallels Christ's sacrifice in the scriptures, which is followed by resurrection. In Dostoevsky work, however, resurrection never follows *prestupleniye*. Instead, it is *nakazaniye*— punishment—that follows. Raskolnikov's crime is, first and foremost, an act of separating himself from humanity by attempting to become a *chelovekobog*. His punishment, among other more temporal things, is that he must live apart from the rest of humanity. He is imprisoned on a "square yard of space" to use his own words. Life on Earth becomes a living hell for Raskolnikov because, as a man-God, he has no place to go. He distances himself from his community by both committing the heinous crime, and more importantly in Dostoevsky's work, by his deification. There are no avenues or escapes—he is utterly alone in his world; alone in his world that, before the murder, he believed would become a heaven on Earth. He wanders aimlessly, both figuratively and spiritually, through the streets of Petersburg, and "a special form of misery had begun to oppress him of late. There was nothing poignant, nothing acute about it; but there was feeling of permanence, of eternity about it; it brought a foretaste of hopeless years of this cold leaden misery, a foretaste of an eternity 'on a square yard of space'" (CP 433). His approximation from the rest of humanity leaves him alone and unable to give or receive love from any of his fellow human beings. Rather than utopia, he has created hell.[19]

This sensation, however, has little effect on Raskolnikov. He continues to hold that his *idea* will be justified by some future good. The approximate freedom he offers all mankind outweighs his one little transgression, and if he discovers that he actually was not permitted to step over and has condemned his soul to eternal perdition, then it makes little difference because he is willing to accept this in the name of the higher good for the rest of humanity. This is one of the key notions that inspired Dostoevsky to write *Crime and Punishment* and most of his other post-Siberian novels. The belief that although he, Raskolnikov, may be damned, the murder can still be justified. Raskolnikov summarizes the misconstrued rationalization as follows: "The old woman was a mistake perhaps, but she is not what matters! The old woman was only an illness . . . I was in a hurry to step over. . . . I didn't kill a human being, but a principle! I killed the principle, but I didn't overstep, I stopped on this side" (CP 278–279). He refuses to acknowledge that he has committed a crime and continues to think that he is participating in a higher moral reality. Redemption is thus impossible for Raskolnikov and he accepts perdition as a martyr, which brings to mind Dostoevsky standing on the scaffold in 1849, waiting and willing to die for his commitment to approximate freedom. The real freedom, for Dostoevsky, appeared in the moment when he was spared.

As has been said, if resurrection does not follow *prestupleniya*, then punishment (*nakazaniya*) does. But Raskolnikov is willing to accept this, at least until he comes to understand what has been said to him at the outset of the novel by Marmeladov, Sonia's father. He is asked near the beginning, "Do you understand, sir, do you understand what it means when you have absolutely nowhere to turn? No, you don't understand yet. . . ." (CP 16). It is not until well after the murder that Raskolnikov can answer this. It means that he must exist in the temporal world, but he must exist as a human being in the human world completely detached from the rest of humanity. Whereas he thought that he would become a Napoleon, a great man, or even a man-God, with the ability to shape the world into some kind of Edenic existence for all mankind, in the end he merely committed a crime against the very people he thought he was freeing. It was, as the Russian in Dostoevsky would say, a violation against the people and a crime against Mother Russia herself.

It is for precisely this reason that Sonia tells Raskolnikov that to make peace with Mother Russia, the Russian people, and with himself, he must:

> Go at once, this very minute, stand at the cross-roads, bow down, first kiss the earth which you have defiled, and then bow down to all the world and say to all men aloud, "I am a murderer!" Then God will send you life again (CP 426).

For Sonia, the shining star of proximate freedom, it is only when Raskolnikov embraces what is most proximate, most embedded, most local, that he can be free. The murderer can re-enter the ranks of humanity if and only if he can accept the love that is freely offered to him by Sonia and by Mother Russia. But Raskolnikov cannot bring himself to do this because he refuses to recognize what it means to live on that "square yard of space." This is the irony of his actions as a liberator. He killed the old woman in the name of freedom but in doing so, has not only failed to provide a single individual with more freedom, but has also removed his own. It is the tragedy and paradox of approximate freedom.

IN THE CLEAR

The pathos of freedom lies precisely in the profound misunderstanding of two types of freedom—between a freedom that abstracts man from man and approximates decent human relations, and a freedom bound up with distinctly human moments of self-sacrifice and compassion. It is in these fleeting and rare moments that proximate freedom lets itself be seen. And this is the key to understanding Dostoevsky's vision of freedom. Proximate freedom is contingent. There is no universal and permanent presence of proximate freedom. Approximate freedom prescribes the appropriate distance between individuals, and between individuals and the governing power. There is no measure of proximate freedom. It simply happens. For Dostoevsky, this distinction was not something he discovered; instead, it happened to him.

Readers of Dostoevsky are familiar with his flirtation with socialist revolutionaries. Also well-known is that Dostoevsky, at the age of twenty-eight years, was put in the Peter and Paul Fortress to await his trial for "conspiring to conspire" with the Petrashevists. He was sentenced to death, there was a mock execution, and then a sentence of four years of penal servitude followed by service in the ranks. Through this ordeal, Dostoevsky held fast to what I have been calling the metaphysics of freedom. Even as he stood on the scaffold, stripped of his outer clothing (not to mention his dignity), having his death sentence read to him, the rifles raised, he held fast to the Western kind of freedom. Dostoevsky's rendition of the incident is telling. In all, twenty-one prisoners were sentenced to death. They were led to Semyonsky Square where a scaffold had been erected in the middle. On the scaffold they were arranged into two lines and, as Dostoevsky describes it:

> The sheriff made his appearance on the scaffold and read out the sentence of death which was to be executed then and there. Twenty times the fatal words were to be repeated: "Sentenced to be shot!" And so indelibly were the words graven into my memory that for years afterwards I would wake in the middle of the night fancying that I heard them being read.... At this moment the sun broke through the clouds, and I thought: "Impossible, they can't mean to kill us!" and I whispered these words to my nearest companion, but instead of answering he only pointed out to a line of coffins that stood near the scaffold, covered with a large cloth.[20]

The most remarkable thing about this mock execution is the fact that Dostoevsky stood on the scaffold unrepentant and ready to die a martyr's death for this understanding of freedom. In *Diary of a Writer* Dostoevsky writes:

> We Petrashevsky stood on the scaffold and heard our sentence without the slightest repentance . . . that the affair for which we were condemned, those concepts which governed our souls, seemed not only to us demanding penitence, but even somehow cleansing for us, a martyrdom, for which many would thank us. And this continued for a long time.[21]

How long this lasted is difficult to say, but Dostoevsky was nevertheless stripped of his factual freedom, put in irons and, along with Durov and Yastrzhembsky, dispatched on the first stage of the long transit to penal servitude in Siberia.[22]

It was not until well after the reprieve that the distinction between approximate and proximate freedom occurred to him—that he realized his Westernizing "freedom" closed him off from humanity. The experiences of his four years in Siberia are recorded in *Notes from the House of the Dead*, a quasi-autobiographical account thinly disguised as fiction. It was a difficult time for Dostoevsky, not least of all because—even as a nobleman in prison for a political crime—he was forced to live in cramped quarters with people from every walk of life, including a handful of other noblemen, and a myriad of criminals ranging from petty thieves to the criminally insane.

The most telling part of the prison experience arises from the fact that Dostoevsky was forced to live and associate with the *muzhiki*, the common peasants. There was an enormous divide between the gentry and the peasantry, and in a letter to his brother on April 22, 1854, he writes:

> Already in Tobol'sk I had got to know the prison-folk, and here in Omsk I settled down to live among them for four years. These folk are coarse, irritating and embittered. Their hatred towards the gentry exceeds all bounds, which is why they meet us, the nobility, with hostility and a malicious joy at our grief. They would have gobbled us up if they had had the chance. However, judge for yourself, how could one defend oneself, when you had to live, drink and eat, and sleep, with these

people for several years, and when you have no chance to complain at innumerable humiliations at every turn. "You nobles, you have iron beaks, you pecked us. To begin with the people were tormented by the master, but now you're worse than us, you want to be our brother...."[23]

The irony, of course, is that it was for the freedom of these people that Dostoevsky and his co-conspirators were conspiring. It was for the freedom of these people that he was sent to Siberia. On the scaffold, Dostoevsky considered himself to be their brother, to be dying a martyr's death so that these people too could enjoy what can only be described as an abstract freedom. In Siberia, however, he quickly discovered that something was amiss.

It was in the prison camp that Dostoevsky began the lessons of proximate freedom. It was there, he tells us, that he learned that "there is not much that our men of learning can teach the common people. I would even say the reverse: it is they who should take a few lessons from the common people."[24] One of the more poignant examples of these lessons in freedom occurred when one day the "common folk" gathered in the square of the prison to voice a complaint about the quality of the food they were being given. Dostoevsky (or the fictional name he had assigned himself in the quasi-fictional work, Aleksandr Petrovich) joined them in the lines, mistakenly thinking that there was an unannounced roll call. On this occasion, Kulikov, one of the common prisoners, took him by the arm, saying "This is no place for you" and escorted him from the ranks. He tells him, "We've our own private business to attend to here and it doesn't affect you. It'd be best if you go off somewhere and wait...."[25] Later, when questioning another convict as to why he was not permitted to take part in the complaint, to go forward with them as their companion, the bewildered convict replies, "But... what kind of companion could you ever be to us?"[26]

From this Dostoevsky came to the grim conclusion that not only did he not know these people and that he was not to be their companion, but it was never to be so. He says, "I realized that I should never be accepted by the men as their companion, not even if I were to be assigned to the special category.... You go your way and we'll go ours; you have your business to attend to and we have ours."[27] For Dostoevsky, this was a shocking revelation because it was for these people that he had conspired and been sent to Siberia. "The old, simplistic conclusions which he had derived from Speshnyov and Chernosvitov about the duty of the intelligentsia to inspire a revolution on behalf of the peasantry seemed to crumble."[28] Freedom, imported from the West, aimed at the abstract "poor folk," simply ceased to make sense.

Dostoevsky's account of this revelation is found in *The Diary of a Writer*. The tale goes as follows: On the occasion of the Orthodox Easter, there was much revelry and celebration in the prison camp. On rare occasions, such as these holidays, the prison officials turned a blind eye on certain infractions of the regulations, including drunkenness. On the second day of the Easter holiday on this particular year there were some fearful scenes in the barracks and Dostoevsky, unaccustomed to such vulgarity, went outside where he met a Polish gentleman, also a political prisoner, who growled, "Je haïs ces brigands!"[29] According to the diary, Dostoevsky immediately turned around and went back to the barracks he had recently fled, climbed on his bunk and pretended to be asleep. He did this often, because he was able to meditate uninterruptedly in this fashion, which were often of personal biographical reflections. On this occasion Dostoevsky began to reminisce about an incident that had occurred on his father's estate when he was a boy of nine years. He recalled thinking that he heard somebody cry out that a wolf was running in the woods in which he was walking. Alone and frightened, the boy ran into a nearby field where the peasant Marei was plowing and was comforted by his father's serf. Dostoevsky recounts his meditation as follows:

> The meeting was a solitary one, in a vacant field, and only God, maybe, perceived from above what a profound and enlightened human sentiment, what delicate, almost womanly, tenderness, may fill the heart of some coarse, bestially ignorant Russian peasant serf, who, in those days, had even had no forebodings about his freedom.... And when I climbed down off the boards and gazed around, I suddenly felt that I could behold these unfortunate men with a wholly different outlook, and, suddenly, by some miracle, all the hatred and anger completely vanished from my heart. I went along, gazing attentively at the faces which I encountered. This intoxicated, shaven and branded peasant with marks on his face, bawling his hoarse drunken song—why he may be the very same Marei; for I have no way of peering into his heart.[30]

And so Dostoevsky came to realize that he knew nothing about the people for whom he had once conspired in revolutionary politics. These people had not even the slightest notion of why he was in prison and did not understand the nature of his crime. It is right then, one might argue, that he caught a glimpse of proximate freedom. It is this moment that he gets a glimpse of the free-life that bonds a people together.

At this moment he came to realize that "the best and most outstanding characteristic of our common people is their sense of justice and their desire for it. The cockerel-like habit of always wanting to be first in every situation, and *at all costs*, and whether one is worthy of it or not—this is unknown among the common people."[31] To be first in every situation means to separate oneself from the pack. This, Dostoevsky realized then and there, is the preoccupation of the "men of learning" and the hallmark of the metaphysics of freedom. Freedom that separates, that makes divisions, that abstracts a man from his neighbor, is unthinkable by the "poor folk." Yet the man of learning pushes for this "at all costs." For the common folk, this cost is too high. The cost is one's community and one's humanity. For the poor folk, the cost of revolutionary politics—the very politics that landed Dostoevsky in Siberia—was, as he later discovered, a sin against the Russian people. The freedom he espied then and there freed him from the metaphysics of freedom. In seeing the connection between the poor folk, the bonds that link them together in their quotidienne struggles in life, Dostoevsky espied for the first time proximate freedom. Freedom, it turns out, is not a measure of interference or mastery, be it of oneself or by the state. Freedom is the moment one is freed of this freedom.

Much later in his life Dostoevsky created a character who makes a similar transformation—from a Westernizing intellectual bringing approximate freedom to Russia, to a man humbled by his experience with the justice of a Russian peasant. In *The Possessed*, Stepan Verkhovensky, near death, realizes that "a man who has no country has no God either. Rest assured that those who cease to understand the people of their own country and lose contact with them also lose the faith of their forefathers and become godless and indifferent."[32] These "godless" people are, of course, those who are indifferent to the real suffering of real people. These are the people who, armed with an abstract notion of freedom, can put a hatchet in an old woman's forehead. They are the revolutionary ideologues who claim to love the people, who want to incite nihilistic revolution on their behalf, but are so abstracted from the reality of their lived experiences that they can only do harm. They are the intellectuals who "don't know a damn thing about the Russian people," and it is "impossible to love something you know nothing about." And if they do purport to serve "the people," it is but an abstraction: "by people [they've] always understood the French people, and at that, only the people of Paris."[33] In the end, these intellectuals "are either despicable atheists or indifferent, vicious human muck."[34]

Dostoevsky, when much later asked by Averkiev whether he considered his sentence unjust (that is, detention in Siberia followed by service in the ranks), replied, "No, it was just, the people would have condemned us."[35] The real injustice is the imposition of a freedom that separates, that divides, that controls. The real injustice is approximate freedom.

NOTES

1. Nikolai Berdyaev, *Dostoevsky* (New York: Meridian Books, 1957), 67. This thought is echoed in what is perhaps the most comprehensive account of Dostoevsky's work by a contemporary political theorist: Dostoevsky, of course, was a consummate artist, but his art seems never to be merely art for art's sake. First and last he was passionately engaged in a no-holds-barred combat for existence in truth and free-

dom—insofar as man, being what he is, the world and society, being what they are, and God, being what He is, make this possible (Ellis Sandoz, *Political Apocalypse: A Study of Dostoevsky's Grand Inquisitor* (Baton Rouge: Louisiana State University Press, 1971), 80).

2. F. M. Dostoievsky, *The Diary of a Writer* (London: Cassell, 1949), see especially his recollection of the peasant Marei, p. 210. For more, see Joseph Frank, *Dostoevsky: A Writer in His Time* (Princeton: Princeton University Press, 2009), William Peter van den Bercken, *Christian Fiction and Religious Realism in the Novels of Dostoevsky* (London: Anthem Press, 2011); Steven Cassedy, *Dostoevsky's Religion* (Stanford: Stanford University Press, 2005); Richard L. Chapple, "A Catalogue of Suffering in the Works of Dostoevsky: His Christian Foundation," *The South Central Bulletin* 43 (1983); A. Boyce Gibson, *The Religion of Dostoevsky* (Philadelphia: Westminster, 1973); Konstantin Mochulsky, *Dostoevsky: His Life and Work,* (Princeton: Princeton University Press, 1967); Ellis Sandoz, *Political Apocalypse: A Study of Dostoevsky's Grand Inquisitor* (Wilmington, DE: ISI Books, 2000); David Walsh, "Dostoevsky's Discovery of the Christian Foundation of Politics," *Religion and Literature* 19 (1987).

3. Isaiah Berlin, "Two Kinds of Liberty" in *Four Essays on Liberty,* (Oxford: Oxford University Press, 1969). On the revival of republican liberty, see Quentin Skinner, *Liberty before Liberalism* (Cambridge: Cambridge University Press, 1998); "The Idea of Negative Liberty: Machiavellian and Modern Perspectives" in Quentin Skinner, *Visions of Politics* (Cambridge: Cambridge University Press, 2002); Quentin Skinner, "Freedom as the Absence of Arbitrary Power" in *Republicanism and Political Theory,* ed. Cécile Laborde and John Maynor (Oxford: Blackwell, 2008); Philip Pettit, *Republicanism: A Theory of Freedom and Government* (Oxford: Oxford University Press, 1997); Philip Pettit, *A Theory of Freedom: From the Psychology of the Politics of Agency* (Oxford: Oxford University Press, 2001); Philip Pettit, "Republican Freedom: Three Axioms, Four Theorems" in *Republicanism and Political Theory,* ed. Cécile Laborde and John Maynor (Oxford: Blackwell, 2008).

4. For more on Dostoevsky's involvement with the Petrashevsky Circle, see Frank, *Dostoevsky: A Writer in His Time,* 129–144 and A. S. Dolinin, "Dostoevsky among the Members of the Petrashevsky Circle," *Russian Studies in Literature* 23 (1987).

5. See Horacio Spector, "Four Conceptions of Freedom," *Political Theory* 38 (2010).

6. Martin Heidegger, *Introduction to Metaphysics* (New Haven: Yale University Press, 2000); Martin Heidegger, "What Is Metaphysics?" in *Basic Writings,* ed. David Farrell Krell (San Francisco: Harper, 1993); Martin Heidegger, "Overcoming Metaphysics" in *The Heidegger Controversy: A Critical Reader,* ed. Richard Wolin (Cambridge, MA: MIT Press, 1991); Martin Heidegger, "Phenomenology and Theology" in *Pathmarks,* ed. William McNeill (Cambridge: Cambridge University Press, 1998).

7. Michael S. Kochin, "How Bodies Read and Write: Dostoevsky's *Demons* and Coetzee's *Master of Petersburg,*" in this volume.

8. Fyodor Dostoevsky, *Crime and Punishment* (New York: P. F. Collier & Son Company, 1917), 65–66. Hereafter cited intext as *CP*. Minor changes to the translation have been made to bring the English closer to the Russian and more modern phrasing.

9. The Crystal Palace is mentioned in *Crime and Punishment* on five occasions: 135, 161, 169, 171, 194.

10. Robert Louis Jackson, *Dostoevsky's Underground Man in Russian Literature,* (The Hague: Mouton & Co., Printers, 1958), 23.

11. F. M. Dostoevsky, *Winter Notes on Summer Impressions* (London: Quartet Books, 1985).

12. A. S. Dolinin, "Nenapecatannye stranicy iz 'Zapisok iz mertvogo doma'. Tekst, istorija otryvka i pocemu on ne byl napecatan" in *Dostoevskij: stat'i i materialy,* ed. A.S. Dolinin (St. Petersburg: n.p., 1922), as cited in Jackson, *Dostoevsky's Underground Man in Russian Literature,* 22.

13. Dostoevsky's Underground Man recognizes this well. He mocks those adherents to approximate freedom, sarcastically saying to them: "And then (all this is being said by you) new economic relations will follow, ready made and also calculated with

mathematical precision, so that all possible questions will disappear in a single instant, since they will all have been provided with answers. And then the Crystal Palace will arise. Then. . . . Well, in short, halcyon days will arrive for mankind." F. M. Dostoevsky, *Notes from Underground* (New York: Bantam Books, 1992), 27.

14. Dostoevsky, *Notes from Underground*, 26.
15. Dostoevsky, *Notes from Underground*, 22.
16. V. I. Ivanov, *Freedom and the Tragic Life: A Study in Dostoevsky* (New York: Noonday Press, 1952), 5.
17. Berdyaev, *Dostoevsky*, 106.
18. For more on what I call Kirilov's Error, see Richard Avramenko, "Bedeviled by Boredom: A Voegelinian Reading of Dostoevsky's *Possessed*," *Humanitas* XVII (2004), 122–126.
19. One is here reminded of Father Zosima's words: "What is hell? . . . The suffering that comes from the consciousness that one is no longer able to love" (F. M. Dostoevsky, *The Brothers Karamazov* (New York: Penguin Books, 1958), 379–380). Further, "*those who love men in general* hate men in particular" (Dostoevsky, *The Notebooks for The Brothers Karamazov*, ed. and trans. Edward Wasiolek (Chicago & London: University of Chicago Press, 1971), 33; pp. 100, 188. Emphasis in original. As cited in Ellis Sandoz, "Philosophical Dimensions of Dostoevsky's Politics," *Journal of Politics* 40 (1978), 669.
20. J. A. T. Lloyd, *Fyodor Dostoevsky* (Brooklyn: Haskell House Publishers Ltd., 1976), 35.
21. Fyodor Dostoyevsky, *The Diary of a Writer* (New York: C. Scribner's Sons, 1949), 195.
22. For a detailed account of this ordeal see Stephen K. Carter, *The Political and Social Thought of F. M. Dostoevsky* (New York: Garland Publishing, Inc., 1991), 62–63.
23. As cited in Carter, *The Political and Social Thought of F. M. Dostoevsky*, 64.
24. Fyodor Dostoyevsky, *The House of the Dead* (London: Penguin Classics, 1985), 191.
25. Dostoyevsky, *The House of the Dead*, 314.
26. Dostoyevsky, *The House of the Dead*, 314.
27. Dostoyevsky, *The House of the Dead*, 320–321.
28. Dostoyevsky, *The House of the Dead*, 321.
29. Dostoyevsky, *The Diary of a Writer*, 206.
30. Dostoyevsky, *The Diary of a Writer*, 210.
31. Dostoyevsky, *The House of the Dead*, 191.
32. Fyodor Dostoyevsky, *The Possessed* (New York: New American Library, 1962), 40.
33. Dostoyevsky, *The Possessed*, 40.
34. Dostoyevsky, *The Possessed*, 40. For more on Verkhovensky and the experience with the peasant woman, see "Dostoevsky's Heroines," in this volume.
35. Konstantin Mochulsky, *Dostoevsky: His Life and Work* (Princeton: Princeton University Press, 1967), 196.

III

Dostoevsky and the Modern Hermeneutic

NINE

Speaking on the Lower Frequencies

Notes from Underground *in Ralph Ellison's America*

Steven D. Ealy

There are many studies of Fyodor Dostoevsky's work that focus on the historical origins of his fiction and on his foils that could be understood as the "efficient causes" of these writings. This essay looks forward, rather than backward, and relates one of Dostoevsky's novels, *Notes from Underground*, to a major work that it helped inspire, Ralph Ellison's *Invisible Man*.[1] Specifically I will examine and compare the narrators of *Notes from Underground* and *Invisible Man*, especially their views of the challenges they confront with regard to human freedom. I will argue that, whatever the similarities between the two—they are both, at least figuratively, underground and invisible—the crucial difference in their view of liberty dooms Underground Man to remain hidden away in his corner but allows Invisible Man the possibility of returning to the social world and resuming a life of social interaction.

The central difference between *Notes from Underground* and *Invisible Man* lies in the relationship of the authors to their narrators. Within the pages of *Invisible Man* Ralph Ellison's voice is never heard, he never speaks over his nameless narrator, so from the reader's perspective the entire story is told by Invisible Man. There is, so to speak, no literary distance between Ellison and his protagonist. Although on other occasions Ellison distances himself from his narrator, within the confines of the novel he never does. Dostoevsky, however, immediately distances himself from his narrator by appending a footnote to the title of the novel's first part, "Underground." In this note Dostoevsky explains that "the author of the diary and the diary itself are, of course, imaginary" (NU 50). In what follows, I will argue that the relationship the authors have with their narrators mirrors the relationship the narrators have with their respective communities. Thus, whereas there is a kind of connection between Ellison and Invisible Man, there is also a connection between Invisible Man and his community—and it is this connection that forms the basis of Ellison's understanding of liberty. Dostoevsky, who begins and ends *Notes from Underground* with an explicit statement of disconnection, sees disconnection as the greatest hindrance to liberty for the Russian people. The Underground Man's disconnect with the Russian people, the *muzhiki*, leaves him alone, in his corner with nothing for company except the abstract principle of liberty he has imported from the West.

THE UNIVERSAL AND AHISTORICAL UNDERGROUND MAN

Underground Man is at war with the world, especially with the world of ideas that shaped the worldview and attitudes of his society. His first words to his reader, and it is unclear whether he intends his reader to be only himself or someone other than himself, are, "I am a sick man . . . I am a spiteful man" (NU 50). He also writes that he is "sufficiently educated not to be superstitious" but that he *is* superstitious anyway (NU 50). Joseph Frank calls him "a well-trained member of the intelligentsia," and throughout we find evidence of his reading in Western philosophy and science with allusions to or quotations from Rousseau, Marx, Darwin, and Mill.[2] We also find references to the Crystal Palace at London's Great Exhibition of 1851 (NU 68, 77, 78) that suggests he has either traveled outside Russia or read about events in other parts of the world. He is, in short, a cosmopolitan man, in touch with and participating in a universal history beyond the parochial boundaries of his native Russia.

Underground Man provides two selections from his *Notes*. The second selection, "Apropos of the Wet Snow," contains three vignettes, one relating to an affair of honor, the second about his relations with former classmates, and a third dealing with his treatment of a young prostitute recently arrived in St. Petersburg from Riga, all of which illustrate the "gloomy, ill-regulated, and solitary" (NU 81) life of the narrator at twenty-four. The first, "Underground," was written some sixteen years after the incidents presented in the second section, and provides the theoretical reflections at the heart of the narrator's world-view and life choices. In this essay I focus on "Underground" rather than his revealing and ultimately self-condemnatory reminiscences, although they will not be totally ignored. Underground Man's "mature" views are based not only on his wide reading, but also on his reflections on his earlier actions. Nevertheless, at the heart of Underground Man's withdrawal from the world into his corner is his inability to reconcile his particular actions and circumstances with his understanding of the so-called universal conditions of human existence that he learned in school. In short, although Underground Man is concerned with questions of his particular individuality and freedom, striking at the heart of these is the "intelligent" world of universalizing and heterogenizing contemporary science and Western culture.

By his own account, Underground Man is "characterless" because every "man in the nineteenth century must and morally ought to be preeminently a characterless creature" (NU 52). The alternative is to be "a man of character," which is to say, "an active man," which is to say, "fools and worthless fellows" (NU 52). The intelligent and characterless man is one of universals, while the man of character and action is "a limited creature." He is limited in that he is tied to the specifics of his time and of his place. The man of action is merely a historical man. The intelligent and characterless man is conscious—especially self-conscious. This self-consciousness lies at the heart of his inaction, or inability to act. While the man of action inevitably encounters a wall, the self-conscious man seems to be caught within a box, the box of modern science. Thus, the ultimate problem for Underground Man appears to be the stifling effect of the "laws of nature, the deductions of natural science, mathematics" (NU 58). Once aware of these laws of nature, the Underground Man argues, the conscious man must live by them; once living by these laws, he becomes a determined man. He is "determined" not in the sense of marshalling one's resources to achieve certain goals, but rather as one whose actions are the result of conditions beyond one's control. After all, as Underground Man cogently argues and concludes, "you have to just accept it, there is no help for it, for twice two is a law of mathematics. Just try refuting it" (NU 58).

This logic, however, does not always sit well with Underground Man. In conversation with himself, he wonders what will happen if the result, i.e., of two times two equals four, is not to my liking. His imagined interlocutors, proponents of scientific rationality, respond, "It is no use protesting; it is a case of twice two makes four! Nature does not ask your permission, she has nothing to do with your wishes, and whether your like her laws or dislike them, you are bound to accept her as she is, and consequently all her conclusions" (NU 58). The seamless linkage in Underground Man's mind appears to move from mathematics to the conclusions of natural science to the laws of nature. All of these are beyond man's ability to control or bend to his will, and thus in reality actually control man. In Underground Man's mind, once the premises are established, a rational, conscious man has no alternative but to accept the conclusions. Just as it makes no sense to argue against the mathematical statement that two times two is four, neither does it make sense to argue against the implications of the view that man "descended from a monkey" (NU 58), once that has been proven.

What are the conditions under which statements like "twice two makes four" or "you descended from a monkey" are proven, or are taken to be proven? The narrator of *Notes from Underground* does not deal with the ultimate foundations of such proof, but investigates (and is caught up in) the implications, especially the psychological implications, of accepting the view that scientific proof can settle the questions of determinism and thus ultimately, questions of human freedom. Underground Man appears to accept a basic equivalence between mathematical statements, statements of "the laws of nature," and statements of scientific theories. Further, Underground Man appears to hold the view that once these premises are accepted, certain conclusions inevitably follow, and that one of the conclusions that follow from this scientific perspective is that free will is an illusion. The tension between Underground Man's acceptance of this model of scientific determinism at the self-conscious "rational" level and his simultaneous "wicked" or spiteful resistance to the implications of this model for his own life is the source of his dissatisfaction and is the impetus that leads to his erratic behavior and ultimate withdrawal into his corner. Joseph Frank captures this dynamic in his analysis of *Notes from Underground*:

> As a well-trained member of the intelligentsia, the underground man intellectually accepts such determinism; it is impossible for him really to live with its conclusions. . . . Reason tells the underground man that guilt or indignation is totally irrational and meaningless, but conscience and a sense of dignity continue to exist all the same as ineradicable components of the human psyche.[3]

The inner tension of Underground Man then is the tension between his "rational" acceptance of a scientific view of man—a view that reduces him to a creature totally determined by stimulus-response mechanisms, as are other animals—and his irrational inability to give up concern for human morality, dignity, and freedom, which his scientific position seems to demand. This tension lies at the heart of Dostoevsky's battle with modernity in general, and the West in particular.

This tension within Underground Man is symbolized by his admission that throughout his life he has been "offended" by the laws of nature (NU 61). He also attributes his inability to act to his understanding of scientific causality. Perhaps following the example of Descartes, Underground Man concludes that before action can be taken all doubt must be eliminated (NU 62), that is, one must have a clear understanding of the primary and secondary causes of action. From his perspective, men of action are able to act only because they are "stupid and limited" which allows them to "take immediate and secondary causes for primary ones" (NU 62). Therefore, they are able to act simply because they do not understand the real foundations of their actions; they are self-deceived. The intelligent and conscious individual, however, is prevented from acting because he realizes he does not, and perhaps on principle cannot, remove all doubt. When Underground Man prepares to act he discovers that he is caught in an interminable search for the ultimate cause of the action he plans to take: "with me every primary cause at once draws after itself another still more primary, and so on to infinity" (NU 62). He concludes that this potentially eternal regress in search of the ultimate cause is "the essence of every sort of consciousness and reflection" (NU 62). This provides another reason why, from Underground Man's perspective, the active man is limited, lacking both consciousness or self-consciousness and thoughtfulness.

Underground Man is concerned not just with the laws of mathematics and natural sciences, not just with the science that might explain the origins of the human species, but also with the laws established by what today would be called the social sciences, especially the science of economics. His discussion of economics begins with allusions to Rousseau and Marx, and a nod toward Aristotle, as he considers man's real interests, real profits, and the good. What, he asks, is profit, and how is it determined? The heart of economics, as he sees it practiced, is once again mathematics, as economics has taken its "whole register of human advantages from the averages of statistical figures and politico-economic formulas" (NU 65). Against this economic approach, however, Underground Man argues there is a "strange advantage [that] does not fall under any classification and is not in place in any list" (NU 65), and that this missing something is man's "most advantageous advantage" (NU 66).[4] Underground Man's imagined interlocutor responds that science (at this point expanded to include economic science) "will teach man . . . that he never really had any caprice or will of his own, and that he himself is something of the nature of a piano key or the stop of an organ, and that there are besides, things called the laws of nature; so that everything he does is not done by his willing it, but done if itself, by the laws of nature" (NU 68). Once these laws are discovered, "man will no longer have to answer for his actions and life will become exceedingly easy for him" (NU 68). That is, an understanding of the laws of nature entails the destruction of human responsibility and accountability.

Only one thing stands in the way of the "extremely easy" life of irresponsibility and determinism, and that is the item neglected in all scientific economic calculations, man's most profitable profit. Underground Man finally identifies this missing element as "one's own free unfettered choice, one's own caprice . . . [this] is that very 'most advantageous advantage'" (NU 69). This free will, according to Underground Man, explodes all systems based on the laws of nature, and at the same time "it preserves for us what is most precious and most important—that is, our personality, or individuality" (NU 71). In other words, Underground Man wants to affirm human freedom, but must combat reductionist science to do so. He challenges the economic approach that finds it profitable for man to pursue "his real normal interests guaranteed by the conclusions of reason and arithmetic" (NU 74). He asks us to expand our horizon when thinking of the pursuit of natural advantages. As he puts it, "it may be the law of logic, but not the law of humanity" (NU 74). This view can be linked to his concern with human personality and individuality, and with his observation that man desires to create and loves destruction. One might even argue that if man is prevented from extending his individuality in creative directions, he will extend it through destruction. This is why free will is ultimately destructive to all deterministic systems.

While Underground Man wants to affirm human freedom, however, he is so caught in the worldview of modern science that he seems incapable of affirming his freedom through his own free actions. Rather, he is able only to withdraw from the world and stew in his own wickedness and spitefulness while crouching in his corner. His rational attachment to science and the laws of nature seem to block him for creative action, and his irrational commitment to human freedom seems to channel him into only destructive paths—destructive of himself and those he interacts with. Within the world presented to us by Underground Man, there seems to be no possibility that he will be able to break out of the intellectual traps he has set for himself and be able to live a free and open life.

THE HISTORICAL AND PARTICULAR INVISIBLE MAN

Ralph Ellison wrote *Invisible Man* with Dostoevsky's *Notes from Underground* in mind. Joseph Frank argues that "*Invisible Man* is more an extrapolation that an imitation of *Notes from Underground*."[5] Frank goes too far with this claim, however. Both works examine common themes, but the narrators' approaches to and resolutions of the problems they confront illustrate crucial differences between the American and Russian mind. Underground Man has trapped himself in his corner by embracing irreconcilable intellectual and ideological positions. Invisible Man, however, is driven underground by historical problems he must resolve. These problems begin with his family history, but must be expanded to include an understanding of the American experience if he is ever to escape his self-imposed exile in an urban cave. Ralph Ellison himself provides the best starting place for understanding the relationship between these two works. In his introduction to the thirtieth anniversary edition of *Invisible Man* he described the narrator of his novel as someone young, powerless, and ambitious but was doomed for failure: "I associated him, ever so distantly, with the narrator of Dostoevsky's *Notes from Underground*" (IM xix).

Near the opening of *Invisible Man* an incident occurs that brings the narrators of these two novels into comparison. In the prologue Invisible

Man recalls an encounter one evening when he bumped into a white man who then uttered a racial slur. Invisible Man grabbed him and demanded an apology.

> . . . I yelled, "Apologize! Apologize!" But he continued to curse and struggle, and I butted him again and again until he went down heavily, on his knees, profusely bleeding. . . . Oh, yes, I kicked him! And in my outrage I got out my knife and prepared to slit his throat, right there beneath the lamplight in the deserted street, holding him in the collar with one hand, and opening the knife with my teeth—when it occurred to me that the man had not *seen* me, actually; that he, as far as he knew, was in the midst of a walking nightmare! And I stopped the blade, slicing the air as I pushed him away, letting him fall back to the street (IM 4).

The parallel with *Notes from Underground* is clear; Ellison is playing with Underground Man's confrontation with the unnamed officer and his inability to act.

Underground Man's confrontation is recounted in the first section of "Apropos of the Wet Snow," which is a series of reflections on incidents from a decade and a half earlier. As a young man of twenty-four, Underground Man had lived a fairly solitary life, but would occasionally wander the city at night pursuing vices (NU 86). On one of his solitary promenades he observed a fight through a pool hall window, and he entered the hall in the hope of getting into a fight himself. He was unable to instigate a fight, but felt humiliated by what did occur, and eventually left to lick his wounded self-image and brood. He describes the event, or non-event, as an encounter with someone who didn't even recognize his existence.

> An officer put me in my place from the first moment. I was standing by the billiard-table and in my ignorance blocking up the way, and he wanted to pass; he took me by the shoulders and without a word—without a warning or explanation—moved me from where I was standing to another spot and passed by as though he had not noticed me. I could have forgiven blows, but I could not forgive his having moved me without noticing me (NU 87).

In Underground Man's mind, he had been insulted by this officer and resolved that he had to settle a point of honor with him (NU 88). He started noticing this officer every time he saw him on the street, and with each sighting his anger and spite seemed to grow. Eventually he began to follow the officer and gather information on him—his name, his address. For two years he gathered his information, and then decided to write the officer—who still didn't even know he existed—a letter in order to bring their "confrontation" to a head, but after writing the letter he was unable to mail it.

Underground Man finally decides to force a confrontation in a public park by intentionally bumping into the officer. His first efforts at this were unsuccessful, for at the last minute he himself would swerve to avoid a collision. Finally, however, he resolves that he must bump shoulders with him by deliberately not stepping aside, and perhaps even giving the officer a shove. "This audacious idea took such a hold on me that it gave me no peace. I was dreaming of it continually, horribly, and I purposely went more frequently to the Nevsky in order to picture more vividly how I should do it when I did do it. I was delighted. This intention seemed to me more and more practical and possible" (NU 90). For the anticipated occasion he purchased new clothes, bought with an advance on his salary, but still he continued to swerve out of the officer's way.

Despairing of success, he finally decided to give up his plan, and visited the park for one last time just to acknowledge his defeat. "Suddenly, three paces from my enemy, I unexpectedly made up my mind—I closed my eyes, and we ran full tilt, shoulder to shoulder, against one another! I did not budge an inch and passed him on a perfectly equal footing! He did not even look round and pretended not to notice it; by he was only pretending, I am convinced of that" (NU 92). While he thought he had taken a worse beating than his "enemy" because he was smaller, he also felt vindicated by the encounter because he had "kept up his dignity . . . and returned home feeling that I was fully avenged for everything" (NU 92). His ecstasy did not last long, however, for within a few days he withdrew into his corner permanently. Even his measly little debauches come to an end. His world is now totally interior, and he appears to be capable of only imagined social contact. Thus while both narrators are invisible, Underground Man, when he finally finds the nerve to act—to take control of both the events of his life and to assert his place in the world—remains invisible. The thrashing Invisible Man hands out after his own bumping incident is simply not available to the sickly, rational and cosmopolitan Underground Man.

This is not to say that Invisible Man is engaged in a purely physical confrontation with his invisibility. Rather, he appears to be nimble enough of mind. He can act in any situation in which he finds himself, and he seems to have especial facility for communicating with crowds. Like Underground Man, Invisible Man's confrontation with his lack of freedom is motivated by a drive to solve a puzzle. Where Underground Man's puzzle is theoretical or philosophical, the Invisible Man's is historical. Invisible Man's puzzle begins with his family history, but can only be resolved by placing this personal history within the context of the larger American history; he must resolve puzzles at both personal and national levels simultaneously. Invisible Man's grandparents had both been born into slavery in the American South, and both were emancipated at the conclusion of the Civil War. On the one hand his grandfather seemed to revel in his freedom, but on the other he appeared to be a docile and law-abiding black man until the end of his life. On his deathbed, however, Grandfather scandalized his very conventional son by claiming that his entire life since emancipation had been one of deception. Living a life of meekness but subservience to white people, the grandfather believes he has lived a life of treachery to the black race (IM 16). The grandfather then gives his son instructions which he steadfastly ignores, but which presents Invisible Man with the puzzle that goaded him through the entire novel: "Live with your head in the lion's mouth. I want you to overcome 'em with yeses, undermine 'em with grins, agree 'em to death and destruction, let 'em swoller you till they vomit or bust wide open" (IM 16). The young grandson could not reconcile his grandfather's outwardly conventional and docile life with the radicalism of his deathbed confession and issuance of marching orders for his son and grandchildren. His last words were, "Learn it to the younguns" (IM 16). As Invisible Man recounts his life—graduation from high school, attending college, moving to New York City and finding employment, and finally escaping underground into an abandoned and forgotten coal cellar to avoid the chaos on the city's streets—he is haunted and driven by the puzzle of his grandfather's deathbed oration. In short, the struggle—the paradox of his freedom—is historical.

The depth of this historical struggle pervades the whole story. The beating of the white man discussed above is emblematic, but examples like this recur throughout the novel. The various events he recounts through the course of *Invisible Man* all originate in the inability or unwillingness of others to extricate him from his (personal and social) history and to see him in his own particular freedom. Whether his antagonists or allies are black or white seems to make no difference; everyone sees him in terms of historical and racial stereotypes rather than as an individual living his own life. The cause of Invisible Man's invisibility is not his lack of character, not his lack of physical or intellectual power, but the historical blindness that prevents them from seeing his presence clearly. Examination of three scenes from the novel illustrates this point well.

As a high school senior Invisible Man delivered the valedictory address at his graduation, and he was invited to give a speech to the town's white elite (IM 17). Rather than being honored for his excellence as a student, however, Invisible Man is subjected to the ignominy of having to participate in a fight among a group of young black toughs for the entertainment of the while elite and the ridicule of these community leaders. He is finally allowed to deliver his speech, which mirrored the words of Booker T. Washington's famous Atlanta Exposition Address (IM 29–30). The rowdy group of white men jeered and joked during his talk until he misspoke and uttered the words "social equality" rather than the intended "social responsibility." At this point the crowd became deathly quiet and intently menacing (IM 31). After correcting himself and convincing the now suspicious group that his misstatement was an accident and not a small rebellion, he finished the speech. At its conclusion the School Superintendent praised him as a good and smart boy (IM 32). He is given two prizes, a calfskin briefcase which he carries with him to the end of the novel, and a scholarship to the state college for negroes.

When Invisible Man arrives at the college, he is selected to be one of the student drivers responsible for guiding the college's white trustees on their visits to campus. One such assignment during his junior year led to disaster. Through a series of missteps Invisible Man first introduced a trustee to a black farmer whose incestuous relationship with his daughter had led to an illegitimate child, and is an embarrassment to the college (IM 46–68). He then entangled the trustee in a bar fight, during which the trustee is injured (IM 89–99). The Invisible Man is expelled from the college and decides that, rather than returning home in disgrace, he will move to New York City to pursue a career.

The third example takes place in New York. After an accident costs him his job, he is befriended by Mary Rambo, who offers him a room in her home until he can get back on his feet. In an early discussion he tells her that he had come to the city to earn enough money to return to college, and she asks what he wants to do with his life. He admits that at one time he had wanted to be an educator, but was having second thoughts (IM 254–55).

Even Mary Rambo, who is supportive and caring, fails to see Invisible Man in his historical particularity, but as a type: "You got to lead and you got to fight and move us all on up a little higher" (IM 255). Mary sees Invisible Man in terms of her plans, as benign as those plans might appear, rather than as an individual seeking his way. His life is inextricable from his history—a history that seems to precede him wherever he goes.

As such, every step that Invisible Man takes has a dual impetus. First, he is continually reflecting on and being goaded by his grandfather's puzzling deathbed statement. At each crisis point, he dreams of his grandfather, whose aim always appears to be to "Keep This Nigger-Boy Running" (IM 33, 147, 573). Second, each of his hopeful steps is undercut by either outright betrayal or by the attempt of someone he mistakenly takes to be a friend concerned with his welfare to simply use him to further their own purposes. So by the end of his long narrative he has no safe haven. He reflects,

> . . . I realized that I couldn't return to Mary's, or to any part of my old life. I could approach it only from the outside, and I had been as invisible to Mary as I had been to the Brotherhood. No, I couldn't return to Mary's, or to the campus, or to the Brotherhood, or home. I could only move ahead, or stay here, underground (IM 571).

His history inhibits his present, it prevents him from having a future. Thus, just as Underground Man withdraws into his corner, Invisible Man literally goes underground, finding shelter in a long deserted coal cellar (IM 565–66, 572). As each of their narratives comes to an end, they seem far removed from the world around, and appear to be reduced to talking to themselves or writing for themselves.

Underground Man ultimately is unable to break out of the paralysis created by his rational acceptance of science and the deterministic laws of nature that rob man of his freedom and his irrational commitment to free will and human creativity. Near the end of "Underground," Underground Man attempts to explain why, since his *Notes* are not intended for an external public, he doesn't "simply recall these incidents in my own mind without putting them on paper?" (NU 80) His response shows how totally internalized his world has become—writing is more imposing than merely thinking, writing of his wickedness provides a harsher self-judgment, he can concentrate on style, and it provides a relief from the stress and boredom of his solitary existence. *Notes from Underground* ends with no hope that Underground Man will come out of his corner and attempt to begin living an active and productive life. The narrator's tale ends abruptly, in mid-sentence, when the true author of the novel, Fyodor Dostoevsky, seems to tire of his creation's droning on that he will write no more. Dostoevsky ensures that Underground Man will write no more by assuring his readers that, in spite of his promise, "the Notes of this paradoxalist do not end here" but that in Dostoevsky's judgment "but it seems to us that we may stop here" (NU 155).

Invisible Man, in contrast to Dostoevsky's protagonist, has at least found a haven in his urban cave, and he makes productive use of his sheltered time (IM 571). So here Invisible Man spends his time working out the historically determining puzzle his grandfather left him. He acknowledges he is still haunted by his deathbed advice (IM 574), but then begins to unravel his grandfather's paradox by reflecting on the dynamics of American history. He considers the possibility that the foundational principle of the American experience was greater than the vicious power exercised by its slaveholders through its early history (IM 574). But then he moves beyond his initial view and wonders whether everyone had to take responsibility for everything because they are the heirs of it (IM 574). And finally, he pushes beyond even this view to one reflecting not merely a connection of historical happenstance but of deep human interdependence (IM 574).

As Invisible Man meditates on the meaning of his grandfather's words for understanding something of the American experience, he also comes to the recognition that his grandfather, who had haunted his dreams for years, had perhaps found the secret to living a free life not driven by a desire for conformity, and he expresses the hope that his newfound knowledge humanizes him (IM 580). Unlike Underground Man who is forever stuck in his corner, Invisible Man prepares to return to the world as the novel comes to an end. On the very first pages of his story he said that he was hibernating (IM 6), but on the novel's penultimate page he announces that this hibernation is over (IM 580). He affirms the possibility of action and the importance of resisting conformity—of becoming the man of action so maligned by Dostoevsky's Underground Man (IM 577). He is finally ready to emerge from his hole, because he has come to think that there is even the possibility for the invisible man to play a socially responsible role (IM 581).

HISTORICAL AND PARTICULAR LIBERTY

I have already noted that within the frameworks established by Ellison and Dostoevsky, each stands in a different relationship to their novel's narrator. Ellison never speaks in his own voice in the pages of *Invisible Man*, although he does write about the novel elsewhere. Dostoevsky, on the other hand, explicitly distances himself from his narrator on both the first and last pages of *Notes from Underground*—it seems clear that we are not to mistake the narrator's voice for Dostoevsky's own. On the contrary, the note at the beginning of "Underground" suggests that we take the narrator as an ideal type, as the sort of person found in contemporary Russia: "He is one representative of a generation still living" (NU 50). Dostoevsky maintains that "such persons as the writer of these Notes not only may, but positively must exist in our society" (NU 50). By the end of the novel, Dostoevsky himself seems to have wearied of his protagonist's ranting, for he himself intervenes in mid-sentence to bring the novel to a close.

Are we to take Dostoevsky's less-than-gentle treatment of his narrator as his ultimate critique of Underground Man's arguments and concerns? Such a conclusion may be more tenuous that it appears at first glance. The most direct way to approach the question is to compare Dostoevsky's own notes in *Winter Notes on Summer Impressions* with Underground Man's notes.[6] *Winter Notes on Summer Impressions* was written just a few years before *Notes from Underground*. This book is an account of his 1862 tour of Europe, a tour that included stops in Berlin, Dresden, Cologne, Paris, Lucerne, Geneva, Florence, Vienna, and, most importantly, London. *Winter Notes*, however, is more than a mere travelogue; it is a spiritual diary in which Dostoevsky reflects on the relationship to Russia to Europe, the impact and importance of the encounter of these civilizations on the Russian soul. In short, *Winter Notes* is not only replete with Dostoevsky's musings on precisely the pathologies that beset Underground Man, it is also similar in tone.[7] I will not provide a detailed study of *Winter Notes* here, but will highlight a few of the similarities of theme between it and *Notes from Underground*.

First, Dostoevsky is concerned with the impact of European civilization on Russia (WN 20). The impact of this European gate-crashing was, unhappily, clear. As Dostoevksy puts it,

> Everything, literally almost everything we can show which may be called progress, science, art, citizenship, humanity, everything, everything stems from there, from that land of holy miracles. The whole of our life, from earliest childhood, is shaped by the European mould. Could any one of us have withstood this influence, appeal, pressure? How is it that we have still not been finally metamorphosed into Europeans? (WN 13)

Clearly, Dostoevsky is not enamored of the so-called progress of the Europeans. If we bear in mind the Great Schism—the Orthodox break from the Latin church, the derisive, and perhaps dismissive, evaluation of the value of Europe for Russia is clear. The reference to the land of holy miracles is an obvious sarcasm.

The tour of Europe also provided Dostoevsky with one his most powerful symbols: the Crystal Palace. In one of his imagined dialogues with his opponents, Underground Man says, "You believe in a palace of crystal that can never be destroyed" (NU 76). The Crystal Palace was the renowned centerpiece of the Great London Exposition of 1851. While in London, Dostoevsky visited this site, which had been incorporated into London's second World's Fair. His evaluation of London and its fair is captured in the title he gives to the chapter detailing the English leg of his tour: Baal. Baal, of course, is the false god of the Old Testament; Baal was fought by Gideon,[8] Elijah,[9] Jehu,[10] and Jeremiah.[11] Dostoevsky's description of the Crystal Palace/Baal is worth quoting:

> The Exhibition is indeed amazing. You feel the terrible force which has brought these innumerable people, who had come from the ends of the earth, all together in one fold; you realize the grandeur of the idea; you feel that something has been achieved here, that here is victory and triumph. And you feel nervous. However great your independence of mind, a feeling of fear somehow creeps over you. Can this, you think, in fact be the final accomplishment of an ideal state of things? Is this the end, by any chance? Perhaps this really is the "one fold"?[12] Perhaps we shall really have to accept this as the whole truth and cease from all movement thereafter? It is all so solemn, triumphant and proud that you are left breathless. You look at those hundreds of thousands, at those millions of people obediently trooping into this place from all parts of the earth—people who have come with only one thought, quietly, stubbornly and silently milling round in this colossal palace; and you feel that something final has been accomplished here—accomplished and completed. It is a biblical sight, something to do with Babylon, some prophecy out of the Apocalypse being fulfilled before your very eyes. You feel that a rich and ancient tradition of denial and protest is needed in order not to yield, not to succumb to impression,

not to bow down in worship of fact, and not to idolize Baal, that is, not to take the actual fact for the ideal (WN 50–51).

Clearly, for Dostoevsky, the Crystal Palace is a vivid and material representation of a society built on mathematics and the scientific laws of nature. It is precisely the kind of world that besets the Underground Man. While he holds himself to be a "man of intelligence," at the same time he declares, unsurprisingly, "I have just rejected the palace of crystal" (NU 77) because what we are likely to find will be a chicken coop rather than a palace (NU 77).

Another similarity between *Notes from Underground* and *Winter Notes* is the use of imagined dialogues between narrator and interlocutor. For example, after his listeners' dismissal of his biblical imagery as nonsense (WN 51), Dostoevsky admits, "I had been carried away by the décor." He then continues pressing his case:

> But if you had seen how proud the mighty spirit is which created that colossal décor and how convinced it is of its victory and its triumph, you would have shuddered at its pride, its obstinacy, its blindness, and you would have shuddered, too, at the thought of those over whom that proud spirit hovers and reigns supreme (WN 51).

The Crystal Palace, with its latest technology, its explicit celebration of liberty brought to mankind from science, technology, industrialization, secularism, and urbanization, makes Dostoevsky shudder. Rather than liberty, he sees slavery. Dostoevsky captures his view of London's masses in a vivid image that also helps relate his concerns to those that drive Ellison's Invisible Man.

Underground Man also sees this contradiction between liberty and slavery. For example, he contrasts the life of man and the life of ants, noting that ants "have a marvelous edifice of that pattern which endures for ever—the ant-heap" (NU 75). Ants, unlike men, are both constant and positive creatures, always aiming toward a goal. Men, however, "is a frivolous and incongruous creature, and perhaps, like a chess player, loves the process of the game, not the end of it" (NU 75). For Underground Man, a rigid focus on achieving "the thing to be attained, which must always be expressed as a formula, as positive as twice two makes four, and such positiveness is not life, gentlemen, but is the beginning of death" (NU 75). This same attitude is captured in traveler Dostoevsky's concern with "a colossal, internal, spiritual regimentation, having its sources in the very depths of the soul" (WN 48) that he finds throughout Europe a desperate yearning ". . . to bow down in worship of Baal" (WN 49). The Crystal Palace—Baal—draws its denizens to it. Its universalistic principles seduce people from around the world. It draws people from their homelands, like pilgrims, to visit. While science and the ideology of Westernism, for Dostoevsky, like the Crystal Palace, might liberate individuals from their parochial and rooted worlds, there is no celebration in this pseudo-freedom.

This is precisely why Dostoevsky wonders if there is "a chemical bond between the human spirit and a man's native land" (WN 14). His central concern is that if Russia's elite, the so-called intelligent class amongst whom Underground Man considers himself, has become so European that the common people regard them as foreigners (WN 29), then there can be no ground for a proper kind of liberty. Without the peasants, for whom are the elite struggling? The disconnect between the Europeanized elite and peasants—the Russians who hold fast to their mystical ties to the soil—lead Dostoevsky to suggest that "we have now reached the point when our contempt for the common people and the basic principles of its being is so profound that even our attitude to it is stamped with a new, unprecedented and kind of supercilious disdain" (WN 29). Underground Man, at least in his rational and scientific moments, fits into Dostoevsky's characterization of the elite separated from the common people and their principles. The tensions within his own existence stem from his inability to give up those concerns rooted in the Russian soil.

All of this speaks to Dostoevsky's concern with questions of freedom, individuality, and community. In *Winter Notes* Dostoevsky offers a penetrating critique of the slogan of the French Revolution: Liberty, Equality, and Fraternity. According to Dostoevsky, the concept Fraternity is the principal obstacle in the West (WN 66). He argues that the Western man speaks of brotherhood but does not know how to realize it (WN 66–67). As a result, fraternity must be created at all costs, although this is an impossibility as brotherhood cannot be artificially created but only exist in nature (WN 67). From Dostoevsky's perspective, which is to say, the perspective of the nineteenth-century Slavophiles in general, brotherhood is organic and rooted in the soil. The tour of Europe only confirmed for Dostoevsky that brotherhood does not exist in the West. Instead, it has been replaced in Europe by "the principle of individuality, the principle of isolation, of intensified self-preservation, of self-seeking, of self-determination within one's own personality of self, of contrast between this self, the whole of nature and the rest of humanity" (WN 67). This Western perspective, this pathology, again seems to characterize Underground Man, who embraces personality and individuality as one's dearest possessions.

Dostoevsky sees brotherhood and individuality as in tension but compatible as long as it is understood that the priority in their relationship is the communal rather than the individual. He even refers to the ant hill in positive terms, by contrasting individual isolation with the need to live in harmony with each other (WN 49). This does not mean that brotherhood requires that individuality be surrendered to achieve happiness, however (WN 68). The individuality Dostoevsky promotes has a spiritualized and self-sacrificing character.

Along the same lines, Dostoevsky thinks that freedom is essential to man. If a man is offered full security in exchange for his freedom, he will refuse the trade, and Dostoevsky sees a paradox in this behavior. The healthy soul, he argues, will reject the so-called liberty of the Crystal Palace because it is merely material liberty. Even if the costs are high, he suggests, we should reject this pseudo-liberty, especially if it results in real suffering. The conflicted Underground Man, like many of the Russian elites Dostoevsky is taking to task, also sees this, but is steadfast in his position. As he says, "Man wants only *independent* choice, whatever that independence may cost and wherever it may lead" (NU 69).[13] Underground Man, like Dostoevsky, and like Russia herself, is drawn to Europe and her progress, but cannot dig himself free of the mystical roots of his Russianness. To be sure, Dostoevsky's relationship to his narrator is not simple or easily delineated. It is, as Joseph Frank puts it, one of "inverted irony."[14]

On the surface at least, the relationship between Ellison and Invisible Man is more straightforward. At the very least, it is not complicated by the author's overt intrusion into his narrator's story by speaking in his own authorial voice. Without reducing the narrator's life story to Ellison's biography, or claiming that Invisible Man is merely a mouthpiece for Ellison's views, I will touch on a common thread in their thought. One important scene in *Invisible Man*, important for understanding both the action of the novel and the development of the narrator, is the funeral of Tod Clifton. A Brotherhood colleague of Invisible Man, Clifton was shot during an altercation with a police officer (IM 436–438). Invisible Man is to deliver a eulogy during the service and, as he looks down on the huge crowd that has gathered in the park, he tries to imagine why they have come. Did they know Tod? Was this simply another opportunity to protest? Invisible Man muses whether politics could ever be an expression of love (IM 452).

The point here is that Ellison, like Invisible Man and his eulogy, regards the novel itself as a political statement. *Invisible Man* was awarded the 1952 National Book Award for fiction, and in his remarks at the award ceremony Ellison articulated a view on love and politics similar to his narrator's musings. Addressing the question of the chief significance of his novel, his response was twofold: "its experimental attitude, and its attempt to return to the mood of personal moral responsibility for democracy" which he thought was characteristic of the best American fiction of the nineteenth century.[15] Near the end of his remarks he returns to the question of democracy. Arguing that we must recognize "our sins against those principles we all hold sacred," Ellison argues that "the way home we seek is that condition of man's being at home in the world, which is called love, and which we term democracy."[16]

As part of this politico-literary experiment, Ellison attempts to capture the rich, colorful, creative, and complex language heard on the streets of the nation. "Our speech I found resounding with an alive language swirling with over three hundred years of American living, a mixture of the folk, the Biblical, the scientific and the political."[17] By employing such language, Ellison is linking liberty with the proverbial soil of America. He is, as it were, bringing liberty home to the historically situated America. This is no abstract, Crystal Palace kind of liberty. For Ellison, a vital American fiction of the present would engage with the same concerns that motivated our greatest writers of the previous century. Such a literature would take "responsibility for the condition of democracy and . . . [embody] imaginative projections of the conflicts within the human heart which arose when the sacred principles of the Constitution and the Bill of Rights clashed with the practical exigencies of human greed and fear, hate and love."[18] For Ellison, in both Invisible Man's moment to speak politically, and in his own at the National Book Awards ceremony, the literary and the political are conjoined: a decade before Martin Luther King, Jr. would publicly share his dream for the nation, Ellison articulated his: "I was to dream of a prose which was flexible, as swift as American change is swift, confronting the inequalities and brutalities of our society forthrightly, yet thrusting forth its images of hope, human fraternity and individual self-realization."[19]

In his study of Dostoevsky and Ellison, Joseph Frank agues that "the invisible man stands in relation to white American culture and *its* ideas and values as Dostoevsky's underground man stands in relation to West European Culture."[20] On this point I think Frank is incorrect. First, as I argued earlier, Invisible Man seems to be universally misunderstood by the characters he encounters, whether black or white. Second, Invisible Man is a part of, and ultimately embraces, an American culture that includes blacks, whites, former slaves and former slave-owners. His novel-long struggle to come to understand this paradoxical situation and to accept it is embodied in and symbolized by his effort to come to terms with his grandfather's deathbed declaration. Third, as a nation we may be guilty of sins against the principles we hold sacred, as Ellison maintained in his National Book Award address, but those principles themselves always contained the promise of "equal treatment before the law" for all, even when our sinful practice denied such equal treatment to some. Thus these principles allow for a self-critique of our actions that over time will allow for self-correction. For Ellison, as for Invisible Man, reconciliation is a national project rooted in a national history. One cannot extricate oneself from slavery by extricating oneself from history. Freedom incorporates history.

While the Invisible Man seems to be universally misunderstood, there is one character in the novel besides his grandfather who sees him for what he is: Brother Tarp. Tarp, who has a long-standing role in the Brotherhood and befriends Invisible Man when he takes over the Harlem chapter, hangs a portrait of Frederick Douglass in Invisible Man's office

(IM 378–79). With this gesture, Ellison is suggesting a parallel between his protagonist and Douglass. Douglass was born into slavery in Maryland in 1818 but as a young adult escaped to Massachusetts, where he became an active abolitionist and outstanding orator. One of his best-known and most powerful speeches was "What to the Slave Is the Fourth of July?" in which he identified the Constitution as a "Glorious Liberty Document."[21] In a similar vein, Invisible Man's final words in the novel are a question to his readers, "Who knows but that, on the lower frequencies, I speak for you?" (IM 581). Invisible Man can, perhaps, speak for all Americans, regardless of color, because he has both feet planted firmly on American soil. Like Douglass, his history and his life are here, in America. His understanding of liberty is domestic. He sees no need to appeal to foreign ideas and foreign people for liberation. This stands in direct contrast to the Underground Man who has one foot in European culture and the other on Russian soil. It is this split, this schism, as it were, that prevents Underground Man from acting. It prevents him from the politico-literary acts of Invisible Man and Ellison himself. Underground Man, by rejecting the organic whole of Russian culture and history, is paralyzed and must therefore keep to his corner.

In the final analysis, Dostoevsky and Ellison share a vision of the importance of embracing one's rich cultural heritage and maintaining a healthy relationship to one's historical roots. Liberty demands nothing less. The differences between their narrators in terms of their ability to act, to finally come out of their hiding places and assume a place in the world of men, can thus be understood in terms of their particular relationship to their culture, history and native soil.

NOTES

1. Fyodor Dostoyevsky, *White Nights: And Other Stories* (New York: Macmillan, 1918), 50. All subsequent references will be cited in-text as NU, with only slight modifications to align the English with the Russian, and to make the English somewhat more current. Hereafter citations to this work will be identified as NU and inserted parenthetically in the text. Ralph Ellison, *Invisible Man* (New York: Vintage International, 1995b) Hereafter citations to this work will be identified as IM and inserted parenthetically in the text. In this essay I refer to Dostoevsky's narrator as Underground Man and Ellison's as Invisible Man.

2. Joseph Frank, *Dostoevsky: The Stir of Liberation, 1860–1865* (Princeton: Princeton University Press, 1986), 319.

3. Frank, *Dostoevsky: The Stir of Liberation, 1860–1865*, 319–320.

4. For an example of an economist who does not reduce questions of profit or value to mere material terms, see Frank Knight, "Ethics and the Economic Interpretation" in *The Ethics of Competition* (New Brunswick: Transaction Publishers, 1997), 11–32. Knight argues that "there is room in the field of conduct for three different kinds of treatment: first, a scientific view, or economics and technology; second, a genetic view, or culture history, and third, for a Criticism of Values. The discussion of the latter will, like literary and artistic criticism, run in terms of suggestion rather than

logical statement, in figurative rather than literal language, and its principles will be available through sympathetic interpretation rather than intellectual cognition" (32).

5. Joseph Frank, "Ralph Ellison and Dostoevsky" in *Through the Russian Prism: Essays on Literature and Culture* (Princeton: Princeton University Press, 1990), 36.

6. Fyodor Dostoyevsky, *Winter Notes on Summer Impressions* (Surrey, England: Oneworld Classics, 2008). Hereafter citations to this work will be identified as WN and inserted parenthetically in the text.

7. Joseph Frank devotes two chapters to *Winter*(chapters 13 and 16) and his chapter on *Notes from Underground* (chapter 21) details the intertextual relationship between these works (Frank, *Dostoevsky: The Stir of Liberation, 1860–1865*, 179–196, 233–248, 310–347). Geri Kjetsaa provides a powerful thumbnail account of the spirit of the earlier work: "One would think that Dostoyevsky would have gotten *something* positive out of this trip, but no, he found simply what he sought: his *Winter WN on Summer Impressions*, published in the first issue of *Time* in 1863, is truly the most damning account of the West ever written by a Russian" (Geir Kjetsaa, *Fyodor Dostoyevsky: A Writer's Life* (New York: Fawcett Columbine, 1989), 143).

8. Judges 6: 25.
9. 1 Kings 18: 16–40.
10. 2 Kings 10: 18–28.
11. Jeremiah 19: 5.
12. See John 10: 16.
13. Vasily Grossman offers a significant critique of the Russian understanding of freedom that suggests Dostoevsky underestimated the importance of the West for Russian freedom: "The implacable suppression of the individual personality—its total, servile subjection to the sovereign and the State—has been a constant feature of Russian history. This too was seen and recognized by the Russian prophets. . . . But along with the suppression of the individual by prince, landowner, sovereign, and State, the Russian prophets sensed a purity, profundity, and clarity unknown to the Western world. They saw a Christlike power—the power of the Russian soul—and they prophesied a great and brilliant future for this soul. . . . They all saw the power of the Russian soul and its significance for the world, but they all failed to see that this soul had been a slave for a thousand years, that its peculiarities had been engendered by the absence of freedom. . . . For a hundred years Russia had been drinking in a borrowed idea of freedom. . . . For a hundred years Russia had been imbibing the work of the thinkers and philosophers of Western freedom" (Vassily Grossman, *Everything Flows* (New York: New York Review of Books, 2009), 175–176).

14. Frank, *Dostoevsky: The Stir of Liberation, 1860–1865*, 236.
15. Ralph Ellison, "Brave New Words for a Starling Occasion" in *The Collected Essays of Ralph Essays*, ed. John F. Callahan (New York: Modern Library, 1995a), 151.
16. Ellison, "Brave New Words for a Starling Occasion," 154.
17. Ellison, "Brave New Words for a Starling Occasion," 152.
18. Ellison, "Brave New Words for a Starling Occasion," 153.
19. Ellison, "Brave New Words for a Starling Occasion," 153.
20. Frank, "Ralph Ellison and Dostoevsky," 35.
21. Frederick Douglass, "What to the Slave Is the Fourth of July?" in *Narrative of the Life of Frederick Douglass, An American Slave, Written by Himself with Related Documents*, ed. David W. Blight (Boston: Bedford/St. Martins, 2003), 169.

TEN

The End of the Ancient World

Dostoevsky's Confidence Game

Ron Srigley

INTRODUCTION

Most scholars agree that the central philosophical ambition of *The Brothers Karamazov* is a depiction, examination, and assessment of the contest between modernity and antiquity in which modernity is exemplified by the politics and philosophy of Ivan Karamazov and antiquity is represented by the Christianity of Zosima and Alyosha.[1] Most also agree that Dostoevsky frames this contest apocalyptically, such that modernity and Christianity are conceived as antithetical accounts of the whole that exhaust the existential possibilities available to us. For instance, Nikolai Berdyaev says that in *The Brothers Karamazov* "every man is offered the alternatives of the Grand Inquisitor or of Jesus Christ, and he must accept one or the other, for there is no third choice: what appears to be other solutions are only passing phases, variations on one or the other theme."[2] Valentina Vetlovskaya argues similarly that the work's hagiographic narrative is driven by a conflict between the "darkness of earthly malice" (Ivan) and the "light of love" (Alyosha) that "is consistently pursued up to the end of the novel."[3] More recently, Bruce Ward and Travis Kroeker have echoed both Vetlovskaya and Berdyaev's interpretations. They argue that for Dostoevsky, "History is characterized by the struggle between . . . two laws—one of death and one of life." These are the laws of "individual egoism" and "Christ" respectively and the contest between them takes place against the backdrop of the "cosmic canvas on which apocalyptic images are drawn."[4]

What is odd about *The Brothers Karamazov*, however, is that despite the overwhelming agreement among commentators about its account of the contest between Christians and moderns, the book has generated no consensus about which side Dostoevsky actually favours. In this regard scholarly opinion is almost equally divided and the contest between these rival interpretations is as antithetically structured as their interpretations of the book itself. On the one hand there are writers like Berdyaev, Ward, Kroeker, Sandoz, Belknap, Catteau, and others who argue that Dostoevsky's chief aim in the book is to defend Christianity from its modern detractors and to depict graphically the nihilism that follows from its rejection. Sandoz's analysis is representative of this type of interpretation: "The Grand Inquisitor spoke *sub specie mortis*, but Dostoevsky has spoken *sub specie aeternitatis*. His Legend points toward the eternal destiny of man. Through parody and caricature he constructs a devastating refutation of the inflated and spiritually diseased supermen of all the ages of history. His concern is with the spiritual crisis of our time and its dangers for men."[5] On the other hand there are V. V. Rozanov, Valentina Vetlovskaya, and D. H. Lawrence, all of whom claim that Dostoevsky was ultimately on the side of Ivan and the Inquisitor and wrote *The Brothers Karamazov* to indicate the profound failure of Christianity to account for the nature of the human condition.[6] D. H. Lawrence's is the clearest and most frank statement of this interpretation: "And we cannot doubt that the Inquisitor speaks Dostoevsky's own final opinion about Jesus. The opinion is, baldly, this: Jesus, you are inadequate. Men must correct you. And Jesus in the end gives the kiss of acquiescence to the Inquisitor, as Alyosha does to Ivan." Dostoevsky's criticism of Jesus is thus "the final criticism, based on the experience of two thousand years . . . and on a profound insight into the nature of mankind."[7]

To make matters worse, both sides can enlist Dostoevsky himself in support of their interpretations. For instance, in a letter to his publisher, Lyubimov, Dostoevsky writes: "My hero [Ivan] chooses a theme I consider irrefutable: the senselessness of children's suffering, and develops from it the absurdity of historical reality." However, only a few sentences later in the same letter Dostoevsky claims just the opposite: Ivan's theme and the critique it provokes is in fact "blasphemy" and that "it will be triumphantly refuted in the next issue [of the *Russian Herald*], on which I am now working with fear, trembling, and veneration."[8]

Interpretations of the type indicated above tend to treat the philosophical ambiguity in Dostoevsky's account as only apparent and therefore resolvable through close readings of the Ivan chapters, appeals to authorial authority, or a combination of both strategies.[9] Though generative of a large body of scholarship, much of it extremely capable and containing genuine insight into the text, such strategies do not adequately address the lingering interpretive questions posed by the opposing side. Sooner or later the doubts raised by Ivan's critique of the Christian theodicy or concerns over the political extremities to which that critique leads Ivan reassert themselves, unsettling the conclusions of both interpretations.

Contrary to the traditional interpretation, I argue that the philosophical alternatives posed by *The Brothers Karamazov* are not real in the sense of being distinct, circumscribable positions, but rather are carefully constructed intellectual traps intended to keep the reader within the range of the philosophical opinion they recognize: namely, modernity and Christianity. Any critique that threatens to expose the limitations of these traditions so as to point to a genuine alternative is carefully and rhetorically undermined by the analysis. Not directly, though. To offer a direct critique would be to acknowledge the possibility of an alternative. Dostoevsky's aim rather is to keep the reader with the orbit of the problematic by making the antitheses on which it rests appear both exhaustive and irresolvable. The book's central interpretive question cannot be resolved because Dostoevsky does not want it to be resolved. It is a contest in which there are no losers. Ivan and Zosima are not opponents properly speaking but two moments of a dialectic whose final ambition is its own perpetual motion.

As to the organization of this chapter, section one explores two attempts to overcome the limitations of the traditional interpretation, those of Robert Belknap and Albert Camus. Though their accounts are only partially successful, Belknap and Camus both clarify the interpretive situation in a way that makes a fuller, more satisfactory reading possible. In section two I explain the nature of Dostoevsky's rhetorical technique through a comparison with Herman Melville's notion of a confidence game. I argue that *The Brothers Karamazov* is a type of confidence game that is amenable to and reinforces the totalizing impulses of the Christian tradition. In section three I outline what I take to be the core of truth in Ivan's critique of the Christian theodicy. Section four explores the manner in which that truth is undermined by Ivan through the political and philosophical excesses with which he saddles his Inquisitor. Section five completes the analysis by examining how Dostoevsky attempts further to undermine Ivan's critique through the creation of a "pure, ideal Christian" in the character of Zosima.[10] I conclude by arguing that the most important consequence of this type of argument is that it effectively removes from view any tradition other than our own and therefore prevents us from acquiring the insights and wisdom that may be generated from such an encounter. For Camus the tradition most immediately affected in this regard is the Greek one. By losing sight of it we deprive ourselves of an image of life that might help us to overcome the excesses and confusions of the modern predicament so clearly exemplified by Dostoevsky's book.

FROM BELKNAP'S THEOLOGY TO CAMUS'S INDECISION: INTERPRETING *THE BROTHERS KARAMAZOV*

Robert Belknap addresses the interpretive ambiguity of *The Brothers Karamazov* directly and offers an explanation of it in his essay, "The Rhetoric of an Ideological Novel."[11] Belknap acknowledges the existence of the two antithetical traditions of interpretation I have described and wonders how we are to make sense of them. He admits that Dostoevsky's intention in writing the book carries more authority than any commentator's opinion and that Dostoevsky's stated intention tends to support the Christian interpretation rather than one favouring Ivan's philosophy. But he also claims that the book's actual rhetorical effect, exemplified by these antithetical styles of interpretation, raises important questions about its meaning. For instance, given the strength of Ivan's argument, Belknap asks whether Dostoevsky was "rhetorically incompetent" or whether he was "consciously or unconsciously lying" about his intention to critique modern nihilism and defend Christianity. Belknap's answer to this question hinges on his account of Dostoevsky's use of sources. Belknap suggests that Dostoevsky's sympathetic portrait of Ivan is an attempt to do justice to Belinsky, Herzen, and Bakunin, three revolutionary figures Dostoevsky admired personally but disagreed with politically and philosophically. "Dostoevsky's fidelity to this aspect of his sources could have made Ivan Karamazov more attractive in his desperate love than seems fitting or strategic if Dostoevsky's letter expressed his real intent."[12] In order to judge the interpretation, Belknap offers a simple test: "If Ivan's greatness is an accidental side effect of Dostoevsky's fidelity to his sources, we should find in the text a series of efforts to destroy one of the most eloquent and convincing arguments in all literature, an argument whose starting point Dostoevsky himself has called irrefutable."[13] And indeed Belknap does find evidence of just such an attempt in *The Brothers Karamazov*. Dostoevsky seduces the reader into identifying with Ivan and then implicates her "in the feelings of guilt, self-consciousness, stupidity, and even savagery" to which his radicalism leads him, thus undermining the brilliance of the argument.[14] In this way he "tempts" his readers in order to lead them "through a death of grace as dangerous as Zosima's in his youth, or Alyosha's when his faith is shaken, hoping he can bring them out beyond as fertile disseminators of grace."[15]

Belknap's frank discussion of this ambiguity in *The Brothers Karamazov* is a welcome addition to the literature. Still, we should wonder whether it explains Dostoevsky's ambition in a way that overcomes the limitations of traditional scholarship, as was his intention.[16] If Ivan's argument is sound on its own terms—"one of the most eloquent and convincing arguments in all of literature," as Belknap says—then why "destroy" it at all, rhetorically or otherwise? Belknap's response to this question is ideologically consistent but dramatically inadequate. He claims that the chapters devoted to Ivan and the Inquisitor are indistinguishably a test of the reader's "faith" and a piece of philosophical "manipulation" designed to undermine the rational inquiry on which the critique of those chapters rests. By calling it manipulation Belknap does not mean it is sophistry, however. His interpretation of *The Brothers Karamazov* follows structurally the basic features of the Christian teaching, according to which sinful, autonomous human reason must die in order to be enlightened by grace and to see the world as it truly is. Belknap's acceptance of this structure explains the ease with which he accepts Ivan's destruction.[17] Ivan insists on reason and is therefore justly damned. A dramatic ambiguity is resolved theologically. It also illuminates Belknap's agreement with the religious wing of traditional scholarship. Ivan's appeal, which Dostoevsky derives from sources like Belinsky, Herzen, and Bakunin, is merely bait for the unwary. In the contest between Christians and moderns, the Christians always win. In this regard the only difference between Belknap's interpretation and that of, say, Berdyaev or Kroeker, is Belknap's more sophisticated account of the mechanism of Ivan's undoing.

I agree with Belknap's claim that Dostoevsky undermines Ivan's argument rhetorically in order to justify the theology of Zosima and Alyosha. What I disagree with is his naive acceptance of this tactic and his corollary assumption that such a reading both legitimizes and settles the contest between Ivan and his Christian protagonists. In part this stance is due to Belknap's own ideological commitments. These cause him to travel the book's rhetorical trajectory in only one direction and thus to misunderstand the significance of the encounter as a whole. Dostoevsky may have attempted to defeat Ivan rhetorically in order to lead readers to embrace the Christianity of Zosima and Alyosha. But like all rhetorical victories, this one is neither definitive nor stable because it does not address the excesses of the Christian account that initially provoked Ivan's rebellion. Sooner rather than later those unaddressed excesses lead the reader to wonder whether Ivan might have been right after all.

I think the dilemma posed by the traditional interpretation of *The Brothers Karamazov* reaches its highest expression in the work of Albert Camus.[18] This does not mean that Camus attempts consciously to solve the dilemma or to supersede it. In fact, as interpretations go, *The Rebel* is in many ways completely conventional. Camus begins by accepting the standard scholarly parameters for interpreting *The Brothers Karamazov* and dutifully attempts to choose between Ivan's modernity and Alyosha and Zosima's Christianity. It is not this effort or the arguments in support of it that distinguish Camus's contribution. What sets Camus apart is rather his inconsistent and contradictory approval of *both* Ivan and Alyosha/Zosima, that is to say, his failure to make the required choice and his unwillingness or inability to cover up the resulting inconsistency. For instance, in the most extended discussion of *The Brothers Karamazov* in *The*

Rebel Camus sides clearly with Alyosha and Zosima and against Ivan. Ivan's denial of the Christian teaching about transcendence and immortality leads him to a metaphysical rebellion that is inherently nihilistic.[19] Yet in the concluding pages of the book Camus drops the charge of metaphysical rebellion altogether and argues instead, and in complete contradiction to his earlier account, that Ivan provides us with an image of "the most pure form of the movement of rebellion"—the desire that everyone be saved.[20] Here Ivan is said to be motivated not by a mad desire to annihilate reality but by "love"—for Camus the highest human motivation and the foundation of all true rebellion.[21] Moreover, in these pages Alyosha and Zosima, earlier Camus's preferred exemplars of virtue and wisdom, are not mentioned at all, nor is the Christianity they represent. Ivan is now presented as the true rebel, who "finds no rest in God or in history."[22]

Camus's uneasy and contradictory assessments of *The Brothers Karamazov* teach us more about that book's meaning than other, more consistent expositions. Why? What Camus recognized, or at least what his analysis demonstrates and what he seems to have felt intuitively, is that one cannot with a clear conscience choose either of the alternatives as Dostoevsky presents them. The reason one cannot do so is that both sides offer insights that make sense experientially but which, as formulated, entail other claims and consequences that one could not possibly accept. To give only one example, Ivan's analysis of the suffering of children demonstrates how frightening and morally disordering the doctrines of divine providence and the final judgement in the afterlife are. This is a criticism one wants to affirm. But Ivan then goes on, in the legend of the Grand Inquisitor, to claim that our moral sensibilities are dangerous fictions that need to be managed by a ruling elite. Thus, the morality appealed to and relied upon in the former case is eliminated as illusory in the latter. And as we will see below, one encounters similar difficulties in the case of Zosima.

In response to this dilemma the most Camus manages in *The Rebel* is a contradictory affirmation of both accounts that leaves the central problematic unresolved. Nonetheless, there is evidence in the book of Camus's dissatisfaction with the resulting position and a suspicion that the real problem has nothing to do with interpretive limitations but rather the manner in which the problematic is framed by Dostoevsky. For instance, usually Camus accepts Dostoevsky's contention that the contest between moderns and ancients is equivalent to the contest between moderns and Christians and that this contest is most clearly embodied in the confrontation between Ivan and Alyosha and Zosima.[23] In this reading modernity is a Christian heresy that derives its form and aspirations from the tradition but rejects its substance or meaning. However, there are moments when Camus argues that the quarrel between Christians and moderns is a red herring and that the real existential and philosophical opposition is between the ancients (understood as all traditions that antedate or are other than the Christian) on the one hand and moderns and Christians on the other. For instance, according to the argument of *The Brothers Karamazov*, the death of the Christian God marked definitively the beginning of the modern era. Yet Camus also writes of this event: "If it is false to say that from that day began the tragedy of contemporary man, neither is it true to say that was where it ended. On the contrary, this attempt indicates the highest point in a drama that began *with the end of the ancient world* and of which the final words have not yet been spoken."[24]

Camus's hunch in *The Rebel* that moderns and Christians share a common philosophical heritage and orientation in contrast to the ancients was an important step forward in his own analysis of modernity.[25] But it is a hunch that never led Camus to revisit *The Brothers Karamazov* in order to test its consequences for that book.[26] That is the ambition of the present chapter.

CRITICISM AND CONFIDENCE GAMES

If the seriousness of any critique is to be measured by the seriousness of the alternative it proposes and the persuasiveness of its argument, then I would argue that Dostoevsky's critique of Christianity is not serious.[27] Despite its sound and at times penetrating psychological insights, *The Brothers Karamazov* is essentially an apologetic work. The book's aim is to defend Christianity against its modern critics, and it does so deftly by employing all the various polemical and rhetorical devices common to this type of literature. Chief among these devices is the figure of Ivan Karamazov. To state the meaning of Ivan's rebellion rather bluntly: what begins as a serious and compelling criticism of the Christian theodicy ends up being a totalitarian revolt against all divinity and all morality about which there is nothing serious at all. Or put differently, Ivan's rebellion is a not a genuine alternative to Christianity, as Dostoevsky would like us to believe—it is a parody of such an alternative, whose purpose is to establish rhetorically the superiority of Christianity to *any* account that might be offered in its place. Dostoevsky's entire account is constructed to this end—to lead the reader to believe that this parody, this nihilistic rebellion, is all that remains should one reject the Christian revelation.[28]

This exclusion of alternatives in *The Brothers Karamazov* is a characteristic feature of all total accounts. It is also a type of confidence game, though not a short con, but a long con in which "distrust is a stage to confidence."[29] The "defects" of the various positions it entails are not genuine; they are there to serve the totality of which they are parts. This means that despite the book's evangelical rhetoric and pious ambitions, it does not really matter where one finds oneself in the cycle of doubt and acceptance, belief and unbelief. Ivan is only a moment away from salvation; and Zosima is Ivan's alter ego. Moving between them is like traveling the circumference of circle where at each point one is equidistant to the center. The point is not to doubt or believe open-endedly or transcendently but to suffer from *these* doubts, to experience *those* hopes, and to fear the loss of *that* meaning and therefore always to remain within the orbit of the center.

The various emotional and intellectual states involved in the account, the arguments and counter arguments, are merely staged events in a single totality designed to deflect one's attention from any reality that transcends it by satisfying those desires in controlled, homeopathic doses. Ivan is their perfect embodiment and therefore Dostoevsky's preferred and most effective evangelist. The chapters on rebellion and the Grand Inquisitor have won far more believers than those devoted to Alyosha and Zosima combined.[30] Of course, in the event that the dialectics, sophistic parodies, and moral posturing fail to silence the reader's intellectual curiosity, there is always the quiet menace of divine punishment in the background that brings real inquiry to an end. It is remarkable the extent to which modern readers still feel that threat and obey it without compulsion. It demonstrates just how much a part of our emotional and mental landscape this type of intellectual thuggishness has become.

There is a charming scene in the final chapter of Melville's *Confidence Man* in which a young con sells an old man, who is already in the process of being conned by a more senior confidence man, two security devices—a portable door lock and a money belt—to protect him against the wiles of the thieves and pickpockets who are ubiquitous on the steamboats of the Mississippi River. The devices are of course themselves a con because they do not provide the security they promise and in fact open the old man up to the potentially more injurious stratagems of the senior confidence man.[31] Nonetheless, the young con offers the old man a "Counterfeit Detector" gratis, a paper that indicates the typical signs of a forged banknote, as an expression of gratitude for his purchases.[32] The old man calls the boy a "public benefactor" and proceeds to try out the Detector on a recently acquired three dollar note. To no avail. The sheer number and microscopic character of the features that need to be considered make the task effectively impossible. Judging one set of symbols by another is possible only if both sets of symbols are visible or intelligible. Failing that, any judgment might seem plausible. In the end the old man favors his banknotes, the invisible over the visible, as it were. But there is a still darker problem. As the ambiguity of the name of the device and the manner in which it was acquired suggest, the Detector's own genuineness is in question.[33] The *true* measure is supplied by a confidence man whose intentions are untrue. Once the mark takes the bait the game's outcome is virtually secure for he now judges the truth of what he sees by a measure whose unreliability is assured by its genesis.

In *The Brothers Karamazov* Ivan plays a similar role. The reader is offered his critique as a measure against which to test the Christian apocalypse for its truth. Ivan argues that the apocalypse is madness on the basis of what he can see or "the facts." However, by sticking solely to the facts—to the visible—he too soon becomes mad. How then do we measure him? By the Christian apocalypse! Escaping this circular reasoning is difficult because the rhetoric is designed to conceal from view all measures of truth other than its own.[34] But no crime is perfect. By following Ivan's initial lead and by clarifying these rhetorical techniques we may find a way out of the confidence game and beyond the restrictive totalities of modernity and Christianity.

IVAN'S REBELLION

There are many ways to gain people's assent. One way is to offer them the truth.[35] Ivan's critique of the Christian apocalypse is such an offer and it is only enhanced by the fact that Ivan is, as Dostoevsky asserts, a "sincere man" (BK, 759). Ivan's sincerity is apparent in several ways, none more powerful than the moral repugnance he experiences when confronted with intellectual dishonesty. Even Father Zosima acknowledges in this regard that Ivan has "a lofty heart" and that he thinks and seeks "higher things" (BK, 61). The object of Ivan's repugnance is the Christian teaching about divine providence and the final judgment. His criticism of these teachings is a critique of Christian theodicy. Ivan claims that if it is true that the events of history move providentially toward their fulfillment, then the divinity that initiated and guides that movement is criminal when considered from the standpoint of human judgment. As such, it is unworthy of human love and respect. His criticism of the Christian teaching about the final judgment has a similar basis. For Ivan the final judgment is both unjust and barbaric.[36] It is unjust because punishing or rewarding people who act as they do under the sway of divine providence is senseless. It is barbaric because eternal punishment is not punishment but vengeance because it does not afford the possibility of betterment. Nor is it vengeance. Vengeance against people who could not act otherwise is not vengeance; it is brutality because no wrong has been committed.

In *The Rebel* Camus offers an interpretation of Ivan's critique of the Christian theodicy. He claims that "it is not the suffering of a child, which is repugnant in itself" that is the source of Ivan's rebellion, "but the fact that the suffering is not justified."[37] For Camus's Ivan, "What is missing from the misery of the world, as well as from its moments of happiness, is some principle by which they can be explained."[38] Suffering and evil are repugnant in themselves, but what is really troubling is the absence of an *idea* to explain them. Here Camus follows Dostoevsky's lead by accepting the Christian problematic as the standard by which the success of all treatments of the problem of evil are to be measured and by which critic and believer alike are to be judged. Ivan accepts the Christian ambition but rejects its solution. He may not consider God or providence to be adequate responses to suffering and evil, but they are the right *kind* of response. Ivan's critique is thus an in-house affair in which rebel and Christian vie with one another for supremacy by arguing the relative merits of their responses to the human desire for totality or completion. Camus summarizes this position: "To kill God and to build a Church are the constant and contradictory purpose of rebellion."[39] Camus is certainly right that Ivan ultimately settles on this type of account, but it is not the type he offers initially. It is in that space, that brief pause between critique and consummation, that we catch a glimpse of something beyond the totalities of the All and the Nothing that ultimately guide the analysis of *The Brothers Karamazov*.

Ivan's best criticism of the Christian teaching is not that it fails to offer an explanation of suffering and evil, but that it does. The suffering and evil he describes transcend us and thus cannot be exhausted by any human category. Of course, there are forms of suffering that are more easily accepted because they are intelligibly related to the order of life. The human nervous system is susceptible to pain, but most of this pain is necessary for the proper functioning of the organism. Without it not only would there be no endeavour, movement, and delight in life, but life itself would not exist. This type of pain we accept gladly as the price of our existence. But our feelings change when it comes to the hard cases Ivan describes. Why do children suffer? Why are they prey to the villainy of adults and to the caprices of fortune?

As we know, the Christian solution to the problem is that suffering makes sense or has a purpose when considered from the standpoint of God's design for the world. This explanation allows our outrage at suffering to exist but relieves it of its most dangerous effects by giving us confidence that reconciliation is possible and that its achievement does not depend on us. According to the teaching, one can be troubled by suffering because it often looks quite bad, but one need not despair because the end of suffering can never be reached, as it lies elsewhere or in the other world. Without such confidence, the end of suffering is reachable but unbearable because it is without meaning. Some more optimistic proponents of modernity resist this final confrontation by expending all their energies alleviating suffering. Ivan's humanitarianism has a similar aim but is more differentiated and differently conceived. He does not avoid that final confrontation himself but for others he offers not cures and therapy but politics and illusions. Politics is power that keeps order, while illusions make human beings happy by preventing them from seeing that their lives are meaningless. But once Ivan starts down this path he cannot stop and must go to the end of suffering, which is nothing. If the end of suffering is nothing then life itself must be nothing too. "Everything is lawful" (BK, 244). Once rebellion reaches this point of lucidity and becomes active it will not be satisfied with appearances and will seek to bring life to the final condition apparent in its nature but which is normally hidden by human weakness and dishonesty. Benevolence or humanitarianism can restrain this movement for only so long because benevolence is a human disposition with no support in nature. This is why Zosima says, "If that feeling [of contact with other mysterious worlds] grows weak or is destroyed in you, the heavenly growth will die away in you. Then you will be indifferent to life and even grow to hate it" (BK, 299–300).

The end of human suffering may be nothing if "something" is defined as personal immortality in the Christian sense. The desire for nothing, however, is not the only human response to such awareness. Kindness, empathy and prudence are also possible. But for Ivan these responses are unlikely without a frank acknowledgement of suffering and evil and an intellectually honest assessment of their nature. Far from obscuring or eliminating our sense of transcendence and distorting our perception of suffering and evil, Ivan's critique is an attempt to restore both by exposing the limiting character of the Christian teaching. Christianity softens our despair over suffering and so manages to elude its worst aspects by creating a totality in which all things are explained or accounted for. "All religions are built on this longing," says Ivan, "and I am a believer" (BK, 225). Because this final accounting is in God's hands, and because its fulfillment is thought to lie in the future, it appears transcendent because it is beyond human control. Ivan's critique, however, teaches us that if we look closer the Christian promise is within easy reach of the normal human desires for consolation and comfort and is therefore far less transcendent or mysterious than it initially appears. That is why Ivan, after declaring his desire for such a resolution, says, "But what pulls me up here is that I can't accept that harmony" (BK, 225). Why not? What prevents him is not a preference for disharmony or a proud refusal to yield to the divine order, but his awareness that the Christian account of these things is not divine enough and perhaps even morally ugly.[40] This is why Ivan tells Alyosha that his criticism is "not blasphemy" (BK, 225). Blasphemy reduces what is high to what is low and therefore harms or denigrates it. Ivan harms nothing; rather, he resists blasphemy because he wants what is high to remain high even if it means confessing his ignorance and his lack of control.[41]

Ivan's objection to Christianity is a moral one. Christianity corrupts human judgment and eliminates transcendence in favor of a totality the main attraction of which is its satisfaction of the human feeling of self-importance. In this regard his criticism is as profound and effective as

Nietzsche's in *The Anti-Christ*: "What sets *us* apart is not that we recognize no God, either in history or in nature or behind nature—but that we find that which has been reverenced as God not 'godlike' but pitiable, absurd, harmful, not merely an error but a *crime against life*. . . . We deny God as God. . . . If this God of the Christians were *proved* to us to exist, we should know even less how to believe in him."[42] For Nietzsche the rejection of the *Christian* God does not entail a loss of *all* transcendence; nor does it require one to abandon all morality and truth. Indeed he argues that a judicious and impartial assessment of the Christian teaching demonstrates that it is the true source of modern nihilism.[43] "If one shifts the centre of gravity of life *out* of life into the 'Beyond'—into *nothingness*—one has deprived life as such of its centre of gravity. The great lie of personal immortality destroys all rationality, all naturalness of instinct—all that is salutary, all that is life-furthering, all that holds a guarantee of the future in the instincts henceforth excites mistrust. *So* to live that there is no longer any *meaning* in living: *that* now becomes the 'meaning' of life."[44] This is essentially Ivan's argument, though Ivan does not make the stronger claim that Christianity is itself nihilistic. When Ivan says that he could not accept the Christian higher harmony "*even if [he] were wrong*," he is making the same argument as Nietzsche only with a little more rhetorical flair. He means that this God is so morally and intellectually absurd that even if he existed he could not accept him (BK, 226). This type of absurdity characterizes all total accounts. The attempt to unify and to rationalize reality forces one to lie about one's experience because life includes much that is discordant and irrational. Ivan's most important insight is his recognition of the totalizing character of Christianity.

As with Nietzsche's later work, Ivan's critique holds out the promise of a genuine alternative to the Christian teaching, one that escapes the Christian presuppositions sufficiently to make possible a new, non-totalizing account of transcendence and the many ways human beings are related to it as well as a restoration of a non-sectarian morality. So why does Ivan not follow through? Why does he settle on a nihilistic totalitarianism that mirrors the worst features of the Christian teaching he has just criticized? And why, against his better judgment, does he accept that teaching's assertion that nihilism is the inevitable and inescapable consequence of its rejection?

Rhetorically Ivan's critique must be serious enough to gain the reader's assent but excessive enough not to be taken seriously. Moreover, its real meaning and consequences must be concealed, otherwise the apology would turn to real criticism and the rhetorical ambitions of the book would be compromised. But how to achieve this effect? Best to have Ivan do it himself, first by slowly retracting the Christian excesses that initially provoked his criticism and then by having him affirm the very nihilism Zosima argued would attend the denial of Christian truth, thus lending a prophetic air to his eventual destruction.[45] The former Dostoevsky accomplishes principally through Ivan's portrait of Jesus in the Inquisitor chapter and Alyosha's description of the life and teachings of Zosima; the latter is the work the Inquisitor himself and is embodied in the regime he offers as an alternative to the teachings of Jesus. I discuss these passages in turn.

IVAN'S UNDOING: THE GRAND INQUISITOR

The Grand Inquisitor's main argument is that Jesus is wrong because he prefers the loving response of the human heart and the freedom to choose between good and evil to the coercion implied by the devil's temptations of "miracle, mystery, and authority" (BK, 236). The Grand Inquisitor, however, knows that human beings need such things, so he proposes to build a political order based on them. This order anticipates the type of totalitarian rule that Dostoevsky saw prefigured in the revolutionaries of his day.[46] Yet despite the Inquisitor's emphasis on nature and the naturalness of the order he proposes, his account still comes off as an attempt to transform the world magically in comparison to the true order of reality represented by Jesus. The Inquisitor claims that human beings are slavish, selfish and weak. Only the very strong among them can bear the truth of the human condition (BK, 242–243). For these few there is philosophy and knowledge; for the rest there is force and fraud. The Inquisitor ameliorates the condition of the many by accommodating their slavish nature rather than trying to improve it. He satisfies their desire for illusion and order by offering them miracle, mystery and authority. Real political and existential order requires illusion because human beings prefer spectacle and power to truth and freedom. According to the Inquisitor, this is the "ancient law" that Jesus ignores in favor of the revolutionary idea that human beings are free to "decide for [themselves] what is good and what is evil" (BK, 235).[47] But human beings do not want this freedom, says the Inquisitor. Freedom is a burden too heavy to bear and the responsibility to choose between good and evil leads only to "confusion," "suffering," and "unanswerable problems" (BK, 235–236). Best to have done with them as quickly as possible while continuing to retain the consoling features of the doctrine. Then "peacefully they will die, peacefully they will expire in Thy name, and beyond the grave they will find nothing but death" (BK, 240). The Inquisitor, like Machiavelli's Prince, knows that he must appear "all mercy, all faith, all honesty, all humanity, all religion," and he knows that "nothing is more necessary than to appear to have this last quality."[48]

Yet all this is very odd coming from the Grand Inquisitor because he is Ivan's creation. Had Ivan wanted to offer a serious criticism of Christianity he would have begun by pointing out that miracle, mystery, and authority—all the things with which he saddles his Inquisitor—are in fact a distinctively Christian phenomena. For instance, had this been his intention he would have said that there is no greater seduction to belief than the Christian miracle of resurrection, in which a dead man comes back to life in his body. He would have argued that there is no greater mystery than the Christian mystery of incarnation, which holds that a man is also God. And finally, he would have pointed out that there is no greater expression of coercion or authority than the Christian notion of a final judgment in which all those who refuse to believe these things will be punished for all eternity. In short, he would have said that all this begins with Christianity, and that if it is bad, it is bad there first of all. He would also have said that all Christian and modern appropriations of these things are the responsibility of Christianity, and Christianity alone.

Everything the Inquisitor proposes is actually first done by Christians. The Inquisitor (and all moderns with him) merely appropriates the Christian miracle, mystery, and authority for his own purposes. The aim in both cases *is* a magical transformation of reality through the establishment of a totality. The reasonable accounts of love and choosing between good and evil are foreign to both teachings. And more important still is the fact that Ivan's criticism of the Christian theodicy makes it amply clear *that he knows this too*. Nonetheless, the Inquisitor's remarks succeed in shifting all the excesses to moderns or to bad Christians (Catholics/Jesuits) while the true, Orthodox Christianity of Zosima stands out as a beacon of sanity in the midst of the general madness.[49]

Why would Ivan say such things? Because the purpose of his rebellion is not to challenge Christianity seriously and fundamentally but to cast it in an ever more favorable light by parodying the alternatives to it, or more precisely, by claiming that there is only one such alternative: nihilism. This is what is most surprising about the Inquisitor's account. He is guilty of the very same totalizing that Ivan found most objectionable in the Christian teaching. Rather than contend with the "confusions" and "unanswered problems" of the world and acquire the virtues that encounter requires and makes possible, the Inquisitor opts against transcendence altogether and in favor of the easy oblivion of the Nothing. Of course, the world is not so ordered and thus Ivan comes to ruin. But what can he do? Even his most sincere critical efforts serve only to guarantee his destruction.

Ivan's nihilism is even more psychologically and dramatically implausible when we consider what he knows about the order of reality. For instance, Ivan knows just as much as Zosima about the importance of love, though he expresses some honest but benign reservations about the Christian idea that all human beings can and should be equally and without distinction, even the most violent and malicious among them (BK, 212). He understands that a greater or transcendent reality—including God—exists beyond his comprehension (BK, 224). And he also understands that one should not blaspheme that reality; he tells Alyosha explicitly that his own criticism of the Christian theodicy is not blasphemy (BK, 225). He knows that the process of life itself, the immediate, uninterpreted world of reality should take precedence over every idea, every meaning with which we seek to explain it, so he is not an ideologue (BK, 212). He knows that justice, though important and necessary in human life, is by itself insufficient. There are higher states of the soul—love, for example—to which the demands of justice are subordinate (BK, 225–26). He knows that all things are somehow connected, but not knowing how, he is inclined to reject all providential accounts that do injustice to the facts as we all know them, such as the fact that children do not deserve to suffer (BK, 224–25). Ivan, however, states this too mechanistically or geometrically, which rhetorically paves the way for Zosima's account of the connection between things as an order of love (BK, 299). And finally, Ivan knows that we should work to reduce human suffering, despite the tragic in human life and despite the fact that we are not be able to overcome it entirely (BK, 226). Given this understanding, Ivan's nihilism seems forced or artificial at best, much more a doctrinal requirement than the dramatic outcome of his own critical insights.

In one sense the Grand Inquisitor simply repeats the excesses of rebellion found in the preceding chapters, but with more rhetorical flourishes and more literary style. But here Ivan concedes even more ground to the Christian account than in his earlier remarks. The demonic element is made even more explicit through his use of passages from John's apocalypse, and the Christian expectation of a miraculous transformation of life wherein everything will be set right is muted to the advantage of Christianity (BK, 232, 238). Of course, Ivan's criticism of divine providence remains, but it loses its force because that providence is now shorn of its excesses, precisely the excesses for which Ivan had earlier criticized it. In its place is a rather modest account of Jesus, whose primary role is to teach human beings that the essence of life lies in love and the free but weighty task of choosing between good and evil. This, of course, is both perfectly reasonable and perfectly inconsistent with the description of Christianity that preceded it, so much so that one wonders why in the world Ivan would even contest it. Reformulated this way, Ivan could accept the teachings of Jesus without reservation. The Christian assertion that Jesus demanded too much from human beings is thus merely a rhetorical device, the aim of which is to imply that here we are confronted with an ethical teaching so elevated that it is beyond the comprehension of unaided human reason (BK, 236). The rhetorical effect is that any teaching offered in its place involves a considerable *lowering* of standards. But again, this is not so. If the excesses of Ivan's rebellion are removed, what remains is something very much like this teaching. One must resist evil and love the good—but entertain no illusions about winning a complete victory either way. That, however, is not Dostoevsky's intention. The whole account aims to reinforce the standard Christian distinction between the natural man and the spiritual man, the man without a revelation and the man with one. And, as always, the man without a revelation is forever letting himself off too easily. He is not really serious about good and evil and human salvation, though he may be concerned with that pathetic thing called human happiness. Dostoevsky adds or subtracts the excesses of the Christian doctrines as necessary to achieve the desired rhetorical effect. But in the end those excesses are always apparent because they are inherent in the teaching itself. This is most clearly seen in Zosima.

SUBDUING THE WHOLE WORLD: ZOSIMA'S CHRISTIANITY

Two short chapters after we learn about Ivan's rebellion and its consequences, Dostoevsky offers us their counter image in Zosima. This placement is intentional. Dostoevsky wrote book 6 of *The Brothers Karamazov* as a "reply to all [the] atheistic propositions" of the preceding chapters. However, he warns that this reply is "not a direct point for point answer to the propositions previously expressed . . . but an oblique one."[50] Rather than arguments, with Zosima Dostoevsky gives us a human being "completely opposite to the world view expressed" in Ivan and the Inquisitor (BK, 762). One would think that one good argument deserves another in a contest of this type, but Dostoevsky excuses his Christian protagonist from answering Ivan directly. Addressed on its own terms Ivan's argument may be unanswerable; better then to shift the ground away from arguments altogether to forms of life.[51] Though this strategy runs the risk of being interpreted as evasion, it also has the benefit of confirming the standard Christian teaching that natural human reason unenlightened by revelation is blind.[52] More important, it creates the impression that the real antidote to Ivan's excesses is wisdom and that wisdom is most perfectly expressed in the Christianity of Zosima. Zosima is nothing if not an exemplar of good judgment and wise counsel—modest, prudent, loving, generous, and insightful. By comparison Ivan is proud, clever, rational, self-centered, and brutal. Ivan's wise criticism of the Christian theodicy leads him to forfeit morality and to become unwise. But because faith is not wisdom and because wisdom is necessary both for life and for responding to modern excesses like Ivan's, Dostoevsky adds wisdom to Zosima's faith and allows the objects of faith which are unwise to recede into the background.

Ivan and Zosima are matched throughout *The Brothers Karamazov*. They see similar things and are similarly troubled by life's injustices, particularly the cruelty done to children and the social hierarchies that justify that cruelty and exacerbate human suffering generally (BK, 294, 298, 295). But whereas Ivan's insight leads him to revolt against reality in an effort to correct creation, Zosima's issues in a wisdom that accepts human partiality and sin without giving way either to cynicism or to moral indifference. Here we have a complete reversal of the initial critical situation. Ivan is now the totalitarian who attempts to change reality magically through force while Zosima is a wise Christian whose acceptance of and openness to life's mystery frees him from this totalitarian ambition and from the resentment on which it rests.

Ivan rejects the Christian teachings about divine providence, the incarnation, and the final judgment because they distort human experience in ways that are morally objectionable and intellectually dishonest. As appealing or comforting as these teachings may be, believing them does not make one wise. However, rather than cultivate this wisdom Ivan instead advocates a totalitarian regime constructed on the very principles he initially rejects as Christian sophistry.[53] Zosima's Christian wisdom is presented as a repudiation of these principles in favor of the free decision of the heart and mind advocated by Jesus in Ivan's poem. Whereas Ivan demands retribution as a condition of human harmony,[54] Zosima claims that we "must shun [the desire for vengeance] above all things" (BK, 300). Whereas Ivan recommends force as a means to achieve moral and political order,[55] Zosima argues that the conscience cannot be coerced and that regimes built on such coercion are unstable and will ultimately come to ruin (BK, 297–298). Whereas Ivan offers rewards and punishments as necessary incentives to action—even eternal rewards and punishments—Zosima tells us to "seek no reward, for great is [our] reward on this earth" (BK, 240, 301). In other words, whereas Ivan conceives order as a construct to be imposed on a world that is at least passively resistant to such efforts, Zosima's wisdom reveals an order that is inherent in reality and apparent in the very movements of life.

Expressed in this way Zosima's account seems comparable to ancient wisdom. Or is it? For the ancients virtue is its own reward. But Zosima speaks and acts as he does because he has assurances. Those assurances are difficult to see because they are more modestly expressed than is customary in orthodox doctrine. Most often Zosima speaks of love, of the freedom to choose between good and evil, and of contact with "other mysterious worlds," all of which suggest an experience of transcendence without further human claim or totalizing expectation (BK, 299). However, once this groundwork is laid and the impression has been created the reasonable account gradually gives way to more conventional expressions of the Christian teachings. While Zosima advocates humility, counsels against the desire for rewards, and repudiates vengeance, he also says that humble love will "subdue the whole world," that "Paradise" awaits the righteous, and that those who reject the Christian teaching will be punished eternally without hope of betterment (BK, 298, 302). Zosima's anticipation of these outcomes does not merely raise the problem of hypocrisy, but compromises the moral value of his teachings fundamentally. To state the matter straightforwardly, humble love employed for the purpose of conquest is not humble; the refusal of some rewards in anticipation of receiving even greater ones is not noble; and forgoing vengeance while receiving assurances that one's enemies will suffer eternally for their wrongdoing is not magnanimous (BK, 302). None of these are real wisdom, because real wisdom is character acquired through engagement with the permanence of the real world. Zosima's wisdom is a temporary disposition based on faith and is designed to hold down the baser desires in anticipation of a future when they will be satisfied more completely. His talk about goodness and morality is therefore more complicated than it appears because the measure of an action changes depending on the world in relation to which it is judged. This dialectical way of thinking is precisely what provokes Ivan's initial criticism of the Christian theodicy—and Zosima teaches him the real price of his rebellion.

Zosima's concluding reflections on the nature of hell are a graphic depiction of the outcome of Ivan's rebellion—not just the earthly torments of his nihilism but his eternal damnation. It is a set up, of course. Ivan's *"even if"* is what makes it possible. As we have seen, Ivan says that he would not accept the Christian teaching *"even if [he] were wrong,"* not even in heaven after the whole thing had been made plain to him (BK, 226). As in *The Antichrist*, this remark is obviously a rhetorical device that Ivan employs for the purpose of emphasis. It means simply that the Christian divinity makes no sense and that Christianity's teachings about providence and the final judgment are so absurd as to be impossible to accept. However, in the context of the Christian apocalypse Ivan's words mean precisely the opposite of what they do in the world of common sense—they mean "I *know* I am wrong but my overweening pride will not allow me to accept the fact." At best they express a type of bad faith; at worst, a demonic resistance to the truth. Whichever the case, they allow Zosima to anticipate imaginatively Ivan's eternal damnation and to paint a vivid picture of the end of all intellectual inquiry that attempts to move beyond the Christian totality.

Zosima's account brings out very clearly the element of force or coercion involved in the Christian teaching: if you do not accept our teaching, even though we offer no explanation of it, you "will burn in the fire of [your] own wrath forever" (BK, 302). Why should this be so? Why could one not simply ask a question, ask for a better explanation, even in the afterlife? As with all after-life stories, this one is based on a conception of life as it is experienced here and now. It reveals a type of human being who, despite his pious speech and elevated humanity, is in fact a brutish character who would see all those who disagree with his account of human life and some of its most perplexing and enigmatic features—love, death, suffering, God, the nature of the soul, truth—damned for eternity.

CONCLUSION

Ivan's critique raises some difficult but honest questions concerning the Christian teachings about divine providence and the afterlife and their tendency to totalize our experience of reality. Far from being nihilistic, these questions open up the possibility of reflecting on our experiences of divinity and mortality without the mediating influence of either modernity or Christianity, or indeed of any tradition. But in the end the opportunity is lost. Dostoevsky answers Ivan's criticism through the Grand Inquisitor and Zosima. Both teach us that these Christian doctrines only appear totalizing because Ivan refuses to understand and practice the ethic of suffering love on which they rest. Of course, that response is merely the same totalizing impulse Ivan had identified once more, only in a gentler, milder form. Its recurrence in the analysis is instructive as to the nature of all total accounts and the manner in which best to respond to them. There always comes a point at which discussion is no longer possible and one chooses instead to make the account an object of analysis. That inability to achieve understanding through dialogue is a genuine loss, but it also warns us not to squander our intellectual resources. As Camus teaches us, beyond the endless rhetorical tricks and tired formulas there are real alternatives to be explored and other, perhaps more interesting conversations to be had.

NOTES

1. James P. Scanlan, "Dostoevsky's Arguments for Immortality," *Russian Review* 59 (2000); Ellis Sandoz, *Political Apocalypse: A Study of Dostoevsky's Grand Inquisitor* (Baton Rouge: Louisiana State University Press, 1971); Nikolai Berdyaev, *Dostoievsky* (New York: Sheed & Ward Inc., 1934), 188; P. Travis Kroeker and Bruce Ward, *Remembering the End: Dostoevsky as Prophet to Modernity* (Boulder: Westview Press, 2001); Vasily Rozanov, *Dostoevsky and the Legend of the Grand Inquisitor* (Ithaca: Cornell University Press, 1972); Jacques Catteau, "The Paradox of the Legend of the Grand Inquisitor in *The Brothers Karamazov*" in *Dostoevsky: New Perspectives*, ed. Robert Louis Jackson (Englewood Cliffs: Prentice-Hall, 1984); Stephen Bullivant, "A House Divided Against Itself: Dostoevsky and the Psychology of Unbelief," *Literature and Theology* 22 (2008); Anna Kaladiouk, "On 'Sticking to the Facts' and 'Understanding Nothing': Dostoevsky and the Scientific Method," *Russian Review* 65 (2006); Victor Terras, *A Karamazov Companion: Commentary on the Genesis, Language, and Style of Dostoevsky's Novel* (Madison: University of Wisconsin Press, 1981); Valentina A. Vetlovskaya, "Alyosha Karamazov and the Hagiographic Hero" in *Dostoevsky: New Perspectives*, ed. Robert Louis Jackson (Englewood Cliffs: Prentice-Hall, 1984).
2. Berdyaev, *Dostoievsky*, 188.
3. Vetlovskaya, "Alyosha Karamazov and the Hagiographic Hero," 288.
4. Kroeker and Ward, *Remembering the End: Dostoevsky as Prophet to Modernity*, 23–24.
5. Sandoz, *Political Apocalypse: A Study of Dostoevsky's Grand Inquisitor*, 237.
6. Rozanov, *Dostoevsky and the Legend of the Grand Inquisitor*; Vetlovskaya, "Alyosha Karamazov and the Hagiographic Hero," 288; D. H. Lawrence, *Selected Literary Criticism* (New York: Viking Press, 1961), 233–41.

7. Lawrence, *Selected Literary Criticism*, 233–41.

8. Fyodor Dostoyevsky, *Complete Letters* (Ann Arbor: Ardis, 1988), Volume Five, to N. A. Lyubimov, June 11, 1879.

9. An interesting feature of Dostoevsky scholarship is that many of the most vigorous defences of the Christian interpretation of *The Brothers Karamazov* are undertaken with very little reference to the chapters devoted to Alyosha and Zosima, the two key representatives of this tradition in the book. See, for instance, Berdyaev, *Dostoievsky*, 205. Berdyaev's explanation echoes Alyosha's own interpretation of Ivan's poem and helps to explain this approach to the text: "'Your poem is in praise of Jesus—not in blame of him—as you meant it to be'" (Fyodor Dostoevsky, *The Brothers Karamazov* (New York: W.W. Norton & Company, 1976a), 241. Subsequent in-text references refer to this translation.

10. Dostoyevsky, *Complete Letters*, to N. A. Lyubimov, May 10, 1879.

11. Robert Belknap, "The Rhetoric of an Ideological Novel" in *Literature and Society in Imperial Russia, 1800–1914*, ed. William Mills Todd III (Stanford: Stanford University Press, 1978).

12. Belknap, "The Rhetoric of an Ideological Novel," 176.

13. Belknap, "The Rhetoric of an Ideological Novel," 177.

14. D. H. Lawrence also recognizes this technique in Dostoevsky. He writes: "Ivan need not have been so tragic and satanic. He made a discovery about men, which was due to be made. It was the rediscovery of a fact which was known universally almost till the end of the eighteenth century, when the illusion of perfectibility of men, of all men, took hold of the imagination of the civilized nations" (Lawrence, *Selected Literary Criticism*, 233–41). Lawrence is right about the diabolical excesses Dostoevsky adds to Ivan's account, but he is too accepting and uncritical of the political ones.

15. Belknap, "The Rhetoric of an Ideological Novel," 201.

16. "This paper treats the ways in which Dostoevsky's social and ideological intentions interacted with certain of his sources in the genesis of Ivan Karamazov and Ivan's Grand Inquisitor. These intentions have eluded some of the best literary minds that have written about Dostoevsky—at least these minds differ so sharply that they cannot all be right" (Belknap, "The Rhetoric of an Ideological Novel," 173).

17. Belknap, "The Rhetoric of an Ideological Novel," 201.

18. Camus was one of Dostoevsky's most serious and perceptive readers. His encounter with Dostoevsky began in the late thirties while Camus was a student at the Lycée in Algiers. The first fruit of that encounter was a theatrical production of Copeau's *The Brothers Karamazov* for the Théâtre du Travail, which Camus had founded in 1936. It was followed by a series of published discussions of Dostoevsky's works in books, essays, and plays such as *The Myth of Sisyphus* (1942), "Helen's Exile" (1946), *The Rebel* (1952), and *The Possessed* (1959).

19. Albert Camus, *The Rebel* (New York: Knopf, 1954), 60.

20. Camus, *The Rebel*, 304.

21. Camus, *The Rebel*, 304.

22. Camus, *The Rebel*, 304.

23. Ron Srigley, *Albert Camus' Critique of Modernity* (Columbia: University of Missouri Press, 2011), 48–80.

24. Camus, *The Rebel*, 102, emphasis added.

25. Srigley, *Albert Camus' Critique of Modernity*, 81–126.

26. Oddly, Camus does better in an earlier analysis of this problem—in his essay "Helen's Exile." Though there he is not discussing *The Brothers Karamazov* explicitly, Camus makes it clear that the excesses of Dostoevsky's "buffoons" stem from their unwillingness to face their human condition. And he traces that unwillingness back to a desire for personal immortality: "Ulysses, on Calypso's island, is given the choice between immortality and the land of his fathers. He chooses this earth, and death with it. Such simple greatness is foreign to our minds today. Others will say that we lack humility, but the word, all things considered, is ambiguous. Like Dostoevsky's buffoons who boast of everything, rise up to the stars and end by flaunting their shame in

the first public place, we simply lack the pride of the man who is faithful to his limitations—that is, the clairvoyant love of his human condition." Here there is no lingering hesitation that the Christian teachings about divine providence and the afterlife are necessary conditions of moral order and correctives to human rebellion (Albert Camus, "Helen's Exile" in *Lyrical and Critical Essays*, ed. Philip Thody (New York: Vintage Books, 1970)). An equally clear analysis can be found in Camus's early work, *The Myth of Sisyphus*.

27. This interpretation challenges fundamentally Dostoevsky's own assessment of his accomplishment: "Even in Europe such force of atheistic *expression* [as exists in the Inquisitor and Ivan's rebellion] does not now exist *nor did it ever*. Accordingly, it is not like a child that I believe in Christ and profess faith in him, but rather, my *hosanna* has come through the great *crucible of doubt*" (Fyodor Dostoevsky, *The Unpublished Dostoevsky: Diaries and Notebooks (1860–81)* (Ann Arbor: Ardis, 1976b), 175).

28. For reasons that should be partially clear now and will become clearer below, I disagree fundamentally with Bakhtin's celebration of the genuinely polyphonic character of Dostoevsky's book: "Dostoevsky was capable of representing someone else's idea, preserving its full capacity to signify as an idea, while at the same time also preserving a distance, neither confirming the idea nor merging it with his own expressed ideology. The idea, in his work, becomes the subject of artistic representation, and Dostoevsky himself became a great artist of the idea." Mikhail Bakhtin, *Problems of Dostoevsky's Poetics* (Minneapolis: University of Minnesota Press, 1984), 130.

29. Herman Melville, *The Confidence-Man* (Oxford: Oxford University Press, 1989), 109. Equally apropos is the confidence man's assertion "that from evil comes good" (ibid.).

30. Berdyaev writes in this regard: "Zosima and Alyosha, in whom [Dostoevsky] gave voice to his positive theories, cannot be numbered among his best-drawn characters; Ivan Karamazov is infinitely more strong and convincing, and his very darkness is pierced by a shaft of strong light" (Berdyaev, *Dostoievsky*, 205).

31. Immediately after the boy has departed the senior confidence man—the Cosmopolitan—asks: "Pray, will you put your money in your belt tonight?" (Melville, *The Confidence-Man*, 303).

32. Such Detectors were in common usage in the period. However, given the sheer number of notes and issuing banks, these documents were often book-length texts and were effectual in the hands of all but a few experts. Stephen Mihm, *A Nation of Counterfeiters: Capitalists, Con Men, and the Making of the United States* (Cambridge: Harvard University Press, 2009).

33. Stephen Mihm, *A Nation of Counterfeiters: Capitalists, Con Men, and the Making of the United States*, 325–330.

34. For a serious though unsuccessful attempt, see Albert Camus, *The Rebel*.

35. This is the strategy employed by Iago in Shakespeare's *Othello*.

36. The extent of the barbarism is apparent in the fact that Ivan has the Virgin Mary plead with God for mercy on the souls of the dead in Hell that their suffering might be relieved. God grants them a small reprieve and justifies his hardness by pointing to the wounds on the hands and feet of Jesus (BK, 228).

37. Camus, *The Rebel*, 101.

38. Camus, *The Rebel*, 101.

39. Camus, *The Rebel*, 101.

40. For an example of this type of reading, see Kroeker and Ward, *Remembering the End: Dostoevsky as Prophet to Modernity*, see especially chapter 1.

41. "'I am a bug, and I recognize in all humility that I cannot understand why the world is arranged as it is'" (BK, 224).

42. F. W. Nietzsche, *The Antichrist* (London: Penguin Books, 1990), 47.

43. "Nihilist and Christian: They Rhyme, and Do Not Merely Rhyme . . ." Nietzsche, *The Antichrist*, 58.

44. Nietzsche, *The Antichrist*, 53.

45. Ivan agrees with Zosima that meaning in existence depends on a belief in God and immortality, thus anticipating the undoing of his own critique. See *The Brothers Karamazov*, 60.

46. See Belknap, "The Rhetoric of an Ideological Novel" for a discussion of these figures.

47. Lawrence spots the excessive rhetoric of Dostoevsky's account but concedes too much ground to the Inquisitor's assessment of humanity's moral sensibilities.

48. Niccolo Machiavelli, *The Prince* (Chicago: The University of Chicago Press, 1998), Book 18.

49. Alyosha responds to Ivan's poem by saying, "That's not the idea of [freedom] in the Orthodox Church. . . . That's Rome, and not even the whole of Rome, it's false—those are the worst of Catholics, the Inquisitors, the Jesuits!" (BK, 241).

50. Dostoyevsky, *Complete Letters*, to E. N. Lebedev, November 8, 1879.

51. In a letter to his editor Dostoevsky writes: "My hero [Ivan] chooses a theme I consider irrefutable: the senselessness of children's suffering, and develops from it the absurdity of all historical reality," Dostoyevsky, *Complete Letters*, to E. N. Lebedev, May 10, 1879.

52. Terms like "intellect alone," "reason alone," and "science" understood as being antithetical to the "spiritual world" are ubiquitous in Zosima's speech (BK, 297, 294, 292).

53. "Miracle, mystery, and authority" (BK, 236).

54. "I must have retribution, or I will destroy myself" (BK, 225).

55. "They will tremble impotently before our wrath, their minds will grow fearful" (BK, 239).

ELEVEN

How Bodies Read and Write

Dostoevsky's Demons *and Coetzee's* Master of Petersburg

Michael S. Kochin

To the memory of Ginat Podrozansky (1978–2011), demon muse.

WHY WRITERS—AND NON-WRITERS—WRITE

Contemporary readers of Dostoevsky's *Demons* tend to take their bearings not from what is in the finished novel, but what was excluded from it, the suppressed chapter "At Tikhon's."[1] In this chapter, the aristocratic antihero Nikolai Stavrogin journeys to a monastery to confess his sins before the holy man Tikhon. Stavrogin confesses to having seduced a young girl, Matryona, and then stood by while she hanged herself in confusion and shame. He confesses to Tikhon by giving him a printed pamphlet resembling a political tract printed by some Russian exile press.[2] Stavrogin asks Tikhon to read the pamphlet to himself, while he sits beside the holy man "silent and motionless."[3]

The narrator, Anton Lavrentievich G___v,[4] prefaces the text of Stavrogin's confession with the following apologia:

> I introduce this document into my chronicle verbatim. One may suppose it is now known to many. I have allowed myself only to correct the spelling errors, rather numerous, which even surprised me somewhat, since the author was after all an educated man, and even a well-read one (judging relatively, of course). In the style I have made no

changes, despite the errors and even obscurities. In any case, it is apparent that the author is above all not a writer.[5]

A number of things are going on in this apologia. Most fundamentally, Dostoevsky—or G___v—is signaling a shift in style, and distancing himself from whatever infelicities the fictional author of the confession has committed. Even Tikhon the holy man cannot quite stomach some of the pamphlet's stylistic monstrosities. Yet there is more to it than style. There is something about the confession, "in the essence," that impels "writers" to put distance between it and them. Stavrogin is the (fictional) author of the confession, but he is not a writer.[6] Dostoevsky, unlike his fictional author Stavrogin, is a writer. Dostoevsky is sufficiently confident in his claim to be a writer that he would publish, subsequent to *Demons*, a one-man journal under the title *Diary of a Writer*.[7]

Stavrogin does not write as a writer, claims G___v.[8] At the heart of the issue here are the motives and purposes of writing. Does Stavrogin write for the same reason a writer would? Out of the same motives as Dostoevsky, or out of the same motives as Dostoevsky's narrator G___v? Out of the same motives as Coetzee, who writes a novel that fictionalizes how Dostoevsky came to write *Demons*? Stavrogin confesses, the reader is to believe, out of a tangle of psychological motives that it takes the entire novel *Demons*, in either its planned or its actual form, to explicate.[9] Tikhon, for his part, takes a shot at explaining Stavrogin's motives in confessing, and is accurate enough that Stavrogin called him a "cursed psychologist."[10] *Demons* attempts to be psychologically realistic—we readers are supposed to find Stavrogin's motives not only explanatory of his confession within the plot, but also motives we could plausibly ascribe to a human being, all the more human, perhaps, because he not a writer.

We need to hold open the possibility that the criteria for being a writer, the motives for writing as a writer, are orthogonal to the motives a reader, if he or she is a non-writer, would find explanatory or compelling. G___v's preface to Stavrogin's confession indicates, but does not answer, the questions: how do writers write, what motives move them to write, and to what end do they write? How and why, in particular, did Dostoevsky write Stavrogin's confession? These are, of course, questions for few readers and none: questions only for those readers who are writers or who wish to understand the phenomenology of writing as an activity of writers. "A crowd isn't interested in fine points of authorship," as Coetzee's Nechaev says to Coetzee's Dostoevsky.[11] Not that this should dissuade from pursuing the question: real writers, it may be said, write for no one, for eternity, or for the dead.[12] For us non-writer readers, it would take a miracle to read either Dostoevsky or Coetzee as a writer would—but to read *Demons* one must in any case hold open the possibility of miracles, of the miracle of repentance and of the resurrection of the body.

One wonders if a writer's life "will bear much scrutiny" as Coetzee's Dostoevsky ponders regarding himself. A writer's life, Coetzee's Dostoevsky claims, is "a life without honor, confession without limit, treachery without end." Why did Dostoevsky write this "book of evil," *Demons*?—"To what end?—To liberate himself from evil or to cut himself off from good?"[13] This is the untamed, wild, or, to use Professor Avramenko's term, "spooky," version of Dominic Head's tame academic-critical question: "What kind of ethical stance can be claimed for the novel?"[14] J. M. Coetzee's *Master of Petersburg* shows non-writer readers why and how writers write. Coetzee's guiding example is Dostoevsky's composition of Stavrogin's confession, and the novel *Demons* of which it was intended to form a part.

In Coetzee's fiction, *Master of Petersburg*, the novelist Dostoevsky, having fled abroad to escape his creditors, returns to St. Petersburg under an assumed name to inquire into the mysterious death of his stepson Pavel Isaev. Dostoevsky moves into Pavel's furnished room, puts on Pavel's white suit, and commences an affair with Pavel's landlady Anna—at the same time playing—at least in his head—with seducing the landlady's young daughter, Matryona.

The bodies of Anna and Matryona, however, are not the only ones to move the writer. Pavel's death, Dostoevsky discovers, is somehow the consequence of his having become entangled with the (historical) nihilist terrorist Sergei Nechaev. Matryona herself is entangled with Nechaev and his followers as well. Indeed, it appears that Nechaev arranged Pavel's death solely in order to lure the writer back to Russia. Nechaev takes Dostoevsky on a tour of the poverty and squalor of underground St. Petersburg.

In Coetzee's novel, it is from this personal encounter with Nechaev, from the writer's fantasies about Matryona, and from his attempts to bring back the dead Pavel in memory that Dostoevsky is moved to compose his great novel, *Demons*. Coetzee goes so far as to have Dostoevsky assert that one can have a hunger for words about the dead: "I have a hunger to talk about my son . . . but even more of a hunger to hear others talk about him."[15] One is tempted to say that "hunger" is a metaphor, but what is being compared to hunger in the usual sense? The passion for words about the dead is felt no less corporeally than hunger is felt for food or thirst is felt for drink. Hunger for words, for disembodied words, is a passion of a body.

The trouble with evoking the dead is that they stay dead even after being evoked. Evoking them out of longing for the dead, the evoker retains the knowledge that the dead are dead. Dostoevsky has only pen and paper, but could do no better with Harry Potter's resurrection stone. In any case, Coetzee's Dostoevsky will be unable to bring back Pavel: "Ultimately it will not be given to him to bring the dead boy back to life. Ultimately if he wants to meet him he will have to meet him in death."[16]

The evocation of the dead will not bring the body back to life. To meet the dead, the writer's body will also have to suffer death. To evoke the dead is to encounter them, in imagination, in writing.

Master of Petersburg is thus not a historical novel. "A historical novel, by definition, is set in a real historical past," as Coetzee says apropos of Philip Roth's *The Plot against America*, also a novel set in a past that never happened.[17] The work of fiction called *Master of Petersburg* offers a less-than-trustworthy phenomenology of how the body writes—and reads—not least since its reconstruction of authorship is emancipated from any fidelity to mere biographical fact—Dostoevsky never met the nihilist terrorist Nechaev. Moreover, Dostoevsky's stepson Pavel, murdered in *Master of Petersburg*, outlived the great novelist in actuality. Coetzee, however, as a writer, takes these liberties with Dostoevsky's real life as a writer to simplify his task of presenting the phenomenology of writing to non-writer readers. We non-writers assume that a writer gets his ideas from what he sees, smells, tastes, or touches. The writer who reads, however, feels what he reads at least as vividly as what he experiences. The historical Dostoevsky made his nihilists live using principally what he read in the newspaper—as he wrote to his editor, M. N. Katkov, "I know nothing at all about Nechaev . . . except from the newspapers."[18] Coetzee assumes that this aspect of a writer's power, to write out of what he reads, is too much for us non-writers to understand, at least until we have thought through how the writer can write out of what he experiences in the flesh, in his own body, when he reads and writes. Of course, Coetzee's fictional phenomenology of writing and reading is simply another fiction, and therefore belongs to the class of writings whose production and reception it is the task of a materialist philosophy of literature to explain.

READING STAVROGIN

Let us put on the virtual dissecting table some preliminary answers to the question of Dostoevsky's motivation in composing Stavrogin's confession. First, Stavrogin's confession is, as Coetzee brings out, an erotic fantasy.[19] Stavrogin is a Byronesque hero, and writer and reader get vicarious sexual pleasure out of contemplating his sexual exploits. Coetzee's Dostoevsky is an aroused observer, aware of the budding breasts of the young Matryona.[20] Indeed, Coetzee's Dostoevsky thinks to himself: "He cannot fail to notice the budding breasts." Either he would be untrue to his vocation as a writer if he did not note those budding breasts and put that observation to work, or he *cannot fail* to notice them: simply put, as a writer and a man, he is constitutionally incapable of not making note of them—presumably in an actual or mental notebook. Coetzee's Dostoevsky "has no difficulty in imagining this child in her ecstasy. His imagination seems to have no bounds."[21] The writer imagines writing a book about his seduction of Matryona, whom in this putative book he seduces by reading to her the tale of her own seduction. Coetzee's Dostoevsky subsequently claims to have written "nothing that could offend a child," but hints that this may not remain the case.[22]

Tales like Stavrogin's confession bring the reader transgressive pleasure. "Reading," says Coetzee's Dostoevsky to the political policeman Maximov, "is being the arm and being the axe *and* being the skull, reading is giving yourself up, not holding yourself at a distance and jeering."[23] Here, in the tale of the seduction of a child by book, there is at least something new, and we readers always want something new, as Plato complains of us. One might compare, from *Demons*, the motive of the party of fools and decadents, including G___v, in going out to enjoy the transgressive pleasure of seeing a suicide—complete with corpse:

> At once the idea was voiced of seeing the suicide. The idea met with support: our ladies had never seen a suicide. I remember one of them saying aloud that "everything has become so boring that there's no need to be punctilious about entertainment, as long as it's diverting."[24]

Dostoevsky's reader, of course, participates in the diversion of contemplating the suicide. This is the same kind of pleasure we get from reading about the machinations of Dostoevsky's fictionalized Nechaev, Pyotr Stepanovich Verkhovensky. In feeding this transgressive pleasure, Dostoevsky is contributing to the very destruction of values aimed at by Nechaev, and by Dostoevsky's Nechaev figure Pyotr Stepanovich Verkhovensky.

Second, Stavrogin's confession might be presented to us as part of a psychological inquiry. As Coetzee shows, a psychologically skilled writer has much to teach even the police about psychopathology and criminal psychology. Coetzee shows us the police official Maximov requesting Dostoevsky's aid as critic of his stepson Pavel's revolutionary *Nachlass*.[25] The police, Coetzee's Dostoevsky tells them, do not know how to read, something of which the police themselves are perfectly well aware. Yet the writer will not do their reading for them—unless they buy his books to learn how to read! Coetzee's Dostoevsky is never on the side of the police: he refuses to reveal his encounters with Nechaev to the police. Moreover, Coetzee's Dostoevsky betrays the police spy Ivanov to the Nechaevists.[26]

Dostoevsky's efforts in understanding the tortured soul of the aristocratic criminal Stavrogin, or any criminal, have in fact made it impossible for sophisticated readers to collaborate in punishing criminals. Dostoevsky's wrestles with this problem in *Diary of a Writer*: "We must call evil evil . . . we must take on ourselves the burden of the sentence."[27] Educated by Dostoevsky's novels of the criminal psyche, we readers understand the environment in which such damaged souls develop and so cannot bear to condemn them.[28] Yet "jurors who acquit right and left are ours," says Pyotr/Nechaev.[29] Coetzee's Dostoevsky makes the appropriate self-diagnosis: "First in his writing and then in his life, shame seems to have lost its power, its place taken by a blank and amoral passivity that shrinks from no extreme."[30] From the point of view of moral seriousness, of Aristotle's serious man (*spoudaios*), Stavrogin's antics are unserious and squalid. A serious man would never read or write a novel like *Demons*, lest he, like Matryona, be seduced to transgressive pleasures—lest he too risk losing his soul to demonic possession.[31]

WRITING STAVROGIN

The writer must give up his soul in order to write.[32] He must give up his soul to become the body writing. While we sometimes still pretend that we understand what the Romantics meant when they spoke of literary works as achievements of the human spirit, we no longer find their dualism of matter and spirit persuasive. What changes for our understanding of the processes of literature when we recognize that it is the body that writes? Roland Barthes and Gilles Deleuze, among others, have sought to develop such a materialist philosophy of literature, but in this line of research it has proven extraordinarily difficult to go beyond gnomic statements such as Barthes's observation that "writing proceeds through the body."[33]

J. M. Coetzee's fiction is rich in the struggles of authors with their bodies in the embodied act of writing.[34] In *Master of Petersburg*, we see Dostoevsky swap his passions for the questionable currency of words on paper; out of grieving for his stepson (and by exploring the fetid basements of St. Petersburg for clues to his murder) Dostoevsky somehow produces the novel *Demons*. Dostoevsky, the cracked bell, is also the Master of Petersburg—for Dostoevsky's St. Petersburg will remain vivid in the imagination of readers after Dostoevsky, Nechaev and Pavel are all dust.[35]

To understand how the body writes we have to separate the question of how the body writes from the tradition of writing about the body. In particular, we need to put aside the whole tradition of writing about the body known as vitalism, which aims to bring the functions of the body into literature. One might think of Rabelais, of Swift, of Kafka, of D. H. Lawrence. What I want to put on the table is not the functions of the body that were once unmentionable in polite company when there was such a thing as polite company, or polite literature when there was such a thing as polite literature. The goal of my physiology is to show the body writing.

Bruno Latour taught us to understand how science produces results, scientific papers or technological devices, by following scientists around as they produce these results in the laboratory.[36] Coetzee suggests that we understand how writers produce writing by following the written product as it is excreted from the writers' body. One could begin with the body not writing:

> Following old habit, [Dostoevsky] spends the morning at the little desk in his room. When the maid comes to clean, he waves her away. But he does not write a word. It is not that he is paralysed. His heart pumps steadily, his mind is clear. At any moment he is capable of picking up the pen and forming letters on the paper. But the writing, he fears, would be that of a madman—vileness, obscenity, page after page of it, untamable. He thinks of the madness as running down through the artery of his right arm down to the fingertips and the pen and so to the page. It runs in a stream; he need not dip the pen, not once. What flows on to the paper is neither blood nor ink, but an acid, black, with an unpleasant green sheen when the light glances off it. On the page it does not dry: if one were to pass a finger over it, one would experience a sensation both liquid and electric. A writing that even the blind could read.[37]

There is a crude vitalism here, where writing is portrayed as a letting of blood-spirit. The activity described in this passage is not writing, but mad scribbling. To preserve himself as a writer, Coetzee's fictional Dostoevsky refuses to open his artery and scribble.[38] To become a writer, we shall see, it is not enough to give up your life's blood.

Of course, both *Master of Petersburg* and *Demons* are about a very peculiar state of the body, demonic possession, which at least Coetzee's Dostoevsky thinks is not the same as being possessed by an idea. "Nechaevism is not an idea. Nechaevism," says Coetzee's Dostoevsky, "is a spirit, and Nechaev himself is not its embodiment but its host, or rather, he is under possession by it."[39] At that moment, Coetzee's Dostoevsky gives that spirit the wrong name: he calls it Baal. Nechaev's spirit's true name, according to the historical Dostoevsky's novel *Demons*, is "Legion." One cannot cast out demons unless one can name each and every one of them correctly.[40]

How does a story, "a private matter, an utterly private matter, until it is given to the world"—how does a story make this transition to the world through the body of the writer?[41] How does the writer write the possessed Stavrogin for us to read? Mike Marais notes that in *Master of Petersburg*, "Like sex, and, indeed, death and epileptic seizures, writing is a falling that ecstatically divests [the writer] of a controlling subjectivity."[42] Yet the writer's loss of subjectivity is ultimately, like the writer's subjectivity, of secondary interest compared to the work: how does the work become an object, a public matter, part of the world because successfully "given to the world"? Insurance executive Wallace Stevens once wrote, "The truth is that the most conspicuous element from the point of view of human interest in the handling of claims is the claim man himself."[43] The dry joke is that, as Stevens explains with a poet's precision, just as for the claim man the most interesting thing in claims work is the claims themselves and their proper disposal, for the reader and the writer the most interesting thing in literature is not the writer but the writing. By *modus tollens*, this implies that the very goal of materialist poetics, of trying to understand how the body writes, is to get outside the "point of view of human interest" on literature.

Thus, to think about how bodies write we must think about how they read.[44] In *Demons*, the exemplary reader is Stepan Trofimovich Verkhovensky, liberal aristocrat and failed historian and father of Pyotr Stepanovich, the Nechaev-like nihilist terrorist. Stepan Trofimovich, like us, is a reader and not a writer. That is to say, he is an indolent or incompetent reader, because he does not put his reading to work as a writer. The most active reader must be a writer, and not just a critic. As Dostoevsky himself once wrote, one needs an artist's vision and capacity in order to read.[45] Likewise, one needs to be a writer to find in the facts of a real incident "a depth that you won't find even in Shakespeare."[46] The fabled inadequacy of art to life is the inadequacy of art—as judged by the artist—to life—as observed by the artist. There is a similar inadequacy of writing to reading by a writer. Coetzee presents what he can of the fullness of his own readings in pastiche or retellings, of which *Master of Petersburg* is the most accomplished.

Stepan Trofimovich is widely read enough to be a great writer and has a sensitive critical palate, even if his tastes are low (the French pulp novelist de Kock instead of the French political scientist de Tocqueville)—but then, as Nabokov liked to point out, so are Dostoevsky's.[47] Stepan Trofimovich is a liberal reader; he loudly and firmly proclaimed that boots are lower than Pushkin, much less Shakespeare.[48] Davison wonders whether Stepan Trofimovich succeeds in moving from the aesthetic to the ethical.[49] Yet the superiority of the ethical to the aesthetic is one of the things we put in question by trying to read *Demons* with J. M. Coetzee, as a writer would.

Stepan Trofimovich's literary judgments as a reader, not a writer, seem excellent. Dostoevsky, a better reader, wrote, "I love my Stepan Trofimovich, after all, and deeply respect him."[50] Stepan is familiar with the major radical works, such as Chernyshevsky's *What Is to Be Done?*, and criticizes them acutely. More astonishingly, he, unlike the writer Karmazinov, sees through the radical chic of the former liberals.[51] Such miraculous power is not given to the non-writing provincial governor's wife Yulia Mikhailovna, or to the retired reader, Stepan's patroness Varvara Petrovna, when she is under the possession of radical chic.[52] Even the writerly narrator of *Demons*, Mr. G___v, is only willing to name names already known to the authorities.[53] Dostoevsky will write later, "The possibility of considering oneself—and sometimes even being, in fact—an honorable person while committing obvious and undeniable villainy—that is our whole affliction today."[54] From that affliction, Stepan Trofimovich is miraculously immune.

Stepan sees through the radicals, but also sees how the radicals have sprung from the liberals, how they are their legitimate children, one could say. Stepan pronounces a father's curse upon the Nechaev figure, his son Pyotr.[55] Yet, if Stepan has the acute vision of the writer, he has a kind of physical indolence that keeps him from writing. This indolence prevents him from giving up his soul, either to radical chic, to writing, or any other kind of possession. Stepan Trofimovich does not *stand* a reproach to the repressive government of Russia—standing for so long is difficult, so instead Stepan Trofimovitch *reclines*. By the time the novel opens, Stepan's indolence has deepened to the point that he hardly even reads.[56]

Stepan Trofimovich is thus an alternative to the radical readers of a later generation—the radicals get everything out of books, unlike Stepan Trofimovich, who brings to books an orientation toward reading acquired from his privileged background and European university education.[57] Yet Stepan the critic cannot compete with the books; he has not been able to transmit his liberalism to his pupils: both the ruined young aristocrats Stavrogin and Liza were his pupils, but neither succeed in crafting a life for themselves, either out of reading or out of any of the choices available to the wealthy, intelligent, young, and beautiful.[58] Stavrogin, the non-writer, is possessed. Like Matryona, the radicals are seduced to transgression by their reading. It is only Stepan Trofimovich, the reader who does not write, who keeps himself together.

THE WRITER'S POSSESSIONS

To write Stavrogin, then, the writer must be open to possession; he must be willing to be seduced by the loss of personality necessary to produce writing that is of other than personal value. The moral danger for the writer—for the writer writing with the body—is this possession. Stavrogin, after all, is not a writer, but he *is* a rapist. Pyotr/Nechaev is not a writer, but he *is* a murderer. To write the possessed, the writer himself must allow his body to be possessed by their demons. He cannot appease these demons with mere blood—as we have seen, the writer must "give up his soul."[59]

Both novels show us this close relation between literature and the extreme mistreatment of bodies at the hands of governments, terrorists, criminals, the self, and demons. Coetzee's Nechaev recognizes this, saying to Dostoevsky in a dripping cellar with two hungry children feeding on a loaf of bread earned by their streetwalker mother: "I suppose you want to hurry home and get this cellar and these children down in a notebook before the memory fades."[60] The suffering of children, he recognizes, is precisely the sort of thing that motivates the writer. Suffering children, like the budding breasts of the young girl Matryona, inspire the writer, that is, both suffering and erotic passion open the writer to possession by demonic spirits. Suffering offers the writer the occasion for indulging the transgressive pleasure of possession. Suffering, or its Latin equivalent, passion, licenses the writer to divest himself of the controlling subjectivity of his non-writer self.

The possession invoked by the spectacle of suffering can motivate the writer and the reader to suffer with the suffering—it can instill compassion. Yet the spectacle of suffering can also move the writer and the reader to revel in the delight in his own power felt by the deliberate perpetrator of suffering. Indeed, the writer thus can present us with the torturer as clearly as he or she can present us with the tortured.[61] Coetzee's Dostoevsky knows well and puts to work in writing Stavrogin's confession that there is generally more "real life" in fictional rapists than in fictional victims.[62] The question that remains is whether the writing itself is conducive to the alleviation of this suffering, or whether it merely affords the reader a view of the spectacle of that suffering from a safe aesthetic distance. Faced with a choice between vitality and morals, every writer will choose vitality—and every serious man will choose morality. One would like to believe that the writer suffers with his victims, and thus his art encourages the serious reader to get out of his easy chair and act to alleviate human suffering. But the real Dostoevsky wrote Stavrogin's confession, and the real J. M. Coetzee wrote *The Master of Petersburg*.

NOTES

For my previous studies of the body writing see Michael S. Kochin, "Literature and Salvation in *Elizabeth Costello*, or How to Refuse to Be an Author in Eight or Nine Lessons," *English in Africa* 34 (2007), 90, 127; Michael Kochin, "Life as Literature: Wright Morris's *Love Among the Cannibals*" (Paper presented at the Annual Meeting of the American Political Science Auguste Association, 2005).

An earlier version of this paper was presented at a panel on "Dostoevsky and the Problem of Western Rights" at the 2011 meeting of the American Political Science Association. I would like to thank my respondent, Dan Mahoney, Donna Orwin, and Anna Kochin for their comments and suggestions.

1. Dostoevsky's editor M. N. Katkov refused to publish "At Tikhon's" when the novel was coming out as a serial, forcing Dostoevsky to rewrite and rethink his plot. In consequence, the suppressed chapter cannot be slotted into the novel as Dostoevsky eventually completed it—indeed the chapter was not published in his lifetime. For details, see Joseph Frank, *Dostoevsky: The Miraculous Years, 1865–1871* (Princeton: Princeton University Press, 1995), 431–434.

2. Fyodor Dostoevsky, *Demons* (New York: Everyman, 1994), 690.

3. Dostoevsky, *Demons*, 690, 705.

4. For the narrator's name, see Dostoevsky, *Demons*, 90, 127.

5. Dostoevsky, *Demons*, 690–691.

6. Dostoevsky, *Demons*, 705 and 710.

7. Fyodor Dostoevsky, *Diary of a Writer* (Evanston: Northwestern University Press, 1994).

8. Early in the book Stavrogin makes an editorial comment on the cliché "I won't be led by the nose" (Dostoevsky, *Demons*, 45) but he acts out that comment rather than write it down.

9. Coetzee explores the paradoxes of confession, with discussions of (*inter alia*) "At Tikhon's" as well as *Notes from Underground*, in J. M. Coetzee, "Confessions and Double Thoughts: Tolstoy, Rousseau, Dostoevsky," *Comparative Literature* 37 (1985), 193–232, reprinted in J. M. Coetzee, *Doubling the Point* (Cambridge: Harvard University Press, 1992), 251–294.

10. Dostoevsky, *Demons*, 706–714.

11. J. M. Coetzee, *The Master of Petersburg* (London: Martin Secker and Warburg 1994), 200.

12. Coetzee, *The Master of Petersburg*, 245. Cf. the subtitle of Nietzsche's *Thus Spoke Zarathustra*: "A Book for All and None."

13. Coetzee, *The Master of Petersburg*, 134, 221, 222.

14. Richard Avramenko, "Bedeviled by Boredom: A Voegelinian Reading of Dostoevsky's *Possessed*," *Humanitas* XVII (2004), 113–138; Dominick Head, *The Cambridge Introduction to J. M. Coetzee* (Cambridge: Cambridge University Press, 2010), ix.

15. Coetzee, *The Master of Petersburg*, 25. *The Master of Petersburg* was published in 1994. Coetzee's son Nicholas died from an accidental fall in 1989, age 23.

16. Coetzee, *The Master of Petersburg*, 238–239.

17. J. M. Coetzee, "Philip Roth, *The Plot Against America*" in *Inner Workings: Literary Essays 2000–2005* (New York: Viking, 2007), 228–243, 241.

18. Quoted in Frank, *Dostoevsky: The Miraculous Years, 1865–1871*, 400.

19. Hayes writes of "the monologic pornography of Stavrogin's confession"; Patrick Hayes, *J. M. Coetzee and the Novel: Writing and Politics after Beckett* (Oxford: Oxford University Press, 2010), 193. Yet Stavrogin's confession does not merely stir the prurient imagination with his description of his rape of a child. In the suppressed chapter "At Tikhon's" the written confession is but a move in dialogue with the comments of G___v and Tikhon himself, as I noted above.

20. Coetzee, *The Master of Petersburg*, 28.

21. Coetzee, *The Master of Petersburg*, 76.

22. Coetzee, *The Master of Petersburg*, 134, 144–145.

23. Coetzee, *The Master of Petersburg*, 47.

24. Dostoevsky, *Demons*, 326.

25. Coetzee, *The Master of Petersburg*, 34–38.

26. Coetzee, *The Master of Petersburg*, 46–47, 92, 147–148.

27. Dostoevsky, *Diary of a Writer*, 1:135.

28. One is here reminded of the education Nietzsche received from reading Dostoevsky's criminals. We know Nietzsche admits his debt to Dostoevsky (Friedrich Nietzsche, *Twilight of the Idols with the Antichrist and Ecce Homo* (London: Wordsworth Editions Limited, 2007), 77), but much less has been made about the kinship between Raskolnikov and the pale criminal in *Thus Spoke Zarathustra*, in a chapter called "The Pale Criminal."

29. Dostoevsky, *Demons*, 420.

30. Coetzee, *The Master of Petersburg*, 24.

31. As Derek Attridge writes: "*The Master of Petersburg* . . . presents a vision of the writing process, and more generally of creativity, of inventiveness, of the achievement of the new, as having nothing to do with traditional understandings of ethics, or with human responsibility—only responsibility to and for the new, unanticipatible, thing that is coming into being"; Derek Attridge, *J. M. Coetzee and the Ethics of Reading* (Chicago: University of Chicago Press, 2004), 132–133. For more on the serious man, see Aristotle, *The Nicomachean Ethics* (Oxford: Oxford University Press, 1980), 1098a, 1099a, 1113a, 1166a, 1169a–1170b, 1176b; Francis Edward Sparshott, *Taking Life Seriously: A Study of the Argument of the Nicomachean Ethics* (Toronto: University of Toronto Press, 1994); Richard Avramenko, "The Gnostic and the Spoudaios: Aristotle, Voegelin and the Drama of Being," *Political Science Reviewer* Forthcoming (2013).

32. Coetzee, *The Master of Petersburg*, 250.

33. Roland Barthes, *Barthes on Barthes* (Berkeley: University of California Press, 1994), 80.

34. See Kochin, "Literature and Salvation in *Elizabeth Costello*, or How to Refuse to be an Author in Eight or Nine Lessons."

35. Coetzee, *The Master of Petersburg*, 140–141. Of course, the title *Master of Petersburg* is also a gesture toward the demon-infested Moscow of Bulgakov's *The Master and Margarita*.

36. See Michael S. Kochin, "What Political Science Needs to Learn from Science Studies" (Paper presented at the Annual Meeting of the American Political Science Association (Toronto, August 2009)); Bruno Latour, *Science in Action: How to Follow Scientists and Engineers through Society* (Cambridge: Harvard University Press, 1987); Bruno Latour and Steve Woolgar, *Laboratory Life: The Construction of Scientific Facts* (Princeton: Princeton University Press, 1986).

37. Coetzee, *The Master of Petersburg*, 18.

38. Contrast Nietzsche in "Of Reading and Writing" in *Thus Spoke Zarathustra*, "Of all that is written, I love only that which is written with one's own blood. Write with blood, and you'll discover that blood is spirit"; Friedrich Nietzsche, *Thus Spoke Zarathustra* (Oxford: Oxford University Press, 2005), 35. This chapter, incidentally, follows directly on "The Pale Criminal."

39. Coetzee, *The Master of Petersburg*, 44.

40. See Luke 8:30; two verses before the beginning of the epigraph to *Demons*; cf. Mark 5:9, Babylonian Talmud, Pesachim 111b; and see Mike Marais, "Death and the Space of the Response to the Other" in *J. M. Coetzee and the Idea of the Public*, ed. Jane Poyner (Athens: Ohio University Press, 2006), 83–99, 87–88. Coetzee disagrees with Avramenko, "Bedeviled by Boredom," about whether Dostoevsky or his creations can be understood without "spooks." As Joseph Frank says, the talk of demons in *Demons* "is meant much more literally than has usually been assumed"; Frank, *Dostoevsky: The Miraculous Years, 1865–1871*, 412. Pyotr Stepanovich is Satan, "the wise serpent," as he is called in the title of the chapter (part 1, chapter 5) in which he introduced; W. J. Leatherbarrow, "*The Devils* in the Context of Dostoevsky's Life and Work" in *Dostoevsky's* The Devils: *A Critical Companion*, ed. W. J. Leatherbarrow (Evanston: Northwestern University Press, 1999), 37–38; Gary Adelman, "Stalking Stavrogin: J. M. Coetzee's *The Master of Petersburg* and the Writing of *The Possessed*," *Journal of Modern Literature* 23 (2000).

41. Coetzee, *The Master of Petersburg*, 40.

42. Sue Kossew, "The Anxiety of Authorship: J. M. Coetzee's *Master of Petersburg* and André Brink's *On the Contrary*," *English in Africa* 20 (1996); Marais, "Death and the Space of the Response to the Other," 93.

43. Wallace Stevens, "Surety and Fidelity Claims" in *Collected Prose and Poetry*, ed. Frank Kermode and Joan Richardson (New York: Library of America, 1997), 796–799, 799.

44. See also Kochin, "Life as Literature: Wright Morris's Love Among the Cannibals."

45. Dostoevsky, *Diary of a Writer*, 1:23.

46. Dostoevsky, *Diary of a Writer*, 1:651.

47. Vladimir Vladimirovich Nabokov, *Lectures on Russian Literature* (New York: Harcourt Brace Jovanovich, 1980), ed. F. Bowers.

48. Dostoevsky, *Demons*, 25, 485.

49. R. M. Davison, "Dostoevsky's *The Devils*: The Role of Stepan Trofimovich Verkhovensky" in *Dostoevsky's* The Devils: *A Critical Companion*, ed. W. J. Leatherbarrow (Evanston: Northwestern University Press, 1999), 126.

50. Dostoevsky, *Diary of a Writer*, 1:550.

51. Dostoevsky, *Demons*, 303–304, 213, 215, 336.

52. Dostoevsky, *Demons*, 300–301, 316–317, 338–339.

53. Dostoevsky, *Demons*, 391.

54. Dostoevsky, *Diary of a Writer*, 1:287.
55. Dostoevsky, *Demons*, 122, 304, 307.
56. Dostoevsky, *Demons*, 12–13, 20, 60.
57. Dostoevsky, *Demons*, 31.
58. Dostoevsky, *Demons*, 40.
59. Coetzee, *The Master of Petersburg*, 250.
60. Coetzee, *The Master of Petersburg*, 186.
61. J. M. Coetzee, *Elizabeth Costello: Eight Lessons* (London: Martin Secker and Warburg, 2003), 204.
62. See Coetzee, *The Master of Petersburg*, 194.

Bibliography

Adelman, Gary. "Stalking Stavogrin: J. M. Coetzee's *The Master of Petersburg* and the Writing of *The Possessed*." *Journal of Modern Literature* 23, no. 2 (2000): 351–357.
Alulis, Joseph. "Dostoevsky and the Metaphysical Foundation of the Liberal Regime: 'Legend of the Grand Inquisitor.'" *Perspectives on Political Science* 38, no. 4 (2009): 206–216.
Anderson, Benedict. *Imagined Communities: Reflections on the Origin and Spread of Nationalism*. New York: Verso, 1991.
Anderson, Susan Leigh. *On Dostoevsky*. Boston: Wadsworth, 2001.
Arendt, Hannah. "Thinking and Moral Considerations." *Social Research* 38, no. 3 (1971): 317–346.
Aristotle. *The Nicomachean Ethics*. Translated by W. D. Ross. Oxford: Oxford University Press, 1980.
Attridge, Derek. *J. M. Coetzee and the Ethics of Reading*. Chicago: University of Chicago Press, 2004.
Avramenko, Richard. "Bedeviled by Boredom: A Voegelinian Reading of Dostoevsky's *Possessed*." *Humanitas* XVII, no. 1 & 2 (2004): 108–138.
Avramenko, Richard. "The Gnostic and the Spoudaios: Aristotle, Voegelin and the Drama of Being." *Political Science Reviewer* Forthcoming (2013).
Bakhtin, Mikhail. *Problems of Dostoevsky's Poetics*. Minneapolis: University of Minnesota Press, 1984a.
Bakhtin, Mikhail, ed. *Problems of Dostoevsky's Poetics*. Minneapolis: University of Minnesota Press, 1984b.
Barthes, Roland. *Barthes on Barthes*. Translated by R. Howard. Berkeley: University of California Press, 1994.
Belknap, Robert. "The Rhetoric of an Ideological Novel." In *Literature and Society in Imperial Russia, 1800–1914*, edited by W. M. Todd III, 173–201. Stanford: Stanford University Press, 1978.
Belknap, Robert. *The Genesis of* The Brothers Karamazov: *The Aesthetics, Ideology, and Psychology of Text-Making*. Evanston, IL: Northwestern University Press, 1990.
Benedict, Saint. *The Rule of St. Benedict in English*. Edited by T. Fry. Collegeville, MN: The Liturgical Press, 1982.
Bercken, William Peter van den. *Christian Fiction and Religious Realism in the Novels of Dostoevsky*. London: Anthem Press, 2011.
Berdyaev, Nikolai. *Dostoievsky*. Translated by D. Attwater. New York: Sheed & Ward Inc., 1934.
Berdyaev, Nikolai. *Dostoevsky*. Translated by D. Attwater. New York: Meridian Books, 1957.
Berdyaev, Nikolas. *The Russian Idea*. Translated by R. M. French. London: Geoffrey Bles & The Centenary Press, 1947.
Berlin, Isaiah. "Two Kinds of Liberty." In *Four Essays on Liberty*. Oxford: Oxford University Press, 1969.
Berlin, Isaiah. *The Hedgehog and the Fox: An Essay on Tolstoy's View of History*. London: George Weidenfeld & Nicolson Limited, 1988.
Berlin, Isaiah. *The Roots of Romanticism*. Vol. 45th A. W. Mellon Lectures in the Fine Arts. Princeton: Princeton University Press, 1999.
Billington, James H. *The Icon and the Axe: An Interpretive History of Russian Culture*. New York: Vintage, 1966.

Bolshakoff, Serge. *Russian Nonconformity: The Story of "Unofficial" Religion in Russia.* Philadelphia: Westminster Press, 1950.
Brazier, P. H. *Barth and Dostoevsky: A Study of the Influence of the Russian Writer Fyodor Mikhailovich Dostoevsky on the Development of the Swiss Theologian.* Eugene, OR: Wipf & Stock Publishers, 2008.
Breger, Louis. *Dostoevsky: The Author as Psychoanalyst.* New York: New York University Press, 1990.
Briggs, Katherine Jane. *How Dostoevsky Portrays Women in His Novels: A Feminist Analysis.* Lewiston, NY: Edwin Mellen Press, 2009.
Buber, Martin. *Between Man and Man.* Translated by R. G. Smith. New York: Macmillan, 1965.
Bullivant, Stephen. "A House Divided Against Itself: Dostoevsky and the Psychology of Unbelief." *Literature and Theology* 22, no. 1 (2008): 16–31.
Burry, Alexander. *Multi-Mediated Dostoevsky: Transposing Novels into Opera, Film, and Drama.* Evanston: Northwestern University Press, 2011.
Camus, Albert. *The Rebel.* New York: Knopf, 1954.
Camus, Albert. *The Rebel: An Essay on Man in Revolt.* 1st Vintage ed. New York: Vintage Books, 1958.
Camus, Albert. "Helen's Exile." In *Lyrical and Critical Essays*, edited by P. Thody, 148–153. New York: Vintage Books, 1970.
Camus, Albert. *The Rebel.* Translated by A. Bower. New York: Vintage Books, 1990.
Carr, Edward Hallett. *Dostoevsky (1821–1881): A New Biography.* Boston: Houghton Mifflin, 1931.
Carter, Stephen K. *The Political and Social Thought of F. M. Dostoevsky.* New York: Garland Publishing, Inc., 1991.
Casey, Michael. *A Guide to Living in the Truth: St. Benedict's Teaching on Humility.* Liguori, MO: Liguori/Triumph Publications, 2001.
Cassedy, Steven. *Dostoevsky's Religion.* Stanford: Stanford University Press, 2005.
Catteau, Jacques. "The Paradox of the Legend of the Grand Inquisitor in *The Brothers Karamazov.*" In *Dostoevsky: New Perspectives*, edited by R. L. Jackson. Englewood Cliffs: Prentice-Hall, 1984.
Chapple, Richard L. "A Catalogue of Suffering in the Works of Dostoevsky: His Christian Foundation." *The South Central Bulletin* 43, no. 4 (1983): 94–99.
Coetzee, J. M. "Confessions and Double Thoughts: Tolstoy, Rousseau, Dostoevsky." *Comparative Literature* 37, no. 3 (1985): 193–232.
Coetzee, J. M. *Doubling the Point.* Edited by D. Attwell. Cambridge: Harvard University Press, 1992.
Coetzee, J. M. *The Master of Petersburg.* London: Martin Secker and Warburg, 1994.
Coetzee, J. M. *Elizabeth Costello: Eight Lessons.* London: Martin Secker and Warburg, 2003.
Coetzee, J. M. "Philip Roth, The Plot Against America." In *Inner Workings: Literary Essays 2000–2005*, 228–243, 241. New York: Viking, 2007.
Comte, Auguste. *Cours de philosophie positive.* 6 vols. Paris: Bachelier, 1841.
Cox, Roger L. *Between Earth and Heaven: Shakespeare, Dostoevksy and the Meaning of Christian Tragedy.* New York: Holt, Rinehart, and Winston, 1969.
Curtis, James M. "Shestov's Use of Nietzsche in His Interpretation of Tolstoy and Dostoevsky." *Texas Studies in Literature and Language* 17 (1975): 289–302.
Davison, R. M. "Dostoevsky's *The Devils*: The Role of Stepan Trofimovich Verkhovensky." In *Dostoevsky's* The Devils: *A Critical Companion*, edited by W. J. Leatherbarrow. Evanston: Northwestern University Press, 1999.
Dolinin, A. S. "Nenapecatannye stranicy iz 'Zapisok iz mertvogo doma'. Tekst, istorija otryvka i pocemu on ne byl napecatan." In *Dostoevskij: stat'i i materialy*, edited by A. S. Dolinin. St. Petersburg: n.p., 1922.
Dolinin, A. S. "Dostoevsky among the Members of the Petrashevsky Circle." *Russian Studies in Literature* 23, no. 3–4 (1987): 137–177.

Dostoevsky, F. M. *The Brothers Karamazov*. Translated by D. Magarshack. New York: Penguin Books, 1958.
Dostoevsky, F. M. *Polnoe Sobranie Sochineii i Pisem*. 30 vols. Leningrad: Nauka, 1972–1990.
Dostoevsky, F. M. *Winter Notes on Summer Impressions*. London: Quartet Books, 1985.
Dostoevsky, F. M. *Notes from Underground*. Translated by M. Ginsburg. New York: Bantam Books, 1992.
Dostoevsky, Fyodor. *The Possessed: A Novel in Three Parts*. London: William Heinemann, 1913.
Dostoevsky, Fyodor. *Crime and Punishment*. New York: P. F. Collier & Son Company, 1917.
Dostoevsky, Fyodor. *The Brothers Karamazov*. Translated by C. Garnett. New York: Modern Library, 1950.
Dostoevsky, Fyodor. *Crime and Punishment*. Translated by C. Garnett. New York: Dutton, 1961.
Dostoevsky, Fyodor. *The Dream of a Queer Fellow and the Pushkin Speech*. New York: Barnes and Noble, 1961.
Dostoevsky, Fyodor. *The House of the Dead*. Translated by H. Sutherland. New York: Dutton, 1962.
Dostoevsky, Fyodor. *The Idiot*. Translated by H. O. Carlisle. New York: New American Library, 1969.
Dostoevsky, Fyodor. *The Adolescent*. Translated by A. MacAndrew. New York: Norton, 1971.
Dostoevsky, Fyodor. *The Brothers Karamazov*. Translated by C. Garnett. Edited by R. E. Matlaw. New York: W. W. Norton & Company, 1976a.
Dostoevsky, Fyodor. *The Unpublished Dostoevsky: Diaries and Notebooks (1860–1881)*. Translated by A. Boyer and D. Lapeza. Edited by C. Proffer. 3 vols. Ann Arbor: Ardis, 1976b.
Dostoevsky, Fyodor. *The Diary of a Writer*. Translated by B. Brasol. Santa Barbara: Peregrine Smith, 1979.
Dostoevsky, Fyodor. *Demons*. Translated by R. Pevear and L. Volokhonsky. New York: Everyman, 1994a.
Dostoevsky, Fyodor. *Diary of a Writer*. Translated by K. Lentz. 2 vols. Evanston: Northwestern University Press, 1994b.
Dostoevsky, Fyodor. *Notes from Underground*. Translated by R. Pevear and L. Volokhonsky, First Vintage Classics Edition. New York: Vintage Books, 1994c.
Dostoevsky, Fyodor. *The Karamazov Brothers*. Translated by I. Avsey. Oxford: Oxford University Press, 1994d.
Dostoevsky, Fyodor. *The Brothers Karamazov: A Novel in Four Parts*. Translated by D. McDuff. London: Penguin Classic, 2003.
Dostoievsky, F. M. *The Diary of a Writer*. Translated by B. Brasol. Edited by B. Brasol. Vol. 1. London: Cassell, 1949.
Dostoyevsky, F. M. *The Brothers Karamazov*. Translated by C. Garnett. 2 vols. J. M. Dent, 1927.
Dostoyevsky, Fyodor. *The Diary of a Writer*. Translated by B. L. Brasol. 2 vols. New York: C. Scribner's Sons, 1949.
Dostoyevsky, Fyodor. *Letters of Fyodor Michailovitch Dostoevsky to His Family and Friends*. Translated by E. C. Mayne. New York: The Macmillan Company, 1961.
Dostoyevsky, Fyodor. *The Possessed*. Translated by A. R. McAndrew. New York: New American Library, 1962.
Dostoyevsky, Fyodor. *Notes from Underground. The Double*. Baltimore: Penguin Books, 1972a.
Dostoyevsky, Fyodor. *Polnoe sobranie sochinenii v tridtsati tomakh*. Edited by V. G. Bazanov. Leningrad: Nauka, 1972b.
Dostoyevsky, Fyodor. *The House of the Dead*. Translated by D. McDuff. London: Penguin Classics, 1985.

Dostoyevsky, Fyodor. *Complete Letters*. Translated by D. A. Lowe and R. Meyer. 5 vols. Ann Arbor: Ardis, 1988.
Dostoyevsky, Fyodor. *The Brothers Karamazov: A Novel in Four Parts and an Epilogue*. Translated by D. McDuff. London: Penguin, 2003.
Dostoyevsky, Fyodor. *Crime and Punishment*. Translated by J. S. Coulson. Oxford: Oxford University Press, 2008a.
Dostoyevsky, Fyodor. *Winter Notes on Summer Impressions*. Translated by K. Fitzlyon. Surrey, England: Oneworld Classics, 2008b.
Douglass, Frederick. "What to the Slave Is the Fourth of July?" In *Narrative of the Life of Frederick Douglass, An American Slave, Written by Himself with Related Documents*, edited by D. W. Blight, 169. Boston: Bedford/St. Martins, 2003.
Dowler, Wayne. *Dostoevsky, Grigor'ev, and Native Soil Conservatism*. Toronto: University of Toronto Press, 1982.
Drouilly, Jean. *La Pensée Politique et Religiuse de F. M. Dostoevsky*. Paris: Libraire des Cinq Continentes, 1971.
Ellison, Ralph. "Brave New Words for a Starling Occasion." In *The Collected Essays of Ralph Essays*, edited by J. F. Callahan, 151. New York: Modern Library, 1995a.
Ellison, Ralph. *Invisible Man*. New York: Vintage International, 1995b.
Fedotov, G. P. *A Treasury of Russian Spirituality*. New York: Sheed & Ward, 1948.
Figes, Orlando. *Natasha's Dance: A Cultural History of Russia*. New York: Picador, 2002.
Frank, Joseph. "Nihilism and 'Notes from Underground.'" *The Sewanee Review* 69, no. 1 (1961): 1–33.
Frank, Joseph. "Dostoevsky: The Encounter with Europe." *Russian Review* 22, no. 3 (1963): 237–252.
Frank, Joseph. *Dostoevsky: The Seeds of Revolt, 1821–1849*. Princeton: Princeton University Press, 1976.
Frank, Joseph. *Dostoevsky: The Stir of Liberation, 1860–1865*. Princeton: Princeton University Press, 1986.
Frank, Joseph. *Dostoevsky: The Years of Ordeal, 1850–1859*. Princeton: Princeton University Press, 1990a.
Frank, Joseph. "Ralph Ellison and Dostoevsky." In *Through the Russian Prism: Essays on Literature and Culture*, 36. Princeton: Princeton University Press, 1990b.
Frank, Joseph. *Dostoevsky: The Miraculous Years, 1865–1871*. Princeton: Princeton University Press, 1995.
Frank, Joseph. *Dostoevsky: The Mantle of the Prophet, 1871–1881*. Princeton: Princeton University Press, 2002.
Frank, Joseph. *Dostoevsky: A Writer in His Time,* Princeton: Princeton University Press, 2009.
Fridlender, G. M., ed. *Polnoe Sobranie Sochinenii*. Leningrad: n.p. 1972–1990.
Fromm, Erich. "Introduction." In *Marx's Concept of Man*. New York: F. Ungar Publishing Company, 1961.
Gellner, Ernest. *Nations and Nationalism*. Ithaca: Cornell University Press, 1993.
Gibson, A. Boyce. *The Religion of Dostoevsky*. Philadelphia: Westminster, 1973.
Gilligan, James. "Shame, Guilt, and Violence." *Social Research: An International Quarterly* 70, no. 4 (2003): 1153.
Girard, Rene. "Superman in the Underground: Strategies of Madness-Nietzsche, Wagner, and Dostoevsky." *MLN* 91, no. 6 (1976): 1161–1185.
Gorodetzky, Nadejda. *Saint Tikhon Zadonsky, Inspirer of Dostoevsky*. London: S.P.C.K., 1951.
Goscilo, Helena. "Feet Puskin Scanned, or Seeming Idee Fixe as Implied Aesthetic Credo." *The Slavic and East European Journal* 32, no. 4 (Winter 1988): 562–573.
Grant, George, Ian Angus, Ron Dart, and Randy Peg Peters, eds. *Theology, Philosophy, and Politics*. Toronto: University of Toronto Press, 2009.
Grass, Karl Konrad. *Die Russischen Sekten*. 2 vols. Leipzig: Druck von C. Mattiesen: J. C. Hinrichs, 1907–1914.

Grossman, Vassily. *Everything Flows*. Translated by R. a. E. C. w. A. Aslanyan. New York: New York Review of Books, 2009.
Guardini, Romano. *Religioese Gestalten in Dostojewskijs Werk*. München: Kösel, 1951.
Hacker, Andrew. "Dostoevsky's Disciples: Man and Sheep in Political Theory." *The Journal of Politics* 17, no. 4 (1955): 590–613.
Hayes, Patrick. *J. M. Coetzee and the Novel: Writing and Politics after Beckett*. Oxford: Oxford University Press, 2010.
Head, Dominick. *The Cambridge Introduction to J. M. Coetzee*. Cambridge: Cambridge University Press, 2010.
Heidegger, Martin. "Overcoming Metaphysics." In *The Heidegger Controversy: A Critical Reader*, edited by R. Wolin. Cambridge, MA: MIT Press, 1991.
Heidegger, Martin. "What Is Metaphysics." In *Basic Writings*, edited by D. F. Krell. San Francisco: Harper, 1993.
Heidegger, Martin. "Phenomenology and Theology." In *Pathmarks*, edited by W. McNeill. Cambridge: Cambridge University Press, 1998.
Heidegger, Martin. *Introduction to Metaphysics*. Translated by G. Fried. New Haven: Yale University Press, 2000.
Hobsbawm, E. J. *Nations and Nationalism since 1780: Program, Myth, Reality*. Cambridge: Cambridge University Press, 1995.
Holquist, Michael, ed. *The Dialogic Imagination*. Austin: University of Texas, 1981.
Howe, Irving. "Dostoevsky: The Politics of Salvation." *The Kenyon Review* 17, no. 1 (1955): 42–68.
Hubbs, Joanna. *Mother Russia: The Feminine Myth in Russian Culture*. Bloomington: Indiana University Press, 1988.
Huizinga, Johan. *Homo ludens*. London: Routledge and Kegan Paul, 1949.
Idinopulos, Thomas A. "The Mystery of Suffering in the Art of Dostoevsky, Camus, Wiesel, and Grünewald." *Journal of the American Academy of Religion* 43, no. 1 (1975): 51–61.
Ilyin, Ivan. *Sobranie sochinenii v desyati tomax*. Moskva: Russkaya kniga, 1997.
Ivanits, Linda. *Dostoevsky and the Russian People*. Cambridge: Cambridge University Press, 2008.
Ivanits, Linda J. "Dostoevskij's Mar'ja Lebjadkina." *The Slavic and East European Journal* 22, no. 2 (1978): 127–140.
Ivanov, Vyaacheslav. *Freedom and the Tragic Life*. Translated by N. Cameron. New York: Noonday, 1952.
Jackson, Robert Louis. *Dostoevsky's Underground Man in Russian Literature*. The Hague: Mouton & Co., Printers, 1958.
Jackson, Robert Louis. *The Art of Dostoevsky*. Princeton: Princeton University Press, 1981.
Jaeger, Werner. *Humanism and Theology*. Milwaukee: Marquette University Press, 1943.
Johae, Antony. "Towards an Iconography of *Crime and Punishment*." In *Dostoevsky and the Christian Tradition*, edited by G. Pattison and D. J. Thompson. Cambridge: Cambridge University Press, 2001.
Jonas, Hans. "Gnosticism and Modern Nihilism." *Social Research* 19, no. 4 (1952): 430–452.
Jonas, Hans. *The Gnostic Religion: The Message of the Alien God and the Beginnings of Christianity*. Boston: Beacon Press, 1958.
Jones, Malcolm. *Dostoevsky after Bakhtin: Reading in Dostoevsky Fantastic Realism* Cambridge: Cambridge University Press, 1990.
Jones, Malcolm V. *Dostoevsky After Bakhtin: Readings in Dostoevsky's Fantastic Realism*. Cambridge: Cambridge University Press, 2005.
Jones, Malcolm V. *Dostoevsky and the Dynamics of Religious Experience*. London: Anthem Press, 2005.
Jones, Malcolm. "Dostoevskii and Religion." In *The Cambridge Companion to Dostoevskii*, edited by W. J. Leatherbarrow, 148–74. Cambridge: Cambridge University Press, 2002.

Kaladiouk, Anna. "On 'Sticking to the Facts' and 'Understanding Nothing': Dostoevsky and the Scientific Method." *Russian Review* 65, no. 3 (2006): 417–438.
Katz, Michael R. "Introduction." In *Devils*. Oxford: Oxford University Press, 1992.
Kaufmann, Walter, ed. *Existentialism from Dostoevsky to Sarte*. Cleveland, OH: Meridian Books, 1968.
Kjetsaa, Geir. *Fyodor Dostoyevsky: A Writer's Life*. Translated by S. Hustvedt and D. McDuff. New York: Fawcett Columbine, 1989.
Knapp, Liza. *Dostoevsky as Reformer: The Petrashevsky Case*. Ann Arbor, MI: Ardis Publishers, 1987.
Knapp, Liza. *The Annihilation of Inertia: Dostoevsky and Metaphysics*. Evanston, IL: Northwestern University Press, 1996.
Knight, Frank. "Ethics and the Economic Interpretation." In *The Ethics of Competition*, 11–32. New Brunswick: Transaction Publishers, 1997.
Kochin, Michael S. 2005. "Life as Literature: Wright Morris's Love among the Cannibals" Presented at Annual Meeting of the American Political Science Association, August 2005. Available at http://ssrn.com/abstract=1121584.
Kochin, Michael S. "Literature and Salvation in Elizabeth Costello, or How to Refuse to Be an Author in Eight or Nine Lessons." *English in Africa* 34, no. 1 (2007): 79–95.
Kochin, Michael S. 2009. "What Political Science Needs to Learn from Science Studies" Presented at Annual Meeting of the American Political Science Association, August 2009, Toronto. Available at http://ssrn.com/abstract=1452022.
Komarowitsch, W. *Die Urgestalt der Brueder Karamasoff: Dostojewskis Quellen, Entwuerfe und Fragmente*. München: R. Piper, 1928.
Kossew, Sue. "The Anxiety of Authorship: J. M. Coetzee's *Master of Petersburg* and André Brink's *On the Contrary*." *English in Africa* 20. no. 1 (1996): 67–88.
Kostalevsky, Marina. *Dostoevsky and Soloviev: The Art of Integral Vision*. New Haven: Yale University Press, 1997.
Kroeker, P. Travis, and Bruce Ward. *Remembering the End: Dostoevsky as Prophet to Modernity*. Boulder: Westview Press, 2001.
Lampert, Evgenii. *Studies in Rebellion*. London: Routledge and K. Paul, 1957.
Langbauer, Laurie. "Ethics and Theory: Suffering Children in Dickens, Dostoevsky, and Le Guin." *English Literary History* 75, no. 1 (2008): 89–108.
Latour, Bruno. *Science in Action: How to Follow Scientists and Engineers through Society*. Cambridge: Harvard University Press, 1987.
Latour, Bruno, and Steve Woolgar. *Laboratory Life: The Construction of Scientific Facts*. Princeton: Princeton University Press, 1986.
Lavrin, Janko. "A Note on Nietzsche and Dostoevsky." *Russian Review* 28, no. 2 (1969): 160–170.
Lawrence, D. H. "The Grand Inquisitor." In *Selected Literary Criticism*, edited by E. Beal. New York: Viking Press, 1956.
Lawrence, D. H. "Preface to Dostoevsky's The Grand Inquisitor." In *Dostoevksy: A Collection of Critical Essays*, edited by R. Welleck, 93. Englewood Cliffs, NJ: Prentice-Hall, 1962.
Lawrence, D. H. *Selected Literary Criticism*. Edited by A. Beal. New York: Viking Press, 1961.
Leatherbarrow, W. J. "*The Devils* in the Context of Dostoevsky's Life and Work." In *Dostoevsky's* The Devils: *A Critical Companion*, edited by W. J. Leatherbarrow, 37–38. Evanston: Northwestern University Press, 1999.
Leatherbarrow, William J., ed. *The Cambridge Companion to Dostoevskii*. Cambridge: Cambridge University Press, 2002.
Leontiev, K. N. *Khram i Tserkov'*. Moskva: Izdatel'stvo, 2003.
Linden, Carl A. *The Soviet Party-State: The Politics of Ideocratic Despotism*. New York: Praeger, 1983.
Lloyd, J. A. T. *Fyodor Dostoevsky*. Brooklyn: Haskell House Publishers Ltd., 1976.
Lloyd, Margie. "In Tocqueville's Shadow: Hannah Arendt's Liberal Republicanism." *The Review of Politics* 57, no. 1 (1995): 31–58.

Lubac, Henri de. *The Drama of Athiest Humanism*. Translated by E. M. Riley. New York: New American Library, 1963.
Lubac, Henri de. *The Drama of Atheistic Humanism*. Translated by E. M. Riley. Cleveland: World Pub. Co., 1949.
Machiavelli, Niccolo. *The Prince*. Translated by H. Mansfield. Chicago: The University of Chicago Press, 1998.
Marais, Mike. "Death and the Space of the Response to the Other." In *J. M. Coetzee and the Idea of the Public*, edited by J. Poyner, 93. Athens, OH: Ohio University Press, 2006.
Masaryk, T. G. *The Spirit of Russia: Studies in History, Literature and Philosophy*. Translated by E. Paul and C. Paul. 2 ed. 2 vols. London: G. Allen & Unwin, 1955.
Matlaw, Ralph E. The Brothers Karamazov: *Novelistic Technique*. The Hague: Mouton, 1957.
Matlock, Jack F. "Literature and Politics: The Impact of Fyodor Dostoevsky." *The Political Science Reviewer* 9, no. 1 (1979): 39–60.
Melville, Herman. *The Confidence-Man*. Oxford: Oxford University Press, 1989.
Merezhkovsky, Dmitry Sergeyevich. *Tolstoi as Man and Artist, with an Essay on Dostoïevski*. New York: G. P. Putnam's Sons, 1902.
Mihm, Stephen. *A Nation of Counterfeiters: Capitalists, Con Men, and the Making of the United States*. Cambridge: Harvard University Press, 2009.
Miliukov, P. N. *Outlines of Russian Culture*. Translated by M. Karpovich, E. G. Davis and V. Ughet. 3 vols. Philadelphia: University of Pennsylvania Press, 1942.
Mochulsky, Konstantin. *Dostoevsky: His Life and Work*. Translated by M. A. Minihan. Princeton: Princeton University Press, 1967.
Moran, John P. "The Roots of Terrorist Motivation: Shame, Rage and Violence in *The Brothers Karamazov*." *Perspectives on Political Science* 38, no. 4 (2009): 187–196.
Moran, John P. *The Solution of the Fist: Dostoevsky and the Roots of Modern Terrorism*. Lanham, MD: Lexington Books, 2009.
Morson, Gary Saul. *The Boundaries of Genre: Dostoevsky's Diary of a Writer and the Traditions of Literary Utopia*. Evanston: Northwestern University Press, 1988.
Murav, Harriet. "From Skandalon to Scandal: Ivan's Rebellion Reconsidered." *Slavic Review* 63, no. 4 (2004): 756–770.
Nabokov, Vladimir Vladimirovich. *Lectures on Russian Literature*. Edited by F. Bowers. 1 ed. 2 vols. New York: Harcourt Brace Jovanovich, 1980.
Niebuhr, H. Richard. *The Meaning of Revelation*. New York: Macmillan, 1941.
Nietzsche, F. W. *The Antichrist*. Translated by R. J. Hollingdale. London: Penguin Books, 1990.
Nietzsche, Friedrich. *Twilight of the Idols; and The Anti-Christ*. Baltimore: Penguin Books, 1968.
Nietzsche, Friedrich. *Thus Spoke Zarathustra*. Translated by G. Parkes. Oxford: Oxford University Press, 2005.
Nietzsche, Friedrich. *Twilight of the Idols with the Antichrist and Ecce Homo*. Translated by A. M. Ludovici. London: Wordsworth Editions Limited, 2007.
Otto, Rudolph. *The Idea of the Holy: An Inquiry into the Non-rational Factor in the Idea of the Divine and its Relation to the Rational*. Translated by J. W. Harvey. New York: Oxford University Press, 1958.
Panichas, George. *The Burden of Vision: Dostoevsky's Spiritual Art*. Grand Rapids: Eerdmans, 1977.
Pattinson, George, and Diane Thompson. *Dostoyevsky and the Christian Tradition*. Cambridge: Cambridge University Press, 2001.
Pattison, George, and Diane Oenning Thompson, eds. *Dostoevsky and the Christian Tradition*. Cambridge: Cambridge University Press, 2001.
Payne, Robert. *Dostoevsky: A Human Portrait*. New York: Knopf, 1961.
Pettit, Philip. *Republicanism: A Theory of Freedom and Government*, Oxford Political Theory. Oxford: Oxford University Press, 1997.

Pettit, Philip. *A Theory of Freedom: From the Psychology of the Politics of Agency.* Oxford: Oxford University Press, 2001.
Pettit, Philip. "Republican Freedom: Three Axioms, Four Theorems." In *Republicanism and Political Theory*, edited by C. Laborde and J. Maynor. Oxford: Blackwell, 2008.
Plato. *The Laws.* Translated by A. E. Taylor, Everyman's Library. London: Dent, 1960.
Poggioli, Renato. "Dostoevski, or Reality and Myth." In *The Phoenix and the Spider: A Book of Essays about Some Russian Writers and Their View of the Self*, edited by R. Poggioli. Cambridge: Harvard University Press, 1957.
Popper, Karl. *The Poverty of Historicism.* New York: Routledge Classics, 2010.
Rad, Gerhard von. *Genesis: A Commentary.* Translated by J. H. Marks. Philadelphia: Westminster Press, 1961.
Rahv, Philip. "The Legend of the Grand Inquisitor." *Partisan Review* 21, no. 3 (1954): 250–260.
Ramsey, Paul. "No Morality without Immortality: Dostoevski and the Meaning of Atheism." *The Journal of Religion* 36, no. 2 (1956): 90–108.
Riemer, Neal. "Some Reflections on the Grand Inquisitor and Modern Democratic Theory." *Ethics* 67, no. 4 (1957): 249–256.
Rosen, Nathan. "Chaos and Dostoyevsky's Women." *The Kenyon Review* 20, no. 2 (1958): 257–277.
Rozanov, Vasily. *Dostoevsky and the Legend of the Grand Inquisitor.* Translated by S. E. Roberts. Ithaca: Cornell University Press, 1972.
Sandoz, Ellis. "Philosophical Anthropology and Dostoevsky's 'Legend of the Grand Inquisitor.'" *The Review of Politics* 26, no. 3 (1964): 353–377.
Sandoz, Ellis. *Political Apocalypse: A Study of Dostoevsky's Grand Inquisitor.* Baton Rouge, LA: Louisiana State University Press, 1971.
Sandoz, Ellis. "Philosophical Dimensions of Dostoevsky's Politics." *Journal of Politics* 40, no. 3 (1978): 648–674.
Sandoz, Ellis. *Political Apocalypse: A Study of Dostoevsky's Grand Inquisitor.* 2nd ed. Wilmington, DE: ISI Books, 2000.
Scanlan, James P. "Dostoevsky's Arguments for Immortality." *Russian Review* 59, no. 1 (2000): 1–20.
Seduro, Vladimir. *Dostoyevski in Russian Literary Criticism, 1846–1956.* New York: Columbia University Press, 1957.
Seeley, Frank Friedeberg. "Dostoyevsky's Women." *The Slavonic and East European Review* 39, no. 93 (1961): 291–312.
Skinner, Quentin. *Liberty before Liberalism.* Cambridge: Cambridge University Press, 1998.
Skinner, Quentin. *Visions of Politics.* 3 vols. Vol. II. Cambridge: Cambridge University Press, 2002.
Skinner, Quentin. "Freedom as the Absence of Arbitrary Power." In *Republicanism and Political Theory*, edited by C. Laborde and J. Maynor. Oxford: Blackwell, 2008.
Solovyov. *A Solovyov Anthology.* Translated by N. Duddington. London: S.C.M. Press, 1950.
Sorsky, Nils. *The Authentic Writings.* Translated by D. M. Goldfrank. Edited by D. M. Goldfrank. Kalamazoo: Cistercian Publications, 2008.
Sparshott, Francis Edward. *Taking Life Seriously: A Study of the Argument of the Nicomachean Ethics.* Toronto: University of Toronto Press, 1994.
Spector, Horacio. "Four Conceptions of Freedom." *Political Theory* 38, no. 6 (2010): 780–808.
Srigley, Ron. *Albert Camus' Critique of Modernity.* Columbia: University of Missouri Press, 2011.
Stevens, Wallace. "Surety and Fidelity Claims." In *Collected Prose and Poetry*, edited by F. Kermode and J. Richardson. New York: Library of America, 1997.
Strakosch, H. E. "Dostoevsky and the Man-God." *Dublin Review* 22, no. 1 (1955): 142–153.

Straus, Nina Pelikan. *Dostoevsky and the Woman Question: Rereadings at the End of a Century*. New York: St. Martin's Press, 1994a.
Straus, Nina Pelikan. "Every Woman Loves a Nihilist: Stavrogin and Women in Dostoevsky's *The Possessed*." *NOVEL: A Forum on Fiction* 27, no. 3 (1994b): 271–286.
Strauss, Leo. *What Is Political Philosophy?* Glencoe, IL: Free Press, 1959.
Sutherland, Stewart R. *Atheism and the Rejection of God: Contemporary Philosophy and The Brothers Karamazov*. Oxford: Basil Blackwell, 1977.
Terras, Victor. *A Karamazov Companion: Commentary on the Genesis, Language, and Style of Dostoevsky's Novel*. Madison: University of Wisconsin Press, 1981.
Terras, Victor. *Reading Dostoevsky*. Madison: University of Wisconsin Press, 1998.
Thompson, Diane. *The Brothers Karamazov and the Poetics of Memory*. Cambridge: Cambridge University Press, 1991.
Thompson, Diane Oenning. "Dostoevskii and Science." In *The Cambridge Companion to Dostoevskii*, edited by W. J. Leatherbarrow, 191–211. Cambridge: Cambridge University Press, 2002.
Trepanier, Lee. "The Politics and Experience of Active Love in *The Brothers Karamazov*." *The Political Science Reviewer* 38, no. 4 (Fall 2009): 197–205.
Turgenev, Ivan. *Fathers and Sons*. Translated by B. Makanowitzky. New York: Bantam Books, 1981.
Turner, Richard Pope, and Judy Turner. "Toward Understanding Stavrogin," *Slavic Review* 49, no. 4 (Winter 1990): 543–553.
Vetlovskaya, Valentina A. "Alyosha Karamazov and the Hagiographic Hero." In *Dostoevsky: New Perspectives*, edited by R. L. Jackson. Englewood Cliffs: Prentice-Hall, 1984.
Voegelin, Eric. "Bakunin's Confession." *The Journal of Politics* 8, no. 1 (1946): 24–43.
Voegelin, Eric. *The New Science of Politics: An Introduction*. Chicago: University of Chicago Press, 1952.
Voegelin, Eric. *Order and History*, 3 vols. Baton Rouge, LA: Louisiana State University Press, 1956–1957.
Voegelin, Eric. *The New Science of Politics: An Introduction*. Chicago: University of Chicago Press, 1987.
Voegelin, Eric. *Modernity without Restraint*. Edited by M. Henningsen, The Collected Works of Eric Voegelin. Columbia, MO: University of Missouri Press, 2000.
Walsh, David. "Dostoevsky's Discovery of the Christian Foundation of Politics." *Religion and Literature* 19, no. 2 (1987): 49–72.
Ward, Bruce K. "Dostoevsky and the Hermeneutics of Suspicion." *Literature and Theology* 11, no. 3 (1997): 270–283.
Ware, Timothy. *The Orthodox Church*. New York: Penguin, 1997.
Wasiolek, Edward. *Dostoevsky: The Major Fiction*. Cambridge, MA: Harvard University Press, 1964.
Wellek, Rene, ed. *Dostoevsky: A Collection of Critical Essays*. Whitefish, MT: Literary Licensing, LLC, 2011.
Williams, Rowan. *Dostoevsky: Language, Faith, and Fiction (Making of the Christian Imagination)*. Waco, TX: Baylor University Press, 2008.
Yacoub, Joseph R. "Children in Dostoevsky: The Case of *The Idiot* and *The Brothers Karamazov*." In *Proceedings of the 2004–2005 Midwest Philosophy of Education Society*, edited by J. Helfer. Bloomington, IN: AuthorHouse, 2007.
Yarmolinsky, Avrahm. *Dostoievsky: A Study in his Ideology*. New York: Publisher Unknown, 1921.
Yarmolinsky, Avrahm. *Dostoevsky, His Life and Art*. New York: Criterion Books, 1960.
Young, Sarah, and Lesley Milne, eds. *Dostoevsky on the Threshold of Other Worlds: Essays in Honor of Malcolm V. Jones*. Ilkeston, Derbyshire: Bramcote Press, 2006.
Zernov, Nicholas. *Three Russian Prophets: Khomiakov, Dostoevsky, Soloviev*. London: S.C.M. Press, 1944.
Zernov, Nicolas. *Eastern Christendom: A Study of the Origin and Development of the Eastern Orthodox Church*. New York: Putnam, 1961.

Zweig, Stefan. *Three Masters: Balzac, Dickens, Dostoeffsky*. Translated by E. Paul and C. Paul, His Master Builders. New York: The Viking Press, 1930.

Index

The Adolescent (Dostoevsky), 16, 73, 130; Versilov, 16, 19, 22
Anderson, Benedict, 57
Anglican Church, 120, 121, 128
Apollo of Belvedere, 25
Aristotle, 94, 185, 227; *Nicomachean Ethics* , 94; *Politics* , 94
atheism (also godless), 3, 9, 31, 34, 37, 45, 51, 59, 64, 73, 80, 83, 85, 88, 93, 94, 95, 96, 99, 100, 102, 107, 161, 176, 216
Avramenko, Richard, 4, 123, 227

Baal, 119, 120, 121, 164, 193, 194, 229
Bahktin, Mikhail, 1, 2, 31–32, 36, 46, 59
Belinsky, Vissarion, 64, 204
Belknap, Robert, 202, 203–205
Benedict, Saint, 52
Bentham, Jeremy, 141
Berdyaev, Nikolai, 75, 77, 79, 81, 83, 85, 87, 96, 97, 105, 116, 131–132, 159, 167, 201, 202, 204
Berlin, 192
Berlin, Isaiah, 51, 56, 159
Bible (also Gospels), 17, 18, 26, 37, 38, 62, 81, 120, 129, 132, 142, 152
bourgeoisie, 115, 120, 122–123, 126, 136
Briggs, Katherine, 75
The Brothers Karamazov (Dostoevsky), 2, 5, 31–47, 51, 53, 60, 64, 68, 73, 78, 93, 94, 95, 96, 99, 106, 159, 201–219; active love, 2, 32, 34, 37, 38–44, 45, 46, 47, 74, 78, 85, 97, 101; Alyosha, 20, 24, 73, 97, 99–101, 106, 107, 108, 201–214; love, 32–46, 53, 57, 58, 59, 62, 64–66, 69; comparison with Camus, 205–207; comparision with Melville, 207–209; Dmitry, 2, 34, 35, 41, 42; moral renewal, 12; romantic, 52, 53, 55–58, 59, 65, 66, 69; Father Ferapont, 52, 53, 67, 68; Father Paisiy, 43, 52, 53, 67, 73; Fyodor, 22, 53–55, 62, 63, 64, 65, 100; Gregory, 63; Grushenka, 32, 35, 41–43, 46, 55–56, 56–57, 65; humility, 68–69; humiliation, 53–55; Ilyusha, 44–45, 56; Ivan, 2, 5, 13, 15, 16–17, 19–20, 22, 32–36, 37, 39–41, 45, 47, 52, 53, 58–63, 64, 65, 66, 67, 69, 95, 97, 98–101, 103, 105, 106, 107, 108, 201–219; Karamazov baseness, 34, 35, 37, 43, 46, 101; Kolya, 35, 44–45; laceration, 34, 35–36, 37, 40, 41, 43, 44, 45, 46; love and memory, 19–20, 44–45; Liza, 40, 63; Markel, 37, 39, 45; patricide, 52, 56, 58, 63, 66, 68; Smerdyakov, 2, 16, 100; nihilism, 53, 60, 62–64; The Legend of the Grand Inquisitor, 2, 3, 5, 16, 17, 19, 23, 31–36, 42, 51, 52, 53, 60–62, 66, 94–102, 104, 105, 109, 115, 201, 202, 206, 208, 213–216, 219; Zosima, 2, 16, 19–20, 32, 37–43, 45, 46–47, 74, 77, 78, 79

Camus, Albert, 5, 99, 100, 203, 204, 205–207, 209, 219; *The Rebel* , 206, 207, 209
capitalism (also free-market), 3, 115–116, 117, 127, 136
Catholic. *See* Roman Catholic
Catteau, Jacques, 202
Chapple, Richard, 74
Chernyshevsky, Nikolai, 230; *What Is to Be Done?* , 230
Christianity: Christ, 2, 9–12, 17–20, 24–27, 32, 33–34, 35, 36, 39, 40, 41, 43, 44, 46, 61–62, 66, 67, 73, 76, 81–82, 95–99, 101, 102, 103, 105, 106–108, 117, 118, 121, 129, 132–134,

169, 170, 201; Church, 24, 25, 27, 52–53, 59, 61, 66–67, 76, 81, 106, 121, 127, 142, 193, 209; faith, 3, 10, 18, 24, 25, 26, 33, 41, 43, 64, 75–76, 77, 78, 79, 80, 81–82, 83, 85–87, 98–99, 101, 102, 103, 107, 107–108, 144, 167, 176, 204, 213, 216, 217; God, 1, 2, 4, 5, 9, 12, 13, 15–16, 17, 18, 20, 24–25, 27, 31, 33, 37, 38, 39, 41–43, 44, 45, 46, 51, 52, 56, 57, 58, 61–62, 64, 65, 66, 67, 68, 73, 76, 77–78, 78–82, 83–85, 87–88, 93, 95, 97, 98–105, 105–108, 126, 127, 131, 132, 134, 141, 144, 145, 148, 154, 156, 167, 168, 169, 170, 171, 172, 175, 176, 205, 206, 209, 210–211, 213, 214, 218; Great Schism, 142, 193; Greek, 94, 142, 159, 203; Holy fool, 80–82; Jesus, 46, 75, 97, 98, 107, 108, 201, 202, 212, 213, 215, 217; Orthodoxy, 1, 21, 24–25, 36, 38, 46, 52, 67, 68, 73, 74, 75, 76, 81, 94, 96, 107, 117, 126, 127, 131, 132, 133, 134, 142, 167, 174, 193, 214; political, 9–12, 66–68. *See also* Protestantism; Roman Catholic
Cleopatra, 124
Coetzee J. M., 1, 5, 224, 225, 226, 227, 228, 228–229, 230, 231, 232; *The Master of Petersburg* , 5, 225, 226, 228, 229–230, 232; Dostoevsky, 225–226, 227, 228, 229, 231, 232; Pavel, 225–226, 227, 228; Maximov, 227
Cologne, 192
conservatism, 3, 26, 31, 53, 115–117, 136, 153
cosmopolitanism, 3, 26, 115, 121, 129, 131, 182, 188
Crime and Punishment (Dostoevsky), 4, 14, 16, 73, 75, 76, 77, 141, 160, 169, 171; Dounia, 146, 170; freedom (approximate), 160–168, 172–176; freedom (proximate), 168–176; Lebeziatnikov, 144; Lizaveta, 148, 149; Luzhin, 146, 168, 169; Marmeladov, 22, 144–145, 146, 160, 168; Pawnbroker, 14, 141, 143, 144, 147, 148, 148–150, 155; Raskolnikov, 4, 14, 16, 73, 74, 75, 76, 77, 78, 79, 97, 141–156, 160–172; Razumikhin,

151–154, 162, 163, 166, 168; Sonia, 4, 141–143, 144, 145, 146, 155, 156, 160, 161, 168, 169, 170
Crimean War, 85

Darwin, Charles, 182
Davey, Ethan-Alexander, 3
deism, 13
The Devils (Dostoevsky), 3, 5, 12, 64, 73–88, 116, 123, 167, 176, 223, 223–232; Anton Laverntievich G__, 223–224, 230; comparison with Coetzee, 224–226, 228–232; compassion (failed), 77–85; compassion (successful), 85–87; Darya, 3, 73, 74, 79–86; Liza, 231; Maria, 3, 22, 74, 75, 76, 79–82, 84, 88; mother earth, 75, 76, 78, 80–82, 85, 86, 88; Rakitin, 41–42, 44, 59; Sonia, 3, 74, 79, 80, 85–88; Stavrogin, 5, 12, 15, 73, 75, 76, 80, 82, 83, 83–88, 223–229, 231, 232; Stephan, 22, 24, 76, 116, 176, 227, 230; Tikhon, 15, 73, 223, 224; women as heroines, 73–87
Diary of a Writer (Dostoevsky), 3, 25, 36, 99, 117, 118, 126, 131, 133, 159, 173, 174, 224, 227
Dostoevsky, F. M.: Christian and political vision, 9–11, 18–23, 37–47, 64–69, 131–135; influence today, 1; on beauty, 116–118; on freedom, 12–17, 160–176; on human duality, 11–17; on Russia, 23–27, 53–54; on women heroines, 73–88; Petrashevsky Circle, 131, 159
Dostoevsky, Masha, 17
The Double (Dostoevsky), 159
Dresden, 192

Ealy, Steve, 4
Ellison, Ralph, 4, 181, 186, 187, 192, 194, 196–198
England, 119, 121, 144
Enlightenment, 21, 33, 34, 35, 36, 69, 96, 124, 126, 128, 174, 204
Europe, 13, 21, 22, 23, 25–26, 36, 54, 59, 66, 69, 76, 77, 85, 99, 117, 118, 126, 135, 142, 144, 160, 192–193, 195, 196, 197, 231

Fige, Orlando, 54
Fonvizana, N. D., 18
France, 4, 36, 85, 119, 122
Frank, Joseph, 128, 144, 182, 184, 186, 196, 197
Fourier, Joseph, 94, 141

Germany, 36, 56, 94
God. *See* Christianity
Gogol, Nikolai, 51, 69, 134; *Dead Souls*, 134
Granovsky, T. N., 64, 127, 134, 135
Guardian, 128

Habib, Khalil M., 4
Heidegger, Martin, 159
Herzen, Alexander, 54, 128, 204
Hobbes, Thomas, 35
The House of Dead (Dostoevsky), 164, 173

The Idiot (Dostoevsky), 17, 73, 81, 86; Myshkin, 17, 73; Nastasya, 73; Totsky, 73
individualism, 24, 37, 42, 73, 78, 86, 88, 121, 145
irrationalism, 100, 151, 163, 184, 186, 191, 211
The Invisible Man (Ellison), 181, 186, 189, 192, 196; Grandfather, 188, 189, 190, 191, 197; Invisible Man, 4, 181, 186, 188–190, 191, 194, 196, 196–197; Mary Rambo, 190, 197
Ivantis, Linda, 75

Jones, Malcolm V., 1
John, St., 215

Kafka, Franz, 228
Katkov, N. N., 226
Kochin Michael, 5, 160
Kock, Charles Paul de, 230
Kroeker, P. Travis, 202, 204

Latour, Bruno, 228
Lawrence, D. H., 61, 105, 107, 202, 228
Lenin, V. I., 116
Leontiev, Konstantin, 130

liberalism, 3, 10, 13, 21, 25, 26, 31, 53, 64, 76, 115–117, 121, 124, 126, 127, 128, 129, 130, 131, 133, 134, 135, 136, 159, 230, 231
London, 120, 122, 164, 182, 192, 193, 194
Lycurguses, 153, 166

Mahomets, 153, 166
Marais, Mike, 229
Marx, Karl, 94, 104, 182, 185
materialism, 73, 76, 86, 88, 94, 122, 126, 127
Melville, Herman, 5, 203, 208; *The Confidence Man*, 5, 208
Mill, John Stuart, 182
Mochulsky, Konstantin, 12
Moran, John P., 2
Morson, Gary Saul, 1
Moscow, 131

Napoleon, 14, 78, 141, 152, 153, 155, 166, 168, 169, 171
nationalism. *See* Russia
Nechaev, Sergei, 64, 131, 224, 225, 226, 227, 228, 229, 230, 231
New York City, 188, 190
New York Times, 128
Nietzsche, Friedrich, 9, 94, 102, 103, 141, 143, 167, 211, 212; *The Anti-Christ*, 218
nihilists, 53, 58, 60, 63, 64, 83, 95, 131, 145, 225, 226, 230
nihilism, 2, 5, 9, 14, 15, 24, 25, 27, 73, 74, 82, 83, 84, 93, 102, 106, 145, 176, 202, 204, 205, 207, 211–212, 214, 218, 219
Notes from the Underground (Dostoevsky), 4, 13, 64, 118, 123, 160, 181, 184, 186, 187, 191, 192, 194; comparison of Ellison's Invisible Man, 186–192; comparison of freedom with Ellison, 192–198; freedom (approximate), 160–168, 172–176; freedom (proximate), 168–176

paganism, 67, 83, 118
Paris, 84, 122, 123, 128, 176, 192
Paul, Saint, 142, 152

Peter and Paul Fortress, 172
Peter the Great, 21
Plato, 3, 13, 20, 93, 94, 99, 101, 136, 227; *Republic*, 94, 136
politics, 1–5; Christian foundation, 9–12, 66–68; Grand Inquisitor, 33–36, 58–62, 93–109, 204–215; humiliation, 51–54; humility, 68–69; love and memory, 44–47; secular humanism, 115–136. *See also* conservatism; cosmopolitanism; liberalism; nihilism; socialism
Poor Folk (Dostoevsky), 159
Popper, Karl, 151
positivism, 94, 99
Potter, Harry, 225
proletariat, 132
Protestantism, 24, 35, 36
Proudhon, Pierre-Joseph, 128, 141
Pushkin, Alexander, 26, 53, 56, 230
Pushkin Speech (Dostoevsky), 26, 107

Rabelais, 228
racism, 4. *See also* United States
rationalism, 2, 9, 10, 14, 18, 21, 22, 32, 33–34, 35, 39–40, 42, 43, 44, 46, 51, 52, 53, 56, 58–61, 62–63, 64, 66, 68, 69, 73, 76, 87, 88, 99, 100, 101, 117, 124, 125, 128, 136, 144, 145, 146, 148, 149, 150, 151, 153, 154, 155, 156, 162, 163–164, 165, 167, 171, 183–184, 185, 186, 188, 191, 195, 204, 206, 209, 211, 215, 216
The Raw Youth (Dostoevsky): Arkady, 22
reason. *See* rationalism; irrationalism
Riga, 182
Roman Catholic, 24, 35, 36, 52, 61, 66, 67, 81, 94, 96, 106, 142, 214; Latin, 142, 193, 231
Roman Empire, 25, 124
romanticism, 2, 52, 53, 55, 56–57, 58, 62, 66, 68, 69, 77, 228
Roth, Philip, 226; *The Plot Against America*, 226
Rousseau, Jean-Jacques, 182, 185
Rozanov, V. V., 202
Russia: aristocracy, 20, 120, 130, 132, 141, 160, 173, 217, 223, 227, 230, 231; Edict of Emancipation, 132, 133; future, 19, 22, 24, 25, 36, 53, 88; humility, 68–69; humiliation, 53–55; intelligentsia, 13, 20, 21, 23, 107, 126–129, 132, 174, 182, 184; Mongol Yoke, 54; nationalism, 55, 57–58, 62, 68, 135; peasantry, 16, 21, 25, 26, 42, 60, 68, 75–76, 80–81, 82, 85–86, 88, 104, 126, 126–128, 130, 133–134, 147, 148, 173, 174–176, 195; serf, 21, 127–128, 132, 132–134, 141, 174, 175

Saint Petersburg, 5, 37, 118, 141, 143, 144, 160, 170, 182, 225, 226, 228, 229, 230, 232
Sand, George, 26, 27
Sandoz, Ellis, 3, 73, 78, 115, 116, 142, 202
secularism, 3, 39, 53, 64, 73, 88, 116, 120, 148, 159, 194
Seville, 33, 61, 97, 98
Siberia, 77, 99, 133, 162, 171, 173, 174, 175, 176
Sieyes, Emmanuel Joseph, 122
slavophile, 26, 75, 81, 132, 195
social democracy, 123, 125, 128
socialism, 3, 9, 10, 13, 21, 24–26, 26–27, 36, 45, 53, 61, 68, 93, 94, 95, 100, 101, 102, 106, 115–118, 121, 122, 123, 124, 125, 126, 128, 129, 130, 131, 133, 135, 136, 141, 151, 159, 161, 172
Solon, 153, 166
Sorsky, Nil, 52
South Africa, 4
Spain, 61, 68
Srigley, Ron, 5
Straus, Nina P., 75
Stevens, Wallace, 229
suffering, 2, 3, 5, 11, 15–17, 19, 22, 25–27, 33–34, 39, 40, 45, 46, 73–88, 95, 96, 98, 99, 100, 101, 105, 107, 108, 118, 120, 123, 132, 142, 145, 149, 164–165, 167, 169, 176, 196, 202, 206, 209–211, 213, 216, 218, 219, 231, 232
Swift, Jonathan, 228

Tocqueville, Alexis de, 230
Tolstoy, Leo, 20, 64
Trepanier, Lee, 2, 74

Turgenev, Ivan, 58, 64; *Fathers and Sons*, 58

United States (also America), 4, 57, 58, 59, 115, 130; race, 186, 188, 191, 196–197
utilitarianism, 3, 4, 14, 59, 101, 141, 143, 144, 147, 148, 149, 150, 155, 156

Vetlovskaya, Valentina, 201, 202
Voegelin, Eric, 94

Walsh, David, 2, 83

Ward, Bruce, 201, 202
Westernizer, 26, 53, 64, 75, 76, 118, 161, 194
Winters Notes of a Summer Impression (Dostoevsky), 3, 118, 119, 120, 128, 164, 192, 194, 195; boredom, 122–130; bourgeoisie, 122–123; Crystal Palace, 119, 120, 121, 122, 123, 124, 125, 129, 164, 165, 168, 182, 193, 194, 196; materialism, 119–121; sources of moral renewal, 130–135

Zadonsky, Tikhon Saint, 98

About the Contributors

Richard Avramenko is associate professor of political science at the University of Wisconsin–Madison. He is author of *Courage: The Politics of Life and Limb* (2012); coeditor of *Friendship and Politics: Essays in Political Thought*; and numerous articles on ancient and continental political thought and literature.

Ethan Alexander-Davey is a doctoral candidate in political science at the University of Wisconsin–Madison.

Steven D. Ealy is a senior fellow at Liberty Fund, Inc., an educational foundation based in Indianapolis. He has published on Robert Penn Warren, Ralph Ellison, the Federalist Papers, and the intellectual foundations and history of American philanthropy.

Khalil M. Habib is associate professor of philosophy and director of the Pell Honors Program at Salve Regina University. Dr. Habib is coeditor *Cosmopolitanism in the Age of Globalization* (coedited with Lee Trepanier). He also has published articles on Aristophanes, Ibn Khaldun, Tocqueville, and Machiavelli.

Michael Kochin is Professor Extraordinarius of political science at Tel Aviv University and founding coeditor with Yoav Peled of *The Public Sphere*. He is author of *Five Chapters on Rhetoric* and *Gender and Rhetoric in Plato's Political Thought*.

John P. Moran is professor of political science and international affairs at Kennesaw State University. He is the author of *The Solution of the Fist: Dostoevsky and the Roots of Modern Terrorism* and *From Garrison State to Nation-state: Political Power and the Russian Military under Gorbachev and Yeltsin.*

Ellis Sandoz is the Hermann Moyse Jr. Distinguished Professor of Political Science and director of the Eric Voegelin Institute for American Renaissance Studies at Louisiana State University. He is the author and editor of numerous books, including *The Politics of Truth and other Untimely Essays, A Government of Laws, The Roots of Liberty,* and *Eric Voegelin's Significance for the Modern Mind.*

Ron Srigley is assistant professor in the Department of Religious Studies and coordinator of the Global Issues Program at the University of Prince Edward Island, Canada. His current research includes a study of the political philosophy of Sophocles' *Antigone* and a monograph on Albert Camus's notion of the sacred.

Lee Trepanier is associate professor of political science at Saginaw Valley State University. He is author of *Russian Political Symbols*, coauthor with Lynita K. Newswander of *LDS in USA: Mormonism and the Making of American Culture*, and editor of several volumes, the latest being *Teaching in an Age of Ideology* (coedited with John von Heyking), *Eric Voegelin and the Modern Continental Tradition* (coedited with Steven McGuire), and *Cosmopolitanism in the Age of Globalization* (coedited with Khalil Habib).

David Walsh is professor of political science at Catholic University of America. He is author of numerous books, the latest being *The Modern Philosophical Revolution*, *The Growth of the Liberal Soul*, and *After Ideology*.

Jingcai Ying is a graduate student in the Department of Politics at the University of Virginia.